UNIFORM RULES FOR EUROPEAN CONTRACT LAW?

Over the last 30 years, the evolution of acquis communautaire in consumer law and harmonising soft law proposals have utterly transformed the landscape of European contract law. The initial enthusiasm and approval for the EU programme has waned and, post Brexit, it currently faces increasing criticism over its effectiveness. In this collection, leading academics assess the project and ask if such judgements are fair, and suggest how harmonisation in the field might be better achieved. This book looks at the uniform rules in the context of: the internal market; national legislators and courts; bridging the gap between common and civil law; and finally their influence on non-member states. Critical and rigorous, it provides a timely and unflinching critique of one of the most important fields of harmonisation in the European Union.

Uniform Rules for European Contract Law?

A Critical Assessment

Edited by
Francisco de Elizalde

•HART•
OXFORD • LONDON • NEW YORK • NEW DELHI • SYDNEY

HART PUBLISHING

Bloomsbury Publishing Plc

Kemp House, Chawley Park, Cumnor Hill, Oxford, OX2 9PH, UK

HART PUBLISHING, the Hart/Stag logo, BLOOMSBURY and the Diana logo are trademarks of Bloomsbury Publishing Plc

First published in Great Britain 2018

A catalogue record for this book is available from the British Library.

Library of Congress Cataloging-in-Publication data

Names: Elizalde, Francisco de, editor.

Title: Uniform rules for European contract law? : a critical assessment / edited by Francisco de Elizalde.

Description: Oxford [UK] ; Portland, Oregon : HART Publishing, 2018. | Includes bibliographical references and index.

Identifiers: LCCN 2018005591 (print) | LCCN 2018005872 (ebook) | ISBN 9781509916306 (Epub) | ISBN 9781509916283 (hardback)

Subjects: LCSH: Contracts—European Union countries. | Obligations (Law)—European Union countries. | Commercial law—European Union countries. | Contracts.

Classification: LCC KJE1640 (ebook) | LCC KJE1640 .U53 2018 (print) | DDC 346.402/2—dc23

LC record available at https://lccn.loc.gov/2018005591

ISBN: HB: 978-1-50991-628-3
ePDF: 978-1-50991-629-0
ePub: 978-1-50991-630-6

Typeset by Compuscript Ltd, Shannon

To find out more about our authors and books visit www.hartpublishing.co.uk. Here you will find extracts, author information, details of forthcoming events and the option to sign up for our newsletters.

CONTENTS

Part III: Uniform Rules to Bridge the Gap between the Common Law and the Civil Law

Part IV: Uniform Rules as a Model for Non-EU Countries

CONTRIBUTORS

The contributors appear in alphabetical order:

Thomas Ackermann holds the chair of Civil Law and European and International Business Law at Ludwig Maximilians Universität (LMU, Germany). He studied law at the universities of Bonn and Cambridge, obtaining his doctorate in Bonn in 1997 with a thesis on the 'rule of reason' in European anti-trust law. In 2004, he completed his habilitation in Bonn with a dissertation on the protection of the reliance interest, a fundamental topic in the law of obligations. In the same year, he was appointed to the chair of German, European and International Civil and Business Law at the University of Erlangen-Nürnberg. His research interests cover the legal constitution of markets, with particular reference to the areas of contract law and competition law. A special focus of his work concerns the European dimension of these subjects. Thomas Ackermann is a member of the editorial board of the *Common Market Law Review*, the leading international peer-review journal in the area of European Union Law. He is a member of the Munich Risk and Insurance Centre and of the Faculty of the International Max Planck School for Competition and Innovation, as well as head of the Munich University Summer Training in German and European Law.

Navin G Ahuja is currently pursuing his doctorate in law focusing on arbitration. He is an in-house legal counsel for a Hong Kong book retailer/wholesaler, advising on various commercial contracts, tenancy agreements and dispute resolution, among other areas. He is also an accredited general mediator of the Hong Kong International Arbitration Centre and Hong Kong Mediation Accreditation Association Ltd. Mr Ahuja managed his family's manufacturing business for 20 years before embarking on a career in law. He completed his master of laws in Arbitration and Dispute Resolution in 2014, during which he participated in the Willem C Vis International Commercial Arbitration Moot and received a moot scholarship. He has been a researcher and a visiting fellow at City University of Hong Kong, and co-coached their team for the Vis Moot in 2016–17. Mr Ahuja is also the editorial assistant for the *Asian Dispute Review Journal*, which covers mediation and arbitration.

Hugh Beale has been a professor of law at Warwick since 1987. Before that he taught at the University of Bristol, University College of Wales, Aberystwyth, and the University of Connecticut. He has been a visiting professor at the universities of Amsterdam, North Carolina, Paris I and Utrecht. He currently holds a visiting professorship at the University of Oxford (2007–).

From 2000 to 2007 professor Beale was on leave from the university while he was a Law Commissioner for England and Wales, with responsibility for the Commercial and Common Law Team. During this period the team worked on projects such as Limitation, Unfair Contract Terms, Illegality in Contracts and Trusts, Registration of Security Interests over Property other than Land, and Insurance Contract Law.

Professor Beale was appointed honorary QC in 2002. He was elected as an honorary member of the Hungarian Academy of Sciences in 2001, and a fellow of the British Academy in 2004.

Francisco de Elizalde (*Editor*) is an associate professor of law at IE University. He focuses on comparative private law, especially contracts and the law of property. He is a visiting professor at Koç University (Turkey) and has previously lectured at FGV Sao Paulo (Brazil), the City University of Hong Kong, and the Law School Global League. He has been a visiting scholar to the University of Cambridge (Centre for European Legal Studies) and Harvard Law School, as well as having conducted research at the Max Planck Institute for Comparative and International Private Law (Germany). He has been co-researcher in national and European-funded projects, and he practised law at the Litigation and Arbitration Department of Garrigues (a major law firm in continental Europe) for several years.

Iñigo de la Maza has been director of the Law and Information Technologies programme at Universidad Diego Portales (Chile) since 2001. He worked as advisor of e-commerce areas at the Ministry of Economy of Chile in 2001–02. He has been speaker at the Annual Conference Latin American and Iberian Law and Economics Association (ALACDE), International Conference on Law and Informatics Havana, and at several universities and institutions in Chile, Peru, Cuba, Argentina, Spain, Colombia and the United States. He has been a principal researcher and co-researcher in several projects related to law and economics, private law specifically contracts, new technologies, among others, funded by universities and institutions from Chile, Mexico and Spain. Professor de la Maza is a co-editor of the proposed Principles of Latin American Contract Law.

Larry DiMatteo is Huber Hurst Professor at the University of Florida. He received his JD from the Cornell Law School, LLM from Harvard Law School, and PhD from Monash University (Australia). He is the former Chair of the Department of Management at the University of Florida and editor in chief of the *American Business Law Journal*. He is the author or co-author of some 120 publications. His books include *Comparative Contract Law: a tale of two legal systems* (with M Hogg, Oxford University Press), *International Law of Sales* (ed, Cambridge University Press) and *The Law of International Contracting* (Kluwer Law). His articles have appeared in the *Harvard International Law Journal, Yale Journal of International Law* and *Vanderbilt Journal of Transnational Law*, among others.

Mateja Durovic is a lecturer in law at King's College London. He was an assistant professor at the City University of Hong Kong. After graduation from the Third Belgrade Gymnasium, he enrolled at the Law Faculty of the University of Belgrade in 2003. He graduated in April 2007 as the Valedictorian, with an average grade of 10.0. He completed LLM studies at the Law Faculty of the University of Cambridge. He pursued his PhD at the European University Institute (EUI) in Florence. Dr Durovic also completed professional training at Stanford and Geneva universities, as well as at the Max Planck Institute in Hamburg. He worked as a consultant in the projects dealing with Serbian and Albanian legal harmonisation with EU law. He is co-editor of the international *Journal of European Consumer and Market Law* (*EuCML*).

Bénédicte Fauvarque-Cosson is a professor of law at the University of Paris II, Panthéon-Assas, where she teaches Comparative Law, Contract Law, Conflict of Laws and European Law. She is President of the *Société de Législation Comparée*, president of Trans Europe Experts, and Vice President of the International Academy of Comparative Law. She is an active member of worldwide famous international and European groups of experts in the field of contract law, and has contributed to drafting the Unidroit Principles of International Commercial Contracts. She is the co-author of *Cases, Materials and Texts on Contract Law, Ius Commune Casebooks on the Common Law of Europe*, (Hart, 2010). Professor Fauvarque-Cosson is the scientific director of the Recueil Dalloz and of the *Revue Internationale de Droit Comparé*. She lectures regularly in several countries.

Juan José Ganuza is a professor of economics and business at Pompeu Fabra University (Spain). He was a visiting researcher at the University California Los Angeles, and Institut D'Economie Industrielle (Toulouse). He has published in the main international economics journals in his research field (*RAND Journal of Economics, International Journal of Industrial Organization, Journal of Industrial Economics, Journal of Economics Management and Strategy*) as well as in general interest economics journals (such as *Econometrica*), law journals (such as the *Journal of Legal Studies*), and business publications (such as *Management Science*). Professor Ganuza has been a consultant on procurement issues for the Spanish government.

Fernando Gómez Pomar is a professor of law at Pompeu Fabra University (Spain). He has lectured at New York University, George Madison University, University of Hamburg and Radzyner School of Law (Israel). He is a member of the editorial boards of several journals, including the *European Review of Contract Law*, the *International Review of Law and Economics* and *InDret*. Professor Gómez Pomar is counsel for the Spanish law firm Uría Menéndez. He is frequently called as an expert witness on aspects of Spanish law in corporate matters before courts in various jurisdictions, such as Delaware Chancery Court, the US Federal Court and the High Court of England and Wales (Queen's Bench Division), as well as arbitration institutions such as the International Chamber of Commerce (ICC), where he has also acted as arbitrator, the Vienna International Arbitral Centre and the American Arbitration Association (AAA). In 2010 he was appointed by the European Commission to its Expert Group on a Common Frame of Reference in the area of European contract law.

Geraint Howells is the current Dean and Chair Professor of Commercial Law at the City University of Hong Kong. He is a member of the board of the International Association of Consumer Law. His publications include *Comparative Product Liability, Consumer Product Safety, Consumer Protection Law, EC Consumer Law, Product Liability, and European Fair Trading Law and the Tobacco Challenge*. Professor Howells often acts as a consultant to the European Commission, the UK Department of Business and the National Consumer Council and was a member of the European Consumer Law Group. He was previously editor of the *Consumer Law Journal*, the *Revue Européene de Droit de la Consommation*, and *European Business Law Library*, and is currently editor of the Markets and Law series for Ashgate publishers and the *Yearbook of Consumer Law*. Professor Howells has taught at the universities of Hull, Keele, Liverpool, Sheffield, Lancaster, Manchester, Tennessee, Würzburg, Münster, Paris XI and Sydney.

André Janssen is an associate professor of law at the City University of Hong Kong. He conducted his academic studies in Münster, Nijmegen, Oxford and Turin. He is an editor of the *European Review of Private Law* (ERPL) and the responsible editor of the German editorial department of the *Contratto e impresa/Europa*. He has taught in Germany, the USA, Italy, Egypt, France, the Netherlands, Poland and China. Professor Janssen is an evaluator for the *Deutscher Akademischer Austauschdienst* (DAAD), and a member of the German working committee of the *Deutsch-Niederländische Juristenkonferenz*. He was the country reporter for Germany within the Study Group on a European Civil Code, Principles of European Private Law: Commercial Agency, Distribution, Franchise and a member of the research and teaching committee of the training and research network 'The Interaction between EU Law and EU Politics and Economy in the Process of European Integration' in Beijing. In addition, he performs advisory work for courts concerning matters of international sales and Dutch private law, product liability and medical law. He also was an advisor for the Committee on the Internal Market and Consumer Protection of the European Parliament concerning issues related to consumer protection.

Işik Önay is an assitant professor at Koç University Law School, Istanbul. He is an expert in civil law with a particular emphasis on contracts and torts. His research interests include European and comparative private law. He holds an LLB from Koç University, an LLM from Queen Mary University of London and a PhD from Istanbul University. Dr Önay is a member of the American Society of Comparative Law and he chaired the organization committee of 2017 Young Comparativists Committee Annual Conference.

Encarna Roca i Trías is a judge of the Constitutional Court of Spain. In 1978 she was the first woman to become a professor of civil law in Spain and in 2011, the first woman to become a fellow of the Royal Academy of Law. She has also served as a judge of the Spanish Supreme Court (1st Chamber, private law matters). In her role as judge she promoted the application of the main European proposals on contract law (PECL, DCFR) as a tool to modernise Spanish private law. Professor Roca has published extensively both nationally as well as in international journals.

Zeynep Derya Tarman is a professor of law at Koç University Law School (Turkey). She earned a doctoral degreee in law in 2007 from the University of Konstanz, School of Law, in Germany (magna cum laude), having previously earned a master's in law and a bachelor degree in law from Istanbul University. Her areas of research and specialisation include international private law, international commercial arbitration, foreign law and foreign investment law.

Bart Wauters is a full-time professor of law at IE University. He obtained his PhD in Legal History at the University of Leuven in 2004, and in that same year his thesis was awarded the Frans Van Cauwelaert Prize by the Royal Flemish Academy of Belgium for Science and the Arts. He was assistant and then professor of Roman law and Legal History at the universities of Leuven and Antwerp, before moving to Madrid, where he has been professor at IE University since 2011. His research activities focus on the history of human rights, the history of the concept of property, the history of legal theory and the history of Church–State relationships. He has also been a member of the board of directors of Miko (NYSE Euronext Brussels: MIKO) since 2013.

TABLE OF CASES

United States

Non-national Cases

Court of Justice of the European Union

International Arbitration Cases

TABLE OF LEGISLATIVE INSTRUMENTS

China

Colombia

France

Germany

Hong Kong

Italy

Malaysia

Netherlands

Paraguay

Peru

Portugal

Spain

Non-domestic Legislation and Instruments

EU Legislation and EU Instruments

European Commission

TABLE OF ABBREVIATIONS

The following table contains a non-exhaustive list of frequently used abbreviations.

CESL	Proposal for a Regulation of the European Parliament and of the Council on a Common European Sales Law[1]
CISG	United Nations Convention on Contracts for the International Sale of Goods[2]
CRD	Directive 2011/83/EU on consumer rights[3]
CJEU	Court of Justice of the European Union
DCD proposal	Digital Content Directive proposal[4]
DCFR	Draft Common Frame of Reference[5]
OSD proposal	Online Sales Directive proposal[6]
PECL	Principles of European Contract Law[7]
PLACL	Principles of Latin American Contract Law
TFEU	Treaty on the Functioning of the European Union[8]
UCC	American Uniform Commercial Code[9]

[1] Proposal for a Regulation of the European Parliament and of the Council of 11 October 2011 on a Common European Sales Law COM(2011) 635 final.

[2] United Nations Commission on International Trade Law, *United Nations Convention on Contracts for the International Sale of Goods* (United Nations, 1980).

[3] Directive 2011/83/EU of the European Parliament and of the Council of 25 October 2011 on consumer rights, amending Council Directive 93/13/EEC and Directive 1999/44/EC of the European Parliament and of the Council and repealing Council Directive 85/577/EEC and Directive 97/7/EC of the European Parliament and of the Council [2011] OJ L304/64.

[4] Proposal for a Directive of the European Parliament and of the Council of 9 December 2015 on certain aspects concerning contracts for the supply of digital content COM(2015) 634 final.

[5] C von Bar and H Schulte-Nölke (eds), *Principles, Definitions and Model Rules on European Private Law: Draft Common Frame of Reference (DCFR)*, outline edn (Sellier, 2009).

[6] Proposal for a Directive of the European Parliament and of the Council of 9 December 2015 on certain aspects concerning contracts for the online and other distance sales of goods COM(2015) 635 final.

[7] O Lando and H Beale (eds), *The Principles Of European Contract Law (Parts I, II, and III)*.

[8] Treaty on the Functioning of the European Union [2012] OJ C326/47.

[9] The American Law Institute and the National Conference of Commissioners on Uniform State Laws, *Uniform Commercial Code UCC*.

UCPD	Unfair Commercial Practices Directive[10]
ULIS	Uniform Law on the International Sale of Goods 1964[11]
UNIDROIT Principles	UNIDROIT Principles of International Commercial Contracts 2010[12]

[10] Directive 2005/29/EC of the European Parliament and of the Council of 11 May 2005 concerning unfair business-to-consumer commercial practices in the internal market and amending Council Directive 84/450/EEC, Directives 97/7/EC, 98/27/EC and 2002/65/EC of the European Parliament and of the Council and Regulation (EC) No 2006/2004 of the European Parliament and of the Council ('Unfair Commercial Practices Directive') [2005] OJ L149/22.

[11] Convention relating to a Uniform Law on the International Sale of Goods from 1 July 1964, The Hague.

[12] UNIDROIT International Institute for the Unification of Private Law, *UNIDROIT Principles of International Commercial Contracts 2010* (UNIDROIT, 2010).

1

The First Stage of Modern European Contract Law

FRANCISCO DE ELIZALDE

The withdrawal of the United Kingdom from the European Union has provoked some of the most serious reflection on the development of the EU for many decades. The official starting signal for this was fired with the Commission's White Paper on the Future of Europe,[1] which aims to steer the debate on how the EU should look in 2025. The White Paper presents five different scenarios that cover various possibilities—from maintaining the status quo, to a change of scope and priorities that would result in further integration, or, by contrast, in the EU gradually being re-centred on the internal market.

In any of those scenarios, such reflections will affect the process of harmonisation of European contract law. The White Paper has triggered the opportunity to assess it critically, a task that could reinforce it, as even before the Brexit vote, various proposals containing uniform rules for European contract law had failed to become hard law. The last one, the Common European Sales Law (CESL), was officially withdrawn by the European Commission in 2014[2] and watered down to two projected directives on digital content (DCD proposal) and online sales (OSD proposal). This was a hard blow, given the efforts made to establish an overarching harmonisation in contract law.

The recent history of European contract law[3] goes back to the Principles of European Contract Law (PECL) drafted by the members of the Commission on European Contract Law, chaired by Professor Ole Lando, which began its work in 1982 and completed it in 2003. The PECL contained model rules addressing general contract law, including formation, validity, interpretation, contents and effects, performance, and breach of contracts.

[1] COM(2017) 2025 of 1 March 2017. I thank Juan Cianciardo for his remarks on the future of the EU. Usual disclaimer applies.

[2] European Commission, Commission Work Programme 2015, COM(2014) 910 final, Annex 2 (n 60).

[3] For a detailed account, see H Beale, 'The story of EU contract law—from 2001 to 2014' in C Twigg-Flesner (ed), *Research Handbook on EU Consumer and Contract Law* (Edward Elgar, 2016) 432–62.

The European Commission moved forward in the construction of common rules with three communications: the 'Communication on European Contract Law',[4] the 'Action Plan on a More Coherent European Contract Law'[5] and 'European Contract Law and the Revision of the Acquis: The Way Forward'.[6] These paved the way for the Draft Common Frame of Reference (DCFR) of 2009 which was prepared by the Study Group on a European Civil Code, led by Professor von Bar, and the Research Group on Existing EC Private Law (Acquis Group), chaired by Professor Schulte-Nölke.

The DCFR was an ambitious project which went beyond contract law to propose model rules also for non-contractual liability, unjustified enrichment, acquisition and transfer of property rights over goods, security in movable assets and trusts. In respect of contracts, the DCFR contained rules for general contract law which incorporated the PECL in a revised form.[7] Additionally, it dealt with specific contracts: sale of goods, lease of goods, services (including, among others, construction, processing, storage and design), mandate contracts, commercial agency, franchise and distributorship, loan contracts, personal securities, and donations.

The DCFR was succeeded by a Feasibility Study, a draft optional instrument, produced by an Expert Group and published in May 2011.[8] The Commission asked the Expert Group 'to select those parts of the DCFR which were of direct relevance to contract law and to simplify, restructure, update and supplement the selected content'.[9] The last proposal in this trend, the CESL, already had a much more restricted scope as it was limited to sales. It derived from the Feasibility Study, was published in October 2011 and, as mentioned above, the European Commission withdrew it in 2014.

Parallel efforts were conducted by other relevant research networks. Among these, there is the work of the Academy of European Private Lawyers (chaired by Professor Gandolfi), which proposed a European Code of Contracts.[10] In turn, the *Association Henri Capitant des Amis de la Culture Juridique Française* and the *Société de Legislation Comparée* prepared the *Principes Contractuels Communs* and the *Terminologie Contractuelle Commune*.[11]

[4] Communication from the Commission to the Council and the European Parliament on European Contract Law of 11 July 2001 COM(2001) 398 final.

[5] Communication from the Commission to the European Parliament and the Council of 12 February 2003, 'A more coherent European contract law—An action plan' COM(2003) 68 final.

[6] Communication from the Commission to the European Parliament and the Council of 11 October 2004, 'European Contract Law and the Revision of the Acquis: The Way Forward' COM(2004) 651 final.

[7] DCFR, pp 30–33.

[8] See 'A European contract law for consumers and businesses: Publication of the results of the feasibility study carried out by the Expert Group on European contract law for stakeholders' and legal practitioners' feedback', ec.europa.eu/justice/contract/files/feasibility_study_final.pdf.

[9] ibid, 5.

[10] G Gandolfi (ed), *Code européen des contrats: avant-projet* (Giuffrè, 2007).

[11] In English, B Fauvarque-Cosson and D Mazeaud (eds), *European Contract Law, Materials for a Common Frame of Reference: Terminology, Guiding Principles, Model Rules* (Sellier, 2008).

The withdrawal of the CESL interrupted this enthusiastic trend. However, the history of successful uniform instruments, such as the UN Convention on Contracts for the International Sale of Goods (CISG), should remind us that achievements follow suffering, reconsiderations and patient wait. This might be the case for European contract law. The opportunities that the White Paper on the Future of Europe may offer should not start from scratch, as the amount and quality of the work that has been done in this field is unparalleled. However, the policies that have guided the harmonisation process and its outputs should be critically analysed before moving forward. The successes and failures of the process ought to be assessed in order to derive from them corresponding lessons for the future. The aim of this book is to offer a modest and necessarily limited contribution to the debate.

The collection is structured in four parts, to a large extent based on the aims of the uniform European rules on contract law set out in the PECL. Part I analyses the need for uniform rules to strengthen the internal market by facilitating cross-border trade. In Part II, the authors reflect on the impact of uniform rules on national legislators and courts. Part III deals with the effectiveness of uniform rules in bridging the gap between the common law and the civil law. Part IV assesses the influence of European uniform contract law in other non-EU countries. In addition to these four parts, Hugh Beale introduces the topic and Larry DiMatteo provides a conclusion.

In Chapter 2 Hugh Beale reflects on the inherent risks of comparative law and proposes ways to mitigate divergent interpretations of uniform rules. To this end, he highlights the importance of making policy choices before drafting a text. Additionally, Professor Beale gives importance to the task of elaborating commentaries of any proposed rules in order to justify and clarify their meaning as well as limiting their scope of application. Based on the comparative experience of English law and the civil law, his chapter then elaborates on the choice of drafting sets of contract rules rather than a unique model rule that does not distinguish between types of contracts or parties involved.

Part I ('Uniform Rules for the Internal Market') begins with Chapter 3, by Bart Wauters, who introduces the reader to the law of the Middle Ages. Professor Wauters illustrates that the *ius commune* (recurrently referred to in modern European private law) was by no means uniform in nature. Instead, he describes the experience of those times as a rich and multi-layered one in which civil, canon, local and merchant laws, among others, interacted with the work of scholars. The development of key concepts of contract law during the Middle Ages on occasion took place over centuries. This timeframe serves as a convenient warning against an impatient expectation of prompt results in respect of the ongoing European harmonisation process.

In Chapter 4, Juan José Ganuza and Fernando Gómez Pomar offer a law and economics perspective to harmonisation. The chapter assesses the efficiency of the process in a variety of possibilities, ranging from full to minimum harmonisation and taking into consideration the hypothesis of a binding or, alternatively, an optional instrument. To this end, the authors contemplate different factual scenarios and relate them to actual proposals for a uniform European contract law to determine whether a specific model is desirable or, instead, if the option should be tailor-made based on the circumstances.

In Chapter 5, Zeynep Derya Tarman conducts a mostly empirical assessment of soft law in jurisdiction and arbitral proceedings, with a detailed analysis of cases. She discusses in depth the relationship of non-state uniform contract rules with *lex mercatoria* and its application even when not expressly agreed by the parties. Professor Tarman's empirical checking of the use of uniform law in practice provides the collection with a factual basis to assess the impact of harmonisation on businesses and lawyers.

Part II ('Uniform Rules for National Legislators and Courts') opens with Chapter 6 by Encarna Roca Trías, who builds on her experience as a judge to highlight the role that courts have in the harmonisation of European contract law. This occurs in two ways. The first, within a clear constitutional framework, is the harmonious application of EU private law, which is to be enhanced by the recourse of preliminary references to the Court of Justice of the European Union (CJEU). The second, which is more controversial, is the use of the European texts of soft law to modernise national law and, at the same time, harmonise it with others in Europe. Professor Roca suggests that both paths may require further judicial cooperation.

The role of judges in the harmonisation of European contract law is further analysed in Chapter 7. Here, Thomas Ackermann reflects on the influence of uniform rules in Germany. He distinguishes between the effectiveness of uniform rules in respect of the legislator and the judiciary. Professor Ackermann offers an interesting perspective. He argues that 'uniform law pays for its legislative appeal as a systematic synthesis of comparative insights'. However, it is his view that the 'lack of the thick descriptions needed for a powerful comparative legal argument in the judicial process' have failed to have a significant impact in the judiciary—an important drawback to harmonisation.

In Chapter 8, Bénédicte Fauvarque-Cosson focuses on the influence of uniform rules on national legislators. In particular, she describes the inspiration that the deep reform of the French law of obligations has drawn from soft law instruments, mainly the PECL, the UNIDROIT Principles of International Commercial Contracts (UNIDROIT Principles) and the DCFR. Based on this fact, she points out the relevance of academics in shaping the law. Accordingly, Professor Fauvarque-Cosson reflects on the need for a 'genuine European teaching of contract law' that will highlight the common pattern of the new codes and legislations in the preparation of future lawyers.

Part III ('Uniform Rules to Bridge the Gap between the Common Law and the Civil Law') begins with Chapter 9, by Geraint Howells and Mateja Durovic. The authors present EU consumer law as an area of success in bridging the gap between different legal traditions. The chapter addresses two traditionally divergent rules and principles (the duty to provide pre-contractual information and the principle of good faith) to highlight the approximation. Additionally, the authors present the criterion of the 'average consumer' as an autonomous European concept that also serves the same end of harmonisation.

In Chapter 10, André Janssen and Navin Ahuja reflect upon the CISG and its merits as a legal hybrid that bridges the gap between the common and the civil law traditions. Besides the relevance of the Convention as a source of hard law, the authors express the paramount influence that the CISG has had in the development of uniform rules in Europe. This may be perceived in binding legal instruments, namely the Consumer Sales Directive,[12] and also in the main proposals of soft law, such as the PECL, the DCFR or the CESL. Moreover, Professors Janssen and Ahuja point out the influence of the CISG in the common development of national law. This amalgam of facts allows the authors to reflect upon the success of the CISG and, based on this, expand the outcome of such an important legal hybrid to the European harmonisation process.

In Chapter 11, Francisco de Elizalde focuses on a particular aspect of general contract law, the terms of contracts, and from this he extrapolates how harmonisation may occur in the margins of uniform rules. The interaction between the common law and the civil law is clearly present in the concept of 'guarantee' as an effect of terms and, less noticeably, in the binding force of pre-contractual information. The chapter emphasises the role of comparative law in building European contract law.

Part IV ('Uniform Rules as a Model for non-EU Countries') opens with Chapter 12, by Mateja Durovic, who introduces the reader to the initiatives that are taking shape in Eastern and South-Eastern Asia under the auspices of prominent scholars. According to the author, the European experience, with its successes and failures, can shed light on relevant decisions that are to be taken regarding Asian proposals for uniform rules, the most relevant of which, the Principles of Asian Contract Law (PACL), are influenced by the PECL. Common issues such as diversity in language, culture and legal traditions, the character of the proposed uniform rules or even concern about an autonomous interpretation of them, are analysed looking to the European harmonisation process.

In Chapter 13, Iñigo de la Maza introduces the Principles of Latin American Contract Law (PLACL) as a syncretism of regional peculiarities, and sees it as a move forward by incorporating rules derived from the main international and European instruments. The uneasy tension between them in the drafting of the PLACL is a difficult task. It is yet to be seen whether the recent abandonment by France of certain well-established concepts in contract law will help to untie certain knots that derive from nineteenth-century dogmatism as understood by the *Code Napoléon*, which was so influential in Latin America.

[12] Directive 1999/44/EC of the European Parliament and of the Council of 25 May 1999 on certain aspects of the sale of consumer goods and associated guarantees [1999] OJ L171/12.

In Chapter 14, Işik Önay reflects on the new Turkish Code of Obligations (TCO) and assesses the influence of EU legislation and the proposals to unify European contract law on it. His critical study selects certain novelties of the TCO which have received a diverse degree of influence (from very direct to indirect or almost none) from the said legislation and proposals. The political drive underlying harmonisation may be clearly perceived in this chapter as black-letter EU contract law legislation—more properly termed consumer contract law—has had a notoriously more important effect on Turkish law compared to European soft law instruments. This is a clear outcome of Turkey's efforts to become a member state of the EU and it highlights that traditional state-originated (or supra-state) law may still be the best tool for harmonisation.

The concluding remarks of the book look to the process of harmonisation from overseas. In Chapter 15, Larry DiMatteo provides an American perspective. After paying homage to those who have most heavily contributed to the harmonisation of contract law, he argues for the importance of scholars in this process. In the same vein, Professor DiMatteo defends the existing efforts to establish European legal education, as this would provide the 'intellectual infrastructure' needed when European contract law matures. Beyond policy decisions (among others, the choice of opt-in or opt-out instruments, or the balance between diversity and uniformity), the chapter concludes with an enthusiastic call to pursue the efforts in European contract law.

The book reunites most of the contributions to an international conference that was organised at IE University (Spain) on 23 and 24 June 2016—coincidentally, as the Brexit vote took place. Both the speakers and the conference attendants represented more than 30 different nationalities, in an uncommon mixture of students, academics, judges and practitioners from around the world. The collection also incorporates the work of scholars who did not take part in the conference but generously agreed to contribute.

The spirit of the conference was one of friendship while maintaining a rigorous academic substance. I am grateful to all the participants for this. I am deeply indebted to my colleagues at IE Law School—Marie-José Garot, Charlotte Leskinen, Fernando Pastor and Víctor Torre de Silva—and to Esteban Leccese for chairing the sessions. Most of them took on even more responsibilities than initially tasked with. Mateja Durovic's advice was crucial at the early stages of the event.

The organisation of the conference enjoyed the invaluable support of a group of students who managed to take care of every detail in a unique way: Vanessa Ardabili, Teresa Artaza, Sarah El Azouzi, David Fåhraeus, Paulina Godinuka, Calum Hedigan, Michelle Meier, Gracia Pujadas, Elena Recla, Adriana Rodríguez, Marie Trapet and Wojciech Zaluska. As always, Elena Peña helped them with enthusiastic commitment.

The conference served as a closing event for the EU Jean Monnet Module 'Towards a Common Private Law of Europe', coordinated by Marco de Benito. I am grateful to him for this opportunity. IE University, IE Law School and

IE University's Centre for European Studies should also be credited for their assistance. In respect of these, my thanks go to Soledad Atienza, Salvador Carmona, Javier de Cendra and Marie-José Garot.

This book would never have seen the light of day without the meticulous work of four bright students who helped throughout the editing process. Led by Wojciech Zaluska, the team also consisted of Sebastian Arnold, Sharai Mpofu and Gracia Pujadas. I am indebted to Hugh Beale for his guidance in preparing this collection. Sinead Moloney and her team at Hart Publishing supported the project from the start – I am very grateful to them. The responsibility for any errors remains, of course, mine alone.

2

The Role for European Contract Law: Uniformity or Diversity?

HUGH BEALE*

I. Introduction

This book is structured around the functions of principles of European contract law identified in the introduction to the Principles of European Contract Law (PECL). What we might call the 'high-level' aims are to strengthen what was then called the European single market (now the internal market) by facilitating cross-border trade, and to provide 'model rules' for national courts and legislators to adopt both inside and outside the European Union. To fulfil these aims, the objective was to provide a legal infrastructure in the form of rules of general contract law on which specific measures could be built; and in particular to bridge the gap between civil law and common law.[1]

The title of this chapter, 'uniformity or diversity', is not intended to call into question the whole project of trying to create a uniform contract law across Europe. Admittedly there are many, particularly in my country, who question whether there is any need for harmonising or unifying measures, especially outside the consumer field. They argue that the differences between the laws cause no problem. I do not agree. I admit that it is very hard to quantify the costs that are caused by differences between the laws of contract in the various member states; and I also accept that the evidence on which the European Commission has sometimes relied has been of little value. For example, while the responses to the Commission's Communication on Contract Law of 2001[2] gave examples

* I am very grateful to Francisco de Elizalde, IE University and the other sponsors of the conference at which this paper was presented for giving us the opportunity to reflect on and assess critically 'the current need for uniform rules in European contract law.' I was particularly honoured to be asked to give my paper as the opening address and a contribution to this book.

[1] PECL Parts I & II, Introduction, xxi–xxiii.

[2] Communication from the Commission to the Council and the European Parliament on European Contract Law of 11 July 2001 COM(2001) 398 final.

of obstacles to cross-border contracts, many of the examples were of obstacles created by particular regulations—for example, particular requirements for insurance contracts—and not of differences between general contract laws. Our colleagues Stefan Vogenauer and Stephen Weatherill conducted an empirical survey and concluded that:

> [T]wo thirds of companies face costly obstacles to trading with others in a different jurisdiction. A major reason for this is the existence of different legal systems ... As to the way ahead, a surprising 83% of businesses view the concept of a harmonised contract law favourably.[3]

Intuitively, moreover, it seems obvious that differences between the laws must cause at least some extra cost to cross-border contracting; and even if the differences are not of great practical importance, the risk of rules being significantly different is likely to form a psychological barrier to businesses which are not familiar with foreign law and cannot afford to take legal advice on it. I note that many of those who say that there is no problem, or who advise their clients to say there is no real problem, are lawyers who have developed expertise and ways—through precedent contracts, for example—to work around the problem. This does not mean that the problem does not continue to cause cost. A sceptic might add that such lawyers have a vested interest in maintaining the status quo.

Nor do I accept that law, and particularly contract law, is so culturally specific that it is impossible to contemplate having uniform rules.[4] I believe that lawyers and business people in any country are perfectly capable of adapting to new systems, even if those systems are very different to those to which they are accustomed. However, we know that when a legal concept is transplanted into a new and different legal environment, the transplant may grow very differently from how it has developed in its original habitat.[5] So when principles are being drafted with the aim of providing model rules for courts and legislators to follow, those courts and legislators must think carefully about how the new concept may fit into their legal system and how it is likely to develop. Equally the authors of the principles must explain very clearly how they envisage the concepts in their draft being applied and how the principles might be expected to develop in various contexts. When uniform rules are being proposed, we must be aware that lawyers from different backgrounds are likely to interpret them and apply them differently, so that

[3] S Vogenauer and S Weatherill, 'The European Community's Competence to Pursue the Harmonisation of Contract Law—an Empirical Contribution to the Debate' in S Vogenauer and S Weatherill (eds), *Harmonisation of European Contract Law: Implications for European Private Laws, Business and Legal Practice* (Hart Publishing, 2006) 105, 136–37; see also S Vogenauer, 'Regulatory Competition through Choice of Contract Law and Choice of Forum in Europe. Theory and Evidence' (2013) 21 *European Review of Private Law* 13.

[4] cp P Legrand, 'European Legal Systems are not converging' (1996) 45 *International and Comparative Law Quarterly* 52.

[5] The literature on legal transplants is vast. Here it suffices to cite G Teubner, 'Legal Irritants: Good Faith in British Law or How Unifying Law Ends up in New Divergences' (1998) 61 *Modern Law Review* 11.

the same rule may have very different effects in various environments; and that rules which work well in one environment may not be suitable for another.

In this chapter I make three basic arguments about 'uniform rules'. First, rules are not enough; they are not sufficiently informative. Secondly, the form of the principles that include the rules may need to vary according to the aim of the drafters. There may be a difference between drafting principles as a model for courts and legislators, and drafting them as a set of rules which are to be applied by the courts or (as soft law) by arbitrators.[6] Thirdly, the diversity of kinds of contract law that we have across the EU is not a purely historical accident. It may reflect not just different ideas but also different needs of the communities that the law is intended to serve. I would like to see uniformity in the sense of the same rules being available to legal actors across Europe, but that does not mean a single, 'one size fits all' measure. I would prefer to see diversity and choice. I end the chapter with a brief look at the current proposals from the European Commission and explain why I hope the Commission will be, as I believe that it will need to be, more ambitious in the future.

II. Rules are Not Enough

When we take a functional approach[7] to contract law, trying to strip out all the differences in concepts and in terminology between the various laws and looking at concrete results, it is evident that the different laws very frequently reach broadly similar results. This is so even when the common law systems are compared to the civil systems. However, I am sure readers are well aware of some of the dangers in making even functional comparisons.

A. False Friends

The first is of course the 'false friend', the concept which seems to be familiar but which is actually applied differently in different systems. For example both French law and English law seek to determine whether the parties have reached an agreement by applying an analysis based on offer and acceptance.[8] This isn't

[6] On these points see also H Beale, 'The Principles of Latin American Contract Law: a Response from an Outsider' in R Momberg and S Vogenauer, *The Future of Contract Law in Latin America* (Hart Publishing, 2017) ch 12.

[7] See K Zweigert and H Kötz, *An Introduction to Comparative Law*, T Weir (tr), 3rd edn (Oxford University Press, 1998) 34 ff.

[8] See the recently revised French Code civil, Arts 1113 to 1122; and any textbook on English contract law, eg E McKendrick, *Contract Law*, 11th edn (Palgrave, 2015) ch 3.

surprising; English law borrowed the concept from Pothier in the nineteenth century.[9] But although we both use offer and acceptance, the notions of agreement in the two legal systems still seem to be very different. My understanding is that French law still requires a meeting of the minds of the parties, at least in principle. English law flirted very briefly with subjective notions and the will theory (and so we find occasional references to the need for a 'consensus ad idem'[10]), but never adopted it.[11] Instead it applies an objective test, or more accurately a 'qualified objective test' to determine whether the parties have reached an agreement. If party A reasonably believes that party B has made an offer, A may accept the offer and there will be a binding contract even if B never intended to make a contract.[12]

B. Differing Techniques

Secondly, the different laws may reach similar results, but by employing very different techniques. Some laws of contract have come to rely very heavily on notions of good faith to develop controls over the behaviour of the contracting parties during negotiation and performance of the contract. This may well be because these controls were not included in the relevant civil code but had to be founded on one of its provisions, for example in German law on § 242 BGB. In other countries, and in particular in the common law, the courts have inherent power to develop the law and rather than rely on general clauses or principles have developed piecemeal solutions to situations that they consider need control.[13]

C. Radical Differences

Thirdly, there are some topics on which there are radical differences. Some of these may be linked to the underlying ideas of the relevant law. An example is when a party makes a mistake over the nature of what is being bought or sold or about its usefulness for the evident purpose of the contract (such as in the French cases where the buyer is mistaken as to the 'constructability' of the land he is buying[14]).

[9] See B Simpson, 'Innovation in Nineteenth Century Contract Law' (1975) 91 *Law Quarterly Review* 247. The borrowing seems first to have been made in the case of *Adams v Lindsell* (1818) 1 B & Ald 681, which introduced the infamous 'postal rule' of English law, that an acceptance of an offer made by post is complete when the letter of acceptance is posted.

[10] See H Beale (Gen ed), *Chitty on Contracts*, 32nd edn (Sweet & Maxwell, 2015) para 3-017.

[11] For a study of the influence of the will theory on the English doctrine of mistake, see C MacMillan, *Mistakes in Contract Law* (Hart Publishing, 2010).

[12] See *Smith v Hughes* (1871) LR 6 QB 597, 607; and for a full discussion, *Chitty on Contracts* (n 10) vol I paras 2-003 and 2-004.

[13] See the well-known explanation given by Bingham LJ in *Interfoto Picture Library Ltd v Stiletto Visual Programmes Ltd* [1989] 1 QB 433, 439.

[14] eg Cass Civ 3.2.1981, D 1984.J.497; B Nicholas, *French Law of Contract*, 2nd edn (Oxford University Press, 1992) 103.

Civil law systems often will give relief on the basis that the party's consent was not fully informed and so the contract may be avoided for mistake. The common law, at least in England and Wales, refuses to give relief in such a case[15] unless the buyer's belief was induced by an incorrect statement (a 'misrepresentation'—which may have been made in good faith and without negligence[16]) by the seller.

These differences mean that the law in each country may start from a very different place, and this may lead two widely diverging interpretations of text of supposedly uniform laws.[17]

D. Reducing the Risks of Different Interpretations

How can this risk be reduced? I think that at least four steps should be taken. First, any group drafting principles should not begin with a proposed text but with a discussion of the policy, the outcomes that it wants to achieve. This was one of the lessons that I was taught when I was appointed to the Law Commission of England and Wales. The Law Commission was very fortunate to be assisted by Parliamentary Counsel, who are highly skilled in drafting. At first I was rather upset to be told that if I put forward my own draft, there was a very great risk that others would interpret my intentions in a completely different fashion from that intended. However, practical experience of testing drafts made me realise that often this was indeed so. The drafter of a text may know what she means, but there is no guarantee that others will interpret it the same way, and so if the policy is not discussed there is a risk that everyone signs up to a form of words that mean different things to different people.

Secondly, it is a good idea to capture the basic approach in the text rather than leaving it to be understood. For example, Article 2:102 PECL provides:

> The intention of a party to be legally bound by contract is to be determined from the party's statements or conduct as they were reasonably understood by the other party.

This is a very important provision because it shows that the PECL also adopts a 'qualified objective' approach.

A third possible approach is to spell out exactly how general provisions are to be applied in as much detail as possible. This is the traditional approach of Parliamentary Counsel. However it can lead to long texts that even English readers, let alone readers who are brought up on the elegance and brevity of Portalis, find completely indigestible. At least for international instruments, it is much more

[15] *Smith v Hughes* (1871) LR 6 QB 597, 604, 608, 610; *Statoil ASA v Louis Dreyfus Energy Services LP (The Harriette N)* [2008] EWHC 2257 (Comm), [2008] 2 Lloyd's Rep 685, [88]–[91].

[16] *Redgrave v Hurd* (1881) 20 Ch D 1. On misrepresentation see eg *Chitty on Contracts* (n 10) vol I ch 7; McKendrick (n 8) ch 13.

[17] See also H Beale, 'The Principles of European Contract Law and Harmonisation of the Laws of Contract' in Andersen, Fejø and Nielsen (eds), *Festskrift til Ole Lando* (GadJura, 1997) 21, 35.

practicable to adopt general clauses or open textured provisions. But then the texts are more open than ever to divergent interpretations.

E. Comments

So I favour a fourth approach, which is to ensure that every article is accompanied by comments, which not only should explain how the article is expected to be applied but also should give examples. The examples should be of two kinds: there should be some 'central' cases, relatively simple applications of the rule, in order to show the basic idea, and then some examples which are more marginal, or even which are NOT intended to be covered, in order to show the intended limits of the provision.

Unfortunately there is a difficulty with comments. EU legislation has to be in a standard format—Articles preceded by Recitals. When the Expert Group,[18] of which I was a member, was working on the first draft[19] of the Common European Sales Law (CESL), we were asked to produce comments,[20] but after the Commission's Legal Services pointed out that these could not be part of the legislation, the idea was quietly dropped. I am sure that one of the reasons that the proposed CESL encountered so much resistance in the European Council was that members of the working group found it hard to understand what the provisions were supposed to mean without an accompanying commentary. The Commission then asked us to produce comments to help them to explain the provisions. Comments on most chapters were eventually drafted and I have been told that they were used by the Commission officials in their negotiations, but the draft comments were never made public. It would have been much better had they been prepared before the proposal was announced and incorporated into the explanatory memorandum, or even just made available as an informal guide to the proposal.

In the Explanatory Memorandum to the recent proposals for directives on digital content ('the DCD') and on online sales ('the OSD'), the Commission says that it has learned lessons from the CESL episode.[21] Unfortunately the lesson about comments and illustrations is not one of the lessons that the Commission appears to have learned. There are quite a number of provisions in the proposals which are very hard to understand without illustrations of what is or is not intended.

[18] Commission Decision (2010/233/EU) of 26 April 2010 setting up the Expert Group on a Common Frame of Reference in the area of European contract law [2010] OJ L105/109.

[19] The draft was published as 'A European contract law for consumers and businesses: Publication of the results of the feasibility study carried out by the Expert Group on European contract law for stakeholders' and legal practitioners' feedback' (May 2011).

[20] *Working Method*, para 1(b). This was a document presented to the Expert Group by the Commission at its first meeting and adopted by the Group.

[21] See p 2 of each proposal.

III. Intended Function and Form

A. Policy Choices

While comments seem to be an essential part of any set of principles, what else is needed may vary according to the function that the principles are intended to serve.

If the principles are intended to serve as a set of rules to govern the relevant transaction (whether as uniform law, as an optional law like the CESL or as 'soft law' that can be applied by arbitrators), what ultimately matters is how the rules are supposed to work, and comments of the kind I have just described may suffice. If however the principles are intended to serve as a model for courts or legislators—for example, in the way that the European Commission seems to have envisaged for the Common Frame of Reference, which was to provide model rules, based on the best solutions found in the laws of the member states' laws and international conventions[22]—more will be needed. Why is the rule proposed the 'best'? What alternatives, whether drawn from existing laws within Europe or elsewhere, were considered? Was any particular methodology, such as economic analysis, used in order to determine which was the best solution? Was it considered to be the best solution in all cases, or only under certain conditions? In other words, as the European Commission accepted during the course of preparation of the Common Frame of Reference, policy choices should be clearly explained, with the reasons for the choice in fact made.

An explanation of the policy choices, and of any conditions or limits on the applicability of the choices, would be particularly valuable if the principles are to be considered as models outside Europe. This is because things that can generally be assumed within Europe may not apply in very different communities. In particular, the legal context may be very different. The machinery of justice and the legal profession may not operate in the ways they do in Europe; there may be no superstructure of rules to protect consumers or employees; and, in terms of the substantive law, the rest of the law—for example, the rules of non-contractual liability and property law, with which the law of contract will necessarily have to interact—may be different. The economic context may also be very different. For example, we tend to assume that there is a fairly well-developed market for goods and services, so that it is not necessary to have controls over prices.[23] That is not an assumption that can be made in all economies.

[22] Communication from the Commission to the European Parliament and the Council of 11 October 2004, 'European Contract Law and the Revision of the Acquis: The Way Forward' COM(2004) 651 final para 3.1.3 p 11.

[23] Thus Art 4(2) of the Directive on Unfair Terms in Consumer Contracts (Council Directive 93/13/EEC of 5 April 1993) [1993] OJ L95/29 provides that the adequacy of the price and remuneration, on the one hand, as against the services or goods supplied in exchange, on the other, may not be assessed for fairness, in so far as the term is in plain intelligible language.

I think an explanation of policy choices is also needed if the principles are to perform another 'infrastructure role', namely to provide definitions for terms and concepts used in EU legislation. This seems to have been another of the Commission's aims for the CFR.[24] Directives and regulations frequently use legal terms without defining them—the classic example being the use of the word 'damage' in the Package Travel Directive.[25] The Court of Justice held that the term should be given an autonomous European legal meaning, not the meaning under the applicable national law. The hope was, first, that courts would draw on the CFR to establish the European legal meaning;[26] and secondly, that legislators might positively indicate that terms should be interpreted in accordance with the CFR unless the legislation provide differently.[27] For either purpose, it would seem desirable that the comments to the principles should explain any alternative definitions that might have been chosen, particularly if in some contexts one of the alternatives might be more appropriate than another.

In other words, if the principles are to be used as 'model rules' for courts and legislators, they should be accompanied by not only comments, but also an explanation of the policy choices that were made. The PECL did not do this for every article. Of course, legislators and courts can draw on the PECL nonetheless—and we have evidence that the PECL were considered extensively in the process of modernising the laws of contract in some countries.[28] However, I think the PECL would have been more useful as a model if there had been more consistent and fuller explanations. In the process of developing the Common Frame of Reference, we made this point to the Commission and the Commission adopted it as a requirement.[29] As a result, in producing the CFR we had to revisit some of the PECL provisions, even if the articles were incorporated into the CFR without any change, to try to reconstruct the reasons for adoption of the article and explain them in the comments. Likewise, when I tried to draft comments on the CESL it

[24] See Commission (n 22) para 3.1.3 p 11.

[25] Case C-168/00 *Simone Leitner v TUI Deutschland GmbH & Co KG* [2002] ECR I-02631.

[26] The PECL and the DCFR have been cited for this purpose in the Court of Justice: Case C-404/06 *Quelle AG v Bundesverband der Verbraucherzentralen und Verbraucherverbände* [2008] ECR 2008 I-02685 para AG44 (citing the PECL in fn 28); Case C-227/08 *Martin v EDP* [2009] ECR I-11939 para AG51; Case 445/06 *Danske Slagterier v Germany* [2009] ECR I-02119 para AG94, fn 57 (both citing the DCFR).

[27] See H Beale, 'The Future of the Common Frame of Reference' (2007) 3 *European Review of Contract Law* 263.

[28] E Clive, 'European Initiatives (CFR) and Reform of Civil Law in New Member States' (2008) XIV *Iuridica International* 18–26; esp I Kull, 'Reform of Contract Law in Estonia: Influences of Harmonisation of European Private Law' (2008) ibid 122; A Kisfaludi, 'The Influence of Harmonisation of Private Law on the Development of the Civil Law in Hungary' (2008) ibid 130; J Rajski, 'European Initiatives and Reform of Civil Law in Poland' (2008) ibid 151. See also N Jansen, 'Legal Pluralism in Europe: National Law, European Legislation and Non-legislative Codifications' in L Niglia (ed), *Pluralism and European Private Law* (Hart Publishing, 2013) 109.

[29] See Report from the European Commission of 23 September 2005 First Annual Progress Report on European Contract Law and the Acquis Review COM(2005) 456 final para 2.6.3.

was not always easy to establish why particular provisions had been adopted in the form in which they appeared.

Some of information about the policy choices that were made, and why, may be gleaned from *travaux préparatoires*. For example, minutes were taken of the meetings of the Expert Group that prepared the first draft of the CFR;[30] and we have (unpublished) minutes of all the meetings of the Commission on European Contract Law and of the Coordinating Committee of the Study Group on a European Civil Code. However, in my experience minutes of this kind are not always helpful in establishing why a particular decision was made. First, the minutes normally reflect only the discussion and the decisions reached. If a text was uncontroversial it would often be accepted without detailed discussion, so the policy choice might not be stated. Secondly, when a choice was debated and either a consensus reached or the choice was decided by vote, it was often the case that members of the group supported a particular solution for different reasons, so a clear rationale is not always evident. And with the CESL there was no public record of the decisions made by the European Commission between the publication of the 'Feasibility Study' draft[31] and the final proposal,[32] either on the changes made to the Expert Group's text (most of which were placed in the Annex) or on the 'chapeau' rules contained in the Regulation itself, which were not subject to consultation before the proposal was made.

The example of the CESL suggests that even a set of rules that is intended to become hard law may need an explanation of the policy choices, not for their ultimate operation but in order to convince legislators that these are the right rules to adopt. So at least temporarily the principles might need a separate 'policy choices' document.

B. Comparative Notes

The third component found in the PECL and the DCFR are comparative notes. These not only set out the sources that have inspired the provision but provide a brief note on the similarities to and differences from the relevant provisions of the laws of the member states. Gathering the comparative information and writing these notes is a long and often painful process, but I think it is important. First, if we are genuinely to treat our principles as resting to any extent on what is common to our various laws of contract, we have to do the comparative work—and demonstrate that we have done it. But secondly, the comparative notes have a lasting value. EU legislators need to know what is 'out there', to what extent the laws of the member states already cover an issue and whether any differences between the

30 Currently the minutes of the Expert Group's meetings seem not to be available on the web.
31 See n 18.
32 See n 19.

laws is likely to cause uncertainty for traders, in order to decide whether EU legislation is needed. Also they have to try to ensure that what is proposed will 'fit' with the various national laws.[33] Conversely, at the national level, comparative notes should help lawyers—whether legislators deciding how to implement directives, courts interpreting the EU legislation or lawyers seeking to understand it—to see how the legislation is intended to affect their law.

The comparative notes also help considerably in the process of establishing a shared legal language in which lawyers can discuss European and comparative contract law. I believe that to date, one of the most significant achievements of the PECL and at least some parts of the DCFR has been to establish a *lingua franca* for European contract law—even if work remains to be done in some other fields.

IV. Diversity in Substance

Do we want rules for contract law that are uniform in substance across the EU? My answer is yes: but not a single set of rules. We need set*s* of rules.

A. Consumer and Employment Law versus General Contract Law

At the national level, lawyers in many member states have to admit that in reality we no longer have a law of contracts: we have several laws, each for a different type of contracts: consumer contracts, employment contracts and, in many member states, housing contracts. I do not know of any member state that has an entirely separate set of rules for each type of contract; the contracts remain subject to the general law of contracts to the extent that the general law is not superseded by the special rules for consumer, employment or housing contracts. But the extent of special regulation at the 'sharp end' of these contracts is such that we can sensibly talk about different regimes. The same would have to be true of any broad legislation at the EU level.

B. Differences Between General Contract Laws

In contrast, in most systems, B2B contracts and contracts between parties neither of which is a business ('C2C' contracts) are governed largely by general contract law; and at present these 'residual laws' vary significantly. Yes, in terms of practical outcomes there is much that is shared, even between systems as different as the common law and the Romanic civil law systems—more than one might at first

[33] See H Beale (n 27) 264, arguing that the Notes provide 'essential background information'.

think. But there are also some dramatic differences in outcome. Let me illustrate this by pointing out some of the differences between the common law of England and Wales and some of the major civil law systems.

I say that there are fewer differences than might appear at first because some apparent differences do not make a lot of practical difference. For example, a peculiar characteristic of the common law is the doctrine of consideration,[34] but in practice this seldom brings a very different outcome. This is because, on the one hand, most contracts involve some sort of exchange—typically, goods or services are exchanged for money, so the doctrine of consideration will be satisfied; and on the other, in the case of a promise to make a gift, the typical case in which the promise will lack the consideration that is required by English law, the promisor has only to put the promise into the form of a deed in order to make it binding.[35] The net effect is really not very different to those systems which say that a promise to make a gift is a contract but that the contract will be unenforceable unless it has been notarised:[36] a gift promise is enforceable if the promisor has taken the correct formal steps. The refusal of English law to require specific performance of a contract unless damages would not be an adequate remedy[37] is perhaps more significant—but here it must be recalled that in many systems, 'enforced performance' can include obtaining performance by a third person at the debtor's expense.[38] Very much the same effect is achieved in English law by allowing the creditor to terminate the contract, obtain a substitute performance from another party and recover damages for the difference in value, plus any other loss.

However, there are at least three substantial differences between the English law of contract and many of the continental laws. They are: (1) the absence of any duty of disclosure, coupled with the absence of any remedy when one party fails to point out even a known mistake of fact to the other and any notion of fraud by silence;[39] (2) the absence of any controls over non-negotiated terms, other than limited controls over clauses that purport to exclude or restrict a party's liability;[40] and (3) the absence of any mechanism for adjusting or terminating contracts that have become very onerous to one party because of an unforeseen change of circumstance.[41]

[34] See eg *Chitty on Contracts* (n 10) vol I ch 4; McKendrick (n 8) ch 5.

[35] See *Chitty on Contracts* (n 10) vol I para 1-136; McKendrick (n 8) 61.

[36] eg French Code civil, Art 931; German BGB § 518.

[37] See eg *Chitty on Contracts* (n 10) vol I para 27-005 ff; McKendrick (n 8) 384.

[38] eg French Code civil, Art 1122; German Zivilprozessordnung § 887.

[39] I have explored this topic at some length in H Beale, *Mistake and Non-disclosure of Facts: Models for English Contract Law* (Oxford University Press, 2012).

[40] Unfair Contract Terms Act 1977; see *Chitty on Contracts* (n 10) vol I ch 15; McKendrick (n 9) ch 11.

[41] cp BGB § 313, and now French Code civil Art 1195 (introduced in 2016). For a comparison before the change to French law, see H Beale, Fauvarque-Cosson et al, *Ius Commune Casebooks for the Common Law of Europe: Cases, materials and text on Contract Law*, 2nd edn (Hart, 2010) ch 24; J Bell and I de Lamberterie, 'The Effect of Change in Circumstances on Long-term Contracts' in D Harris and D Tallon, *Contract Law Today: Anglo-French Comparisons* (Clarendon Press, 1989) 195.

I have not included the absence of a doctrine of good faith in my list. This is because, as I have explained, I see the doctrine primarily as a technique by which the courts achieve results, and I think many of the results that continental courts reach by applying good faith could equally be reached by English courts.[42] However, the fact remains that, quite apart from in relation to the points already listed, English courts have been much more reluctant to require parties to have reasonable regard to the other party's interests than have many continental courts. To give just a single example, I doubt many Supreme Courts would follow the example of the Privy Council on an appeal from Hong Kong, in allowing a seller of land to terminate the contract, and also to forfeit the 10 per cent deposit already paid by the buyer, because the buyer was 10 minutes late in paying the price.[43] This reluctance seems to be a fourth difference, and arguably the one that underlies the other three.

Although these differences are few in number, they are very significant. I have argued elsewhere[44] that they are not just the result of historical accident; the courts have developed other areas of private law in radical ways, and they could have done the same here. Either English courts are seriously misguided and English law is seriously defective, or, as I believe to be the correct explanation, it is operating on different assumptions and is trying to achieve something different.

C. Different Approaches to Contract Law

First, the English courts seem to expect a much greater degree of self-sufficiency from the parties. The parties are expected to ask questions before they make a contract, not to rely on the other to tell them; they are expected to read and consider the terms of the contract before they sign, and to object to what they do not like; and they are also expected to consider how the contract may be affected by future changes and, if they think it will need adjustment, to include suitable hardship or adjustment clauses in their agreement.

Secondly, English law places greater emphasis on protecting reasonable reliance.[45] As we saw earlier, a party cannot escape from a contract because it was mistaken as to the nature of the subject matter, or its usefulness, unless its mistake was caused by the other party. Similarly with the other 'vitiating factors'; English

[42] cp the often-quoted dictum of Bingham LJ in *Interfoto Picture Library Ltd v Stiletto Visual Programmes Ltd* [1989] QB 433, 439: 'In many civil law systems, and perhaps in most legal systems outside the common law world, the law of obligations recognises and enforces an overriding principle that in making and carrying out contracts parties should act in good faith … English law has, characteristically, committed itself to no such overriding principle but has developed piecemeal solutions in response to demonstrated problems of unfairness.'

[43] *Union Eagle Ltd v Golden Achievement Ltd* [1997] AC 514.

[44] H Beale, 'The Impact of the decisions of the European courts on English contract law: the limits of voluntary harmonisation' (2010) 18 *European Review of Private Law* 501.

[45] The classic article is J Steyn, 'Contract Law: Protecting the Reasonable Expectations of Honest Men' (1997) 113 *Law Quarterly Review* 433.

law does not look at whether A's consent was free, but at whether B's behaviour was somehow so improper that B should forfeit the right to rely on the contract. For example, duress or undue influence by a third person is not a ground on which the victim may avoid a contract unless the other party to the contract knew or had constructive notice of the facts.[46]

Thirdly, when the English courts do interfere, they tend to do so on specific grounds, so that, for example, controls over the negotiating process are less intrusive than in continental systems.[47]

Fourthly, the reluctance to adopt broad standards of control is often based on a fear that broad standards will be applied in different ways by different judges, so that outcomes will be uncertain. This creates risk for the parties, and, the courts argue, may result in more litigation.[48]

Fifthly, the relationship between the law and the parties seems to be conceived differently in England and in many continental countries. The law of contract is seen as merely reflecting what the parties probably wanted, rather than as laying down standards to which they ought to adhere.[49] It is symptomatic that the obligations of a seller to deliver goods of a proper quality[50] are not seen as standards, but as implied terms, ie terms based on what the parties would normally want; and there seems to be much less concern over deviations from the legislative norms.[51]

[46] See the line of cases concerning 'surety wives' beginning with *Barclays Bank Plc v O'Brien* [1994] 1 AC 180; and in particular *Royal Bank of Scotland v Etridge (No. 2)* [2001] UKHL 44, [2002] 2 AC 773. cp French Code civ Art 1142; for German law, see H Beale, Fauvarque-Cosson et al (n 41) 599.

[47] So there is no general rule against breaking off negotiations at the last moment even if you know that the other party is relying on a contract; but if you have carelessly told the other party that the draft contract is certain to be approved by Head Office when in fact there is no chance of that, you may be liable in tort for misrepresentation: see *Box v Midland Bank Ltd* [1979] 2 Lloyd's Rep 391. An appeal on the question of costs only was allowed: [1981] 1 Lloyd's Rep 434.

[48] See the useful discussion in McKendrick (n 8) 217–22, esp 219.

[49] cp BGB § 307(2) para (1).

[50] Sale of Goods Act 1979, ss 13–15. Until 2015 these provisions also applied to consumer contracts, although the consumer could not contract out of them even the consumer wanted to do so: Unfair Contracts Terms Act 1977, former s 6(2). In the Consumer Rights Act 2015, the 'implied terms' have been replaced by terms that are 'to be treated as included' in the contract: for goods contracts, see ss 9–18.

[51] It is true that if a term falls within the provisions of the Unfair Contract Terms Act 1977, for example because it excludes or restricts a party's liability for breach of contract, and is enforceable only if it satisfies the requirement of reasonableness, it is for the party claiming that the term satisfies the requirement of reasonableness to show that it does: s 11(5). But in practice in most B2B contracts the courts have no hesitation in upholding terms that exclude or restrict liability. The current opinion seems to be that the parties' apparent choice should be respected: 'Where experienced businessmen representing substantial companies of equal bargaining power negotiated an agreement, they may be taken to have had regard to the matters known to them. They should, in my view, be taken to be the best judges of the commercial fairness of the agreement which they have made; including the fairness of each of the terms of that agreement' (Chadwick LJ in *Watford Electronics Ltd v Sanderson CFL Ltd* [2001] EWCA Civ 317, [2001] Build LR 143, [63]). See *Chitty on Contracts* (n 11) paras 15-110 and 15-111. In contrast, if a term has a harsh effect that neither party contemplated because they did not foresee the events that occurred, it may be held to be unreasonable: eg *Britvic Soft Drinks Ltd v Messer UK Ltd* [2002] EWCA Civ 548, [2002] 2 Lloyd's Rep 368.

Lastly, the role of the judge in contract cases may be understood differently. It is not to investigate in full the rights and wrongs by some abstract sense of justice, but to dispose of the dispute as speedily as possible. The objective principle itself may be the product of trying to make trials simpler—how can subjective intention be proved, when 'the devil himself knoweth not the mind of men'?[52] Little else than a desire to limit what has to be investigated and so to make trials simpler can explain exclusionary rules such as that, when the court is seeking to interpret the contract, it may not consider either what was said in the course of negotiating the contract[53] or the behaviour of the parties after the contract was made.[54] And the parties are allowed, even encouraged, to limit what the court wants to consider even further, for example by employing 'merger' (or 'entire agreement') clauses in order to deny effect to any agreements that were not in the written documents[55] and 'no reliance' clauses to exclude any evidence that one party might have given incorrect information to the other party.[56]

D. Rules that are Appropriate for the Legal Subject

Such a scheme of contract law is obviously very different from many continental laws, and indeed from the PECL. But is it 'better' or 'worse' than the PECL? I do not think we can answer that without knowing, 'better' or 'worse' for what? What is the economic context in which the law will be operating—will there, for example, be a developed and competitive market? What kinds of contract and of dispute will the law have to cope with? Who will typically be the parties?

I have argued elsewhere that one of the reasons that English contract law seems to assume such a degree of self-sufficiency among contracting parties is that the parties who typically appear before the higher courts fit that model.[57] Partly because of the high cost of litigation, contract disputes will seldom be heard at this level unless significant sums are at stake. This means that the contracts are normally between businesses of some size. They may have in-house counsel who will have overseen the making of the contract, or they may have taken external legal advice before entering it. In addition they are often 'repeat players', for whom contracts of the relevant type are routine and who therefore can be presumed to

[52] Brian CJ in 17 Edw IV, *T Pasch case*, 2 (1477), cited in *Brogden v Metropolitan Railway Company* (1877) 2 App Cas 666, 692.

[53] *Chartbrook Ltd v Persimmon Homes Ltd* [2009] UKHL 38, [2009] 1 AC 1101.

[54] *James Miller & Partners Ltd v Whitworth Street Estates (Manchester) Ltd* [1970] AC 572, 603.

[55] See *McGrath v Shah* (1989) 57 P & CR 452; *North Eastern Properties Ltd v Coleman* [2010] EWCA Civ 277, [2010] 1 WLR 2715 [55], [82]–[83]. Entire agreement clauses are discussed in *Chitty on Contracts* (n 10) para 13-107.

[56] See *Chitty on Contracts* (n 10) para 7-144. The courts seem very ready to uphold these clauses, see eg *Springwell Navigation Corp v JP Morgan Chase Bank* [2010] EWCA Civ 1221, [2010] 2 CLC 705.

[57] See n 41.

have a very good idea of what they are doing. That is not to say that they are always of equal bargaining power, but they will have a good idea of the risks they have in signing up to terms dictated by the other party, even if they cannot bargain for much of an improvement in them. Between such parties, the old notions of freedom and sanctity of contract, and of self-reliance—'*qui dit contractuel dit juste*'[58]—are quite plausible. These are parties who can be expected to know what information they need before they enter the contract, and to ask for it; to be well aware of the risks of relying on getting a contract before the documents have been signed; to read and understand the terms of the contract even if the terms were drafted by the other party; who can be expected to think about how the contract will work out and what 'tricks' the other party might get up to, and draft clauses to prevent them; and, in long-term contracts, to anticipate changes in the circumstances and to draft their own clauses to deal with them. And if the party had not done any of those things—well, this was just one contract, the losing party will have learned valuable lessons for next time.

The emphasis on certainty and predictability of the outcome is probably explained by two factors. The first is that the higher the sums involved, the greater the risk caused by uncertainty. The second is that often the contracts are in volatile markets, such as the commodities or charter-party markets, and there is a great deal of money at stake because of a major shift in market conditions since the contract was made. The real issue becomes whether one party has the right to escape from the contract that has turned out unfavourably. Parties who are each convinced that the court will side with them may even end up investing more in litigation than the dispute is worth.[59] Trying to get out of a contract on the basis of a slight breach by the other party when your real motive is to escape a bad bargain may seem to be contrary to good faith or to be an abuse of right. The English courts have sometimes applied relatively flexible standards to prevent such abuses;[60] but often they have applied a rigid approach, that a breach of contract may justify termination even if the consequences are not serious on the basis that this must be what the parties would have wanted—a rigid, 'bright line' rule under which the parties will supposedly know exactly when their legal rights are.[61]

[58] A Fouillée, *La science sociale contemporaine*, 2nd edn (Hachette, 1885) 410: see L Rolland, '«Qui dit contractuel, dit juste.» (Fouillée) … en trois petits bonds, à reculons' (2006) 51 *McGill LJ* 765, 771.

[59] G Priest, 'Breach and Remedy for the Tender of Non-conforming Goods' (1978) 91 *Harvard LR* 960.

[60] *Hong Kong Fir Shipping Co Ltd v Kawasaki Kisen Kaisha Ltd* [1962] 2 QB 26, CA.

[61] *Bunge Corp v Tradax Export SA* [1981] 1 WLR 711, HL. However, the Law Commission rightly points out that when a rigid rule seems to produce a very unjust result, the courts have a tendency to fudge the issue, for example by finding that there was no breach in the first place: Law Commission, *Sale and Supply of Goods* (Law Com No 160, 1987) para 4.1. An example is *Cehave NV v Bremer Handelsgesellschaft mbH* [1976] QB 44, the effect of which had to be corrected by amendments to the Sale of Goods Act 1979; see the report cited and ss 14(2) and 15A of the 1979 Act.

E. Why not Include Protections that are Applied Cautiously?

It can be argued that every law should contain controls, such as general clauses that can potentially be applied to any contract, but then should exercise restraint, very seldom applying them to B2B contracts. I understand that this is what happens in the Nordic systems, whose contracts acts contain a general clause[62] that, outside cases of mistake,[63] is applied only in fairly extreme circumstances. But in England it is often argued by commercial lawyers that if a party can challenge a clause, they may be able to use the challenge as a delaying tactic, even though the challenge is almost bound to fail.[64] For example, the lessee of a machine under a finance lease which is having difficulty meeting the schedule of payments might, when sued for the payment, trump up an allegation that the machine was defective. It would then argue that the lessor was responsible for the defect and is therefore not entitled to the payments, even if the contract clauses make it clear that it is the supplier, not the finance lessor, to whom the lessee should look to in the case of a defect, and the supplier had in fact given a guarantee that would cover the alleged defect. In a summary judgment it will not be possible to decide either whether there was a defect or whether the clauses are valid.

F. Choosing Appropriate Rules

In other words, a legal system that is dealing much more frequently with commodity contracts and charter parties is likely to develop different characteristics from one that deals regularly with contracts made by small businesses or private individuals who acted without legal advice. So legislators and courts considering a set of principles or indeed a national law of contract as a model should consider carefully: who will be the audience for/the subjects of the intended law? Do we want all the controls that were built into, say the CESL?

But even more pertinently to my theme, I believe that parties should be entitled to choose the law that they consider is the most suitable for their purposes. Some are arguably unsuitable for certain types of transactions. It is well-known that some large industrial firms in Germany have been using Swiss law for their export contracts, to avoid the extensive controls that the BGB gives the courts over standard contract terms. Conversely, it is certainly arguable that English law currently fails to provide adequate protection for small businesses, because the Unfair Contract Terms Act (UCTA) 1977 gives protection only against a narrow range

[62] Nordic Contracts Act s 33. See also O Lando et al, *A Restatement of Nordic Contract Law* (Djøf Publishing, 2016) § 4–5.

[63] Discussed in H Beale (n 39), 66–67. See also S Whittaker and R Zimmermann, *Good Faith in European Contract Law* (CUP, 2000) 230–33.

[64] See Law Commission, *Unfair Terms in Contracts* (Law Com No 292, Scot Law Com No 199, 2005) para 4.10.

of clauses.[65] My prime objection to proposals for a single, uniform European law of contract is that 'one size does not fit all'. To me, one of the great advantages of the CESL proposal was that it would have allowed B2B parties to select a regime that was appropriate to their needs. Had it been adopted, I would have urged the UK Government to exercise its option to make the CESL available for non-cross-border contracts,[66] and to have encouraged small businesses to ask for it when making contracts.

G. Will Protective Sets of Rules Ever be Chosen?

As I have argued elsewhere,[67] there would certainly have been a question about whether the CESL would ever have been used. Would the other party—a large business, say—ever have agreed to contract on the terms of the CESL? The CESL provided extensive protection to the other party. That would have meant the larger business facing increased costs if it agreed to contract on the CESL. For example, a business which usually contracts on its own standard terms and insists on the contract being governed by English law would suddenly have found that the other party would be able to challenge those terms on the grounds of unfairness—with the result, for example, that the larger business might have been unable to rely on a price increase clause to increase its prices freely. It might have had to disclose information that it does not have to disclose under current English law. Its behaviour might have been challenged in ways that were not possible under its earlier contracts. The larger business might well have been reluctant to contract on the CESL unless it was paid enough extra, or obtained the goods or services that it wanted at a sufficiently lower price, to compensate for the increase in costs and risk. In other words, use of the CESL might have entailed the SME paying a 'premium' to the larger business for getting the contract on the CESL and therefore obtaining the legal protection that the SME wanted.

Would an SME be prepared to pay this sort of premium? I think the answer is yes: SMEs, or at least some SMEs, might well think that it is worth paying the premium. The increased cost is likely to be relatively low, and I think the SMEs would view it as a kind of insurance—pay a small premium and get protection against a range of 'contractual accidents'. Basic law and economics then tells us that if the SME is prepared to 'pay' the premium (or, as the case may be, to accept slightly lower prices for its products), the larger firm will find it worthwhile offering the

[65] Clauses that purport to exclude or restrict liability for breach of contract (and in some cases, only where the terms was part of one party's written standard terms of business) and clauses that purport to allow the proferens of written standard terms to perform in a way that is substantially different from what was reasonable expected—or not to perform at all.

[66] CESL Art 13(b).

[67] See H Beale, 'A Common European Sales Law (CESL) for Business-to-Business Contracts' in L Moccia (ed), *The Making of European Private Law: Why, How, What, Who* (Sellier, 2013) 65, 73–75.

CESL as a way of attracting SMEs which otherwise would not contract. There is room, in other words, for an efficiency gain that will leave both parties better off: a win-win situation. Of course, not every SME will want to pay the premium.[68] Some SMEs may prefer keener prices over increased protection. Let them opt for a law which doesn't offer them protection, like English law. That is their choice. The great advantage of the CESL, and in particular its advantage over further harmonisation of general contract law, was precisely that the CESL would have been optional. No business would have needed to use it if they didn't want to.

The position where an SME is dealing with another SME is perhaps less clear. Would they then still wish to use the CESL, when it might well have resulted in their own terms being challenged, or their own behaviour being claimed to be contrary to good faith and fair dealing, or the other party being able to escape because of a mistake? Of course in many legal systems this can happen already. But even with SMEs that are used to dealing with each other on the basis of an 'unprotective' law like English law, I believe that many of them might still prefer to adopt the CESL. By and large, they can ensure that their terms are fair and that their own behaviour is inscrutable. They cannot be so sure about the other party's terms and behaviour. I think they may be more concerned about losing because of what the other party gets up to, than because of what they do themselves. They too, then, will prefer the CESL. In addition, it may well be that they will view their own willingness to adopt the CESL as a sign that 'we are a good company; our terms are fair so challenges to them need not concern us; our behaviour is impeccable'. The CESL might have become a badge of 'contractual reliability'.

But larger businesses may well not want this kind of protection for contracts with other larger firms. Indeed, if the English Law Commission is correct, there are many international businesses that do not want any kind of control over unfair terms. Unfair Contract Terms Act 1977 section 26 provides that the Act does not apply to international supply contracts, and section 27 provides that the Act does not apply to any contract that is only subject to English law because the parties have chosen that law. In proposing this exception from what was to become UCTA 1977, the Law Commissions argued simply:

> The effect of imposing our proposed controls in relation to those contracts might well be to discourage foreign businessmen from agreeing to arbitrate their disputes in England.[69]

So the UK's 'law for export' has deliberately been kept even closer to the classical, individualistic model than the law for domestic consumption.

[68] See generally M Trebilcock, 'An Economic Approach to Unconscionability' in Reiter & Swan (eds) *Studies in Contract Law* (Butterworths, 1980) 379, 412–19.

[69] Law Commission, *Second Report on Exemption Clauses in Contracts* (Law Com No 69, 1975) para 232.

H. Do We Need Further Sets of European Rules?

It may be that there would be little interest in developing a uniform 'law for commercial contracts'. In sales, we already have the CISG, even if it does not deal with any of the issues on which I have shown that there are key differences; and we have the UNIDROIT Principles of International Commercial Contracts (UNIDROIT Principles). The UNIDROIT Principles do not have quite such extensive controls over unfair terms as do the PECL and the CESL: there is no general test of fairness. However, there is a provision guarding against 'surprising clauses'. I have argued elsewhere that when we take into account the circumstances in which it seems appropriate to intervene in B2B contracts, even when one is a small business, the surprise clause provision deals with many of the cases.[70] So it may be argued that the European contract law should continue to follow the protective model adopted in the PECL and the CESL, and businesses that want something different should simply be left free to use English law or the law of others jurisdictions that take a similar, minimalist approach. But Germany has recently shown interest in attracting legal business to its courts;[71] and competition from other legal systems was one of the reasons for the recent modernisation of French contract law. So there might be interest in exploring an alternative, hard-nosed contract law for Europe to sit alongside any successor to the CESL.

V. The Future

Given the fate of the CESL proposal, and the very limited scope of the 'targeted full harmonisation' proposals on digital content (DCD proposal) and online sales (OSD proposal), is there any point in discussing uniform laws of contract across Europe? Certainly the current political climate of distrust of the EU, and indeed of doubt whether the twin crises over the euro and migration will cause the whole EU project to collapse, seems to offer very little hope of broad harmonisation being acceptable in the next few years. But if we can get through these crises, then I think there is a chance that fuller harmonisation will come back onto the agenda.

A. Weaknesses of the Current Proposals

First, I am very sceptical as to how far member states will be prepared to accept full harmonisation even in the consumer field. The draft Directive on Digital

[70] See H Beale, '"Surprising" or "Unfair"? Controls over Standard Terms' in UNIDROIT (ed), *Eppur si muove: The Age of Uniform Law—Essays in honour of Michael Joachim Bonell* (UNIDROIT, 2016) 975.

[71] See H Kötz, 'The Jurisdiction of Choice: England and Wales or Germany?' (2010) 18 *European Review of Private Law* 1243.

Content seems to be broadly acceptable to the working groups in the European Council,[72] or at least to meeting little opposition there. I think this is because it is widely accepted that the law on the supply of digital content differs so much between member states, and in many member states is so unclear, that everyone can see that we really need targeted and appropriate rules on digital content; and given that only two member states, the Netherlands (which has extended sales rules to cover digital content[73]) and the UK,[74] have modern law and that the proposed directive is broadly similar to what the UK has, there is a feeling that there is nothing to lose from full harmonisation. But the proposal on online sales seems to be running into much more opposition, because for many member states it would result in significant reductions in consumer protection and would mean that distance and on-premises sales would be governed by different regimes. The Commission may have learned lessons from the failure of the CESL proposal;[75] it seems to have forgotten the fate of much of the original proposal for the Consumer Rights Directive (CRD),[76] which had to be narrowed down enormously because some member states objected to the resulting reduction in protection for their consumers that would result.

I think that creating an optional instrument like the CESL that could be used for cross-border sales, but would leave domestic law untouched for those businesses and consumers who want to use it, was a much better approach. I am still at a loss to understand why it generated so much opposition among consumer organisations. If it would have resulted in consumers who had agreed to use the CESL suffering significant reductions in consumer protection, I too would have been opposed to it; but the proposal in fact gave a high level of protection and I saw no sign that the Commission was prepared to water it down, as the consumer organisations predicted would happen. Nor do I think consumers would have been confused by the choice between domestic law and the CESL. It is hard to think of a scheme that is more confusing than the combination of the national law chosen by the trader and the mandatory rules of the consumer's habitual residence that frequently results from Article 6 of the Rome I Regulation.

However, I have two other reasons for hoping that sooner or later, more extensive harmonisation of contract law will come back onto the agenda.

[72] See Note from the Presidency to the Council 2015/0287 (COD) of 2 June 2016, Brussels, data.consilium.europa.eu/doc/document/ST-9768-2016-INIT/en/pdf; and see Committee on the Internal Market and Consumer Protection Committee on Legal Affairs, Working Document on the directive of the European Parliament and of the Council on certain aspects concerning contracts for the supply of digital content of 23 June 2016, www.europarl.europa.eu/sides/getDoc.do?pubRef=-//EP//NONSGML+COMPARL+PE-585.510+01+DOC+PDF+V0//EN&language=ES.

[73] See European Parliament Research Service, *Briefing, EU Legislation in Progress, April 2016, Contracts for supply of digital content to consumers* (European Union, 2016) 3.

[74] Consumer Rights Act 2015 ch 3.

[75] See the Explanatory Memorandum to each proposal, 2.

[76] Proposal for a Directive of the European Parliament and of the Council of 8 October 2008 on consumer rights COM(2008) 614 final.

B. Reducing Legal Differences in B2C Contracts[77]

The European Commission's current proposals, like the CESL, have two goals. One is to give consumers the confidence to make full use of the internal market by ensuring that wherever the trader with whom the consumer contracts with is based, the consumer will enjoy a high level of consumer protection. The other is to make it easier for traders to sell across borders. We need to consider the extent to which the new proposals meet the apparent aims of the exercise.

The proposed Directive on Digital Content ('the DCD') will provide consumers with rights and remedies that are accessible and, for the most part, suitable. Indeed in some respects (eg public enforcement; stricter liability for digital services) the DCD provides more protection to the consumer even than the recent legislation in the UK.[78] As few member states yet have specific provisions on digital contents, full harmonisation of this topic will not result in major reductions in consumer protection.[79] The proposed Directive on Online Sales ('the OSD') will also result in consumer protection beyond the minimum required by the Directive on Consumer Sales[80]—even though in some member states the full harmonisation requirement will result in a significant loss in consumer protection. But both directives are quite limited in their scope of coverage. They are targeted at only the topics which the Commission thinks are most likely to give rise to disputes.

In this respect there is a major difference between current proposals and the CESL. The CESL sought to provide provisions on all the issues that were likely to arise in the making and performance of a contract. Recital 6 stated:

> Differences in national contract laws therefore constitute barriers which prevent consumers and traders from reaping the benefits of the internal market. Those contract-law-related barriers would be significantly reduced if contracts could be based on a single uniform set of contract law rules irrespective of where parties are established. Such a uniform set of contract law rules should cover the full life cycle of a contract and thus comprise the areas which are the most important when concluding contracts. It should also include fully harmonised provisions to protect consumers.

The range of issues that will be fully harmonised by the proposed directives is much narrower than would have been covered by the CESL. So the number of differences between the laws of the member states that may continue to worry

[77] This section of my chapter draws heavily on a Briefing Paper on Scope of application and general approach of the new rules for contracts in the digital environment that I prepared for the Legal Affairs Committee of the European Parliament in February 2016.

[78] The Consumer Rights Act 2015 ch 3 deals mainly with conformity and remedies.

[79] This is on the assumption that certain clarifications and improvements are made—in particular (1) that the opening words of Art 6(2) are deleted: they seem to allow traders to write their own minimum standards in the small print of their terms; and (2) that it is made clear that Art 14, which gives consumers the right to damages for damage to their digital environment, does not affect their rights under national law to compensation for other kinds of loss.

[80] Directive 1999/44/EC of the European Parliament and of the Council of 25 May 1999 on certain aspects of the sale of consumer goods and associated guarantees [1999] OJ L171/12.

traders will be greater under the current proposals than they would have been had the CESL been adopted.

In terms of substance, it is probably correct that the two proposals do address the issues that are most likely to arise in the context of cross-border contracts for online sales and the supply of digital content.[81] Moreover, I certainly do not suggest that the instruments should cover as many topics as the CESL, which in effect would have provided an almost complete 'law of contract', because for the transactions with which the directives are dealing, some of the issues that were covered in the CESL seem unlikely to arise. One issue is threats;[82] I simply cannot imagine traders exercising duress over consumers via the Internet. Another issue is mistake. There is almost no scope for mistakes as the nature of what is being bought[83] to arise when the buyer is a consumer because the consumer has to be given so much information by the trader.[84] I also wonder whether we need provisions on unfair exploitation—the Internet is one place where price comparison is relatively easy. But before deciding, we would need to find out whether problems of exploitation have occurred in practice.

However, there are some areas of law in which possible differences between the traders' law and the mandatory rules of the consumer's state of habitual residence might still worry traders. Thus the laws on damages and on limitation vary substantially between one member state and another; some laws allow the price for the goods or digital content to be challenged;[85] and even the law on when a contract is formed and the effect of a mistake over the price or other terms, whether by the consumer or the trader, is not the same everywhere.

Even more importantly, the hindrance to cross-border contracts caused by differences between the laws of contract is probably as much psychological as it is real. It seems likely that traders, and in particular SMEs which cannot afford to take legal advice, are put off by 'the fear of the unknown' as much as by actual differences between the various laws. The wider the coverage of the instrument, the greater the reassurance to the trader that it will not meet some unexpected legal rule, and so the greater the encouragement to try selling to consumers in other member states. One of the virtues of the CESL was the number of issues it resolved.

Which of the two is more likely to solve the problems faced by traders interested in selling to consumers across borders? The current approach of 'targeted full harmonisation', or the 'optional instrument' approach of the CESL, which dealt with so many more issues? It is arguable that an optional instrument, coupled with a minimum harmonisation directive on the supply of digital content in order to

[81] See the Explanatory memorandum to each proposal, p 2.

[82] cp CESL Art 50.

[83] cp CESL Art 48.

[84] See Art 6 of the Consumer Rights Directive.

[85] See H Schulte-Nölke, C Twigg-Flesner and M Ebers (eds), *Consumer Law Compendium* (Sellier, 2008) 232.

ensure that consumers purchasing digital content are protected by rules that are accessible and appropriate, would be a better way forward.

C. B2B Contracts

Even more importantly, the DCD and the OSD are limited to B2C contracts. This is understandable, as at least some of the opposition to the proposed CESL seems to have been generated by the proposed inclusion of B2B contracts. Moreover, those consulted supported dealing with B2C contracts only.[86] It can also be said that the differences between the laws of contract in the various member states are less problematic for B2B transactions because there are fewer mandatory rules. However, the number of mandatory rules and the controls over B2B contracts vary substantially between member states. The CESL proposal contained substantial protection for SMEs (in particular, controls over unfair terms that were not individually negotiated), which of course made it appear more threatening to national laws that have few controls—even though their domestic law would have remained untouched.

However, I believe that to leave B2B contracts entirely to one side would be to miss a real opportunity to provide a simple system by which traders may make simple online purchases without having to worry about withdrawal rights, inadequate information or unfair terms. This would make it significantly easier for traders, particularly SMEs, to do business with each other across borders, and thus would contribute to the development of the internal market.

D. Online B2B Sales

A preliminary point is that in practice it will be very hard for a trader who is running a website to know whether the customer is a consumer or an SME, particularly if the SME is not a corporation. Many businesses are run from home rather than from an obvious business address, and there is no guarantee that the means of payment (such as a debit or credit card) will enable the trader to detect that the customer is a business. Therefore I suspect that in practice, most traders who operate a website that is open to consumers do not differentiate between consumers and business buyers, except that the terms and conditions offered may distinguish between consumers and business buyers.

I am not suggesting that, even in a set of rules designed for SMEs, we should assume that business buyers should be given exactly the same protection as consumers. For example, I think that a trader selling to another trader should be entitled to limit its liability for losses caused by non-conformity of the goods or by

[86] See DCD Explanatory Memorandum p 7.

delay in delivery, provided that this is done in a transparent manner. However, I believe that some of the differences between business-to-consumer and business-to-business sales—even in the CESL—were inappropriate.

Some rules about website trading in the CESL applied to any trader using a website (the rules derived from the E-Commerce Directive[87]).[88] However the rules derived from the Consumer Rights Directive (CRD) naturally were applied exclusively to business to consumer contracts. With hindsight I believe that this was unjustified. In particular I now think that a business buyer who contracts over the Internet should have a right to withdraw from the contract (at least as a default rule), and should be provided with the same pre-contractual information as a consumer.

The rationale for allowing a consumer to withdraw from a distance contract, or to withdraw an offer to buy, is that the consumer will not have had the chance to examine the goods before buying them. This will often be the case also with a business buyer. In addition, if I am correct that traders find it very difficult to distinguish between consumers and business buyers, then in practice many web traders must allow the buyer to cancel the order whether not the buyer is a consumer, either under the terms of the trader's contract or as a voluntary concession. However, I do not think that a business buyer over the Internet should have to check the trader's terms to see whether the trader extends this right to business buyers, nor rely on the trader's goodwill. I think that it would actively encourage B2B sales over the Internet if there were normally a right of cancellation.

It is true that a right of cancellation is not needed on every occasion, because the buyer may be buying goods which the buyer has bought before. This is particularly likely when the buyer is a business, as it is more likely to have bought the same goods on a previous occasion. Nonetheless, I would give trader buyers a right of cancellation, at least as the default rule. First, if buyers do not need the right to cancel, they will seldom exercise it, and therefore it will cost the trader very little. Secondly, it would be possible to allow the business buyer to waive their right of cancellation, perhaps in exchange for a small discount on the price in order to encourage them to do so. The magic of IT can easily be used to ensure that a business buyer can waive the right to cancel, by having to click on a separate pop-up acknowledgement, perhaps at the time that they choose the delivery method. The pop-up box might also require buyers to 'self-certify' that they are traders, with a warning that trying to obtain a trade discount when not a trader amounts to fraud.

Similarly, it seems sensible to require a trader who offers to sell to both consumers and business buyers over the Internet to provide the same information for both types of buyer. Whatever is required, the seller is likely to emphasise the positive

[87] Directive 2000/31/EC of the European Parliament and of the Council of 8 June 2000 on electronic commerce [2000] OJ L178/1.

[88] eg CESL Art 24, Additional duties to provide information in distance contracts concluded by electronic means.

aspects of the product as a way of encouraging sales. It is the negative aspects—for example, whether digital content may not be compatible with the buyer's hardware or other software—which is less likely to be revealed and which therefore should have to be disclosed. It is of course true that a business buyer is likely to be better informed and more sophisticated than a consumer and therefore might ask more questions. However it seems to me that it would encourage B2B Internet sales if business buyers could have the same confidence that they have been given the information they need, and that the information is correct, as would be the case with a consumer buyer. Moreover, in practice the trader will be providing the required information anyway for consumer buyers—so there would be no extra cost in providing it for business buyers also.

E. B2B Digital Content

A large business buying digital content—such as a university negotiating a site licence for its staff and students to use a software program—can perhaps be expected to ensure that the terms of the contract set out clearly the supplier's obligations as to conformity and possibly even the remedies that the buyer will have for non-conformity. But many business buyers of digital content will be SMEs, who do not have the sophistication to do this. Moreover, if a business is buying a small quantity of software, it is in no one's interests to spend time and effort negotiating over such matters. Businesses in all member states (including the UK) need a clear and up-to-date set of rules to govern the supply of digital content. This might be left to each member state, but given the importance of cross-border contracts for the supply of digital content, it would make much more sense to have European legislation that applied to B2B contracts as well as consumers. This could be a directive, but an optional instrument would fulfil much the same aims while not limiting the parties' choice.

VI. Conclusions

I do not think that we should be trying to harmonise the laws of the member states in the old sense of requiring all states to adopt the same rule for both domestic and cross-border contracts for business to business contracts, even for online sales or the supply of digital content. For the reasons I have explained earlier, I think that what is needed for B2B transactions is an optional instrument. Optional instruments are currently out of favour, but I hope that, in the longer term, the idea will be revived; and I have reasons to think that if we are at all serious in our belief that reducing the differences between the laws of contract will lower the costs of cross-border contracting, and so can contribute to the functioning of the internal market, we will need to come back to the idea.

This will not be something that happens immediately. But we also need to recognise that investigating thoroughly what optional instruments are needed and drawing them up, complete with the comments, explanation of policy choices and comparative notes that I have asked for, takes a long time. So does proper consultation and revision. Even if optional instruments will not be back on the agenda for a decade or more, we need to work on them now. And since the Commission cannot realistically be expected to have long-term goals in mind, the task falls to us as academics.

Part I

Uniform Rules for the Internal Market

3

Ius Commune and Contract Law

BART WAUTERS

There are evident similarities between the purposes of the Principles of European Contract Law (PECL) and the influence on the development of the law in Europe of the medieval *ius commune*, that body of Roman and canon law texts that were the object of learned glosses and commentaries from civilians and canonists. The PECL have the long-term objective to help bring about the harmonisation of general contract law within the European Union, and there can be no question that the medieval *ius commune* came very close to bringing about just that: the development of a common core of legal principles across multiple jurisdictions.[1]

In the field of contract law however, which is the area of law that concerns us here, the development towards a general law of contract was not straightforward. Medieval law was more pluralistic than the twenty-first-century lawyer is accustomed to, and even if a general theory of contract was the final outcome of the development that started in the medieval *ius commune*, by no means was it clear from the outset that such theory would be the result: we must beware of a teleological reading of the past.

In this chapter we will focus on two issues: the interaction between the principles of contract law as developed by the medieval *ius commune* and local law, and the development of the general contract theory itself. A close look at these two issues, which are related to each other, allows us to draw some conclusions that can be useful when assessing the role of PECL and other proposals for uniform rules for contract law.

I. Roman Contract Law

Roman law did not provide a general theory of law, only a *numerus clausus* of defined contracts. For an agreement to be a contract, it had to fulfil the specific requirements of a particular type of contract, such as sale or lease. The oldest of

[1] General information on the history of the private law sources in Europe can be found in B Wauters and M de Benito, *The History of Law in Europe: an Introduction* (Edward Elgar, 2017).

Roman contracts, the *stipulatio*, was based on the ritualistic exchange of a question and an answer between the promisor and the promisee. The matching of the verbs used in the question and answer pronounced by respectively promisee and promisor was what brought the *stipulatio* into existence. As such it was a strict and unilateral contract. Its formality and rigidity partly explain why the origins of the *stipulatio* are situated in Rome's archaic past and why it is likely that from the *stipulatio* most other Roman contracts evolved: only when in a given situation the *stipulatio* was inefficient would the praetor create a new legal remedy.[2]

The classical jurist Gaius, followed by the Justinian *Institutes*, classified the Roman contracts into four categories: verbal contracts, of which the *stipulatio* was the most important; literal contracts, another strict form of contract that was obsolete by the end of the third century AD, and which arose by means of the double entry of financial transactions into the daybook and then the ledger by the *pater familias*; real contracts, which implied that one party conveyed a thing to another party, and which included *mutuum* (loan for consumption), *commodatum* (loan for use), *depositum* (deposit) and *pignus* (pledge); finally the four consensual contracts, *emptio venditio* (sale), *locatio conductio* (lease), *mandatum* (mandate) and *societas* (partnership).[3] Apart from these standard contracts, the Roman jurists also distinguished 'innominate' contracts, certain agreements for mutual services (eg barter) that fell outside the four categories and that were enforceable when one of the parties had performed his part of the bargain. On top of the standard and innominate contracts, Roman texts also speak of 'pacts', informal agreements that nevertheless received a certain degree of legal recognition: they were not directly actionable, but could be raised as a defence. This is the meaning of Ulpian's famous text: 'nuda pactio obligationem non parit, sed parit exceptionem'.[4]

To make things complicated, the texts also contain examples of pacts that were made directly actionable by the praetor and imperial legislator, such as the promise to make a gift (*pactum donationis*) or the promise to give dowry (*pactum dotis*).

[2] A Watson, *Roman Law & Comparative Law* (The University of Georgia Press, 1991) 124; A Watson, *The Evolution of Western Private Law*, expanded edn (The Johns Hopkins University Press, 2001) 36.

[3] More information on the Roman law of contracts can be found in the comprehensive volume of R Zimmermann, *The Law of Obligations. Roman Foundations of the Civilian Tradition* (Oxford University Press, 1996), and in most textbooks of Roman private law, eg M Kaser and R Knütel, *Römisches Privatrecht*, 20th edn (CH Beck, 2014); P du Plessis, *Borkowski's Textbook on Roman Law*, 5th edn (Oxford University Press, 2015); B Nicolas, *An Introduction to Roman Law* (Clarendon Press, 1962); WW Buckland, *A Text-Book of Roman Law from Augustus to Justinian*, P Stein (ed), 3rd edn (Cambridge University Press, 1963).

[4] T Mommsen et al (eds), *Institutiones and Digesta*, 16th edn (Weidmann, 1954) Dig 2.14.7.4. In this chapter I will use the citation system for Romano-canonical texts as in JA Brundage, *Medieval Canon Law* (Longman, 1995) 190–205. The standard edition of the Latin text of the *Corpus Iuris Civilis* is still that of T Mommsen et al (eds), *Institutiones and Digesta*, 16th edn (Weidmann, 1954); T Mommsen et al (eds), *Codex*, 11th edn (Weidmann, 1954); T Mommsen et al (eds), *Novellae*, 6th edn (Weidmann, 1954). Despite its shortcomings, the standard edition of the basic medieval canon law texts is still that of E Friedberg (ed), *Corpus Iuris Canonici* (Lawbook Exchange, 2000).

The consensual contract—the idea that an arrangement is legally enforceable only because the parties involved agree on its terms, without necessity of further formalities—is one of the Roman jurists' great legacies. However, the development of four consensual contracts did not imply a general theory of consensualism. The absence of such theory can be explained, not only by the notable reticence of Roman jurists towards defining abstract legal concepts and theories,[5] but also by the existence of the *stipulatio*, which allowed for any promise to be made enforceable, provided some—relatively easy—formalities were complied with.[6] There is much to say for Alan Watson's suggestion that the *stipulatio* was the archaic Roman version of a general contract.[7] In a very traditional society such as the Roman one, modifications to the inheritance of the past were not that evident. In the mindset of Roman jurists, contracts based on consent and mutually binding on the parties, were in a way deviations from the formalistic and unilateral *stipulatio*. This mindset barred the development of a general theory of contract by the Romans, as exemplified by their refusal to make bare 'pacts' actionable.

II. The Civilians

When the medieval civilians, first in Bologna and increasingly all over Europe, started to study the Justinian texts again from the early twelfth century onwards, they sought to bring the variety of Roman contracts into a rational scheme. One of the first victims of their effort was the *stipulatio*, which lost its position as a central institution of contract law. Medieval glossators were confused by the texts they found on the *stipulatio* in the *Corpus Iuris Civilis*, which contained on the one hand the classical transaction as described above, but on the other hand incorporated the post-classical practice of written requirements that were added in Justinian's time.[8] The medieval civilians, who thought that Justinian's texts were authoritative as they stood and did not read them as the result of a millenarian evolution with different historical layers, concluded that the *stipulatio* was a highly technical transaction that could only be entrusted safely to professional document-writers such as notaries. This conclusion guaranteed the marginalisation of the *stipulatio* in medieval practice and doctrine.[9]

[5] Dig 50.17.202: 'Omnis definitio in iure civili periculosa es; parum est enim, ut non subverti posset'. See A Watson, *The Spirit of Roman Law* (The University of Georgia Press, 1995) 146.

[6] KP Nanz, *Die Entstehung des allgemeinen Vertragsbegriffs im 16. bis 18. Jahrhundert* (J Schweitzer Verlag, 1985) 18–22.

[7] Watson (n 2) *Roman Law & Comparative Law* 288.

[8] Zimmermann (n 3) 78–82, 546–47; Nanz (n 6) 36; R Volante, *Il sistema contrattuale del diritto comune classico. Struttura dei patti e individuazione del tipo. Glossatori e Ultramontani* (Giuffrè, 2001) 21.

[9] Zimmermann (n 3) 547.

The loss of the central position of the *stipulatio* in medieval doctrine created in a way a vacuum. For the Romans, the *stipulatio* had been the default contract with which any promise could be made actionable if the parties wished to do so, but in the Middle Ages this was no longer a practical option. It was therefore logical that the civilians sought other ways to enforce promises that did not fall within the scope of one of the Roman contracts. This they tried by creatively analysing Ulpian's statement that *pacta nuda* (mere, bare or 'naked' pacts) did not create an obligation. The nudity of the pact was taken as a metaphor for an agreement based on consent alone, but that was not actionable. But the Roman texts also contained examples of *pacta* that were actionable in court, such as the donation or the promise to give dowry. These *pacta* were considered by the glossators to be '*vestita*', clothed. The theory of the clothes was a very successful one, up to the point that some civilians interpreted the *pacta* to be the all-encompassing category of Roman contract law, to be split up in two subcategories: the *pacta nuda*, on the one hand, and the *pacta vestita* on the other hand.[10] The *pacta vestita* were then thought to contain every agreement that was actionable: the *numerus clausus* of contracts, the innominate contracts and the enforceable *pacta*. The civilians were more willing to consider an agreement as a vested one than the Romans had been. By the time Accursius (d 1263) wrote what would become the standard gloss on the Digest, the category of the *pacta vestita* had expanded greatly,[11] and by the end of the Middle Ages there were civilians who even advocated for civil courts to enforce performance of naked pacts (even if only under a canonical remedy).[12]

The civilians lived in a paradoxical situation. On the one hand, they held fast to the authority of the Roman texts, on the other hand they saw that actionability of bare agreements was a real demand from society. Their solution was some kind of middle ground, by stretching the Roman law texts far enough to cover most common day-to-day situations in which bare agreements should lead to actionability. There was however a text in the Digest that said that all contracts require consent.[13] But the civilians largely ignored it and concluded that consent to a contract created an obligation only under the *ius gentium*, not under the *ius civile*.[14] At the level of legal theory the civilians were not yet ready to take the step towards consensualism.

[10] H Dilcher, 'Der Typenzwang im mitteralterlichen Vertragsrecht' (1960) 77 *Zeitschrift der Savigny-Stiftung für Rechtsgeschichte: Romanistische Abteilung* 270, 274.

[11] Accursius, Glossa ordinaria [Venetiis 1488] ad Dig 2.14.7.5, v° Quinimo: '(after listing the "vested" pacts in several categories): Sic videtur quod nullum pactum sit nudum cum quodlibet habeat consensum, unde vestiri consensu videtur'.

[12] W Decock, *Theologians and Contract Law. The Moral Transformation of the Ius Commune (c 1500–1650)* (Martinus Nijhoff, 2013) 114.

[13] Dig 2.14.1.3.

[14] ibid; see J Gordley, *Foundations of Private Law. Property, Tort, Contract, Unjust Enrichment* (Oxford University Press, 2006) 291.

III. The Canonists

Canon law was the second pillar of the medieval *ius commune*. Many civilians had studied canon law at the university and were familiar with its concepts, values and institutions. Faith to the given word was one such moral value. Theologians such as Saint Augustine (d 430) or Saint Jerome (d 420) thought that non-compliance with promises was a sin, and early examples of canon law legislation, such as the fourth council of Toledo (633), showed the concern of church authorities for compliance with the given word.[15] Gratian included the Toledo canon in his ground-breaking collection,[16] but otherwise did not dedicate much attention to contract law. Another example of the Church's concern for the given word was the oath, *iuramentum*. Jesus had not encouraged swearing, and therefore oaths attracted careful scrutiny from the canonists, including Gratian, who picked up a text from Saint John Chrysostom (d 407) that said that there should be no difference between speaking under oath and normal speaking, or between lying and perjury.[17]

One of the greatest and most original commentators on Gratian's *Decretum*, Huguccio (d 1210),[18] combined several strands of earlier canonistic thought to develop a new theory on the *pacta nuda*. He said that even if a promise (*nuda promissio*) was not embedded within the solemnities of a *stipulatio*, and as a consequence could not be enforced according to Roman law (*civiliter*), the promisor would commit a sin if he did not fulfil his promise. The reason was that God did not distinguish between simple promises and promises under oath with respect to their observance. The promisor could not use the lack of the formalities as an

[15] P Landau, 'Pacta sunt servanda. Zu den kanonistischen Grundlagen der Privatautonomie' in M Ascheri et al (eds), *'Ins Wasser geworfen und Ozeane durchquert'. Festschrift für Knut Worfgang Nörr* (Böhlau Verlag, 2003) 457, 461; F Spies, *De l'observation des simples conventions en droit canonique, étude suivie de quelques recherches concernant l'influence du principe canonique de l'observation des simples conventions sur le droit coutumier français* (Recueil Sirey, 1928) 28; J Roussier, *Le fondement de l'obligation contractuelle dans le droit classique de l'Église* (Domat-Montchrestien, 1933) 63; P Bellini, *L'obbligazione da promessa con oggetto temporale nel sistema canonistico classico: con particolare riferimento ai secoli XII e XIII* (Giuffrè, 1964).

[16] On Gratian and his *Decretum*, see A Winroth, *The Making of Gratian's Decretum* (Cambridge University Press, 2000); HJ Berman, *Law and Revolution: the Formation of the Western Legal Tradition* (Harvard University Press, 1983) 143. The canon can be found in C 12 q 2 c 66.

[17] See C 22 q 5 c 12; RH Helmholz, *The Spirit of Classical Canon Law* (The University of Georgia Press, 1993) 145; P Prodi, *Il sacramento del potere. Il giuramento politico nella storia costituzionale dell'Occidente* (Il Mulino, 1992) 124; M David, 'Parjure et mensonge dans le Décret de Gratien' (1955) 3 *Studia Gratiana* 116; J Gaudement, 'Le Serment dans le droit canonique médiéval' in R Verdier (ed), *Le Serment. Vol. II Théories et devenir* (Éditions du CNRS, 1991) 63; J Hallebeek, 'Actio ex iuramento: the legal enforcement of oaths' (1990) 17 *Ius commune. Zeitschrift für Europäische Rechtsgeschichte* 69.

[18] On Huguccio, see WP Müller, *Huguccio. The Life, Works, and Thought of a Twelfth-Century Jurist* (The Catholic University of America Press, 1994).

excuse not to fulfil his promise.[19] Johannes Teutonicus (d 1245), the author of the ordinary gloss to the *Decretum Gratiani*, went a step further and found that the promisee should have a claim in court. He used Huguccio's equation of the observance of simple promises with that of promises under oath as the basis for that action, the *condictio ex canone.*[20] A few decades later the *Liber extra* (1234), one of the most important official medieval collections of papal decretals, stated that pacts, however naked, were to be observed.[21] It was the legislative embodiment of a principle that had been in the making for decades.[22]

However, Johannes Teutonicus' *condictio ex canone* and the legislative initiative in the *Liber extra* did not generate much enthusiasm, not even among canonists. The main problem[23] was that, as it stood, the principle represented a major risk for secular jurisdiction, because it assigned to the ecclesiastical jurisdiction unlimited responsibility over all kinds of promises, even commercial ones. This was certainly not to the liking of secular courts, who would always guard themselves against too invasive ecclesiastical claims to jurisdiction. In England the Constitutions of Clarendon said as early as 1164 that jurisdiction over sworn promises to pay debts belonged exclusively to the royal courts (and thus not in the tribunals of the Church).[24] In France the *Ordonnance de Villers-Cotterêts* (1539) made an end to ecclesiastical jurisdiction over all disputes between lay persons,

[19] Huguccio ad C 12 q 2 c 66: 'licet stipulatio non intervenerit, obligatur enim nuda promissione saltem et si non civiliter unde tenetur ad promissum persolvendum ... peccaret enim quis nisi nudum pactum observaret honestum tamen licet nulla sollempnitas intervenerit', as cited by Landau (n 15) 462.

[20] J Teutonicus, Glossa ordinaria ad C 12 q 2 c 66: 'Videtur quod aliquis obligetur nudis verbis ... quod verum est et potest dici quod competit actio ex nuda promissione scilicet condictio ex canone illo: Juramenti', as cited by Landau (n 15) 469; Rousier (n 15) 137. See also J Teutonicus, Glossa ordinaria (Venetiis 1496) ad C 22 q 5 c 12, v° Distantiam: 'Distantiam quantum ad hoc cum mortaliter peccat: qui simpliciter dicit falsum sicut qui sub iuramento dicit falsum. Magis tamen peccat peierando quam mentiendo. Solidius subsistit ubi iuramentum interponitur: ut supra q.1.c.1 sed tamen plus operatur sacramentum quam simplex promissio ut extra de iureiurandum debitores [X 2.24.6]. Item hic est argumentum quod ex nudo pacto oritur actio ut [C 12 q 2 c 66]'.

[21] X 1.35.1.

[22] For the origin of this text, see Landau (n 15) 458.

[23] Another problem was that, if carried far enough, the canonical principle that bare pacts are binding would also give rise to an obligation even if the person who had uttered the words did not have the intention to. To tackle that problem, the canonists used the notion of *causa*. In this chapter we will not discuss the history of the *causa*; useful material about the *causa* in the Middle Ages can be found in A Brito Guzmán, 'Causa del contrato y causa de la obligación en la dogmática de los juristas romanos, medievales y modernos y en la codificación europea y americana' (2001) 23 *Revista de estudios histórico-jurídicos* 209; J Gordley, *The Philosophical Origins of Modern Contract Doctrine* (Clarendon Press, 1991) 49–57. About the link between the *causa* and the common law doctrine of consideration, see DJ Ibbetson, *A Historical Introduction to the Law of Obligations* (Oxford University Press, 1999) 141; DJ Ibbetson, 'Consideration and the Theory of Contract in Sixteenth Century Common Law', in J Barton (ed), *Towards a General Law of Contract* (Duncker & Humblot, 1990) 67.

[24] RH Helmholz, 'Contracts and the Canon Law' in J Barton (ed), *Towards a General Law of Contract* (Duncker & Humblot, 1990) 49, 58.

including contracts.[25] From the twelfth to the sixteenth century, many canonists (but not all of them)[26] warned that a too expansive ecclesiastical jurisdiction would erode legitimate lay jurisdiction, an evolution they did not find desirable.[27] The generally held opinion was the one expressed by Baldus (d 1400), who said that the *condictio ex canone* was only applied between clergymen, or among citizens who lived in the lands under the temporal jurisdiction of the Church, such as the Papal State.[28] This seems to be confirmed by late medieval practice in the ecclesiastical courts, where promises between laypersons were dealt with only if they had been made under oath.[29]

The addition of an oath to a promise continued to be the key to open the doors of ecclesiastical tribunals for lay parties who sought to enforce them. That was explicitly included in the *Liber sextus*, the collection of papal decretals promulgated by Pope Boniface VIII in 1298.[30] The jurisdictional basis to get access to the ecclesiastical courts was that the oath was a spiritual element; as such there was not an inroad into secular jurisdiction. From research in late-medieval archives of church courts from England, Aragon, France and Scotland we know that church courts each year dealt with a surprisingly high number of cases involving oaths over promises, to the point that it would not be an exaggeration to say that some church courts had become agencies for the collection of petty debts.[31] Practice in the courts of the Church thus seems to have matched the standard doctrine of canonists: no enforcement of bare promises as a general rule, only enforcement of promises made under oath.

It would be an exaggeration to say that the medieval canonists developed a sophisticated general law of contract. Their focus was on unilateral promises, not on consent. To all practical effects the ecclesiastical courts would only hear cases on promises with a formal element attached, the oath, and not so much on bare agreements. But canonical doctrine at least showed that there were potential deontological incongruities in maintaining the difference between statements under oath and bare promises, and as such the origin of the principle that *pacta sunt servanda* can be firmly grounded in medieval canon law.

[25] Francis I, *Ordonnance sur le fait de la justice* (first published, Villers-Cotterêt, 1539) Art 1: 'C'est à savçoir que nous avons défendu et défendons à tous nos sujects, de ne faire citer, ni convenir les laïcs pardevant les juges d'église, ès actions pures personnelles, sur peine de perdition de cause et d'amende arbitraire'. Text published in M Isambert et al (eds), *Receuil général des anciennes lois françaises, depuis l'an 420, jusqu'à la révolution de 1789* (Belin-Leprieur, 1828) vol XII, 601; Spies (n 15) 217.

[26] We do not discuss Innocent IV's '*denunciatio evangelica*' as remedy to enforce bare promises and means to establish general ecclesiastical jurisdiction over pacts, because it would lead us too far. See Roussier (n 15) 165; Landau (n 15) 468; KW Nörr, *Romanisch-Kanonisches Prozessrecht. Erkenntnisverfahren erster Instanz in civilibus* (Springer, 2012) 64.

[27] For instance Hostiensis, quoted in Landau (n 15) 471.

[28] Decock (n 12) 128.

[29] Helmholz (n 24) 55.

[30] VI 2.2.3.

[31] Helmholz (n 24) 57.

IV. The Interaction Between the *Ius Commune* and the Local Law

Generally speaking, to use a well-chosen image, the relationship between the *ius commune* and the local law in the Middle Ages was like the one between the sun and the planets in the solar system.[32] Roman and canon law, together with the body of learned commentaries on the basic texts, were like the sun that sends warmth and light to the different systems of local law, the planets. To a larger or lesser extent, the local systems of law took the *ius commune* as the gravitational centre of their orbits. Even if the medieval *ius commune* did not develop a general theory of contract, it is possible to discern the influence of separate strands of civilian or canonical thoughts into local law. In what follows, we will see examples of the courts merchant, of local statutory law, and of local custumals. We will also zoom in on the English common law.

Since the nineteenth century it became a dominant idea that during the Middle Ages there was a well-functioning, efficient, flexible and transnational *lex mercatoria* that governed most commercial transactions across Europe and provided equitable and uniform standards based on Roman law.[33] In spite of many excellent studies that argue the contrary, the myth is difficult to get away with.[34] In the Middle Ages there was no such thing as a uniform and universal *lex mercatoria*. What did exist were courts throughout Europe that allowed for the settlement of conflicts between merchants. Those courts were very diverse between one and another: some of them, such as fair courts or guild courts, were almost private mercantile systems where the judges were elected among merchants and merchant custom was applied. These mercantile customs varied geographically and further differed on the type of trade the merchant was engaged in. In other places merchants had to go to the normal civil courts that were instituted by local authorities, such as towns or feudal lords, and that applied predominantly local statutes or local customs, although some of these would under certain circumstances allow for merchant customs as well.[35] The merchant law in the Middle Ages, then, was much more diverse than the myth of a *lex mercatoria* seems to imply.

[32] M Bellomo, *The Common Legal Past of Europe, 1000–1800* (The Catholic University of America Press, 1995) 192.

[33] Berman (n 16) 333, 342. For the nineteenth-century construction of the idea of a medieval *lex mercatoria*, see D de Ruysscher, 'La lex mercatoria contextualisée: tracer son parcours intellectuel' (2012) 90 *Revue historique de droit français et étranger* 499.

[34] KO Scherner, 'Lex mercatoria—Realität, Geschichtsbild oder Vision?' (2001) 118 *Zeitschrift der Savigny-Stiftung für Rechtsgeschichte, Germanistische Abteilung* 148; C Donahue Jr, 'Medieval and Early Modern *Lex mercatoria*: An Attempt at the *Probatio Diabolica*' (2004) 5 *Chicago Journal of International Law* 21; JH Baker, 'The Law Merchant and the Common Law before 1700' (1979) 38 *Cambridge Law Journal* 295.

[35] E Kadens, 'Order within Law, Variety within Custom. The Character of the Medieval Merchant Law' (2004) 5 *Chicago Journal of International Law* 39; E Kadens, 'The Medieval Law Merchant: The Tyranny of a Construct' (2015) 7 *Journal of Legal Analysis* 251.

On the other hand, it was true that merchants preferred to settle their conflicts according to their own customs, that they preferred a swiftly operating legal infrastructure and that, in varying degree, many towns were willing to accommodate them to attract the business they brought with them. In spite of the diversity of proceedings, rules, courts and judges across Europe, there was a certain coherence in merchant practices. Therefore it was not surprising that learned authors such as Bartolus (d 1357) and Baldus discussed practices in merchant courts as if they belonged to a different order, and gave it names like the *ius mercatorum* or *consuetudo mercatorum*.[36]

For our purposes it is interesting that there seems to have been an agreement between authors that merchants could make binding agreements *ex nudum pactum*. Bartolus was one of the first authors to point to that fact:[37] 'In merchant courts, where a case can be decided by equity, this exception cannot be raised: a *stipulatio* has not been made but it was a bare agreement only.'[38] Bartolus' comments created school, and he was followed by Baldus and others.[39]

Why did Bartolus make this observation?[40] This law of the Digest declared that under certain circumstances a surety (*fideiussor*), in order to preserve his own reputation and avoid shame (*verecundia*), could recover from the principal debtor the interest he had paid on the debt. In Roman law, interest had to be established with a *stipulatio*; when creditor and debtor established the interest with a formless pact the principal debtor could use the lack of formalities as an excuse to escape the obligation to pay.[41] When in that situation the creditor approached the surety, this last one, in order to preserve his own reputation, might feel compelled to pay the interest anyway. The preservation of a good name was the main reason why the Roman jurists would allow for it, and the ordinary gloss referred to other places in the Digest where consideration was given to honour and reputation.[42] For medieval businessmen, reputation was also important: the same men met each other often at successive trade fairs, sometimes travelled together for better protection, and regularly used the same pool of intermediaries and brokers who channelled

[36] Kadens (n 35) 'Order within Law' 43.

[37] Nanz (n 6) 57.

[38] Bartolus de Saxoferratus, *In ius universum civile commentaria* (Basilea, 1562) 745, ad Dig 17.1.48.1: 'in curia mercatorum, ubi de negotio potest decidi bona aequitate, quod non potest opponi ista exceptio, non intervenit stipulatio sed pactum nudum fuit' (own translation).

[39] Baldus, *Super codice commentaria* (Lugduni, 1539) III, 96, ad C 4.35.10: '[In D 17.1.48 Bartolus] dicit quod in curia mercatorum ubi negocia debent decidi de bona aequitate non potest opponi exceptio ista, "non intervenit stipulatio sed fuit nudum pactum", quia verecundia est recusare alicui quod pacto nudo convenit seu promisit, secundum eum', also quoted in C Donahue Jr, 'Equity in the courts of merchants' (2004) 72 *Tijdschrift voor Rechtsgeschiedenis* 1, 9; Baldus, *In Decretalium Commentaria* (Venetiis, 1595), ad X 1.35.1: 'Ex pacto etiam nudo agunt mercatores, et nummularii inter se, ut [Nov 4.1] et si artifices faciunt statutum inter se, quod agatur ex nudo pacto, tale statutum valet'.

[40] In his comment on Dig 17.1.48.

[41] Donahue (n 39) 7.

[42] Accursius, Glossa ordinaria [Venetiis 1488] ad Dig 17.1.48, v° Existimationem: '[id est] bonam famam conservandam sic ponitur [in Dig. 50.13.5.1: Existimatio est dignitatis illaesae status, legibus ac moribus comprobatus, qui ex delicto nostro auctoritate legum aut minuitur aut consumitur]'. Further references to Dig 50.12.6.1; Dig 12.3.4.pr; Dig 19.1.51.pr; Dig 16.3.31.1.

gossip and news.[43] In a way, then, it was logical that Bartolus offered his observation on the enforcement of bare agreements in merchant courts to Dig 17.1.48. That law included sureties, a concept that was used among merchants. Reputation was another link between Dig 17.1.48 and the merchants. And, finally, the conflict underneath that law was caused by a debtor who did not want to pay up what he owed under a *pactum nudum* and used the lack of formalities as an excuse to not to pay the creditor.

Even if the association of ideas (surety—reputation—merchants—naked pacts) might in itself be sufficient to explain Bartolus' remarks to this particular law in the Digest, a further question can be asked about the role of canon law as a possible source for Bartolus' comments to Dig 17.1.48. After all, he stated that merchant courts were ruled by equity, a concept particularly well elaborated by the canonists. Moreover, the accursian gloss to Dig 17.1.48 compared '*pudor*' (sense of honour) with that of a situation where no one was to be compelled to commit perjury,[44] and perjury, as we have seen, was an important subject for the canonists as well. Finally, some of the words that Bartolus uses ('non intervenit stipulatio …') match the words used by Huguccio ('stipulatio non intervenerit').[45] Granted, equity was not the monopoly of the canonists, as Roman law texts included many references to the concept and were discussed by the civilians as well.[46] Furthermore, the accursian reference to perjury should not necessarily have prompted Bartolus to link it with the canonical discussion on the enforceability of naked pacts, just like Accursius had not done so himself.

Should we then exclude the possibility of canonical influence on Bartolus' comments on Dig 17.1.48? Not entirely. A 1348 legislative text of the Kingdom of Castile, the *Ordenamiento de Alcalá*, may shed some light on the question. The *Ordenamiento de Alcalá* was promulgated in 1348 and was the outcome of negotiations between the king and the representatives of clergy, nobility and town oligarchies assembled in the *Cortes* on a wide variety of issues affecting the kingdom. During the first half of the fourteenth century the Kingdom of Castile was the witness of increased legislative activity, especially during the reign of Alfonso XI (1312–50), which resulted in a long series of *Ordenamientos*, such as the *Ordenamientos de Burgos* of 1315 and 1338, the *Ordenamiento de Villa Real* of 1346, the *Ordenamiento de Segovia* of 1347 and, finally, the *Ordenamiento de Alcalá* in 1348. Of all these (and other) *Ordenamientos*, the 1348 text is the most

[43] See the important caveats of Kadens (n 35) 'The Medieval Law Merchant' 275.

[44] Accursius, Glossa ordinaria [Venetiis 1488] ad Dig 17.1.48, vº Pudori: 'Nota argumentum emptorem posse de evictione agere, etiam si de calumnia non iuret, cum sciat rem pertinere ad actorem, quia non debet compelli perierare'.

[45] See (n 19), (n 38) for full reference.

[46] As in Dig 1.1.1.pr: 'Ius est ars boni et aequi'. For further references, see F Pringsheim, 'Bonum et aequum' (1932) 52 *Zeitschrift der Savigny-Stiftung für Rechtsgeschichte: Romanistische Abteilung* 78; P Landau, '"Aequitas" in the "Corpus iuris canonici"' (1994) 20 *Syracuse Journal of International Law and Commerce* 95.

important one, especially because it brought order in the system of legal sources: traditional Castilian municipal law or *Fueros*, royal law and *ius commune.*[47]

For our purposes it is important to note that title XVI of the *Ordenamiento de Alcalá* contains a single law, *Paresciendo*, which relates to promises:[48]

> If it appears that a man wanted to be bound to another by a promise, by some contract, or in some other way, then he will be bound by it to those he bound himself to. That the promise was not made via *stipulatio* (that is, a promise with certain solemnities) cannot be raised as an exception … because more valid is the fact that the obligation or the contract were made in any such way that made clear that one wanted to be bound to someone and make contract with him.

The 1348 text makes an end to the rigid, Roman law-based regime of the *stipulatio* as picked up some 75 years earlier by the *Siete Partidas.*[49] From the sixteenth century onwards, *Paresciendo* was considered to have been foundational in the introduction of consensualism, and as such might have played a role in the development of a general theory of contract by essentially Spanish authors in the sixteenth century.[50]

But the contractual theory in *Paresciendo* is not that much of a novelty, as the law returns to Castile's own traditions from before the *Partidas*,[51] and reading

[47] F Tomás y Valiente, *Manual de historia del derecho español* (Tecnos, 1983) 242–48; JA Escudero, *Curso de Historia del Derecho. Fuentes e Instituciones Político-administrativas* (Edisofer, 2003) 455; A Pérez Martín, 'El Ordenamiento de Alcalá (1348) y las glosas de Vicente Arias de Balboa' (1984) 11 *Ius Commune. Zeitschrift für Europäische Rechtsgeschichte* 55; G Sánchez, 'Sobre el Ordenamiento de Alcalá y sus fuentes' (1922) 9 *Revista de Derecho Privado* 353.

[48] Own translation. The original in Castilian reads as follows: 'Paresciendo que se quiso un Ome obligar à otro por promision, ò por algund contracto, ò en alguna otra manera, sea tenudo de aquellos à quienes se obligò, è non pueda ser puesta excebcion que non fue fecha estipulacion, que quiere decir: prometimiento con ciertas solepnidades del derecho … mas que sea valedera la obligacion ò el contracto que fueren fechos en qualquier manera que paresca que alguno se quiso obligar à otro, è façer contracto con el', in I Jordán de Asso y del Río and M de Manuel y Rodríguez (eds), *El Ordenamiento de Leyes, que D. Alfonso XI hizo en las Cortes de Alcalá de Henares el año de mil trescientos y cuarenta y ocho* (Joachin Ibarra, 1774) 26. The *Ordenamiento de Alcalá* of 1348 was also published in *Cortes de los antiguos reinos de León y de Castilla* (Real Academia de Historia, 1861) vol I, 492–593. It is clear that a new critical edition is desirable, see Pérez Martín (n 47) 58. The law *Paresciendo* was incorporated, with changes in its text, in later legislative compilations in Castile, more in particular in the *Ordenamiento de Montalvo* (1484), Lib III, tit VIII, ley 3; the *Nueva Recopilación* (1567), Lib V, tit XVI, ley 2; and the *Novísima Recopilación* (1805), Lib X, tit I, ley 1.

[49] JA Arias Bonet, 'Recepción de formas estipulatorias en la Baja Edad Media. Un estudio sobre las promisiones de las Siete Partidas', (1966) 42 *Boletim da Faculdade de Direito Universidade de Coimbra* 285. On the *Siete Partidas* in general, see, among many others, Bellomo (n 32) 100.

[50] A Guzmán Brito, 'La promesa obligacional en las "partidas" como sede de la doctrina general de las obligaciones' (2007) 34 *Revista Chilena de Derecho* 395; Decock (n 12) 162.

[51] The *Fuero Real* (1255) had already introduced the idea that unwritten contracts should be enforced, lib I, tit XI, l.1: 'Todo pleito que entre algunos derechamientre fuere fecho, quier sea por escripto, quier sin escripto, maguer que pena non sea hi puesta, firmemientre sea guardado, et el alcalle fagalo guardar. Et si en el pleito pena fuera puesta, qui contra el pleito veniere, pecha la pena, asi como fue puesta en el pleito', in A Pérez Martín (ed) *El Fuero Real de Alfonso X El Sabio* (first published 1836, Agencia del Boletín Oficial del Estado, 2015) 28. Pérez Martín (n 47) 80; Arias Bonet (n 49) 295.

it as the legislative basis of consensualism is anyway a step too far.[52] *Paresciendo* only allows naked pacts to be enforced. In that sense it is interesting to notice the strong parallel between the wording of the text of *Paresciendo* 'non pueda ser puesta excebcion que no fue fecha estipulacion' with Bartolus' remark 'non potest opponi ista exceptio: non intervenit stipulatio'. Is it possible that Bartolus' remark somehow was picked up by the drafters of the *Ordenamiento*?

That seems unlikely. Bartolus died in 1357. Even if we are not sure when he published his comments on the *Digestum vetus*,[53] it is not until the second half of the fourteenth century that the first Bartolian manuscripts are circulating in Spain,[54] meaning that it is unlikely that there were any works of Bartolus available in the Iberian Peninsula before the *Ordenamiento de Alcalá* was actually drafted.

The gloss to the *Ordenamiento*, composed between 1390 and 1394—more than four decades after the promulgation of the *Ordenamiento*—is not very helpful either. It refers to Bartolus and Cinus de Pistoia (d 1337) but only to their comments on last wills, which the glossator thought to cover the words 'in some other way' of *Paresciendo*.[55]

However, when we look at the persons who actually drafted the text, we can identify as one of its authors Gil Álvarez de Albornoz (d 1367). He was Archbishop of Toledo and chancellor to Alfonso XI, and, more importantly, had studied canon law in Toulouse.[56] This canon law background of the *Ordenamiento*'s main drafter possibly explains why canonical ideas had their influence on the final draft of the *Ordenamiento*'s chapter on the law of contracts. It would also fit the overall moralistic approach of the *Ordenamiento*, which is ascribed to canon law influence on the drafters of the text.[57] But the overall fit would not by itself explain the word-for-word similarity between the text of the *Ordenamiento* and Bartolus' comments about the actionability of agreements in merchant courts.[58]

[52] Rafael Núñez Lagos, *La estipulación en las Partidas y en el Ordenamiento de Alcalá* (Real Academia de Jurisprudencia, 1950) 58.

[53] He lectured on the *Digestum vetus*, probably for the first time, in January 1344, when he was professor in Perugia; he again lectured on the *Digestum vetus* in December 1347 and in 1352/53. It was very common that the works of glossators circulated for a time as student notes before they were 'revised' by the professor. The first dated manuscript of Bartolus' lecture on the *Digestum vetus* was written in 1347. See FK von Savigny, *Geschichte des römischen Rechts im Mittelalter*, 2nd edn (Heidelberg Mohr, 1850), vol 6, 145, 163. More biographical data on Bartolus in CN Sidney Woolf, *Bartolus of Saxoferrato. His position in the History of Medieval Political Thought* (Cambridge University Press, 1913); H Lange and M Kriechbaum, *Römisches Recht im Mittelalter. Band II. Die Kommentatoren* (Beck, 2007) 687, 723.

[54] A García y García, 'Bartolo de Saxoferrato y España' in A García y García, *Derecho común en España. Los juristas y sus obras* (Universidad de Murcia, 1991) 99, 117.

[55] Pérez Martín (n 47) 174; cp the exegesis of Núñez Lagos (n 52) 56.

[56] About Gil Álvarez de Albornoz, see E Duprè Theseider, 'Albornoz, Egidio de' in *Dizionario Biografico degli Italiani* 2 (Istituto dell' Enciclopedia Italiana, 1960).

[57] Núñez Lagos (n 52) 59; Tomás y Valiente (n 47) 243.

[58] A working hypothesis is that both Bartolus and the *Ordenamiento* went back to an as yet unidentified common source, who himself possibly made use of Huguccio. To find that source, I see basically two options. The first option is the investigation of the 'French connection' between Álvarez de Albornoz and Bartolus. Álvarez de Albornoz had studied in Toulouse and Bartolus, via his master Cinus de Pistoia, was familiar with the works of authors from the school of Orléans, such as Pierre de

The overall picture of canon law influence on the local law, as exemplified by the *Ordenamiento de Alcalá*, fits also developments in other parts of Europe. French custumals of the thirteenth century capture a trend to recognise a general concept of contracts based on consent, a trend that probably goes back to canon law. On the other hand, the custumals would not go so far as to include the idea that bare agreements were directly actionable. Philippe de Beaumanoir's *Coutumes de Beauvaisis* (1280) includes famously the idea that 'toutes convenances sont a tenir, et pour ce dit on: "convenance vaint loi", exceptees les convenances qui sont fetes par mauvaises causes'.[59] This article is possibly the result of fusing Roman law elements such as Dig 50.17.23 ('legem enim contractus dedit'—'for a contract imposes a law')[60] with canon law elements such as using '*conventus*' instead of '*contractus*' or '*pactum*'.[61] To be fair, it is unlikely that this article matched contemporary practice in Beauvais. In fact, it is almost the only statement regarding general contract theory in the 74 articles that Beaumanoir dedicates to agreements. All other articles refer to specific contracts, where Beaumanoir linked the effectiveness of bare agreements to the observance of certain formalities as indications of the serious intention of the parties to bind themselves.[62] Nevertheless, it is a clear indication of canon law influence on some of the authors of the custumals.

The influence of the *ius commune* on the development towards a general law of contracts in England is not as clear as the examples of Castile and France. That is not a surprise, of course, as in the solar system of the *ius commune*, few planets are farther away from the sun than England.[63] There is little direct evidence from common lawyers who stated that they borrowed their ideas from Roman or

Belleperche (d 1308) and Jacques de Révigny (d 1296). On the relationship between Bartolus and the School of Orléans, see among others CH Bezemer, 'Word for word (or not). On the track of the Orleans sources of Cinus' lectura on the Code' 68 *Tijdschrift voor Rechtsgeschiedenis* 433; P Legendre, 'La France et Bartole' in D Segoloni (ed) *Bartolo da Sassoferrato. Studi e documenti per il VI centenario* (Giuffrè, 1962) 131. The second option is the investigation of the interactions between the civilian and canonical discussions of the surety (*fideiussor*). Bartolus had delivered his comments on the *curia mercatorum* on a law dealing with a problem between principal debtor and surety, while canon law would allow actionability of naked pacts regarding similar problems between debtor and surety. See X 3.22.3–5; Innocent IV, *Commentaria super libros quinque decretalium* (Francofurti ad Moenum, 1570), ad X 3.22.3, v° solvat: '[Fideiussor in quatuor casibus potest agere contra principalem debitorem] Primus est, si reus dilapidat bona sua. Secundus, si fideiussor condemnatus est creditori. Tertius, si ex pacto hoc convenit a principio [C 4.35.10]. Quartus, si diu stetit in obligatione [Dig 17.1.38; Dig 17.1.45.5; Dig 13.6.5.15]'. On surety in Roman law, see Zimmermann (n 3) 139–41; on surety in canon law, see K Pennington, 'The Ius Commune, Suretyship, and Magna Carta' (2000) 11 *Revista internazionale di diritto commune* 255, 269.

59 Philippe de Beaumanoir, *Coutumes de Beauvaisis*, Am Salmon (ed) (Alphonse Picard et Fils Éditeurs, 1899), vol II, 2.

60 The full passage reads: 'Sed haec ita, nisi si quid nominatim convenit (vel plus vel minus) in singulis contractibus: nam hoc servabitur, quod initio convenit (legem enim contractus dedit), excepto eo, quod Celsus putat non valere, si convenerit, ne dolus praestetur: hoc enim bonae fidei iudicio contrarium est: et ita utimur'.

61 See X 1.35.1. On the civilian approach to the term 'conventio', see Volante (n 8) 47.

62 Nanz (n 6) 62.

63 The metaphor is adapted from Pennington (n 58) 274.

canon law. But there are some indirect hints. In his discussion on the writ of debt, Glanvill (d 1190) probably made use of Roman law.[64] But the influence of the *ius commune* was likely more felt via the canon law; not so much the doctrine, but rather the practice in the ecclesiastical courts. There are some suggestive indications that the rise of assumpsit as the central contractual remedy in the beginning of the sixteenth century coincides in time with the Church courts losing their competence to enforce promises. Furthermore, there were some similarities in the pleadings and language used in the ecclesiastical courts and that of the royal courts.[65] Even more conclusive is the evidence for the application of canonical principles in the Court of Chancery to remedy deficiencies of the common law of contracts. Medieval chancellors were often bishops, and as such familiar with canon law. Procedure at equity was based on the Romano-canonical procedure. And there were features of the contract law that were identical at the Chancery and ecclesiastical courts.[66]

V. Conclusion

If we look at the role of the medieval *ius commune* in the development towards a general law of contract, there are several conclusions to be drawn that can help to assess the value of initiatives like the PECL.

First, once a text becomes the object of learned commentaries, it is difficult to predict in advance where the interpretative efforts of commentators will lead to. The civilians tried to interpret the basic text in such a way as to adjust it for greater enforceability of naked pacts, even if in the end they did not do away with the Roman *numerus clausus*. The canonists were more flexible and some of them developed wide-reaching remedies to enforce all sorts of promises, but while doing this they focused more on unilateral promises than on consensus. It was on these traditions that the Spanish theologians founded their general theory of contracts. But that result was certainly not written in the stars at the beginning of the twelfth century, when Irnerius and Gratian developed the basic texts of Roman and canon law.

Second, the *ius commune* was not something uniform. There were obvious differences between the civilian and the canonical traditions, and within each

[64] RC Van Caenegem, *Royal Writs in England from the Conquest to Glanvill: studies in the Early History of the Common Law* (Selden Society, 1959) 379; Ibbetson (n 23) *Law of Obligations* 17. On the writ of debt in the development of the English law of contract, see J H Baker, *An Introduction to English Legal History*, 4th edn (Butterworths, 2002) 317; AWB Simpson, *A History of the Common Law of Contract. The Rise of the Action of Assumpsit* (Oxford Univeristy Press, 1975) 75; J Barton, 'The Medieval Contract', in J Barton (ed), *Towards a General Law of Contract* (Duncker & Humblot, 1990) 15.

[65] Helmholz (n 24) 62; RH Helmholz, 'Assumpsit and Fidei Laesio' (1975) 91 *LQR* 406.

[66] Helmut Coing, 'English Equity and the Denunciatio Evangelica of the Canon Law' (1955) 71 *LQR* 223; J Barton, *Roman Law in England* (Giuffrè, 1971) 50; Helmholz (n 24) 60.

tradition there were a variety of opinions as well, that changed over time. The most interesting and dynamic ideas were found in the academic debates among civilians, canonists and between them; debates which often were conducted over several generations before they could lead to widely accepted and mature conclusions. It is not a coincidence that the example of statute law that we investigated in more detail, the *Ordenamiento de Alcalá* of 1348, borrowed word-for-word from a learned author, not from one of the *libri legales.*

Third, as the metaphor of the solar system seems to imply, there is sometimes a trend to consider the *ius commune* as the senior partner over the local law. That image is not wrong. But the relationship was certainly not unidirectional. The *ius commune* incorporated many elements of the local practice. We saw how the civilians tried to stretch their basic texts far enough to cover enforceability of agreements in most commonly occurring situations. Bartolus referred to the practice in merchant courts. As to canon law, the canonists realistically acknowledged that the practical enforcement of a remedy such as the *condictio ex canone* was inherently limited in scope, because of the foreseeable opposition of lay courts. And it was the practice of ecclesiastical courts, and not so much doctrine, that introduced the English to the canonical principle of enforceability of promises. It is this interaction between local law and *ius commune*, between practice and doctrine, that triggered new readings of the basic texts.

For a twenty-first-century observer it is not always easy to understand the plurality of the medieval legal landscape. There was the legal science centred around Roman and canon law; there was also royal law, urban law, feudal law, rural law, merchant law, etc. Some of it was statute law; most of it was customary, even if law practitioners started increasingly to record customs. Courts and arbiters used all of this material in a wide variety of ways. Generally, courts felt much less constraints than nowadays in using material that did not directly resort under their jurisdiction. If the material was helpful, why not use it? As we are breaking away from the model of the nation-state (in fits and starts, admittedly), the need for helpful material that grasps legal principles across several jurisdictions will only increase. For a legal historian, it is difficult to predict what the impact, results or outcome of PECL will be, but the medieval example shows that the journey itself can be very rewarding.

4

Optimal Standards for the Single Market: A Law and Economics Approach

JUAN JOSÉ GANUZA AND FERNANDO GÓMEZ POMAR

I. Introduction: Legal Diversity and the Single Market

Among the fundamental reasons for its existence, and among the major sources of policies and activities of the European Union, the establishment and implementation of an internal market are pre-eminent. The notion of what constitutes the internal market is now set out in Article 26 of the Treaty on the functioning of the European Union (TFEU), according to which:

1. The Union shall adopt measures with the aim of establishing or ensuring the functioning of the internal market, in accordance with the relevant provisions of the Treaties.
2. The internal market shall comprise an area without internal frontiers in which the free movement of goods, persons, services and capital is ensured in accordance with the provisions of the Treaties.

Goods, services, capital and persons move across national borders, typically through economic interactions that are not free from the reach of legal rules and regulations. The presence of different legal orders, and the diversity of rules and standards to which those transactions and the underlying goods and services are subject, could be a relevant source of costs for smooth cross-border economic interaction.

There does not seem to be any overwhelming body of evidence showing the significance of legal diversity as an obstacle to international trade, although several studies have addressed the issue. One study[1] on the matter was indicative, but not totally conclusive, on its relevance and on the magnitude of costs at stake.

[1] S Vogenauer and S Weatherill, *The Harmonisation of European Contract Law: Implications for European Private Laws, Business and Legal Practice* (Hart Publishing, 2006).

An empirical study,[2] using the data of 25 OECD countries, found that the similarity of legal systems may be capable of producing between 50 and 80 per cent more cross-border trade. In another paper[3] it is estimated that legal similarity can increase trade among OECD countries by up to 65 per cent, controlling for transportation costs, common culture and language, and similar factors. However, using Eurobarometer survey data,[4] one study questions how large the hampering effect of legal disparities across European countries is on firms' cross-border activity. Despite this, recent Eurobarometers still show that European consumers are substantially less willing to buy online from sellers in a different European country, a reluctance that is likely inspired to a not insignificant extent by differences in legal rights and outcomes. Recently, a paper[5] commissioned by the EU Policy Department for Citizens' Rights and Constitutional Affairs, looked at how home acquisitions in some European states face important obstacles due to diverse legal rules dealing with all dimensions of real estate transactions, although the paper did not provide a quantification.

The choice of legal order by the parties to the transaction, and healthy rivalry among competing legal systems—regulatory competition—may improve matters and reduce the negative consequences of legal disparities across European systems for the functioning of the internal market. These mechanisms, however, are not always expected to do all the work, and cannot provide, in all circumstances, the desired outcome. There are, undoubtedly, important costs, both natural or man-made, linked to their functioning that sometimes may, perhaps, be large enough to prevent adequate choice of legal rules and regulatory competition.

There are various reasons for this. Sometimes the relevant choice of a course of action by firms which are subject to the legal rules must be made before any choice of legal order can be effectively made by the parties to the transaction. The outcome of such choice can hardly be anticipated by the firm. This is particularly likely to happen with respect to goods and services produced for mass consumer markets, and with respect to dimensions that cannot wait—for technological or economic reasons—to be determined at a later stage, when the question of the applicable law has been sorted out.

Additionally, the choice of applicable law may be subject to significant transaction costs of different kinds. Parties, especially such inexperienced ones as consumers, will not be informed on alternative legal rules, and may be distrustful of legal rules and standards from other countries. Moreover, in consumer markets,

[2] F den Butter and R Mosch, *Trade, Trust, and Transaction Costs* (2003) Tinbergen Institute Working Paper No 2003-082/3.

[3] A Turriniand and T Van Ypersele, *Legal Costs as Barriers to Trade* (2006) Center for Economic Policy Research Discussion Paper Series Paper No 575.

[4] WHJ Hubbard, 'Another Look at the Eurobarometer Surveys' (2013) *Common Market Law Review* 187.

[5] Sparks et al, 'Cross Border Acquisitions of Residential Property in the EU: Problems Encountered by Citizens' (2016) *European Union Directorate-General for Internal Policies.*

mistakenly or not, legal rules significantly restrict the choice of governing law, and essentially subject the transaction to the laws of the consumer's home country.[6] Article 12 of the European Product Liability Directive[7] forbids contract clauses excluding or limiting liability. This is considered to include choice of law clauses that lead to the application of a legal order that is not harmonised according to the rules set out in the directive.

In other circumstances, given the goal of the parties, legal fragmentation simply cannot be overcome by choice of law or regulatory competition, since the transaction is multi-jurisdictional and is intended to produce effects in a set of different member states, where legal requirements differ (eg formality requirements for documents or pre-requisites for registration).

Thus, legal disparities across member states are likely to impose costs (of varying extents, depending on the circumstances) on firms and other economic agents intending to transact across national borders, both firms willing to serve several foreign markets, and consumers willing to be served by sellers from other states.

II. The Role of Harmonisation of Legal Rules and Standards

Although their size remains hard to quantify, given the costs for firms, consumers, and economic agents in general that arise from the disparity of legal orders, some degree of approximation or harmonisation of the diverse legal and regulatory standards of various national legal systems may be a policy alternative worth considering. That would serve to eliminate or, at least, reduce the costs of regulatory diversity affecting cross-border transactions. Unsurprisingly, the EU has been granted powers to adopt measures for the approximation of the provisions laid down by law, regulation or administrative action which have as their objective the establishment and functioning of the internal market (Article 114 TFEU).

The negative effects of legal and regulatory fragmentation for a single transnational market are probably higher in the area of mass transactions.[8] Goods and services produced and distributed in mass markets are typically less individualised, also with respect to the applicable legal and regulatory standards—as to the specificities of a particular transaction. In addition, in large inter-firm deals,

[6] See Arts 6.1 and 6.2 of the Rome I Regulation, based on the principle that the protection granted by the mandatory law of the consumer's habitual residence cannot be excluded by choice of law clauses.

[7] Council Directive 85/374/EEC of 25 July 1985 on the approximation of the laws, regulations and administrative provisions of the Member States concerning liability for defective products [1985] OJ L210/29.

[8] See also EA O'Hara, 'The limits of Contract Law Harmonization' (2012) 33 *European Journal of Law and Economics* 505.

since firms are repeat players with more at stake overall, they will have greater opportunities to learn how to overcome the disadvantages of legal diversity, and also greater incentives to incur the costs of doing so. Consumers, on their part, for many transactions at least, are just one-shot players, facing higher costs of learning and significantly lower incentives to invest in reducing the effects of legal fragmentation.

Harmonised European rules for those mass markets have the potential to reduce the costs of doing business in different national markets. If a firm plans to launch a product in several member states, the costs of compliance with legal constraints are obviously higher in the presence of different legal requirements than with a single set of legal conditions for a business campaign.[9]

Legal and regulatory diversity will not dissipate entirely, even if a harmonised legal body of rules and standards for the single market were put in place. Law is not a one-dimensional product, but a complex one. Even if the legal standard is, on the books, set jointly for all national legal orders, the law as an outcome may well differ, due to the impact of courts and other adjudicators, legal procedure, legal culture and environment in general, which remain national. Also, the need to adapt to local market conditions will always impose costs on cross-border activities by firms.

A few years back, a proposal was advanced by some commentators[10] with the idea of allowing firms to sell and distribute consumer goods in compliance with, not one of the 28 legal regimes in the EU, but with a new, entirely 'European' set of rules and regulations governing those transactions, which would apply across the single market. Firms would see their cost of selling goods all over the European market dramatically reduced, since they would no longer need to take into account the national standards in each of the markets they serve, as it would be safe to comply only with the European ones. Consumers in various member states, relying on being adequately protected under the European rules, would be willing to enter into transactions governed by the European standards, and not by the regulations in their home countries. Cross-border trade in the single market would thus be enhanced.

This is not solely a theoretical or scholarly possibility. An optional set of European contract law rules[11] was presented by the European Commission in

[9] See S Grundmann, 'European Contract Law of What Colour?' (2005) 1 *European Review of Contract Law* 184; K Riesenhuber, 'System and Principles of EC Contract Law' (2005) 3 *European Review of Contract Law* 303.

[10] See H Schulte-Nolke, 'EC Law on the Formation of Contract-from the Common Frame of Reference to the Blue Button' (2007) *European Review of Contract Law* 333 for a presentation by the original creator of the idea of the 'Blue Button' (the term refers to the colour of the European flag in the context of e-commerce, one in which the proposal is presumed to be more relevant for reducing transaction costs in cross-border trade). Along similar lines see H Beale, 'The Future of the Common Frame of Reference' (2007) *European Review of Contract Law* 257.

[11] Common European Sales Law (CESL).

2011 to the EU member states, on the basis of a draft and feasibility study prepared by an expert group.[12]

The determination of what should be the content of legal rules or standards that harmonise legal diversity across member states is, naturally, a key dimension, both theoretically, and for the interests of the affected firms and consumers. There are several important elements in the setting of the content of the European rules at this point in time. One is whether the European standards should simply reflect the current minimum level of protection contained in the directives already in force, or whether they would correspond to the minimum, average, or maximum levels of consumer protection now observed in the different national legal systems.[13] Another refers to the relationship between the European standards—given, at least hypothetically, that their content corresponds to the desirable level—and the pre-existing national standards. The European standards may try to entirely replace the prior national standards, but they may also attempt, more modestly, to set a minimum level that national standards should need to comply with. Additionally, the harmonised legal standard may be conceived purely as an alternative, and in no case as a replacement.

It is well known in EU law that some consumer directives have been conceived as preventing member states from keeping or adopting rules that depart from those of a relevant directive. For instance, the Consumer Rights Directive (CRD) opted for full harmonisation (Article 4), banning all divergent national rules.[14] The recent proposals for a directive on certain aspects concerning contracts for the online and other distance sales of goods (OSD proposal) of 9 December 2015 (Article 3), and for a directive on certain aspects concerning contracts for the supply of digital content (DCD proposal) of 9 December 2015 (Article 4) have also been formulated as maximum harmonisation instruments.

Most consumer directives, however, have followed a less intrusive minimum harmonisation approach, whereby the European rules simply set a required floor for the national standards. This is still alive, as the still recent Directive[15] 2013/11 on alternative dispute resolution for consumer disputes of 21 May 2013 sticks to the minimum harmonisation.

Optionality, in turn, has been less used in EU law-making, and the most relevant example of such an approach to harmonisation in the single market, the CESL Proposal (see Article 8 for the optional application clause), is no longer on the EU legislative agenda.

[12] It must be disclosed that one of the authors was a member of the expert group.

[13] See M Hesselink, *SMEs and European Contract Law* (2007) Centre for the Study of European Contract Law, University of Amsterdam Working Paper no 2007/03.

[14] Except for minor issues such as information disclosure requirements for contracts that are not distance or off-premises contracts (Art 5).

[15] Directive 2013/11/EU of the European Parliament and of the Council of 21 May 2013 on alternative dispute resolution for consumer disputes and amending Regulation (EC) No 2006/2004 and Directive 2009/22/EC (Directive on Consumer ADR) [2013] OJ L165/63.

The brief comparison in approaches, however, shows that the relationship between harmonised legal standards with pre-existing diverse national ones may be tackled in various ways.

In this chapter we try to offer some economic insights on the European debate concerning the merits and modes of building harmonised rules in private law (thinking mainly of consumer, contract, and tort provisions that may affect cross-border trade). This is an area dealing with the different avenues of convergence of legal systems, the possible though unlikely adoption of the Common European Sales Law, and the general characterisation of the relationship between higher level harmonising standards and the national level. Here we emphasise the details of various harmonisation regimes and how they would influence the content of European standards.

Crucially, whether the technological parameters and the parameters for consumer protection are independent or correlated, and the sign of the correlation, if it exists, determine whether the optimal standard is intermediate between the existing national standards, equals the more exacting standard, or even, counter-intuitively, exceeds the toughest standard among the national laws.

Our second basic set of findings refers to the modes of harmonisation: full harmonisation is very powerful for obtaining gains from trade, but it may sacrifice preference satisfaction at the local level that diverse national standards were able to serve better. Minimum harmonisation needs to be complemented with other measures, such as a full or limited country of origin principle, that guarantee some degree of firm entry into foreign markets to achieve some meaningful degree of harmonisation. We show, however, that co-existence of harmonised and national standards, when the harmonised standard allows entry of foreign firms, is always at least as good as minimum harmonisation, and often is better in terms of implementing first best outcomes. Rigidities in technology choice due to economies of scale or other reasons that prevent the effective use of more than one standard by firms play an important role in the relative desirability of softer (co-existence) or blunter (full harmonisation) modes of harmonising rules and standards.

In what follows we will be assuming that the legal rules and standards are produced or, at least, supported, by governmental authorities or bodies. This qualification affects both the rules that predate the harmonisation exercise, and those that result in the common or convergent legal standards. Obviously, the substantive content of the rules, let alone the expertise or input embodied in it, may have been originated by private bodies (firms, NGOs, other lobbying groups, experts), but we opt to restrict ourselves to legal rules and standards sponsored and enforced by the public authorities or political entities or countries. We do not deny that competition of legal rules may come from private actors who may be able to sell their 'private legal systems'[16] to social and economic players, and that there may

[16] See G Hadfield, *Rules for a Flat World. Why Humans Invented Law and How to Reinvent It for a Complex Global Economy* (Oxford University Press, 2016) ch 10.

be also non-national or transnational legal rules and standards, both privately and publicly supplied.

These are obviously extremely interesting issues, both theoretically and practically, but we think, perhaps erroneously, that the issues that we explore here are complex enough even in the traditional sphere of the diverse legal systems of the nation-states, and the common or harmonised standards that may be adopted on top of or in parallel to them (albeit forcing adaptation and change, if needed, of the national legal systems). Most of what we say, though, will find application when those added complexities are included in the picture, since at least in the medium term, boundaries and nation-states will persist and will be able to exercise some degree of control on legal elements of transactions taking place within the territories over which they have control.

III. Full vs Minimum Harmonisation and Co-Existence of Standards

The most desirable substantive content for a set of rules intending to produce a harmonising effect in the single market is something that cannot be determined independently of whether the harmonised standards should replace, or co-exist with, the pre-existing national standards.

In EU law, and especially in EU consumer law, this issue commonly presents itself as the full versus minimum harmonisation dilemma. This perception does not fully capture the scope and dimension of its relevance. Obviously, the problem is not limited to EU law, since it emerges in any exercise in harmonisation where pre-existing legal rules covering the matter existed before the common standards were designed and eventually implemented. It is, thus, a general problem in legal harmonisation (unless no previous rules existed, an extremely unlikely scenario).

Moreover, theoretically the range of alternatives and policy choices is larger than the EU debate commonly assumes, because on the one hand, minimum harmonisation allows for a wide variety of accompanying conditions for cross-border trade once the (minimum) harmonisation measure has been adopted; while on the other hand, softer (than minimum harmonisation) approaches exist, such as pure co-existence of the pre-existing national standards with the newly created common or harmonised ones.

It is clear that maximum harmonisation is causing a complete displacement and abrogation of the national standards that do not entirely coincide with the harmonised rule. Regardless of whether the former are higher or lower than the latter, it implies the strongest or most aggressive form of harmonisation in terms of the relationship of the output of the convergence exercise with the pre-existing situation of legal diversity. In the area of EU consumer law, and usually in the name of preserving high levels of consumer protection, as well as respecting heterogeneity of societal preferences in that respect, full harmonisation has often been criticised by the European legal academic community.[17]

The harmonised standard may simply set a mandatory floor in the relevant variable, parameter or behaviour to which the legal rules refer, but allowing the affected countries (in the EU, the member states) to keep, or to create in the future, more exacting standards along the relevant dimension (in EU consumer law, higher requirements for the protection of consumers). Thus, only legal rules with standards lower than those ordained by the common rule would be eliminated. In a material sense, only the standards (and the countries having them in their legal systems) below the level in the harmonising instrument are actually 'bound' by the common rule, and the rest remain unaffected, except for the elimination of the choice, previously unconstrained, to change their laws in the direction of going below the floor set by the harmonised rule (in the EU context, the level adopted in the Minimum Harmonisation Directive).

In theoretical terms, however, it must be noted that minimum harmonisation is not at all equivalent to pure co-existence of standards. Under minimum harmonisation, standards lower than the harmonised one will be out of the picture, and will be replaced by the harmonised standards. In the second case, the harmonised standard does not replace or erode, at least in an explicit or formal way, any of the existing ones, regardless of whether they were higher or lower than the newly adopted harmonised legal standard.

Under minimum harmonisation, however, countries with a higher national standard are allowed not only to keep it, but essentially to 'ignore' the harmonised standard, since firms operating in that national market would be forced to comply with the stricter national standard. Thus, under minimum harmonisation, unless there is some possibility of entry into the markets with standards that are different from those mandated by the national authorities, there will be no chance of cross-border trade.

If, despite the adoption of a common rule with minimum harmonisation effects (repealing lower national standards), the markets of the affected countries remain entirely isolated, the harmonisation exercise as such becomes moot and worthless. If harmonisation is intended to have some bite on cross-border transactions, it would be necessary to complement minimum harmonisation with some possibility of entry of foreign firms using the harmonised standard in a national market other than their own.

The conditions of entry of firms from another country in the local market may differ, thus affecting the likely outcomes and levels of penetration and cross-border trade (which, in turn, should ideally have an impact on the chosen levels of the harmonised standards).

[17] T Wilhelmsson, 'Full Harmonisation of European Consumer Contract Law?' (2008) *16 Zeitschrift fuer Europäisches Privatrecht* 221; C Twigg-Flesner and D Metcalfe, 'The Proposed Consumer Rights Directive—Less Haste, More Thought?' (2009) 5 *European Review of Contract Law* 368–91; M Loos, *Full Harmonization as a Regulatory Concept and its Consequences for the National Legal Orders: The Example of the Consumer Rights Directive* (2010) University of Amsterdam Working Paper no 2010/03.

One would conjecture that, at a minimum, entry by firms from another country will be possible in those markets where the local standard is not higher (it will be equal to, given the assumed minimum harmonisation exercise) than the harmonised one. Then, firms using a standard that is at least as high as the national level of protection are able to enter that national market.

Think of two countries, A and B, which are affected by minimum harmonisation with this kind of imperfect or incomplete entry under harmonised standards at least as high as the local ones. Imagine that the minimum harmonisation standard is intermediate (or I) between those of country A (low level, or L) and country B (high level, or H). If minimum harmonisation is complemented with an entry measure that allows firms to enter a foreign market but only under standards that are at least as high as those in the receiving country, firms from country A, using standard I (due to minimum harmonisation the standard L has been eliminated from the scene, even in country A) could not enter country B, whereas firms from country B, using standard H would be able to serve their own country (B), under its local standard, but also country A, since they are operating under a standard that is at least as high (in fact, higher) than the local one (remember, H is larger than I).

The above scheme corresponds to a kind of imperfect or asymmetric 'country of origin' regime that would allow cross-border trade only under standards that are higher than that of the import country, but not the reverse.

The conditions of entry accompanying minimum harmonisation of legal rules and standards may be even more favourable to foreign firms. If minimum harmonisation is supplemented with full 'country of origin' or 'mutual recognition' principles, which would allow firms from other countries—remember, now using at least the minimum harmonised standard—to enter the market of those countries who have preserved a standard higher than the harmonised one, as long as they operate and serve clients under the standard of their country of origin, which, following minimum harmonisation is at least equal to the harmonised level. A similar outcome would happen in practice when the firms from the country with the higher standard, using the freedom of movement of capital could at zero or relatively little cost, re-incorporate in a country with the lower standard—this local standard now, after minimum harmonisation, has at least the same level of the harmonised standard—and re-enter their old national market as a foreign firm, benefiting from the country of origin or mutual recognition principle.

As already mentioned, an even weaker or less intrusive form of harmonisation exists, as far as the existence and the level of pre-existing national standards are concerned. Such mode of harmonisation does not seek to replace or affect the existing national standards. This softer harmonisation exercise would operate through a supplementary set of rules under which firms could enter a foreign market, and compete with local firms (which would likely still use the national standard). One could label such a scheme pure co-existence of harmonised and national standards, since the harmonised set of rules would not replace at all the existing ones in each of the national markets, regardless of whether the national standards are higher or lower than the level imposed in the harmonised rule.

Again, co-existence of standards allows, in theory, for various possibilities of implementing the harmonisation process. The choice between standards may be given to the governments of the countries involved in the exercise, or rather to the firms deciding to operate in a given national market.

In the first case, we have essentially an additional set of rules that countries may voluntarily adopt on top of their own standards, or replacing their existing rules. Such an optional approach to harmonising rules in European private law has been proposed by some commentators on a European instrument on contract law.[18] To have some bite, this harmonised optional standard should allow firms from the country adopting the harmonised standard (together with, or as a replacement of, their pre-existing rules) and that operate under it, to be able to enter, under such standard, the national markets of other countries. Otherwise, there is no incentive to make use of the harmonised standard in the national legal system, and no country that cared about its own firms would ever adopt the harmonised standard: adopting the new, common standard would not enhance the ability of these firms to serve foreign markets and, for the purely domestic market, one could assume or hypothesise that the pre-existing national standard was better tailored to the preferences of the local population and the cost structures of the local firms. It is true that it is possible to imagine a national government opening up its own local market to foreign firms operating under the new harmonised standards, but it is unlikely to happen in practice unless such a move was reciprocal, and the latter in fact means that firms from a country adopting the harmonised standard and operating with it are able to enter a foreign market.

In a given harmonisation process, the option between a national standard (that will still be in force) and a new harmonised standard may eventually be given not to the governments, but to the firms. Firms will be able to decide under which legal or regulatory standard to operate—their national one, or the new harmonised standard, or even under both, if that is technologically feasible—more on this later. Again, if the harmonised standard is to acquire some bite in cross-border trade, the firms using the harmonised standard need to be allowed to enter any national market of the countries participating in the harmonisation exercise. Otherwise, the option granted to the firms is moot, since in their own local market they could always stick to the pre-existing national standard (remember, under pure co-existence such standards still remain in force).

The model of pure co-existence with an option granted to the firms essentially corresponds to the 'blue button' proposal that was described above, and to the

[18] See S Grundmann, 'The Optional European Code on the Basis of the Acquis Communautaire—Starting Points and Trends' (2003) 10 *European Law Review* 698–711; S Grundmann and W Kerber, 'An Optional European Contract Law Code: Advantages and Disadvantages' (2005) 2 *European Journal of Law and Economics* 215–36.

optionality of the proposed (and failed) Common European Sales Law.[19] These regimes can be fully replicated when the option is given to national governments, when countries may give their firms the choice to operate under the national standard or the harmonised one, a regime that one could label as a dual standards regime.

The previous characterisation shows that the number of harmonisation regimes is larger and more complex than is commonly assumed in literature. For the purpose of assessing the effects of a harmonisation process, having regard to the substantive content of the common rules and standards is insufficient, since how the harmonised rules relate to the national ones, and how they allow firms in each of the participating countries to enter the domestic markets of the other states is a crucial element to understand the welfare effects of the process. The taxonomy of harmonising modes, as we have tried to show, is also more complicated than one would initially have in mind, and this creates an additional layer of complexity in the analysis of legal harmonisation.

IV. A Preliminary Assessment of the Various Modes of Harmonisation

In order to approximate the welfare consequences of the different harmonisation modes (with all the accompanying dimensions as to possibilities of entry in a foreign market) it is useful to make a simplifying assumption. In order to abstract from the additional (and no doubt real) complexities deriving from a large number of countries participating in the process, we will assume that only two countries, A and B, are involved in the harmonisation exercise. This simple setting allows us to focus on the basic logic explaining how the various alternatives as to the modes of harmonisation affect welfare through their impact on the level of the harmonised standard and the outcomes in terms of cross-border trade. The basic logic remains essentially unaltered when the number of countries increases, though the process becomes more intricate and the outcomes less certain. Obviously, this suggests a note of caution as to the generalisation of the implications from the two-country setting to more complex ones, but the fundamental features of the different modes of harmonisation regarding the effects on cross-border trade persist.

Moreover, it is also necessary to distinguish two different scenarios. In one of them, firms are able to operate and do business serving their customers under more than one standard. In our two-country setup, this means that a firm can, at a

[19] Arts 3 and 4 of the Regulation Proposal determined the optional nature of the rules and the cross-border transactions subject to them, and Art 8 set the details of the option to be binding on the parties. Art 13 granted member states the ability to extend the scope of the harmonised rules to purely domestic transactions, albeit always preserving the optional character.

reasonable cost, produce and sell locally under its own national standard, and sell in the foreign market using the harmonised standard.[20] In many circumstances, this scenario may not be implausible when one is thinking of legal rules such as those in contract law, including consumer contract law, since a firm may be able to adapt the terms of the contract to the local or the harmonised standard without too much added cost or too much of a disruption in its production and commercialisation operations. Obviously, when one increases the number of countries from our setting of just two, this scenario of firms' flexibility regarding legal standards becomes less plausible, perhaps even becoming unrealistic to imagine when the size of the group of countries reaches a certain threshold. This would mean that our first scenario (firms are able to use more than one standard in their dealings with customers) is a less likely one when we depart from our simple basic setting of two countries building a harmonised standard.

The second scenario is the opposite one, in which firms are constrained to employ in their production and/or commercialisation processes just one 'technology', and thus, can be in compliance with only one standard, be it their own national one, or the harmonised set of rules.

Again, this setting in which firms cannot reasonably at a low cost operate under different standards, and are forced by cost considerations to only do business under one single set of rules and standards, is plausible even in a two-country setup. Examples include standards governing the quality of raw materials in production processes, or safety standards as to mass-produced products (and thus likely to show significant economies of scale). Again, clearly this second scenario becomes more likely as one increases the number of countries and markets involved, since the added number of standards would imply a likely larger impact on the cost functions of the affected firms.

Before we start considering separately the two scenarios, it is important to bear in mind that we will be assessing different modes of harmonisation, and thus, we are not comparing them with the background alternative of no harmonisation. We are focusing our analysis on the assessment of the various modes of harmonisation with respect to one another, and thus, we do not intend to claim in a general way that the preferred mode of harmonisation is more desirable than refraining from harmonising at all. Clearly, diversity of legal rules and standards may not be hindering cross-border trade, or if it is, only minimally. This may be the case both when cross-border trade is healthy despite legal diversity, and when very little or no cross-border trade is to be expected even when there are no legal disparities, due to non-legal barriers, be they economic, cultural or of other types. It is very unlikely then that harmonisation will be worthwhile, at least for purposes of

[20] Obviously, not (for legal or practical reasons) under the national standard of the foreign country, since if this were the case any legal harmonisation effort would be totally wasted, as firms would already be able to enter the foreign market with the existing national rules (abstracting from tariffs or other similar barriers, but these are outside the scope of legal harmonisation of substantive rules and standards).

promoting cross-border trade. Whether this is actually the case or not in a given context is largely an empirical matter and we do not risk passing judgement on this, either with respect to the EU, or to other regional or international settings.

Let us start with the scenario in which firms in country A are able to use their own national standard (A), but also the harmonised one (H), and firms in country B are able to use their own national standard (B), and also the harmonised one (H).

Intuitively, in this setting pure co-existence[21] appears as a natural candidate for the most desirable mode of harmonisation in terms of welfare and promoting cross-border trade. When technology does not bind in terms of forcing firms to use a single standard, a regime of harmonised standards (optimally set) that do not replace the pre-existing ones, but simply allow entry of firms into foreign markets by effect of using the harmonised standard, seems to be appealing. First, it is less intrusive on pre-existing standards (which we assume were tailored to the local population's preferences and local firms' cost parameters in satisfying legal requirements) than minimum harmonisation (remember, this wipes out the lower pre-existing standard, however fitting they were to the local populations of individuals and firms), let alone full harmonisation, that does away with all national standards and only allows the harmonised standard in its place.

This feature of pure co-existence is an important one, since preserving the low national standard may be desirable to allow a better match of the standard with the preferences of the population in the country with the low standard. Imagine that country A has the low standard (A<B), but that firms in country A are more efficient—have lower costs of serving consumers, taking into account the satisfaction of the legal standard—so they are going to enter the market of country B if cross-border trade is possible. Pure co-existence is able to implement the first best in these circumstances: firms in country A would serve consumers in that country under standard A (the lower of the national ones), and consumers in country B under standard H (which, by the way, if set optimally will be higher than B, due to the entry of firms with lower costs than the local firms in B). This is the best, most desirable scenario both in terms of satisfaction of preferences of the populations and enjoying the advantages of cross-border trade.

This outcome is not possible under minimum harmonisation, in all its forms, because it totally eradicates the standards that fall short of the harmonised level (in our case, at least A, since under minimum harmonisation the optimal harmonised standard is not necessarily going to be as high as under pure co-existence). Under full harmonisation only the common standard survives, and thus the satisfaction of preferences is necessarily worse than under pure co-existence and under minimum harmonisation. Thus, in some sets of circumstances, co-existence, by bringing the possibility of entry into foreign markets under the umbrella of the

[21] We will not distinguish between the two forms (optionality for governments or for firms), since with the first one we can replicate the second.

harmonised standard, allows the full realisation of the gains from trade, and simultaneously preserves local standards where entry by foreign firms, due to firms' cost considerations, is not an issue.[22]

There is, however, one circumstance (always in the scenario where firms are able to operate under more than one standard) where an unconstrained (more on this below) pure co-existence scheme may experience disadvantages compared with minimum harmonisation, and will not lead to the most desirable outcome in terms of preference satisfaction. Imagine that country A has the low standard (A<B), but that firms in country B are more efficient—have lower costs of serving consumers, taking into account the satisfaction of the legal standard—so that firms in country B are going to enter the market of country A if cross-border trade is feasible. Under pure co-existence, firms from country B will enter market A under the harmonised standard (H), which will be intermediate between A and B. It would be optimal in terms of welfare and preference satisfaction that they serve their own local market (B) with the standard B, since this is the one best adapted to the combination of the population's preferences and firms' costs in country B. However, since standard H is lower (and thus less costly for firms) than B, and pure co-existence as such would not prevent them from doing it, they would prefer to use H also locally, a standard that is less fitting to the preferences of the local population in B.

This may explain why some national governments were reluctant to adopt the Common European Sales Law, worried about their own national high standards being replaced locally by lower harmonised standards. The concern is legitimate in theory, but not when one actually considers the complete scheme contained in the Common European Sales Law, since it allowed standards to co-exist for cross-border trade, but not domestically (or at least not domestically if the relevant government did not opt-in to use the Common European Sales Law also for purely national transactions).

This sub-optimal outcome, however, will be curtailed by limiting the use of the harmonised standard to cross-border trade (as Article 4 of the Regulation Proposal on the Common European Sales Law did[23]). If that happens, firms from country B would only be able to use standard H in market A, but would be forced to use B in their domestic market, the outcome that is the best allocation in terms of social welfare.

This same (desirable) outcome would also happen under minimum harmonisation (both with partial entry and full country of origin principle, although not

[22] If the harmonised standard is set optimally by the countries, it can be shown that pure co-existence is even superior to no harmonisation when the costs of the harmonisation process as such are trivial, or can be disregarded.

[23] The fact that Art 13 granted member states the option to expand the scope to domestic trade does not weaken the finding in the text, since governments that care about social welfare would not do so in the circumstance described in the text. If a government does not care about social welfare, then there is no reason to think that the national standard was a good one to start with.

when there is no entry), since in this case the standard that is replaced is only A (the lower one, and which is dominated by H when market B is served by the more efficient firms from country B), and firms from B, under minimum harmonisation, cannot use H (which, remember, is intermediate and lower than B) in their local market of country B.

What does all of the above imply for a general assessment of harmonisation regimes in the scenario where firms are not constrained to operate just under one standard? Here, the implications are reasonably clear-cut.

With co-existence, when limited to cross-border trade, it is possible to implement the first-best standard, which thus dominates (weakly, that is, is always as good as, and sometimes better than) any other mode of harmonisation. Non-constrained co-existence, however, is not always able to induce the most desirable situation in terms of welfare, since in the circumstance described immediately above (firms from the country with the higher standard are more efficient), minimum harmonisation (with partial entry or full country of origin principle) performs better.

This should not lead us to think that minimum harmonisation (even with full country of origin principle) is superior generally to pure co-existence. It is not. When we are in the first situation described above (firms from the country with the lower standard are more efficient), co-existence of standards, both constrained and unconstrained, dominates minimum harmonisation in all its versions and forms.

In turn, with minimum harmonisation, coupling it with the full country of origin principle dominates the other versions of this mode of harmonisation, since it facilitates entry of efficient firms, without sacrificing high national standards (obviously, assuming the harmonised standards are properly set taking into account the existence of the full country of origin principle).

Let's now turn to the second scenario, where firms in both countries are constrained to use only one standard, that is, they cannot use both a local standard in their home market, and the harmonised standard in the foreign market. They are forced to operate in all markets they decide to serve under just one standard. Which (single) standard they will prefer depends on their convenience, but also on the harmonisation regime: for instance, under full harmonisation, only the harmonised standard remains in place; under minimum harmonisation, they have to use the local standard, unless its own country adopts the harmonised standard as the national one.

This second scenario is more complex, and a full-blown analysis would exceed the scope of this chapter. The gist of the argument is as follows: the comparison between the different harmonisation regimes hinges on whether or not the harmonisation process in fact will result in enhanced cross-border trade (in our simple setting, whether or not the more efficient firm enters the foreign market). If no entry is expected to take place, then it is clear that full harmonisation cannot be desirable, since it eliminates the pre-existing national standards (that are better fitted to the preferences and the cost functions of the two countries as separate markets), bringing no benefits at all, since there will be no enhanced trade due to the introduction of the harmonised standard. The other regimes are indeed superior, and can be adjusted to this situation of no added entry and trade following harmonisation. Clearly, though, this is a situation where no harmonisation at all is to be preferred, since the whole point of the harmonisation exercise is to enhance the possibility of entry, with its accompanying benefits, so when no entry is to be expected, harmonisation becomes entirely moot, and any cost involved in the process are simply wasted.

When firms can just operate under a single standard, and entry can be expected to happen, then full harmonisation is desirable, and in fact leads to the best allocation feasible. Minimum harmonisation, under any of its varieties, is unable to replicate this outcome, and co-existence may approximate it, but only under further assumptions that would require an even greater foresight on the part of the lawmakers designing the harmonised standards.

In summary, when firms are constrained to do business solely under a single standard, one is again confronted by the fundamental dilemma of choosing between gains from trade produced by full harmonisation and between engaging in a process of building common standards that may in the end fail to bring additional cross-border transactions, while sacrificing a better matching of legal standards to national consumers' preferences and local firms' costs considerations. This dilemma does not have a general answer, but our analysis, we believe, may be helpful to better understand the performance of the different harmonisation modes.

V. Conclusions

Setting harmonised standards against the background of national standards already in place in national legal systems is a very complex task, as the previous analysis shows. However, if legal disparity is proven to have relevant negative effects on cross-border transactions, and the benefits of a larger market without borders and national barriers are large enough, then it may be the case that the unavoidable effort to obtain those gains is worth while.

In the harmonisation process, setting the level of the standards involved at the right level in terms of substance (eg in contract law, determining the relative rights and obligations of the parties) is crucial, although this is not the only relevant dimension. The way in which the harmonised standards relate to the prior national standards is of primary importance, both theoretically and in policy terms. Full harmonisation is of course a very powerful tool to overcome barriers to trade, but it may require important sacrifices in terms of matching the standards to the local preferences and cost considerations. Thus, softer forms may be appealing, because they may be capable of bringing gains from trade (ideally, to the same extent as full harmonisation) while at the same time being flexible enough to better accommodate the preferences and conditions in the various countries involved in the harmonisation exercise. Although an acknowledgement of the different modes of harmonisation (full vs minimum, but also the mere addition of harmonised standards as options) is well established in the literature, their theoretical underpinnings in terms of the welfare effects of the various modes, and how they impact the substantive levels of the standards, has not previously been explored in a systematic way.

Building on a formal model of harmonisation,[24] we have tried in this chapter to characterise different modes of harmonisation, how they affect the optimal choice of harmonised standards, the efficiency of their induced outcomes, and the factors that may affect their performance. Further analysis and some empirical corroboration of our claims remain for future work.

[24] JJ Ganuza and F Gomez, 'How to Build Optimal Standards for Contract and Consumer Law: An Economic Analysis' (2015) *Universitat Pompeu Fabra Department of Economics and Business.*

5

Non-national Rules in the Arbitration of Commercial Contracts

ZEYNEP DERYA TARMAN

I. Introduction

The increasing globalisation of markets has made cross-border contracts a common feature of practice for most lawyers. Those lawyers lacking specific experience in cross-border transactions may face difficulty with a number of rather complicated issues that do not arise when dealing with contractual matters solely within national borders. Rules governing contracts between companies from the same country (or domestic contracts) are contained in the national law of the parties. The relevant courts having jurisdiction in the event of a dispute under a domestic contract will be those determined by the national law of the parties, unless alternative dispute resolution is selected. When the contract is international, however, the situation becomes much more complicated.[1]

In the absence of an adequate legal framework for cross-border transactions, one of the main issues arising with respect to cross-border contracts is the applicable law. Presently, no law addressing cross-border contracts has priority over domestic legal systems applicable to international contracts. All national legal systems have rules regarding the determination of the law relating to issues involving a foreign element, i.e. that are not merely domestic. These rules (called conflict of law rules) make it possible to apply domestic laws to international matters, particularly when the domestic law appears to be more appropriate to govern these situations. When a dispute is brought before a national court, there is no doubt that the court must apply its own conflict of law rules. Therefore, when a court must determine the applicable law with respect to a contract, it will base its decision on the domestic system of private international law. However, conflict of law rules differ from one country to another. This variance creates uncertainty and tends to produce contradictory results. If courts of different countries apply different

[1] N Ekşi, *Milletlerarası Ticaret Hukuku*, 2nd edn (Beta, 2015) 135.

conflict of law rules to the same situation, they may arrive at different conclusions. For example, if one country has a rule stating that the law of the place of conclusion of the contract shall apply, while another country's rule states that the law of the place of performance of the contract shall apply, the courts may resolve the dispute quite differently. In this context, it is usually in the parties' interests to take advantage of the opportunity granted to them to designate the law best suited to their particular transaction and relationship within their contract.

This chapter considers whether or not, and in what circumstances, non-national rules can be applied to international commercial contracts before the national courts pursuant to the Rome I Regulation on the Law Applicable to Contractual Obligations (Rome I Regulation)[2] and before arbitral tribunals pursuant to various domestic statutes and institutional arbitration rules.

II. Law Applicable to the Substance of the Case

A. Choice of Law Principle

The basic principle that parties may choose the law governing their contractual relationship has become widely accepted.[3] It is a reflection of the well-received freedom of contract principle in international private law.[4] The liberty to choose the applicable law ensures that the parties enjoy predictability, legal certainty, safety, and simplicity.[5] In other words, by choosing the applicable law in advance, parties are able to know how the contract will be regulated in the event of a dispute. In order to meet the above expectations, academic study groups have conducted research with the purpose of unifying the substantial rules for international contracts at the European level. The Principles of European Contract Law (PECL), Draft Common Frame of Reference (DCFR), and Common European Sales Law (CESL)[6] can be mentioned in this regard. These rules aim to act as an important source of international commercial and private international law. In addition to the aforementioned instruments, the International Institute for the Unification of Private Law (UNIDROIT) prepared the UNIDROIT Principles of

[2] Regulation (EC) 593/2008 of the European Parliament and of the Council of 17 June 2008 on the law applicable to contractual obligations (Rome I) [2008] OJ L 177/6.

[3] As an example of this principle see Art 24 of the Turkish Private International Law (PIL) Code; Art 116 of the Swiss PIL Code; Art 3 of the Rome I Regulation; Art 187(1) of the American Restatement (Second) on Conflict of laws.

[4] C Şanlı, E Esen and İ Ataman-Figanmeşe, *Milletlerarası Özel Hukuk*, 4th edn (Vedat, 2015) 252; E Nomer, *Devletler Hususi Hukuku*, 21st edn (Beta, 2015) 312–13.

[5] ibid (Nomer) 316.

[6] HL MacQueen, 'The Europeanisation of Contract Law: The Proposed Common European Sales Law' in LA DiMatteo, S Saintier and K Rowley (eds), *Commercial Contract Law: Transatlantic Perspectives* (Cambridge University Press, 2013) 529–58.

International Commercial Contracts (UNIDROIT Principles). The purpose of these non-national rules is to provide a set of rules that can be applied to all types of international commercial contracts. These rules are intended to create an equal and fair situation for both parties, and are suitable for the needs and development of international commercial relations. According to the drafters, it is in the interest of international businesses that these non-national rules be generally applicable to agreements concerning commercial relations.

However, the incorporation of such non-national rules into international commercial contracts, or choice of them as the applicable law to a contract, is not a very widespread practice among the international business community. The reason for this is probably scepticism concerning the application of the non-state rules by national courts and even arbitral tribunals.

B. Application of Non-national Rules at State Courts

Article 3 of the Rome I Regulation stipulates that a contract shall be governed by the law chosen by the parties. Interpreting the meaning of law in light of Recital No 13, it can be said that the Rome I Regulation does not permit choice of law other than national laws.[7] Consequently, national courts can only apply national laws and the parties must therefore agree upon the application of a national law to the substance of the dispute. Codes and rules of law such as UNIDROIT Principles or Principles of European Contract Law (PECL) are not considered a valid choice of law under the Rome I Regulation. The choice of non-national rules by the parties can be interpreted as an incorporation of such rules of law to the contract. They can be respected as contract terms but they will be binding only to the extent they do not conflict with the mandatory provisions of the applicable national law. In other words, the contract as a whole (including the incorporated rules) remains governed by a state's law.[8]

The Hague Principles on Choice of Law in International Commercial Contracts approved on 19 March 2015[9] have taken a modern, novel approach by allowing the choice of non-national rules. Article 3 of these principles allows parties to choose rules of law defined as 'rules that are generally accepted on an international, supranational or regional level as a neutral and balanced set of rules'.[10] It remains to be

[7] H Heiss, 'Party Autonomy: The Fundamental Principle of European PIL of Contracts' in F Ferrari and S Leible (eds), *Rome I Regulation: the Law Applicable to Contractual Obligations in Europe* (Sellier, 2009).

[8] *Channel Tunnel Group Ltd v Balfour Beatty Construction Ltd* [1993] 1 AC 334, 347 (HL). The parties referenced the principles of international law as the applicable law. PECL was applied by the English court through incorporation.

[9] *Principles on Choice of Law in International Commercial Contracts* (HCCH, 2015).

[10] G Saumier, 'The Hague Principles and the Choice of Non-State Rules of Law to Govern an International Commercial Contract' (2014) 40 (1) *Brooklyn Journal of International Law* 1.

seen whether lawmakers will adopt the principles to change their current conflict of law rules on party autonomy.

C. Application of Non-national Rules in Arbitration

The restriction of choice to national law only is not applied in arbitral proceedings. The applicable law to the merits of a case is designated by the national arbitration laws of the states. Since many arbitration laws have been guided by the UNCITRAL Model Law,[11] the main focus of this chapter will be the provisions of this Model Law.

The application of non-state rules in arbitration is examined in two parts: the first part considers the application of non-national rules when they are explicitly chosen as applicable law by the parties in their agreements. The second part interrogates whether or not the non-state rules could be used as applicable law when parties have not made any express choice of law in their agreement.

i. Choice by the Parties: Explicitly or Referring to International Law or Lex Mercatoria

Arbitral proceedings generally allow parties to choose non-national rules to be applicable to their contracts. The provisions of national arbitration laws and institutional arbitration rules regarding the law applicable to the substance of the dispute usually authorise parties to choose non-national rules.

In ad hoc arbitrations, the parties may select the law pertaining to the ad hoc procedure. In such cases, the law applicable to the substance of the dispute must be determined according to the relevant provision of the arbitration rules chosen by the parties. If the parties have not chosen which law will be applicable to the ad hoc arbitration procedure, then the law applicable to the substance will be determined according to the law of the place of arbitration.

According to Article 28 of the UNCITRAL Model Law, the arbitral tribunal shall decide the dispute in accordance with such 'rules of law' as chosen by the parties as applicable to the substance of the dispute. Failing any designation by the parties, the arbitral tribunal shall apply the 'law' determined by the conflict of law rules that it deems most suitable. Due to this difference in terminology, it is accepted that parties may choose non-national rules as applicable 'rules of law', and that non-national rules can be applied independently of any national law. The parties are free to choose a combination of law rules from different jurisdictions or designate the application of non-state rules or *lex mercatoria* to

[11] *UNCITRAL Model Law on International Commercial Arbitration 1985 with Amendments as Adopted in 2006* (United Nations, 2008).

their contracts.[12] However, while many practitioners are familiar with non-state rules such as the UNIDROIT Principles, few choose to apply them in cross-border contracts. In a study conducted among 500 lawyers dealing with international commercial arbitration, 60 per cent of the participants stated that they were aware of the UNIDROIT Principles, while 30 per cent of the lawyers applied them in their contracts. However, these percentages dropped dramatically when the same study was conducted in the UK. Only 3 per cent of the lawyers in the UK applied the UNIDROIT Principles in their practice, although 45 per cent of the lawyers were aware of the rules.[13]

Similarly, Article 46(1) of the English Arbitration Act, Article 1051(1) of the German Arbitration Act (part of the ZPO), Article 1496 of the French Civil Procedure Act, Article 1054 of the Dutch Civil Procedure Act and Article 12C of the Turkish International Arbitration Act provide that the arbitral tribunal shall decide the dispute according to the 'rules of law' chosen by the parties.

It may be concluded that provisions of arbitration laws which do not limit the choice of law of the parties with the term 'law', but rather use the term 'rules of law', allow for the application of non-national rules if chosen by the parties. The use of the term 'rules of law' aims to authorise parties to choose non-national rules of law as well as national laws as applicable law to their contracts. Consequently, parties' reference to non-national rules such as PECL or UNIDROIT Principles must be taken into account, and the arbitrators are obliged to apply these rules of law to the substance of the dispute.

In institutional arbitration, the arbitration rules of the institution are the primary point of reference for the determination of the law applicable to the substance. According to Article 21(1) of the International Chamber of Commerce Arbitration Rules, the parties shall be free to agree upon the rules of law to be applied by the arbitral tribunal to the merits of the dispute.

Similarly, Article 22.3 of the London Court of International Arbitration Rules, Article 22(1) of the Stockholm Chamber of Commerce Arbitration Rules and Article 27(1) of the Austrian Federal Economic Chamber of Arbitration Rules refer to 'rules of law' agreed upon by the parties. It can thus be concluded that arbitration rules of the leading arbitral institutions permit the choice of non-national rules by the parties.

There are a number of arbitral awards based on the UNIDROIT Principles. An arbitral tribunal formed under the auspices of the International Arbitration Court of the Chamber of Commerce and Industry of the Russian Federation applied the UNIDROIT Principles in its award numbered 233/2012 and dated 3 October 2013. In this case, the sales contract between a company from

[12] M Heidemann, *Does International Trade Need a Doctrine of Transnational Law? Some Thoughts at the Launch of a European Contract Law* (Springer, 2012) 9.

[13] S Lake, 'An Empirical Study of UNIDROIT Principles International and British Responses' (2011) 16 *Uniform Law Review* 669, 692.

Liechtenstein and a Russian company contained a choice of law clause referring to the application of the UNIDROIT Principles.[14] In another case, the arbitral tribunal inaugurated by the Lausanne Chamber of Commerce and Industry, in its award of 31 January 2003, based its decision on the UNIDROIT Principles. The contract between the parties contained conflicting provisions as to the applicable law. However, at the beginning of the arbitral proceedings, the parties agreed on the application of the UNIDROIT Principles.[15]

In line with those decisions, the arbitral tribunal formed under the aegis of the International Chamber of Commerce decided to apply the UNIDROIT Principles as the law applicable to the substance of the dispute in its award of 6 January 2003. The parties involved in the case did not make an explicit reference to the UNIDROIT Principles; instead, they alluded to 'international trade usages' in their contract. The arbitral tribunal interpreted the contractual reference to international law by stating that the parties' intention was to exclude the application of any domestic law in favour of general principles of law and *lex mercatoria* and consequently applied the UNIDROIT Principles as the central component of such general principles and *lex mercatoria.*[16] In this case the arbitral tribunal denied the application of PECL by stating that PECL constitutes an academic research that at the current stage was not widely known to the international business community and that its principles are a preliminary step to the drafting of a future European Code of Contracts to be applied instead the UNIDROIT Principles.

ii. In the Absence of Choice of Law by the Parties

According to Article 28 of the UNCITRAL Model Law on International Commercial Arbitration, the arbitral tribunal shall decide the dispute in accordance with such 'rules of law' as are chosen by the parties or, failing any designation by the parties, apply the law determined by the conflict of laws rules which it considers applicable. According to this wording of the provision it can be concluded that the arbitral tribunal shall decide according to the 'law' in the absence of choice of law by the parties. National arbitration acts inspired by the Model Law, such as the Turkish International Arbitration Act Article 12C, or the English Arbitration Act Article 46(3), adopted the same language to ensure the application of national laws by the arbitrators. In the event that the national legislator made a distinction between 'rules of law' and 'law', and made a reference to 'law' in the absence of choice of law by the parties, it is not possible to elect non-state rules as the applicable law. I believe that the relevant provision of the Model Law should

[14] International Arbitration Court of the Chamber of Commerce and Industry of the Russian Federation Case No 233/2012, dated 3 October 2013, www.unilex.info/case.cfm?id=1793.

[15] Arbitration Court of the Lausanne Chamber of Commerce and Industry, Arbitral Award, dated 31 January 2003, www.unilex.info/case.cfm?id=862.

[16] ICC Case No 12111, dated 6 January 2003, www.unilex.info/case.cfm?pid=2&do=case&id=956&step=FullText.

be revised to bring it in line with modern views. At the moment, this provision forms an impediment to the progress of contemporary international arbitration culture and practice.

Some national arbitration laws, however, such as the Swiss International Private Law Act Article 187 or the Dutch Civil Procedure Act Article 1054, provide that the arbitrators may apply the appropriate 'rules of law' in the absence of choice of law by the parties. Similarly, the most widely used institutional arbitration rules also provide that the arbitrators may apply the 'rules of law' as applicable law. Article 21(1) of the ICC Arbitration Rules, in the absence of choice of law by the parties, the arbitral tribunal shall apply the rules of law which it determines most appropriate. Likewise, Article 22.3 of the LCIA Arbitration Rules as well as Article 22(1) of the SCC Arbitration Rules state that the arbitral tribunal shall select and apply the most appropriate laws or rules of law. All these arbitration rules authorise arbitrators to apply non-national rules to the merits of the dispute in the absence of choice of law by the parties. Arbitrators may decide in accordance with the UNIDROIT Principles or PECL, on the basis that they are the most suitable law.

Regarding the selection of law, the most appropriate law is that which ensures equity between the parties and includes the most sophisticated and detailed provisions concerning the subject matter of the dispute. Since national laws are prepared on the basis of national relations, they may be insufficient to deal with the needs of international business transactions. The application of non-state rules will require less time and effort, compared to the determination of the most closely connected national law, and will ensure fair resolution. Furthermore, the application of such rules will put the arbitrators from different legal backgrounds on an equal footing.

There are several examples of arbitral awards based on non-national rules, mainly UNIDROIT Principles. In these events, the arbitrators applied the Principles as the applicable law, even though they were not chosen by the parties as such. For instance, the arbitral tribunal formed under the auspices of the International Chamber of Commerce, in its award numbered 15089 and dated 15 September 2008, applied the UNIDROIT Principles even though the contract relating to high-technology based services entered into by businesses from two Middle Eastern countries was silent as to the law of the contract. The arbitral tribunal stated that the UNIDROIT Principles receive wide recognition in international arbitration practice and set out the basic principles of modern contract law.[17] In its award of 1995 (ICC Case No 7110), the arbitral tribunal formed under the aegis of International Chamber of Commerce, similarly held that the UNIDROIT Principles are a reliable source of international commercial law in international arbitration.[18] Likewise, the arbitral tribunal formed under the auspices of ICC,

[17] ICC Case No 15089, dated 15 September 2008, www.unilex.info/case.cfm?id=1440.

[18] ICC Case No 7110, First Partial Award, dated June 1995, www.unilex.info/case.cfm?pid=2&do=case&id=713&step=Abstract.

in its award of 2004 (ICC Case No 13012), decided to apply the UNIDROIT Principles as part of *lex mercatoria.*[19]

iii. Interpreting or Gap Filling of CISG or National Laws

Article 7 of the CISG sets forth that national judges applying CISG to disputes arising out of international relations shall consider the international character of the dispute. That means judges must employ an international perspective when international transactions are at issue. Regarding issues covered but not explicitly regulated by CISG (internal gaps), a reference to non-state rules is common practice.[20]

The arbitral tribunal aligned with the Vienna International Arbitration Centre, in its award dated 15 June 1995, held that the awarded interest should be calculated on the basis of Article 7 April 9 of the UNIDROIT Principles.[21] Likewise, ICC award of 1995 Case No 8128[22] made a reference to the same article of the UNIDROIT Principles to fill the contractual gap regarding the interest rate.

Apart from filling the gaps of CISG, arbitral tribunals also refer to non-state law in order to interpret the applicable national laws. For example, the arbitral tribunal formed under the auspices of the International Chamber of Commerce, in its award numbered 9078, exercised the UNIDROIT Principles in order to make up for the damages for lost opportunities in German law.[23] Similarly, a gap regarding the right to require performance of non-monetary obligations in Russian law was bridged applying the UNIDROIT Principles Article 7.2.2.[24]

There are also arbitral awards referring to PECL as an instrument to interpret and meet the shortcomings of CISG and national laws. For example, the arbitral tribunal formed under the auspices of the Netherlands Arbitration Institute, in its award dated 10 February 2005, made a reference to the PECL 2:104(1) in order to fill the gap regarding the incorporation of the general conditions containing an arbitration clause.[25] PECL 5:101:3 was similarly referenced in order to apply the duty of cooperation between parties in a contract of association.[26] Although at the moment the number of cases making reference to PECL remains low, it is expected to increase in the future.

[19] For the same view see ICC Case No 7375; ICC Case No 8261; Permanent Court of Arbitration Case No 45863, www.unilex.info.

[20] LA DiMatteo, *Law of International Contracting*, 2nd edn (Kluwer International, 2009) 151.

[21] Vienna International Arbitration Centre Case No SCH-4366, dated 15 June 1994, cisgw3.law.pace.edu/cases/940615a3.html.

[22] ICC Case No 8128 (1995), cisgw3.law.pace.edu/cases/958128i1.html.

[23] ICC Case No 9078, dated July 2001, www.unilex.info/case.cfm?pid=2&do=case&ID=1059.

[24] International Arbitration Court of the Chamber of Commerce and Industry of the Russian Federation Decision No 64/2008, dated 9 April 2009, www.unilex.info/case.cfm?id=1803.

[25] Netherlands Arbitration Institute, Arbitral Award, dated 10 February 2005, www.unilex.info/case.cfm?pid=1&do=case&id=1235&step=Abstract.

[26] *Andersen v Andersen* [1999] 10 *American Review of International Arbitration* 451; LA DiMatteo (n 20) 219.

III. Conclusion

The application of non-national rules is generally accepted in arbitral proceedings either when the parties have chosen them as the applicable rules of law to the merits of their dispute or, in the absence of such choice of law, as the most appropriate law. However, state courts still require further time to respect the choice of non-national rules.

It is expected that the application of non-national rules will become more widespread among international business actors, since there are increasingly strong voices defending them. It will be seen that their application will ensure fairer, faster, and less costly resolutions compatible with the expectations of modern merchants and the needs of international trade. As illustrated above, arbitral tribunals commonly accept the application of the UNIDROIT Principles. However, the application of the European set of rules such as PECL, DCFR and CESL remains limited, and begs more time.

Part II

Uniform Rules for National Legislators and Courts

6

The Modernisation of the Law of Obligations Using the Principles of European Contract Law

ENCARNA ROCA TRÍAS

I. Introduction

Law is a cultural product. It responds to particular needs and follows very specific aims. Cultural motivations may be used both to demonstrate the need for codification as well as to reject a general uniform private law. In this sense, an argument arises between continental law and common law. Even the most reluctant scholars must recognise that the two different sets of legal experience, those of continental law and the common law, have something in common that affects the nature of legal reasoning, the systematic method used, the nature of the legal rules, the different role that facts play in each system and, above all, the meaning of rights as regards the actions. European directives have been considered as a tool for creating a uniform European law as well as harmonising European private law and they have certainly introduced general criteria in particular fields, but not without some difficulty. This is the case of directives concerning consumer law, sale of goods and the regulation of new technologies such as electronic commerce, which have also shown the need to break with the traditional schemes of legal thought due to the requirement of transposition to domestic law. Many areas of domestic law are currently affected by the entry into force of European directives and in some cases their application by domestic courts is done in accordance with the aims of those directives, rather than by following the interpretation of domestic law.

Therefore, the main criterion concerning the *functionality* of current European law cannot be reduced to efficiency or purely economic reasons, but must be measured in accordance with the values linked to the general category of welfare.

II. Advantages and Disadvantages of a Uniform Contract Law

In a paper presented at a meeting held in Florence in 2008,[1] Fabrizio Cafaggi said that the private law policy causes one of the main problems in private law in the European Union. The issue of a future European private law has been the subject of a number of resolutions in the European Parliament, and publications by the Commission, however no decision has been taken on it thus far. Currently, the debate is approached on an academic level, seeking what Cafaggi identifies as 'The search for a common core of principles on the rationalisation of the acquis communautaire, and the advantages and disadvantages of codification of private law'.[2]

However, the current problems are not limited to this issue: they extend far beyond this, since a common European law exists, comprised of the body of directives, but the lack of a clear European policy on this subject creates a great divide. My approach points out the need for a new methodology in the field of European private law, which focuses on the following:

(a) Avoiding complete harmonisation and encouraging the use of general clauses—although we must accept that the use of a complete regulation would 'minimise the risks of conflicting interpretations'.[3] A 'rule-based legislation'[4] increases the cost of adaptation.
(b) 'The improvement of the modes of coordination among national judiciaries',[5] since 'adequate judicial training becomes a precondition for implementation of policies based on judicial governance'.[6]

In my opinion, the subject of European contract law must be focused on two issues. The first refers to the convenience of a single European text on contract law. The second issue refers to the need to establish several clear means through which to achieve a progressive approach among European judges on matters related to the interpretation of the law, not only European law but also internal law derived from European sources. I will restrict my arguments to the second topic—how judges apply European law.

Directives have long been considered a tool for harmonising European law and have certainly introduced general criteria in certain fields. However, in some

[1] F Cafaggi, 'Internal Market, Contract Law and New Governance' (2008) 26 *European University Institute*.
[2] ibid 1.
[3] ibid.
[4] ibid.
[5] E Roca (quoting Fabrizio Cafaggi), 'Private Law: Reforming the Law of Obligations in Europe' (lecture held at the Munster University Law Faculty, March 2013) 8.
[6] ibid.

situations it becomes very complicated for judges to interpret European law in accordance with the aims provided by any directive. It has been correctly stated that directives lead to unification at the EU level, but also dispersion at a national level. The system is very complex and remains a work in progress.

III. Judicial Governance

It is true that checking how much European law is applied is a difficult task, but it is also crucial. '[Judicial] governance would be perceived not only as an institutional response to cultural differences, associated with national identities in order to make them compatible by creating an internal market but also as a comprehensive answer to market and governmental failures'.[7] Under this idea, judges become 'key actors to implement policies defined through European legislation'.[8] Therefore, judicial governance is not only about the EU acting to develop its policies in areas over which it has powers, which could be defined as a first level of action, but is about these policies being effective due to their actual application by judges, who are the main targets. This would represent the second, and likely most important level of action since any reluctance by the judges to apply European laws would destroy the system.

It is absolutely imperative to grant judges an important role in the gradual unification of private law in Europe. It is true that even if a single legislation was reached and the different private systems were harmonised, only judges would hold the key to the effectiveness of European legislation, as the application of directives has already shown. In the Introduction of the Draft Common Frame of Reference (DCFR), it is said that:

> shortly after their publication, the Principles of European Contract Law (PECL), which the DCFR (in its second and third Books) incorporates in a partly revised form, received the attention of many higher courts in Europe and of numerous bodies charged with preparing the modernisation of the relevant national law of contract.[9]

Among these courts were the Spanish Supreme Court as well as Spanish lower courts. The role of the European judge must be examined from two viewpoints, which are not incompatible, but complementary. As regards current European law of contract, the participation of judges is witnessed through the use of preliminary rulings to the Court of Justice of the European Union (CJEU). Additionally, at an internal level, the said judicial action is noticed through the use of European texts, both hard and soft law, as interpretative tools to resolve internal conflicts. I shall briefly outline the Spanish experience on both aspects.

[7] Roca (n 5) 10.
[8] ibid (quoting Cafaggi).
[9] 'Introduction' in DCFR 8.

A. The Use of Preliminary Rulings

The objective of preliminary rulings is to clarify the meaning and interpretation of EU law which is applicable to a particular national litigation. The mechanism of the preliminary ruling

> mainly aims to place a European institution, the Court of Justice, in a position to set common directives which must be considered by national judges and courts when ensuring that the correct, uniform development of European law is observed, maintaining the agreement achieved at the stage of producing regulations to its effective enforcement.[10]

The CJEU sets forth a uniform doctrine which must be respected by the courts of EU member states. This is because EU law takes precedence and enjoys direct effect under certain circumstances.

'The main problem lies in cases where Member States do not correctly fulfil their obligations under a directive, or when they have not made any attempt to fulfil them at all'.[11] Another problem with the preliminary ruling lies in the fact that its case law only refers to European law, and this explains why the CJEU is empowered to establish the correct interpretation. This is not useful to achieve certain interpretative unification in other aspects of private law, when it has its origin in the member states.

I can highlight recent examples from the Spanish courts regarding the interpretation of European consumer law in dealing with enforcement proceedings in mortgages. The economic crisis had a great impact on the payment of long-term mortgages, a major part of these loans having been contracted by people in order to buy their homes. In 2013 a Spanish judge filed a preliminary ruling requesting clarification of the meaning of unfair terms in mortgages contracts according to the Unfair Terms Directive.[12] The aim of the Directive is to protect consumers. The CJEU considered the buyer as a consumer subject to the protection granted by the Directive.[13] The questions in the preliminary ruling referred to the right of the consumer to stop the enforcement proceedings of the mortgage when the contract contained unfair terms. The *Aziz* case[14] established that:

> Council Directive 93/13/EEC of 5 April 1993 on unfair terms in consumer contracts must be interpreted as precluding legislation of a Member state, such as that issue in the

[10] Roca (n 5) 11.

[11] N Reich, 'The Public/Private Divide in European Law' in H Micklitz and F Cafaggi, *European Private Law after the Common Frame of Reference* (Edward Elgar, 2010) 57.

[12] Council Directive 93/13/EEC of 5 April 1993 on unfair terms in consumer contracts [1993] OJ L95/29.

[13] In the same way as Directive 2014/17/EU of the European Parliament and of the Council of 4 February 2014 on credit agreements for consumers relating to residential immovable property and amending Directives 2008/48/EC and 2013/36/EU and Regulation (EU) No 1093/2010 [2014] OJ L60/34, not yet transposed in Spain.

[14] Case C-415/11 *Mohamed Aziz v Caixa d'Estalvis de Catalunya, Tarragona i Manresa (Catalunyacaixa)* [2013] 3 CMLR 5.

> main proceedings, which, while not providing in mortgage enforcement proceedings for grounds of objection based on the unfairness of a contractual term on which the right to seek enforcement is based, does not allow the court before which declaratory proceedings have been brought, which does have jurisdiction to assess whether such a term is unfair, to grant interim relief, including, in particular, the staying of those enforcement proceedings, where the granting of such relief is necessary to guarantee the full effectiveness of its final decision.

The ruling opened up a series of preliminary rulings requested by Spanish courts—the *Peñalva* case,[15] and, principally, the *Sánchez Morcillo* case.[16]

It is however important to keep in mind that this system affects only European law, although it binds the national court inasmuch as it applies this law in order to avoid a loss of efficiency which would exactly contradict the European law aim of unification. Other unresolved problems remain, since the level of harmonisation sought later is only achieved in issues pertaining to European law, which is sectorial. In addition to this we face the question of whether or not European fundamental rights reign supreme, as contemplated in the *Melloni*[17] and *Akerberg*[18] cases. Notwithstanding the complexity of this issue, we turn now to the experience of Spanish judges in the interpretation of conflicts.

B. Interpretation by Means of Resorting to European Instruments of Soft Law

Since 2005 the Spanish Supreme Court has used the technique of integrating the Principles of European Contract Law in order to interpret the regulations in the Spanish Civil Code. Thus, in the judgments[19] of 10 October 2005, 5 April, 20 July, 31 October and 22 December 2006, Article 8:103 PECL was used to determine if a fundamental non-performance had existed or not, ending a long discussion about the meaning of Article 1124 of the Spanish Civil Code. The judgments[20] from 4 and 11 July 2006 used Article 1:201 PECL regarding the concept of good faith and fair dealing. That[21] of 5 January 2007 used Article 13:102 PECL for the concept of set-off, while that[22] of 27 September 2006 used Article 7:103 PECL regarding the

[15] Case C-8/14 *BBVA SA v Pedro Penalva Lopez and Others* [2015] ECLI:EU:C:2015:731.

[16] Case C-169/14 *Juan Carlos Sanchez Morcillo and Maria del Carmen Abril Garcia v Banco Bilbao Vizcaya Argentaria SA* [2014] ECLI:EU:C:2014:2099.

[17] Case C-399/11 *Stefano Melloni v Ministerio Fiscal* [2013] Digital Reports (Court Reports—General), ECLI:EU:C:2013:107.

[18] Case C-617/10 *Aklagaren v Akerberg Fransson* [2013] ECLI:EU:C:2013:105.

[19] STS (1ª) 10 October 2005 (RJ 2005, 6005); STS (1ª) 5 April 2006 (RJ 2006, 2364); STS (1ª) 20 July 2006 (RJ 2006, 6030); STS (1ª) 31 October 2006 (RJ 2006, 6429); STS (1ª) 22 December 2006 (RJ 2006, 7943).

[20] STS (1ª) 4 July 2006 (RJ 2006, 4079); STS (1ª) 11 July 2006 (RJ 2006, 4453).

[21] STS (1ª) 5 January 2007 (RJ 2007, 1).

[22] STS (1ª) 27 September 2006 (RJ 2006, 5497).

concept of early performance. The judgment[23] of 11 July 2007 used Article 5:102 PECL regarding the interpretation and relevant circumstances; the judgment[24] of 27 July 2007 used Article 8:108 PECL regarding the excuse due to impediment and Article 8:106 PECL for the notice fixing additional period for performance; finally, that[25] of 31 October 2005 used Article 10:102 PECL regarding joint and several obligations. Spanish law was applicable in all of these contracts, except in the judgment of 4 July 2006, where German law was applicable. In the last rulings[26] related to information in contracts such as swaps, the Civil Chamber of the Supreme Court referred to the Principles of European Contract Law (STS 28 October 2015 and 12 February 2016). In the recent judgments[27] it did so as regards information duties (8 September 2014; 20 October 2015 and 12 February 2016); control of transparency in unfair clauses (STS 8 September 2014); *rebus sic stantibus* clause (STS 15 October 2014);[28] 'escrow' contracts (STS 24 October 2014; 8 November 2014);[29] the application of the principle of good faith and fair dealing in banking contracts (STS 7 July 2015; 29 September 2015, 12 February 2016),[30] and finally, the concepts of mistake and deception (STS 3 February 2016;[31] 7 July 2015, 29 September 2015).

In these cases, the PECL, the UNIDROIT Principles, as well as the DCFR are rather used as a basis to consolidate court case law; the DCFR are sometimes lacking convincing legal support, although providing for answers similar to those enshrined by the PECL. Leaving aside this collateral concern, the use of the PECL in Spanish courts seems to be a consistent decision to develop the judicial application of the law of contracts. This is not only because this contributes both to the prevalence of PECL in Spain and to enhancing the cross-border commercial relationships, but also because it provides coherent and sensible solutions to private law cases, even when national law applies.[32]

We must question which juridical reasons permit judges to use private (soft law) texts. They are neither binding rules, as it is not possible to cite them as a law in force, nor as case law. They belong to a category known as 'doctrine'. Cortese qualified them as 'unrecognised citations', which are produced by private discussion among highly recognised scholars. As a consequence, judges cannot base their rulings on the grounds of European private (soft law) texts, or take the principles

[23] STS (1ª) 11 July 2007 (RJ 2007, 5005).

[24] STS (1ª) 27 July 2007 (RJ 2007, 888).

[25] STS (1ª) 31 October 2005 (RJ 2005, 6651).

[26] STS (1ª) 28 October 2015 (RJ 2015, 4583); STS (1ª) 12 February 2016 (RJ 2016, 361).

[27] STS (1ª) 8 September 2014 (RJ 2014, 3903); STS (1ª) 20 October 2015 (RJ 2015, 4338); STS (1ª) 12 February 2016 (RJ 2016, 361).

[28] STS (1ª) 15 October 2014 (RJ 2014, 5090).

[29] STS (1ª) 24 October 2014 (RJ 2014, 4811).

[30] STS (1ª) 7 July 2015 (RJ 2015, 3882); STS (1ª) 29 September 2015 (RJ 2015, 4286); STS (1ª) 12 February 2016 (RJ 2016, 361).

[31] STS (1ª) 3 February 2016 (RJ 2016, 92).

[32] F Cortese, 'Los principios europeos de la responsabilidad civil en la jurisprudencia. El problema de las "citas no reconocidas"' in MJ Herrador Guardia (ed), *Derecho de daños* (Sepin, 2011) 113–25.

of European private law, or UNIDROIT, with the aim of substituting the law in force. Judges can only quote the European law principles in order to update the old laws in force with the aim to modernise them.

The PECL as well as DCFR and the UNIDROIT Principles have influenced Spanish case law in the field of contract law through:

(a) unification of cases dealing with the breach of contract;
(b) disappearance of fault as a requisite for the breach of contract;
(c) more unified system for remedies in the case of breach of contract;
(d) risk as a crucial element in the doctrine of liability for breach, and
(e) frustration of the aim of the contract as the target of breach.

These developments have been observed in rulings interpreting Article 1124 of the Spanish Civil Code (remedies for breach) through the use of the PECL as a tool for interpreting the law in force leading to a modernisation of the old system of contracts.

The outcomes achieved by case law in using these tools can be summarised as follows:

(a) The reinforcement of interpretations held by the Supreme Court in previous case law.
(b) The interpretation of new laws whose origin is European law, as has happened in commercial agency contracts.
(c) The creation of a tool to facilitate the application of general clauses, such as good faith and fair dealing.

However, this technique also raises obvious problems for the aim proposed in this forum. The first is that it uses exclusively private texts of soft law as its basis, although authors from several countries have contributed to its drafting and it constitutes to a certain extent the common core of European contract law. The rules are far from safe, as they have not been officially accepted, so they can never be anything more than interpreting criteria which cannot change national law. The second disadvantage is the slow pace at which we would achieve an effective unification, since thus far it has only been approached on an interpretation level. It is based on the goodwill and knowledge of some learned judges.

However, these techniques should be discussed at a European level, to facilitate a meeting point between national judges to enable them to solve certain problems, common to all the European legal systems, in a uniform manner.

IV. Final Thoughts

At the moment, the European Union faces many challenges, of diverse nature, some of them directly related to the harmonisation of private law. In order to advance further along the road to legal integration, EU member states should act in accordance with the principle of trust. The role of judges is of great relevance, as are the roles played by legislators and scholars, in the building of this trust.

In this regard, it is important to highlight the key role that national judges play in the application of European legislation. Consumer law and CJEU judgments in the field provide examples of the essential role of judges in boosting the domestic application of European law in a uniform way. As these examples demonstrate, the European legal landscape would greatly benefit from harmonisation mechanisms for the interpretation of European and domestic legislation by national judges.

7

Uniform Rules as Guidelines for National Courts and Legislatures: The German Experience

THOMAS ACKERMANN

I. Introduction

Hopes for a uniform European contract law have never rested exclusively on EU legislation. Instead of a top-down approach to harmonisation, there has always been the alternative vision of a gradual convergence between national contract laws, driven by insights and inspiration in national legislatures and courts gained from foreign contract laws. Uniform laws that represent not only the common core of national contract laws, but which also make an informed choice between different concepts and solutions offered by national laws, can ideally be said to represent the essence of comparative wisdom. They may thus serve as a short cut to those looking for directions from outside for the development of their domestic laws. The Principles of European Contract Law (PECL) were clearly drafted with this purpose in mind, as stated in the introduction to the full text published in 2000:

> The Principles are thus available for the assistance of European courts and legislatures concerned to ensure the fruitful development of contract law on a Union-wide basis. Even beyond the borders of the European Union, the Principles may serve as an inspiration for the Central and Eastern European legislators who are in the course of reforming their laws of contract to meet the needs of a market economy.[1]

In order to test the hypothesis that uniform contract laws such as the PECL provide valuable guidelines for national courts and legislators for the development of

[1] PECL p xxii; see also p xxiv: 'The court or arbitrator may adopt the solution provided by the Principles knowing that it represents the common core of the European systems, or a progressive development from that common core. Equally the solutions of the Principles may be adopted by legislators reforming their contract law. The Commission hopes in particular that the principles will be of service to those charged with reform of contract law in the newly-emerged democracies of Europe.'

their own domestic contract laws, Germany is a suitable candidate for two reasons. First, Germany's economic and political conditions generally seem to favour the ability and willingness to adapt domestic trade-related law, including contract law, to superior solutions that can be found in foreign or in uniform laws. Considering Germany's high level of external trade and the comparably strong German commitment to European integration, the receptiveness for new concepts of contract law in Germany should at least in theory be high, in particular if they can be said to have welfare-enhancing effects. Second, and more specifically, from Ernst Rabel's pioneering work[2] to the prolific contemporary output of academics at German universities and research institutions, the development of uniform contract law itself is due in no small part to efforts originating in German academia, thus creating an environment in which the introduction of rules and concepts from uniform law into the domestic legal system is not really a legal transplant but the reception of ideas that many participants in the German legal discourse can easily recognise as their own.

Against this background, this chapter sets out to explore and to explain the impact that uniform law has had on German legislation in the field of contract law, and on the way German courts have interpreted their domestic contract law. As this chapter will show, there is a striking divergence between the legislative and the judicial reception of uniform law in Germany: while uniform law was successful as a model for the reform of the German law of obligations (*Schuldrechtsreform*) in 2002, it has failed to make any significant impact on the judicial interpretation of the provisions of the German Civil Code (*Bürgerliches Gesetzbuch* = BGB) affected by this reform. As an internationally minded academic, one is easily tempted to attribute this divergence to defects of the judicial system, such as time and cost constraints of litigation, a lack of exposure to uniform law among judges and lawyers in their legal education, or simply a home bias preventing practitioners from thinking outside the domestic box. However, while some or all of these reasons may be true, an equally important reason for the lack of attention to uniform law in German courts is that uniform contract law is of little or no assistance to judges trying to solve particular issues in the interpretation of provisions of the BGB even if these provisions were inspired by uniform law. Rather, densely descriptive factual scenarios and legal arguments that produced certain results in different legal orders are needed in order to make comparative legal research fruitful for judicial decision-making. In selecting and synthesizing these results in a systematic way, drafters of uniform law provide a valuable service to legislators, but at the same time (and notwithstanding accompanying comments and notes) they make the substance underlying these results largely invisible. This makes uniform law unappealing to judges looking for help in narrowing down the abstract terms of a

[2] E Rabel, *Das Recht des Warenkaufs*, vol 1 (Walter de Gruyter, 1936); ibid vol 2 (Walter de Gruyter and Mohr Siebeck, 1958).

provision of their national codification to a solution of a concrete issue even if this provision is copied from uniform law.

The first part of this chapter will address the legislative aspect of this story, ie the reception of uniform contract law by the German legislature in its reform of the law of obligations. The second part is devoted to the judicial response in Germany, examining a very small number of cases where uniform law has played a role, but perhaps more importantly explaining the much larger body of case law where it has not. The third part will develop the argument that the divergence between the legislative and the judicial reception of uniform contract law in Germany has at least one of its roots in the ambivalence of uniform law. The author's point is that uniform law pays for its legislative appeal as a systematic synthesis of comparative insights with a lack of the detailed descriptiveness needed for a powerful comparative legal argument in the judicial process.

II. The Reception of Uniform Contract Law in the Reform of the German Law of Obligations

From its beginning, the idea of uniform contract law has been embraced by academics at German universities and research institutions. As is well known, Ernst Rabel's pioneering work on the sale of goods had a decisive influence on the Uniform Law on the International Sale of Goods (ULIS) finalised at The Hague in 1964. German scholars of comparative law were also heavily involved in the preparation and in the discussion of further evolutionary steps in uniform law, namely the Convention on Contracts for the International Sale of Goods (CISG), the UNIDROIT Principles of International Commercial Contracts (UNIDROIT Principles), the Principles of European Contract Law (PECL) and the Draft Common Frame of Reference (DCFR). However, while internationally renowned, for a long while, German comparative law scholarship had no significant impact on the development of domestic German contract law. Throughout the twentieth century, the codification of contract law in the first two books of the BGB remained essentially unchanged. New developments, in particular provisions for the protection of weaker parties, were introduced through separate parliamentary acts. They were not inspired by uniform law, but were either developed autonomously (such as the former statute on the control of standard form clauses)[3] or owed their existence to EC directives (such as the statute on doorstep-selling).[4]

This era came to an end with the reform of the law of obligations that came into force on 1 January 2002. This reform was triggered by the need to implement three

[3] Gesetz zur Regelung des Rechts Allgemeiner Geschäftsbedingungen, BGBl I 1976 p 3317.

[4] Gesetz über den Widerruf von Haustürgeschäften und ähnlichen Geschäften, BGBl I 1986 p 122.

EC directives, namely the E-Commerce Directive,the Late Payment Directive, and most importantly, the Consumer Sales Directive, into German law.[5] However, on this occasion, the legislature went much further and introduced a complete overhaul of the general part of the law of obligations and of the statute of limitations. The core element of the reform was a new regime for remedies for breach of contract that was heavily influenced by the system of remedies that could be found in the ULIS and subsequently in the CISG and in the PECL.

Before giving some examples of how this influence affected provisions of the BGB and its underlying system, it is appropriate to explain why the German legislature embraced the model of uniform law, after having left the core of contract law intact for a century. The main reason was not that the decisions courts reached under the original provisions of the Civil Code were regarded as unjust, inefficient or wrong for any other conceivable reason. The main reason was rather that the provisions of the Civil Code relating to breach of contract were widely perceived as inadequately systematising the law as it stands, and sometimes even misleading students of German civil law about solutions to legal issues that had been found by the courts. At this point, uniform law, as represented by the ULIS and later the CISG, came into play. At least in the eyes of a late twentieth-century lawyer, uniform law seemed to satisfy the desire for a simple, clear and complete set of rules much better than the German provisions originating from the late nineteenth century. The idea that the system of uniform law provides a better understanding of contractual remedies than the original structure of the Civil Code owes its success mainly to an academic who later came to regret his support for the reform, but could not stop a development that was inspired by his own work. His name is Ulrich Huber. In a *Festschrift* dedicated to Ernst Rabel's pupil Ernst von Caemmerer in 1978, Huber wrote an article in which he compared the rules of breach of contract provided by the BGB and by the ULIS.[6] His result was that on the basis of the BGB, a doctrine had emerged that isolated different instances of breach of contractual duties such as impossibility, late performance or deficient performance. As a consequence, the fundamental idea that, apart from the breach of a duty of care, contractual liability was simply based on non-performance of a contractual duty was obscured. Huber concluded that the system of remedies in the ULIS, while not producing results that were fundamentally different from German law, much better reflected this basic idea. Shortly after this publication, in 1980, the Federal Ministry of Justice published reports on a reform of the law of

[5] Directive 2000/31/EC of the European Parliament and of the Council of 8 June 2000 on certain legal aspects of information society services, in particular electronic commerce, in the Internal Market [2000] OJ L178/1; Directive 2000/35/EC of the European Parliament and of the Council of 29 June 2000 on combating late payment in commercial transactions [2000] OJ L200/35; Directive 1999/44/EC of the European Parliament and of the Council of 25 May 1999 on certain aspects of the sale of consumer goods and associated guarantees [1999] OJ L171/16.

[6] U Huber, 'Zur Dogmatik der Vertragsverletzungen nach einheitlichem Kaufrecht und deutschem Schuldrecht' in *Festschrift für Ernst von Caemmerer* (Mohr Siebeck, 1978) 837.

obligations, and Huber provided the part on non-performance, which was heavily influenced by the idea that the legislative model of the BGB should follow the example of uniform law.[7] This idea remained intact when the Commission for the Reform of the Law of Obligations that was subsequently mandated by the Federal Ministry of Justice published a draft for the reform of the law of obligations in 1992.[8]

However, this draft was criticised by practitioners and academics. Therefore, the Federal Ministry of Justice refrained from taking any further steps towards the fundamental changes of the BGB envisaged by the Commission for the Reform of the Law of Obligations during the 1990s. It was widely believed that this project had been buried, until it surprisingly resurfaced in 2000 when the Federal Ministry of Justice decided to embed the implementation of the E-Commerce Directive, the Late Payment Directive and the Consumer Sales Directive in the framework of the reform proposed in 1992. With the help of a new Commission, the Ministry developed a revised draft into a bill for the reform of the law of obligations, which was passed by parliament in 2001 and came into force on 1 January 2002. At the time, the reform met with strong resistance. In particular, many German professors of civil law protested against it, including Ulrich Huber, who turned from an early supporter of the reform into a protagonist of the resistance against it.[9] One of the arguments against the reform was that, by building on the draft published in 1992 that was inspired by uniform sales law, it ignored more recent developments in the field of uniform law such as the PECL. Indeed, the references to uniform law in the bill that was finally submitted to parliament are mainly references to the CISG, while only a few references to the PECL can be found that were apparently inserted in order to counter the criticism that the draft was not out of step with the development of uniform law.[10]

Some examples of these references to uniform law in the reform bill serve as an illustration of the influence that concepts of uniform law had, via Ulrich Huber's earlier work and the work of the subsequent commissions, on the German legislation.

1. A central feature of the law of obligations that came into force in 2002 is the introduction of a general provision for damages for breach of any duty arising from an obligation in section 280 BGB (except for damages for breach of contract in cases of initial impossibility, which are specifically covered by section 311(2) BGB). The very broad category of 'breach of duty' is meant

[7] U Huber, 'Leistungsstörungen' in *Gutachten und Vorschläge zur Überarbeitung des Schuldrechts*, vol 1 (Bundesanzeiger Verlag, 1981) 647.

[8] Bundesminister der Justiz (ed), *Abschlußbericht der Kommission zur Überarbeitung des Schuldrechts* (Bundesanzeiger Verlag, 1992).

[9] See U Huber, 'Das geplante Recht der Leistungsstörungen' in W Ernst and R Zimmermann (eds) *Zivilrechtswissenschaft und Schuldrechtsreform* (Mohr Siebeck, 2001) 31.

[10] Entwurf eines Gesetzes zur Modernisierung des Schuldrechts BT-Drs 14/6040 of 14 May 2001.

to encompass all cases of non-performance of contractual obligations (and, in addition to that, the breach of duties arising from non-contractual, in particular pre-contractual relationships). In this regard, the reform bill explicitly refers to the rules on non-performance in Articles 45, 61 CISG as an equivalent.[11] This reference lends credibility to a concept that was highly controversial before the reform, not least because this idea has significant historical roots in the legal thinking of Heinrich Stoll, who tried to establish his over-arching concept of *Leistungsstörungen* (disturbances of performance) as part of a national socialist law reform in the 1930s.[12] The reference to uniform sales law thus not only served the purpose of establishing the rationality of a general provision on breach of duties arising from contract and other sources of obligations, but also had the effect of decoupling this idea from its unfortunate connection with Germany's dark past.

2. Apart from its impact on the general structure of the rules on non-performance, uniform law was referred to as a repertoire of solutions for particular problems that occurred under the original set of rules that came into force as part of the BGB in 1900. One of these problems was the relationship between termination and damages as remedies for breach of contract. In the pre-reform German law of obligations, the relationship between termination and damages was deemed mutually exclusive.[13] This was highly unsatisfactory, because once a creditor had declared a contract terminated after a breach by the debtor, the creditor was barred from claiming damages for breach of contract from the debtor. In particular in cases where a creditor did not receive legal advice, there was a significant risk that she would inadvertently lose her right to damages if courts could not help but interpret her reaction to a breach of contract by the debtor as a termination of the contract. This was changed by section 325 BGB, which now allows for a combination of termination and damages. So even after termination of the contract, the creditor remains entitled to damages for non-performance of duties arising from the contract. Articles 45(2) and 75–76 CISG served as a source of inspiration for this solution.[14]
3. Another fitting example of the impact of uniform law on the German law of obligations is the statute of limitations. The pre-reform statute of limitations in the general part of the Civil Code was widely regarded as lacking coherence and leading to arbitrary distinctions. The reform enacted in 2001 sought to remedy this defect by introducing a new statute of limitations that follows the model of the PECL. Inspired by Article 17:102 and Article 17:105 PECL,[15] the German legislature opted for a three-year-period of limitation as a standard

[11] ibid 92.

[12] cp H Stoll, *Die Lehre von den Leistungsstörungen* (Mohr Siebeck, 1936).

[13] This followed from pre-reform ss 325 and 326 BGB.

[14] Entwurf eines Gesetzes zur Modernisierung des Schuldrechts (n 10) 93, 188.

[15] ibid 103.

rule (section 195 BGB), beginning at the end of the year in which the claim arose and the obligee obtained knowledge of the circumstances giving rise to the claim and of the identity of the obligor, or would have obtained such knowledge if he had not shown gross negligence (section 199(1) BGB).

4. A somewhat ambiguous inspiration was drawn from uniform law for new answers to the perennial question as to which impediments to performance qualify as an excuse from performance. While not abolishing specific rules on impossibility and impracticability, the reform of the law of obligations substantially remodelled these rules. Reversing the previous default rule, section 311a(1) BGB states that impossibility or impracticability do not prevent a contract from being effective, even if the obstacle to performance exists when the contract is entered into. Moreover, according to section 275(1) BGB, a claim for performance is excluded in all cases of impossibility. Finally, cases of impracticability are covered by two complex rules in sections 275(2) and (3) BGB. According to section 275(2) BGB,

   > the obligor has a right to refuse performance to the extent that performance requires expense and effort which, taking into account the subject matter of the obligation and the requirements of good faith, is grossly disproportionate to the interest in performance of the obligee. When it is determined what efforts may reasonably be required of the obligor, it must also be taken into account whether he is responsible for the obstacle to performance.

   And according to section 275(3) BGB,

   > [i]n addition, the obligor may refuse performance if he is to render the performance in person and, when the obstacle to the performance of the obligor is weighed against the interest of the obligee in performance, performance cannot be reasonably required of the obligor.

   In particular, section 275(2) BGB has a functional parallel in Article 9:102(2)(a) PECL, which refers to 'unreasonable effort or expense', and in Article 7.2.2(a) of the UNIDROIT Principles, which refers to cases where performance is 'unreasonably burdensome or expensive', as was recognised by the drafters of the section 275 BGB.[16] However, in these cases, the drafters were critical of the lack of precision of uniform law and called the cited provisions 'a negative counter-example'.

5. A fifth illustration of the impact of uniform law is the way the drafters of the reform of the German law of obligations approached the question of the threshold for the termination of a contract after non-performance. In this regard, it was noted that Article 25 CISG and Article 6.3.1 PECL refer to the requirement of 'fundamental breach' and 'fundamental non-performance', respectively.[17] This was taken as evidence that a minimum degree of seriousness of non-performance is necessary in order to allow the creditor to

[16] ibid 129.
[17] ibid 181–82.

terminate the contract. However, while agreeing with this general idea, the drafters did not adopt the wording ('fundamental') from the CISG and from the PECL, but chose a different terminology and a different legislative technique by stipulating that in cases of part performance, the contract may only be revoked if the creditor has 'no interest' in part performance (section 323(5) first sentence BGB), while in cases of non-conformity, termination is excluded if the breach is 'trivial' (section 323(5) second sentence BGB).

6. Last but not least, the fault requirement in sections 280(1) and 276 BGB serves as a counter-example where the drafters of the reform consciously refrained from following the guidance provided by uniform law. As is well known, uniform law (in particular Article 79 CISG and Article 9:501(1) PECL) bridges the gap between continental fault and common law strict liability by introducing an intermediate regime that starts from the principle of strict liability, but mitigates this principle by introducing elements of fault liability. The drafters of the new German law were of course aware of this approach, but decided to stick to the fault requirement as an established principle of German civil law.[18]

III. The Lack of a Judicial Response to Uniform Law

Turning from the legislative to the judicial reception of uniform contract law in Germany, I have found only two judgments in the Federal Supreme Court's jurisprudence on the new law of obligations that discuss the impact of provisions of uniform contract law.

The first case concerned the termination of a building contract for a shopping mall.[19] Before performance was due, there were serious doubts as to whether the debtor was able to perform in time. The creditor was therefore keen to terminate the contract. Under section 323(1) BGB, this requires the expiry of a *Nachfrist* (a period of grace). The creditor thus specified a *Nachfrist*—however, before performance was due. This was rejected as premature by the Federal Supreme Court. Against this background, the creditor relied on another basis for termination. According to section 323(4) BGB, the creditor may terminate the contract before performance is due if it is obvious that the requirement for termination is met. However, the Federal Supreme Court held that the provision is only applicable if performance is not yet due and it is clear that the debtor will not perform. Once performance has become due (as was the case in the dispute before the Federal Supreme Court), the general *Nachfrist* requirement applies. In order to support this interpretation of section 323 BGB, the Federal Supreme Court pointed out that this is also the unanimous view on Article 72 CISG.

[18] ibid 131.

[19] Bundesgerichtshof (Federal Supreme Court), judgment of 14 June 2012, VII ZR 148/10.

In the second case, the Federal Supreme Court dealt with termination in case of a defective performance.[20] As has already been mentioned, under section 323(5) second sentence BGB, termination is excluded if the breach is 'trivial' or 'insignificant'. As a rule of thumb, the Federal Supreme Court accepted that the delivery of non-conforming goods is a significant breach and thus allows the creditor to terminate the contract if the cost of repair exceeds 5 per cent of the price. This threshold is much lower than the threshold courts derive from the requirement of fundamental breach in Articles 25 and 49(1)(a) CISG. The Federal Supreme Court recognised that the termination of international sales contracts may often be inefficient and should be limited accordingly, but refused to extend this rationale to domestic German law, all the more so as the German legislature chose a wording (the breach must not be 'trivial' or 'insignificant') that clearly differs from the CISG (where a 'fundamental' breach is required), and a legislative intention to follow the model of the CISG could not be ascertained.

Fifteen years after the reform of the German law of obligations came into force, two judgments rendered by the Federal Supreme Court that engage in a discussion of the relationship between new provisions of the BGB and uniform contract law represent, at first view, surprisingly slim pickings, if we consider the much more significant impact of uniform law on the legislative level. This leads to the suspicion that courts have been either unable or reluctant to engage in a more thorough examination of uniform law as a source of inspiration for the interpretation of the German law of obligations. Be that as it may, it should not be overlooked that, when faced with problems of the interpretation and application of new provisions of the BGB, courts would often not find any guidance in the rules of uniform law even if they tried. Even taking account of notes and comments accompanying uniform model laws, they often lack the specificity required by a national judge for the solution of an issue before the court. Against this background, it is understandable that the Federal Supreme Court has been far less influenced by uniform law than the drafters of the provisions of the BGB interpreted and applied by the Federal Supreme Court.

The rules on contract damages provide a suitable illustration of this point.[21] Provisions of uniform law, such as Articles 74–77 CISG, Articles 9:501–10 PECL or Articles III.-3:701–13 DCFR contain sets of rules on damages as a remedy for breach of contract that start from the undeniable premise that contract damages must primarily cover the creditor's expectation interest, ie the creditor's total loss caused by the breach (*damnum emergens* as well as *lucrum cessans*) must be compensated so that the creditor is put into the position she would have been in if the debtor had performed his contractual duty. However, for courts dealing with a domestic law in which this premise has long been established, this is a fairly trivial point that does not have to be established by venturing into the sphere of uniform

[20] Bundesgerichtshof (Federal Supreme Court), judgment of 28 April 2014, VIII ZR 94/13.

[21] For a closer examination of the findings I briefly summarise here, see T Ackermann, 'Beyond Expectations?—An Assessment of the DCFR Rules on Contractual Damages' in G Wagner (ed), *The Common Frame of Reference: A View from Law & Economics* (Sellier, 2010) 35.

law. Legal issues of contract damages that come before German courts are more intricate than this, and frequently, no answers can be gleaned from uniform law that could inspire the courts. A case in point is a dispute about the impact of the debtor's opportunity to remedy defects on the creditor's right to damages. If a defect is remediable, it is common ground between German and uniform law that the creditor is precluded from claiming damages for the period which the debtor is allowed to remedy the defect. Any cost of remedy incurred by the creditor can only be claimed as damages if the debtor failed to remedy the defect during the period allowed to him by the creditor, or if the creditor did not need to allow the debtor an opportunity to remedy.[22] Accordingly, a creditor who prematurely had a defect remedied by a person other than the debtor, because she did not know of the debtor's right to remedy, will not be able to recover her costs as damages. As this result leaves the debtor (who is spared the effort of remedying the defect) with a windfall profit, the argument has been made under German law that the creditor should be allowed to claim this benefit (eg under the rules of unjust enrichment). However, this view was rejected by the Federal Supreme Court, in a heavily disputed decision,[23] mainly because such a consolation prize for the creditor would undermine her incentive to allow the debtor an opportunity to remedy, which is not merely a formality but can be regarded as a means to prevent moral hazard. Without going into the details of this discussion about domestic German law, it is safe to say that neither the Federal Supreme Court nor academics who criticised the court could have gained any significant insights in this case by the study of uniform law, simply because this issue was not on the radar of the drafters of uniform law. There are more issues where the same lack of orientation by the rules of uniform law is evident.[24] The upshot is that even if they tried, German courts could not have gained much inspiration from uniform law for the solution of issues that came before them under the new law of obligations, even though the legislation that introduced the new rules was heavily influenced by concepts of uniform law.

IV. Uniform Contract Law: A Model for Legislatures, but not for Courts

The striking divergence between the legislative and the judicial responses to uniform contract law in Germany leaves us with the question of whether there is a defect in the enterprise of uniform law that can be cured, or whether the lack of

[22] cp ss 437 No 3, 280(1), (3); -281–83 BGB; Arts III.-3:202–03 DCFR.

[23] BGHZ 162, 219. An example of the fierce criticism this decision met with in academic circles is an annotation by S Lorenz, 'Voreilige Selbstvornahme der Nacherfüllung im Kaufrecht: Der BGH hat gesprochen und nichts ist geklärt' (2005) *NJW* 1321.

[24] See Ackermann (n 21).

appeal for national courts is a concomitant feature of the attractiveness uniform rules hold for national lawmakers. It is submitted that the latter hypothesis is correct. While it is true that national legislatures and national courts can both profit from looking beyond their domestic context, their requirements as to the kind of comparative research that supports them vary to such a great extent that it is all but impossible to conceive of an instrument of uniform law that serves both the interests of legislatures and the interests of courts equally well, and thus manages to kill two birds with one stone.

Let us first look briefly at the requirements of national legislatures and the way uniform law supports them. Despite persistent criticism and talk of crisis, contract law legislation outside the common law world is still based on the idea of a codification. In a nutshell, a codification is a piece of legislation that claims to be the sole source of law within its scope.[25] As this is a normative claim, a codification does not require its drafters to anticipate 'all the answers to all possible questions'.[26] Rather, it is the primary task of the drafters to provide a set of systematically coherent and terminologically consistent provisions from which courts can derive rules that solve issues the drafters did not anticipate. A high level of abstraction is not detrimental to this purpose. To the contrary, too much detail is likely to harm the usefulness of codifications in the judicial process, as can be seen from excessively fine-grained pieces of legislation such as the much-maligned and ultimately unsuccessful Prussian *Allgemeines Landrecht* of 1794. It goes without saying that a systematic synthesis of insights of comparative contract law that is put into the form of a model codification is helpful for such an enterprise. From a legislative perspective, a lack of detail in uniform law is not a defect, but can be a virtue as long as the provisions of uniform law meet sufficiently high standards of systematic coherence and terminological consistency. Against this background, all the time and expense spent on the drafting (rather than on the substance) of provisions of uniform contract law is worthwhile, as these efforts provide national lawmakers with the input they require for a codification of contract law.

Turning to national courts, a completely different picture emerges. Unlike national legislatures, national courts must provide answers to all questions, but to actual rather than potential questions arising from the disputes that reach the courts and must be decided by them. If courts act within the framework of a codification such as the BGB, they are bound by the legislature to develop their answers exclusively from within the codification as the sole source of law within its scope. But this does not prevent courts from taking account of concepts and arguments that have emerged in comparable cases under foreign laws as a source of inspiration, in particular if they have to deal with issues that were not anticipated by the domestic legislature. Returning to the example of the recovery of the cost of

[25] cp F Wieacker, 'Aufstieg, Blüte und Krisis der Kodifikationsidee' in *Festschrift für Gustav Boehmer* (Röhrscheid, 1954) 34; G Gilmore, 'Legal Realism: Its cause and cure' (1961) 70 *Yale LJ* 1037, 1043.

[26] ibid, as famously put by G Gilmore.

cure for defective goods, German courts could possibly learn from how courts in other legal systems handle concerns of moral hazard in such a situation. However, even if uniform laws can be said to reflect the condensed wisdom of comparative research on contract law, they hardly provide the detail required by courts in order to fulfil such a task. What courts actually need is a close-up view of the relevant details of the raw material of comparative contract law and thus the opposite of the synthesis (and sometimes the innovation) the drafters of uniform law derive from this material. Such a close-up view would ideally not only include an account of the reasoning of a foreign court in a comparable case, but also of the legal and factual (cultural and socio-economic) context in which it is situated. Borrowing a phrase made famous by the American anthropologist Clifford Geertz,[27] I would like to call this technique of comparative research a thick description. Without engaging in the theoretical and practical challenges posed by such an approach and also without claiming that there is anything novel about it, I would merely point out that this is exactly not what the *grands projets* of uniform law aim at. Instead of highlighting legal details, uniform rules are hiding them, and instead of putting legal rules into context, they are de-contextualising them. Seen from a legislative perspective, this is a feature, not a bug. Only if we look at uniform law from a judicial perspective, is the reverse true.

V. Conclusion

My account of the reception of uniform contract law in Germany is not a story of failure or success. It is a story that illustrates the inherent limitations of uniform contract law. It seems that a trade-off is inevitable in the field of comparative law. The more comparative research caters to the requirements of legislatures by providing them with model rules, the less appealing it becomes from a judicial perspective as it strips off the details and the context from the idiosyncratic material from which these rules are drawn. To be sure, the systematic and terminological rigour of a well-executed model codification can be as intellectually admirable as a sophisticated comparative case study. However, the question remains as to what is the most effective use of limited academic resources. Considering that political support for an expansion of supranational and international institutions that generate a demand for uniform contract law is not exactly on the rise, a redeployment of academic resources from legislative to hermeneutical efforts seems quite likely.

[27] C Geertz, 'Thick Description: Toward an Interpretive Theory of Culture' in *The Interpretation of Cultures: Selected Essays* (Basic Books, 1973) 3.

8

National Reforms: New Instruments Towards Converging Rules within Europe? The Example of the French Contract Law Reform (2016)

BÉNÉDICTE FAUVARQUE-COSSON

I. Introduction

Over the last two decades, one of the most striking phenomena in European private law has been the proliferation of soft law instruments which reflect a common core. The development of this common core, as well as of European legal thinking, has led to a first radical change: research in the field of law is no longer national, but European and international. Ten years ago, the idea of a European Civil Code, promoted by European groups of scholars and judges, was on the agenda of the European Union. For many reasons, it is no longer on the agenda. Yet, paradoxically, the rise and fall of the European projects (Draft Common Frame of Reference, Common European Sales Law) has revived the issue of recodification of 'good old civil codes'. These re-codifications, instead of favouring legal nationalism, are the instruments of new convergences. Many factors explain this: the rise of English as the *lingua franca*, the necessity to have a modern and adapted new contract law, the circulation of legal instruments and, above all, the new prominent role played by comparative law.

The context in which the French contract law reform took place illustrates this new tendency well. While interpreting some of the new provisions, French judges will be expected to draw inspiration from the soft law instruments which inspired the French legislator, among which the UNIDROIT Principles on International Commercial Contracts (UNIDROIT Principles) and the Principles on European Contract Law (PECL), as this inspiration was officially mentioned in the Rapport au Président de la République, published together with the Ordonnance.[1]

[1] Rapport au Président de la République relatif à l'ordonnance n° 2016-131 du 10 février 2016 portant réforme du droit des contrats, du régime général et de la preuve des obligations; Ordonnance

In this chapter I will first present some preliminary reflections on the European context; secondly, I will explain the context in which the French reform took place, and thirdly I will give some illustrations, based upon provisions which relate to party autonomy, of some of the new convergences fostered by the French contract law reform.

II. Preliminary Reflections on the European Context

Contract laws in Europe are based on common philosophical origins, among which the principles of autonomy and *pacta sunt servanda* come first. While, mainly for political reasons linked to the various crises that the European Union has faced and is still facing, the perspective of a uniform European law now seems unlikely, national reforms, enacted in new civil codes, are the most appropriate tools to foster convergences. They Europeanise our legal reasoning and help national judges to develop new attitudes, which is a *sine qua non* condition for a general law in Europe to exist once more.[2] Only a genuine European teaching of contract law can allow future generations of jurists to be fully aware of this common legal identity. Legal education should be based on an enlarged vision of comparative law, which encompasses national codifications, case law, European instruments, international conventions and, last but not least, soft law instruments.

In the move towards a common private law of Europe, one could ask the following question: why give contract law—which is only one of the branches of the law of obligations, together with tort and unjust enrichment—such a privileged position? Contract law is essentially of a non-mandatory nature (excluding the rules which apply to consumer law), and this means that the parties may disregard the rules, whether from a national or a European origin. Furthermore, in an international commercial context, the parties may, by virtue of the principle of contractual autonomy, codified in Article 3 of the Rome I Regulation, designate the law of their choice. In actual practice, this freedom of choice could weaken the force of the arguments put forward by the European Parliament, soon followed by the European Commission when it launched its series of communications on

n° 2016-131 du 10 février 2016 portant réforme du droit des contrats, du régime général et de la preuve des obligations, www.legifrance.gouv.fr/affichTexte.do?cidTexte=JORFTEXT000032004539.

[2] See R David, 'Le Droit Continental, la *Common Law* et les Perspectives d'un *Jus Commune* Européen' and R Sacco, 'Droit commun de l'Europe et composantes du droit' in M Cappeletti (ed), *Nouvelles Perspectives d'un Droit Commun de l'Europe* (Sithoff et Bruylant, 1978); H Coing, 'Europäisierung der Rechtswissenschaft' (1990) *Neue Juristische Wochenschrift* 937 ff; G Van den Bergh, 'Jus Commune, a History with a Future?' in B De Witte and C Forder (eds), *Le Droit Commun de l'Europe et l'Avenir de l'Enseignement Juridique* (Kluwer, 1992). On contemporary civil codifications, see R Zimmermann, 'Codification. The Civilian Experience Reconsidered on the Eve of a Common European Sales Law' (2012) 8 *European Review of Contract Law* 367 ff.

European contract law, which rest on the idea that the diversity of laws constitutes a barrier to the internal market. Prima facie, contract law does not appear to be the subject matter for which European harmonisation is the most urgently required.[3] In spite of this, European scholars have invested much time and energy in this enterprise, thus paving the way for the legislator. Is this purely a waste of time or, in spite of the apparent abovementioned contradiction, are there good arguments for engaging in this codification of European contract law? There are indeed various arguments in favour of the codification of contract law:

— First, the subject lends itself to unification because of the international dimension it has acquired: contracts contain more and more frequently a foreign element which gives them a European or international dimension.
— Secondly, the disadvantages of a sectorial approach, denounced by the European Commission itself, call for a coherent and more complete set of rules to govern contracts.
— Thirdly, contract law is not entirely made up of non-mandatory rules. There are many provisions which are mandatory, for various reasons (protection of a weak party, competition law, etc).
— Last but not least, contract law is a core subject in all countries from the continental law family and the law of contract has a highly symbolic dimension, which goes far beyond pure legal education.

The debate on European contract law appeared in an important phase of expansion of the European Union, an expansion which was both geographical (the enlargement of the EU) and substantial (more and more subjects fell within the ambit of EU law). An important financial and economic crisis shook the world. The EU faced a major political crisis, with increasing criticism of its role in different areas, including law. This context was not favourable to the development of European contract law, and many dreams have not been realised.

However, a remarkable and well-known 'spill-over' effect of this whole enterprise has been the emergence of a genuine 'collective legislative doctrine',[4] which developed in trans-border groups which either met in constantly changing venues or became sedentary. Some of these groups have developed 'doctrinal codifications' close to the 'Restatements' model which are now famous worldwide. Others purported to contribute to the elaboration of European private law by the identification of common principles.[5]

The diffusion, by the European Commission, of several consultations on European contract law has greatly contributed to creating a framework within

[3] W van Gerven, 'The ECJ Case-law as a Means of Unification of Private Law?' in Arthur Hartkamp et al (eds), *Towards a European Civil Code* (Ars Aequi Libri and Kluwer Law International, 2004) 101 ff.

[4] P Deumier, 'La Doctrine Collective Législatrice: Une Nouvelle Source de Droit?' (2006) *Revue Trimestrielle de Droit Civil* 63 ff.

[5] The Common Core of European Private Law: see www.jus.unitn.it/dsg/common-core/meeting_13html.

which European jurists became capable of influencing the European legislator, either collectively or individually. This phenomenon became more institutionalised when the Commission officially asked the 'network of excellence' to develop a Common Frame of Reference for contract law. In carrying out its mission, European scholarship had no pretension of replacing the legislator, but intended to become a major source of inspiration. This was particularly well explained in the introduction of the PECL, which is a non-binding model drafted independently of any political project and has contributed greatly to the new emergence of a true common legal culture in Europe. By claiming and fully embodying its role as a guide to the European legislator, legal scholarship has strengthened its standing and, more importantly, has revived history: let us not forget that, historically, 'the European jurist preceded European law'.[6] In past decades, important new sets of rules applicable to the private law aspects of international transactions have been published, and this has not given rise to such a debate, because it was not within a European context. In particular, the UNIDROIT Principles, first published in 1994, have not become a worldwide reference. As observed by E Allan Farnsworth, a leading academic and the US member of the first working group, 'No lawyer who practices in this area can afford to be ignorant of either'.[7] Today, most writings on international commercial law or transnational law refer to the UNIDROIT Principles.[8]

The modernisation of the law of obligations by using the PECL, the UNIDROIT Principles, or other models (including the CISG) demonstrates the importance of soft law. As within Europe many countries have engaged, (Eastern Europe, France) or will engage (Spain, Belgium), in a major reform of their civil code, the role of these models is paramount. They contribute to the 'hybridisation' of the law and help to bridge the gap between the common law and the civil law.

In France, the new law of obligations, which has modified a considerable part of the *Code civil*, testifies to this and it leaves no doubt that in the future, judges will seek help from these soft law models to interpret the new rules of the *Code civil*, particularly those which relate to party autonomy and leave some scope for interpretation.

[6] H Coing, 'European Common Law: Historical Foundations' in M Cappelletti (ed), *New Perspectives for a Common Law of Europe* (Sithoff, 1978) 31, 44 ff. Some academic initiatives, particularly the Draft Common Frame of Reference, have indeed come under severe attack from those who had other views on the development of European private law, both in terms of methodology and substance. Criticism also came from those who opposed any further form of European integration. The following question has often been raised, particularly after the DCFR was published: why should European private law be unified, why should our national and regional diversity be erased, and what would be the benefits?

[7] EA Farnsworth, 'An International Restatement: The UNIDROIT Principles of International Commercial Contracts' (1996) 26(3) *University of Baltimore Law Review* 1.

[8] H Beale et al, *Cases, Materials and Texts on Contract Law*, 2nd edn (Hart Publishing, 2010); M Reimann et al, *Transnational Law: Cases and Materials* (West, 2013) 822 ff, 860 ff.

III. Uniform Rules: A Source of Inspiration for the French Legislator

Title III of Book III of the French Civil Code, *Des contrats ou des obligations conventionnelles en general*, remained largely unaltered from 1804 to 2016. Yet, French contract law has evolved over this period, and this is mainly due to the creativity of French judges. This, in itself, shows that the division between civil law (codified systems) and the common law (case law) is not as clear-cut as it used to be years ago. In many fields, the Cour de cassation created new rules (for instance, for pre-contractual negotiations, offer and acceptance) and sometimes, it has even changed their meaning. The Cour de cassation modernised other rules and even gave a practical application to some academic concepts, notably to those of *obligation de moyens* and *obligation de résultat* (these concepts have since been 'codified' within the UNIDROIT Principles)—obligation of best efforts or specific results, respectively, Articles 5.1.4(1), 7.4.1(1)) and are used as a criterion for evaluating performance (Articles 5.1.4(2), 7.4.1(2)). In France, other codes also have rules which relate to contract law: the Commercial Code has very important provisions (notably on abuse), and a consumer code was promulgated in 1993.

In spite of the fact that the necessity for a reform had been highlighted in 1904, and despite several attempts, contract law rules remained mainly untouched until the 2016 reform. From 1804 to 2016, the underlying principles of contract law have changed profoundly. In 1804, the rules on contracts were inspired by the ideas of individualism and liberalism. They reflected the spirit of the Enlightenment and of the newly gained freedom and equality. Two centuries later, many argued that greater contractual fairness was needed and that more balance between the parties' reciprocal obligations had to be ensured—a challenge which could not be met purely by the mere development, within French cases, of the principle of good faith. It was felt that in order to counterbalance the freedom of the parties, the public interest and fundamental rights had to be more adequately preserved. However, this view was not shared by all and, as such, was an insufficiently strong enough incentive to engage into such a symbolic reform.

In reality, the reason for the reform arose from the European and international context. Strikingly, it is the prospect of having a European contract code (or, even more frightening for French lawyers who are very proud of their French *Code civil*, a European Civil Code) which was the main engine for the French reform of the *Code civil* which took place in 2016.

The need to take into account the surrounding international and European legal environment constituted the main motivation for the French lawyers who, under the leadership of Pierre Catala, drafted the *Avant-projet de réforme du droit des obligations et de la prescription* (draft bill reforming the law of obligations and of prescription) and submitted it to the French Minister of Justice (this project is known by the name of its chairman, Pierre Catala, and thus often referred to as the *Avant-projet Catala)*.[9] This project, published just after the bicentenary of the *Code civil*, is a form of 'resistance' to the European unification of the law. Instead of 'bridging the gaps' with the common law tradition, it rather reinforces some of the specificities of French contract law, which, over the centuries, have become important markers of the civil law tradition. In particular, the French concept of *cause* was retained.

Another academic group, chaired by Professor Francois Terré, prepared another draft which took much more inspiration from the European models as well as from the UNIDROIT Principles, and has had much more influence on the subsequent work of the Ministry of Justice.[10]

When the Ministry of Justice started to prepare its own drafts, it drew inspiration from the European and international context. In particular, it analysed carefully the Principles of European Contract Law, the UNIDROIT Principles, the DCFR, and some other academic codifications, including those of the French group constituted within the Network of Excellence (*Terminologie contractuelle commune* and *Principes contractuels communs)*.[11] Over the years, the UNIDROIT Principles, the PECL and, subsequently, the DCFR, but also the *Terminologie contractuelle commune* and *Principes contractuels communs*, which had been elaborated by the Association H Capitant and the Société de législation comparée,[12] became the main sources of inspiration for all those involved in the reform.[13] From 2004 to 2016, a wide-ranging and lively debate took place in France, during which the soft law models (UNIDROIT Principles, or PECL) became famous.

The French reform, in force since 1 October 2016 (but not systematically applicable due to its important transitory measures) was made by way of an *ordonnance* (delegated legislation).[14] The decision to use this method of adoption gave rise

[9] P Catala, *Avant-projet de réforme du droit des obligations et de la prescription* (La Documentation française, 2006). The Catala project was translated into English by J Cartwright and S Whittaker: www.justice.gouv.fr/art_pix/rapportcatatla0905-anglais.pdf. It was also translated into English by A Levasseur (Louisiana): www.henricapitant.org/sites/default/files/Traduction_definitive_Alain_Levasseur.pdf. It is interesting to compare and contrast the two translations. For an English commentary, see B Fauvarque-Cosson and D Mazeaud, 'L'avant-projet de réforme du droit des obligations et du droit de la prescription' (2006) XI *Uniform Law Review* 103.

[10] F Terré (ed), *Pour une Réforme du Droit des Contrats: Réflexions et Propositions d'un Groupe de Travail sous la Direction de François Terré* (Dalloz, 2009).

[11] Association H Capitant and Société de Législation Comparée (ed), 'Projet de cadre commun de référence. Terminologie contractuelle commune' (2008) 6 *Collection Droit Privé Européen et Comparé*; Association H Capitant and Société de Législation Comparée (ed), 'Projet de cadre commun de référence. Principes contractuels communs' (2008) 7 *Collection Droit Privé Européen et Comparé*.

[12] ibid.

[13] See F Ancel, B Fauvarque-Cosson and J Gest, *Aux sources de la réforme du droit des Contrats* (Dalloz, 2017).

[14] The translation into English of the French provisions of the first version of the *Ordonnance* was officially requested by the director of the *Direction des Affaires Civiles et du Sceau* of the Ministry of Justice. The task was entrusted to J Cartwright and S Whittaker, who had previously translated the *Avant-projet Catala*, as well as to myself. Other translations have been made, notably under the auspices of the *Fondation pour le Droit Continental*. Available at: www.textes.justice.gouv.fr/art_pix/THE-LAW-OF-CONTRACT-2-5-16.pdf.

to fierce criticism, particularly the French Senate, which expressed its opposition by rejecting the first *habilitation*.[15]

The *Ordonnance* was adopted on 10 February 2016 and published one day later in the *Journal Officiel de la République française* (JORF n°0035 du 11 février 2016 texte n° 26), together with a report to the President of the French Republic, which explained the history of the reform, its purposes and its content. The reform made by this *Ordonnance* is not confined to contract law. It is wider and its impact is on Title III, Title IV, Title IV *bis* of Book III of the Civil Code. As of 1 October 2016, the new *Code civil* is thus organised:

- Title III 'Of sources of obligations' has three subtitles for the three main sources of obligations.
  - Subtitle I: *Le contrat* (the contract).
  - Subtitle II: *La responsabilité extracontractuelle* (non-contractual liability), but this is not included in the reform.
  - Subtitle III: *Les autres sources des obligations* (other sources of obligations). These include *gestion d'affaires* (management of another's affairs), *paiement de l'indu* (undue payment), and *enrichissement injustifié* (unjustified enrichment).
- Title IV deals with the *régime général des obligations* (a systematic presentation of the general principles of obligations and how they relate to each other). It contains, for instance, texts on conditional obligations, plural obligations, extinction of obligations (by satisfaction, set-off, impossibility of performance, release of debts, merger) as well as provisions on assignment of rights, debts and contracts, on novation and delegation, and on restitution.
- Title IV *bis* deals with proof of obligations.

The many divisions and subdivisions (chapters, sections, subsections) make it easy to understand what the text is about, in spite of the fact that, contrary to the UNIDROIT Principles or the PECL, each article does not have a specific title. When the government decided to abolish the French concept of *cause*, the fact

[15] See F Ancel and B Fauvarque-Cosson and J Gest, *Aux sources de la réforme du droit des Contrats* (Dalloz, 2017). See also the Rapport au Président de la République relatif à l'ordonnance n° 2016-131 du 10 février 2016 portant réforme du droit des contrats, du régime général et de la preuve des obligations, which explains well the spirit and content of the reform and regularly refers to these soft law instruments. In the first bill the Government issued, on 27 November 2013, on the modernisation and simplification of law and procedures in the areas of justice and home affairs (*Projet de loi du 27 novembre 2013 relatif à la modernisation et à la simplification du droit et des procédures dans les domaines de la justice et des affaires intérieures*), the *exposé des motifs* (explanatory statement) gave a detailed explanation of the reasons for the reform. It emphasised the constitutional goal of 'intelligibility of the law', the necessity to reinforce legal certainty and the influence and attractiveness of French law. Following this first bill, an impact assessment was published on November 2013. This document establishes a list of foreign recent reforms of the law of obligations and insists on the influence of the UNIDROIT Principles on the law of Quebec and China. It also mentioned, as an ongoing reform in Africa, the '*avant-projet d'acte uniforme de l'OHADA*' (p 73) and it contained a long list of all the projects which aim at harmonising European and international contract law, and this list first quotes the UNIDROIT Principles (p 74).

that this concept was not present in those soft law instruments played its part, although the main reason for this deletion was the obscurity which surrounded the concept.[16] However, in order to compensate for this and also to better align the new provisions of the *Code civil* on the international and European models, the *Ordonnance* has kept the main functions of the cause in various new provisions. Judicial interpretation of these new provisions will most certainly be inspired by the soft law models which have themselves inspired the French legislator.

IV. Soft Law Instruments: A Source of Inspiration for the Application of the French Reform—Selection of Issues Related to Party Autonomy

Article 1102 of the Civil Code is part of a first chapter titled 'Preliminary Provisions': it takes place after the definition of the contract by Article 1 and before a series of definitions (Articles 1104–11).

Together with Articles 1103 and 1104, it sets the fundamental principles of French contract law, which are, in substance, the same as in many legal systems: binding force of the contract between the parties (Article 1103 restates Article 1134(1), except that it mentions contracts and not 'conventions') and the wide-ranging principle of good faith, which applies for the negotiations and formation (this is new in the *Code civil* but not in the French law of contracts) and for the performance of the contract (former Article 1134.3). Some inspiration was taken from the main European and international projects: PECL, Article 1:201; Draft Common Frame of Reference, Article 1-1:102 and III-1:103; UNIDROIT Principles (Articles 1.7 and 1.8).

Interestingly, Article 1102 affirms the principle of freedom of contract and also specifies its limits: parties are not allowed to derogate from rules of public policy. The new Article 1102 draws inspiration both from Article 6 of the *Code civil* (although it does not keep the concept of *bonnes moeurs*) and from the international and European models, particularly insofar as it specifies that it is mandatory ('parties are not allowed to derogate from rules of public policy'). The previous draft *Ordonnance* had an interesting and innovative, but also controversial, provision on the infringement of fundamental rights and freedoms. It encountered several objections and has been deleted.

[16] The requirement of *cause*, one of the distinguishing features of the French family of legal systems, raised many difficulties and created some uncertainty: though broad, the concept was imprecise, and 'anti-causalist' arguments had been developed for a long time (notably by Planiol). It was widely acknowledged that *cause* covered two very different types of situation: situations in which there are neither *cause* nor dramatically unbalanced reciprocal obligations, and situations in which the *cause* is illicit.

Article 1110, which belongs to Chapter 1 on *Dispositions liminaires* is of the utmost importance in the new French law of contract. This provision introduces into the *Code civil* the distinction between bespoke contracts (*contrats de gré à gré*) and non-negotiated contracts, or *contrats d'adhésion* (cp UNIDROIT Principles, Article 2.1.19 'Contracting under standard terms'; the definition of both types of contract made by Article 1110 is still subject to debate and criticism and when referring to it, French judges could usefully look at Article 2.1.19(2) of the UNIDROIT Principles).

This provision is of the greatest importance. It affects the core notion of contract and it may become the major distinction of general French contract law. Based on this distinction, a specific regime, more protective of non-negotiated contracts, will emerge, as it has in other countries (cp German law). With these new provisions, the French *Code civil* opens the door to a general control of terms in a *contrat d'adhésion* and a dual 'general' regime. Some important consequences are further drawn from this distinction, both as regards unfair terms (Article 1171) and interpretation of the contract (Article 1190).

Article 1171 regulates 'contractual terms which create a significant imbalance in the rights and obligations of the parties to the contract' (*clauses abusives* or unfair terms), while for B-to-C contracts, the provisions are in the French consumer code, which integrated EU law in this respect. Article 1171 is inspired by the EU Directive on Unfair Terms in Consumer Transactions,[17] and by the PECL which enable the courts to strike out unfair terms in B-to-B or C-to-C contracts. Article 1171 introduces a provision on unfair terms, which is only applicable to non-negotiated contracts (*contrats d'adhésion*) or standard-form contracts,[18] as opposed to 'bespoke' contracts. Drawing inspiration from Article 4:110 PECL a former version of this text, which previously was Article 1169 of the draft *Ordonnance*, had introduced the regulation of unfair terms in all B-to-B contracts (cp Article 3.2.7 of the UNIDROIT Principles on 'gross disparity'). However, it appeared that this provision is perhaps the most controversial provision of the whole project and, as a compromise, new Article 1171 is limited to unfair terms which were not individually negotiated. For negotiated contracts, the general principle of good faith (Article 1104) and the provisions on interpretation of the contract may still come into play.

Under French law, contracts must be interpreted by seeking the common intention of the parties. Article 1188(1) reiterates this basic rule: a contract is to be interpreted according to the common intention of the parties, rather than according to the literal meaning of its terms. Article 1188(2) then adds: 'Where the common intention of the parties cannot be discerned, a contract is to be interpreted in the

[17] Council Directive (EC) 93/13/EEC on unfair terms in consumer contracts [1993] OJ L95/29 (Unfair Terms Directive).

[18] As noted in our translation, 'Standard-form contract' translates as *contrat d'adhésion*, or more literally, 'a contract to which one adheres', and whose conclusion therefore involves no or little choice.

sense which a reasonable person placed in the same situation would give to it'.[19] Other rules on interpretation form part of Chapter III. Article 1190, which has been the subject of particular criticism, adopts the principle of interpretation *in favorem*[20] and applies it to negotiated contracts.[21] Traditionally, under French law, interpretation is limited in scope: clear and precise terms may not be interpreted (Article 1192 *Code civil*). There is no rule, in this chapter, similar to that of the UNIDROIT Principles on supplying an omitted term; such a rule is encompassed in the provision dealing with the binding force of the contract and reformulates Article 1135 of the *Code civil* (now Article 1194).[22]

The rules on change of circumstances and unilateral termination of contracts clearly show the influence exerted by both the PECL and the UNIDROIT Principles. Before this reform, France was still one of the few European countries (together with Belgium, Luxembourg and England) which did not allow courts to modify or terminate the contract when there had been an exceptional change of circumstances. The reason for this was the binding force of the contract, itself related to parties' autonomy: since parties are free to decide what they want, they should organise contractually the risk of a change of circumstances and specify what consequences it entails. The PECL (6:111) and the UNIDROIT Principles, on the other hand (Articles 6.2.1 to 6.2.3), have provisions which enshrine this judicial power. There is some originality in the French provisions, particularly in new Article 1195 on change of circumstances ('Hardship' in the UNIDROIT Principles):

> If a change of circumstances that was unforeseeable at the time of the conclusion of the contract renders performance excessively onerous for a party who had not accepted the risk of such a change, that party may ask the other contracting party to renegotiate the contract. The first party must continue to perform its obligations during renegotiation. In the case of refusal or failure of renegotiations, the parties may by common agreement terminate the contract as from a date and subject to such conditions as they shall fix, or ask the court to set about the adaptation of the contract. In the absence of an agreement within a reasonable time, the judge may, if one party asks the court to do so, adapt the contract or terminate it, as from a date and subject to such conditions as it shall determine.

The important and remarkable section 5, entitled '*L'inexécution du contrat*', draws some inspiration from international models. Article 1217 enumerates the 'remedies' for which a party may apply, thus bringing greater clarity to this part of contract law. Unlike the PECL, CISG and the UNIDROIT Principles, it does not

[19] cp PECL, Art 5:101; UNIDROIT Principles, Art 4.1.

[20] cp UNIDROIT Principles, Art 4.6; *contra proferentem* rule.

[21] C Witz, 'L'interprétation du contrat dans le projet de réforme du droit des contrats' (2015) *Recueil Dalloz* 2020.

[22] cp PECL, Art 5:103 and Art 5:104; UNIDROIT Principles, Art 5.1.2 on implied obligations.

include a provision granting the aggrieved party a right to immediate termination in case of an anticipated fundamental non-performance (see CISG Article 72, PECL Article 9:304, and UNIDROIT Principles, Article 7.3.3). Article 1221 on *L'exécution forcée en nature* ('enforced performance in kind') states a new rule, consistent with the PECL (Article 9:102) and the UNIDROIT Principles which limits the right to seek performance in kind 'where there is a manifest disproportion between its costs to the debtor and its interest for the creditor' (Article 1221).

There are many more innovations whose inspiration is at least partially drawn from European and international trends, as well as from the common law world. For instance, where the non-performance is sufficiently serious, termination by notice (also called 'unilateral termination') is permitted (Article 1224)—judicial termination by the court used to be the only mode of termination absent a termination clause. This is the reason why termination by notice to the debtor requires compliance with strict conditions, set out in Article 1226.

There are many other interesting provisions in this French reform which also deal, among other matters, with the general regime of obligations (*régime general*) and the proof of obligations. A systematic comparison with the PECL, the DCFR or the UNIDROIT Principles is impossible but one can anticipate that French judges will use these models as guidelines in order to find the solution to the problems raised before French courts. They will thus ensure a European-oriented development of contract law and contribute to the reinforcement of the bridge that has been constructed between the civil law and the common law.

Obviously major differences will remain, notably in terms of legal structure, reasoning and classifications. But it seems that, in spite of Brexit, fundamental concepts and legal policies are often converging. The fact that these convergences derive from soft law models and evolutions in our codified legal systems (rather than from EU new instruments enacted after Brexit), all translated into English, should be an incentive for British judges to look at them.

A crucial question remains unsolved, as it is in fact impossible to solve: what place is left, under these new internal rules on contracts, to party autonomy and to what extent are the rules mandatory or non-mandatory? The provisions do not specify whether or not they are mandatory (with a few exceptions, such as Article 1104 on good faith). Since general contract rules are usually not mandatory, it could be inferred that unless otherwise provided by the rule itself, the French provisions are non-mandatory (*supplétives*). This would be an overly simplistic interpretation of the reform. French judges may decide whether or not a provision is mandatory and when they do so, they look at the factual circumstances of the case. In an international context, French courts are also free to decide whether a rule is a '*loi de police*' (overriding mandatory rules) which should apply irrespective of the law chosen by the parties (in determining whether to qualify a provision as an 'overriding mandatory rule', they could take guidance from Article 1:103 of PECL and Article 1.4 of the UNIDROIT Principles, as well as to the comments that usefully explain the meaning of these texts).

V. Conclusion

This re-codification of French contract law has had a great impact in France and beyond. An enormous amount of literature has been published on this reform, including exhaustive commentaries. The law of torts should also be modernised (*droit de la responsabilité délictuelle*) in the coming years.

No longer may legislators remain indifferent to the forces which affect those matter in which it is intended to reform the law. No longer may judges ignore important evolutions within other jurisdictions. Legislative reforms and innovative cases are often promoted by authors whose comparative works give the necessary distance to assess which changes ought to be accomplished.

Part III

Uniform Rules to Bridge the Gap between the Common Law and the Civil Law

9

The Rise of EU Consumer Law between Common Law and Civil Law Legal Traditions

GERAINT HOWELLS AND MATEJA DUROVIC

I. Introduction

EU consumer law, where contract law provisions play an essentially important role, has managed to emerge and evolve in spite of the significant differences which exist among the diverse contract law traditions of the EU member states. Moreover, EU consumer law has had material effects on the development of national contract laws. To some extent it has been possible to reconcile differences among the contract law traditions, at least in the area of consumer contract law, and to arrive at unified European contract law solutions.

Contract law has traditionally been seen as a part of national identity. The pride in different codifications, some of which represent living legal monuments, may explain why some member states are reluctant to accept any modifications of their national contract laws.[1] Nevertheless, EU consumer law has demonstrated that convergence between different contract law legal traditions is possible to some extent. However, EU harmonisation has been successful almost exclusively in the area of consumer contract law. In that sense, EU consumer law can be seen as a bridge between common law and civil law. The process of harmonisation of consumer contract laws has taken place in a subtle manner in order to avoid different obstacles imposed by the member states.[2] This history is worth exploring in its own right, to ascertain if there are any lessons to assist the broader harmonisation of European private law.

[1] R Michaels, 'Code vs Code: Nationalist and Internationalist Images of the Code civil in the French Resistance to a European Codification' (2012) 8 *European Review of Contract Law* 277.

[2] M Durovic, 'The Subtle Europeanization of Contract Law: The Case of Directive 2005/29/EC on Unfair Commercial Practices' (2015) 23 European Review of Private Law 5, 715.

II. Three Different Approaches towards Harmonisation

From the perspective of EU consumer law, three different approaches towards convergence of national contract laws can be observed. The first approach envisages only minimum EU mandated standards, with member states being left to develop further additional rules. That is the case with Directive 1999/44/EC on Consumer Sales, which is based on the minimum harmonisation principle.[3] It only requires the adoption of a minimum level of consumer protection among the member states. Consequently, member states can maintain their existing rules or develop their own national rules on consumer sales, having in common just the same legislative basis.

The second approach covers the situation when only the minimum standards have been adopted, but additional harmonisation has been promoted actively through the case law of the Court of Justice of the European Union (CJEU). That is the case with Directive 1993/13/EEC on Unfair Contract Terms,[4] where only minimum standards have been required, but the CJEU has provided very fruitful case law which has contributed significantly to a higher level of convergence between common law and civil law. It has done this by fleshing out responsibilities deriving from the core obligations of the directive—whether it be interpreting the unfairness test to promote taking account of the consumer's interests,[5] or requiring practical rather than mere formal transparency[6] or requiring courts to consider unfairness ex officio.[7] Although formally the same as the first approach, the active role of the court merits attention in some areas.

Ultimately, the third approach includes the situation where EU consumer law has also imposed maximum standards, besides the minimum standards, leaving the least freedom to the member states to develop national rules. That is the case, most famously for example, with Directive 2005/29/EC on Unfair Commercial Practices (UCPD)[8] which is based on the maximum harmonisation principle.

[3] Directive 1999/44/EC of the European Parliament and of the Council of 25 May 1999 on Certain Aspects of the Sale of Consumer Goods and Associated Guarantees [1999] OJ L171/12.

[4] Council Directive 93/13/EEC of 5 April 1993 on Unfair Terms in Consumer Contracts [1993] OJ L95/29.

[5] Case C-415/11 *Aziz v Caixa d'Estalvis de Catalunya, Tarragona i Manresa (Catalunyacaixa)* [2013] 3 CMLR 5.

[6] Case C-92/11 *RWE Vertrieb v Verbraucherzentrale Nordrhein-Westfalen EV* [2013] 3 CMLR 10.

[7] Joined Cases C-240/98 to C-244/98 *Océano Grupo Editorial SA v Roció Murciano Quintero and Salvat Editores SA v José M. Sánchez Alcón Prades, José Luis Copano Badillo, Mohammed Berroane and Emilio Viñas Feliú* [2000] ECR I-4941; Case C-168/05 *Elisa María Mostaza Claro v Centro Móvil Milenium SL* [2006] ECR I-10421.

[8] Directive 2005/29/EC of the European Parliament and of the Council of 11 May 2005 concerning Unfair Business-to-Consumer Commercial Practices in the Internal Market and amending Council Directive 84/450/EEC, Directives 97/7/EC, 98/27/EC and 2002/65/EC of the European Parliament and of the Council and Regulation (EC) No 2006/2004 of the European Parliament and of the Council ('Unfair Commercial Practices Directive') [2005] OJ L149/22.

In the contract law field less examples follow this model, but Directive 2008/48/EC on Consumer Credit[9] adopted it as a basic principle (subject to several exceptions).

III. Harmonisation of Contract Law in the European Union

Of the 28 member states of the European Union it is possible to make distinctions among the 29 national contract law regimes. Each of the member states has its own contract law regime, with the exception of the United Kingdom, which has two: English and Scottish contract law. These national contract laws belong to diverse legal traditions: common law, civil law and mixed legal tradition, each with its own historical development and particularities.[10] Accordingly, English and Irish contract laws are part of the common law tradition, Cypriot, Maltese and Scottish contract laws belong to the mixed legal traditions, whereas the contract laws of Austria, Belgium, Bulgaria, Croatia, Czech Republic, Denmark, Estonia, Finland, France, Germany, Greece, Hungary, Italy, Latvia, Lithuania, Luxembourg, the Netherlands, Poland, Portugal, Romania, Slovakia, Slovenia, Spain and Sweden all represent civil law legal traditions.

Consequently, a huge diversity of private law traditions may be observed. The process of strengthening the development of the European Union has also been closely linked to a strengthening of the tendency to harmonise different private laws of member states, a phenomenon particularly present in the field of contract law. At a certain stage, this trend has even focused on the attempt potentially to adopt the European Civil Code, a project which turned out to be overambitious and for which political support of the member states was clearly missing. Nevertheless, the process of Europeanisation of contract law through a more piecemeal approach and legal instruments that regulated only certain aspects of contract or types of contracts has continued.

One of the main challenges of the process of Europeanisation of contract law was related to the question of how to overcome the differences which exist among different contract laws, and which are deeply embedded in the particular legal traditions. This is why the goal of all the different projects on the Europeanisation of contract law has always been to reconcile the differences that exist between common and civil law approaches towards contract law. In that context, the pioneer was certainly the publication of the Principles of the European Contract Law (PECL).

[9] Directive 2008/48/EC of the European Parliament and of the Council of 23 April 2008 on credit agreements for consumers [2008] OJ L133/66.

[10] K Zweigert and H Kötz, *An Introduction to Comparative Law*, 3rd edn (Oxford University Press, 1998) 63 ff.

At the beginning of the process of Europeanisation, the entire possibility of overcoming the differences between common law and civil law had been questioned by arguing that the convergence between different contract law traditions was simply not possible due to the presence of fundamental irreconcilable differences.[11] These views have, rightly, been exposed to severe criticism.[12] Eventually, the subsequent development of European contract law has proven that convergence is in reality possible, albeit a partial and not a full harmonisation, as the European private law today consists primarily of consumer law provisions.[13] But this shows convergence is possible; though the extent to which the consumer context assisted this needs to be considered. The piecemeal approach was the secret of the success of European private law. All of the overambitious projects have failed, including the one that was supposed to deal in a more holistic way with consumer contract law, by codifying several core elements into a single piece of legislation.[14] Initially, the process of harmonisation was rather slow, but subsequently there were increasing calls for further harmonisation of national contract laws.[15]

However, it turned out to be difficult to reach consensus among the different legal traditions on general rules on consumer contracts, such as those on formation or execution of the contract, primarily originating from the national contract law sources. In the area of commercial contract law, the harmonisation of contract law is a much more difficult task due to substantially different principles, values and foundations on which the common law and civil law have been based.[16] The CISG, in that sense, represents an exception of partially successful harmonisation. Its failure to achieve full success lies primarily in the fact that it is not a complete contract law instrument and that it has achieved much more success in practice in civil law jurisdictions than the in the common law ones. Even so, 87 countries throughout the world (as of July 2017) have become party to the CISG, which makes CISG the most successful international legal instrument ever adopted.

As a consequence of all these efforts and ambitious work, the European Commission initiated and/or, directly or indirectly, supported several projects on European contract law, among which the most important outcomes are the published Principles of European Contract Law (PECL) and the Draft Common

[11] P Legrand, 'European Legal Systems are not converging' (1996) 45 *International and Comparative Law Quarterly* 52.

[12] JM Smits, 'Contract Law in the European Union: Convergence or Not?' (2008) 1 *Sammelband 4. Europäischer Juristentag TICOM Working Paper Series on Comparative and Transnational Law* 45–65.

[13] S Weatherill, *EU Consumer law and Policy*, 2nd edn (Edward Elgar Publishing, 2013) 188 ff.

[14] European Commission Proposal for a Directive of the European Parliament and of the Council of 8 October 2008 on Consumer Rights COM(2008) 614 final.

[15] E McKendrick, 'Harmonisation of European Contract Law: The State We Are' in S Vogenauer and S Weatherill (eds), *The Harmonisation of European Contract Law—Implications for European Private Laws, Business and Legal Practice* (Hart, 2006) 28.

[16] G Cordero Moss, 'International Contracts between Common Law and Civil Law: Is Non-state Law to Be Preferred? The Difficulty of Interpreting Legal Standards Such as Good Faith' (2007) 7 (1) *Global Jurist* Art 3.

Framework of Reference (DCFR). However, they never managed to result in a real European contract code or a European civil or even a Common European Sales Law (CESL), but have only remained outstanding examples of legal scholarship, used as important reference points in debates on the Europeanisation of contract law.[17]

Today, the body of European consumer contract law is rather fragmented and dispersed throughout several directives.[18] The area of contract law affected by the process of Europeanisation is still relatively small. It is well described as an archipelago of small islands in the wide seas of national laws.[19] Some might even argue that the most important Europeanisation of contract law has been performed through the provisions of a non-contract law instrument: the UCPD 2005/29/EC. This directive, despite its formal separation from contract, has had a material influence on the Europeanisation of contract law in the European Union and some of the national contract law concepts.[20]

In the process of harmonisation of contract law and reconciliation among the different approaches of civil law and common law, the CJEU in Luxembourg has played a fundamentally important role. The CJEU has been providing an autonomous meaning of the notions of EU consumer law. The CJEU confirmed that the terms used in EU consumer law have their own European and autonomous meaning that differs from the related concepts in the national legal systems.[21]

In that sense, the CJEU may be classified as the engine of Europeanisation.[22] Interestingly, the CJEU played an important role not only in the development of consumer contract law but also in the development of commercial contract law. For instance, in *Granarolo SpA v Ambrosi Emmi France SA*,[23] the CJEU provided

[17] C Twigg-Flesner, *Europeanisation of Contract Law*, 2nd edn (Edward Elgar, 2013) 175.

[18] Council Directive 93/13/EEC of 5 April 1993 on unfair terms in consumer contracts [1993] OJ L95/29; Directive 1999/44/EC of the European Parliament and of the Council of 25 May 1999 on certain aspects of the sale of consumer goods and associated guarantees [1999] OJ L171/12; Directive 2008/48/EC of the European Parliament and of the Council of 23 April 2008 on credit agreements for consumers and repealing Council Directive 87/102/EEC [2008] OJ L133/66; Directive 2008/122/EC of the European Parliament and of the Council of 14 January 2009 on the protection of consumers in respect of certain aspects of timeshare, long-term holiday product, resale and exchange contracts [2008] OJ L33/10; Directive 2011/83/EU of the European Parliament and of the Council of 25 October 2011 on consumer rights (CRD), amending Council Directive 93/13/EEC and Directive 1999/44/EC of the European Parliament and of the Council and repealing Council Directive 85/577/EEC and Directive 97/7/EC of the European Parliament and of the Council [2011] OJ L304/64; Directive 2015/2302 of the European Parliament and of the Council of 25 November 2015 on package travel and linked travel arrangements amending Regulation (EC) No 2006/2004 and Directive 2011/83/EU of the European Parliament and of the Council and repealing Council Directive 90/314/EEC [2015] OJ L326/1.

[19] H Collins, *The European civil code—the Way Forward* (Cambridge University Press, 2008) 40.

[20] See M Durovic, *European Law on Unfair Commercial Practices and Contract Law* (Hart Publishing, 2016).

[21] Case C-122/10 *Konsumentombudsmannen (Ko) Ving Sverige AB* [2011] ECR I-03903 para 32.

[22] J Stuyck, 'The European Court of Justice as motor of Private Law' in C Twigg-Flesner (ed), *The Cambridge Companion to European Union Private Law* (Cambridge University Press, 2010).

[23] Case C-196/15 *Granarolo SpA v Ambrosi Emmi France SA* [2016] ECLI:EU:C:2016:559.

the interpretation of what is to be understood as a contract under European contract law.[24]

The process of harmonisation of contract law and the reconciliation among the differences of different legal traditions can be best observed on the examples of the duty of information, the principle of good faith and the average consumer.

A. Duty of Information

The duty of information represents probably the best example of how a unified European solution in consumer contract law had been adopted despite the fundamentally different approaches to this matter in the general law of contract in common law and civil law. Since the very beginning of the development of EU consumer law, the duty of information has been seen as the most important instrument for the protection of consumers. It aims to secure that the consumer is in a position to make a fully informed choice.[25] Whether this is the correct policy will not be examined here, as we are only concerned with the harmonisation process. Starting from the first directive in the area of consumer contract law, Directive 85/577/EEC on Doorstep Selling,[26] and in all subsequent directives in this area, the duty of information has taken a central place in the regulatory mechanism for protecting consumers; its importance had only been enhanced subsequently.[27]

Accordingly, the duty of information has been included in all of the European directives dealing with consumer contract law.[28] However, at the beginning, no general pre-contractual duty of information existed. It only applied to specified types of consumer contracts. In that context, one of the most important features of Directive 2011/83/EU on Consumer Rights (CRD)[29] has been the passing of the new harmonised European contract law rules on pre-contractual consumer information requirements.[30] In case of off-premises and distance selling contracts, the harmonised pre-contractual information requirements are based on

[24] U Grusic, 'Long-Term Business Relationships and Implicit Contracts in European Private Law' (2016) 12(4) *European Review of Contract Law* 395.

[25] S Weatherill, *EU Consumer law and Policy*, 2nd edn (Edward Elgar, 2013) 92.

[26] Council Directive 85/577/EEC of 20 December 1985 to protect the consumer in respect of contracts negotiated away from business premises [1985] OJ L372/31.

[27] C Poncibo, 'The Consumer Rights Directive and the proposal for a regulation on a Common European Sales Law (CESL): Do they promote consumer confidence?' (2013) 2013-1/10-COLSI *Istituto Universitario di Studi Europei Working Papers Series* 16.

[28] T Wilhelmsson and C Twigg-Flesner, 'Pre-contractual Information Duties in the Acquis Communautaire' (2006) 2 *European Review of Contract Law* 441.

[29] Directive 2011/83/EU of the European Parliament and of the Council of 25 October 2011 on Consumer Rights (CRD), amending Council Directive 93/13/EEC and Directive 1999/44/EC of the European Parliament and of the Council and repealing Council Directive 85/577/EEC and Directive 97/7/EC of the European Parliament and of the Council [2011] OJ L304/64.

[30] E Hall et al, 'The Consumer Rights Directive—An Assessment of its Contribution to the Development of European Consumer Contract Law' (2012) 8(2) *European Review of Contract Law* 139.

the maximum harmonisation principle.[31] Contrary to this, in case of on-site contracts, pre-contractual information requirements are based on the minimum harmonisation principle.[32]

The process of harmonisation of contract law is most difficult in areas where the differences among the national legal traditions are greatest and connected with some of the fundamental values and ideas on which contract law is based. The example of the CISG demonstrates that well, as the CISG contains no rules, for instance, on liability for break-off negotiations, validity of contract and its terms or consent defects. This is why it is even more surprising that the duty of information, as the element of contract law where the differences among jurisdictions are the most present, can today be observed as one of the areas of contract law where the process of Europeanisation has been most complete in the consumer field.

However, the general duty of information in consumer contract law was imposed even before the adoption of Directive 2011/83/EU, through a non-contract piece of legislation: the UCPD 2005/29/EC.[33] Prior to the adoption of this directive, there was concern about the divergences that existed among the national contract laws of member states in relation to the recognition of the duty of information as well as the possible impact that this duty may have on national legal systems.[34] This directive, by imposing public law duties, made the notion of pre-contractual disclosure a recognised feature of all national legal landscapes. It also introduced the notion that it was wrong to mislead consumers by omission of a core value.

The principle of prohibiting the provision of false information through the active behaviour by one party to the other during contract formation dates back to ancient laws.[35] In national contract laws, it is emanated principally through contract law rules on consent defects, and in particular through provisions on fraud. They are named in different manners depending on the legal system (dol, misrepresentation, dolo), but they all aim to provide a remedy in case of provision of false information and thus they represent functional equivalents.[36]

This is uncontroversial. But once one moves on to positive duties to provide information, more differences emerge between legal systems. It is true that the general principle of *caveat emptor*,[37] developed in ancient Roman law, remained applicable for many centuries in the majority of national legal systems of member states. This notion applied to *Emptio-Venditio* contracts, ie the fact that in sale-purchase contracts the buyer was the one who was expected to take care of

[31] CRD Art 6.

[32] CRD Art 5.

[33] Directive 2005/29/EC (UCPD) Art 7.

[34] G Howells et al, 'Towards a better understanding of unfair commercial practices' (2009) 51 *International Journal of Law and Management* 69 ff.

[35] RC Van Caenegem, *An historical introduction to private law* (Cambridge University Press, 2003) 180–81.

[36] M Michaels, 'Functional Method' in M Reimann and R Zimmermann (eds), *The Oxford Handbook of Comparative Law* (Oxford University Press, 2006) 342.

[37] 'Let the buyer beware'.

potential defects of the object of contract, and that a seller was not obliged to disclose them to a buyer.[38] However, increasingly, continental civil law systems developed legal rules requiring disclosure as part of the negotiation process.

Contrary to the approach of the majority of European legal systems, English law has been very reluctant to recognise a positive duty to provide information. In England, the courts were faced with the same question as those in France: whether misrepresentation can arise from passive behaviour. The answer to this question is radically different to that given in some of the civil law legal systems. English law is very strong on its general position that misrepresentation can arise exclusively by active behaviour, and not by passive behaviour or silence. This is because the simple omission of a party in the form of mere silence is not considered to be a representation, since it does not represent the statement of fact and, therefore, it is not a conduct, pursuant to English law which attaches liability and responsibility exclusively to conduct.[39]

The refusal to make any changes in that aspect is explained by English lawyers on the basis that an imposition of a duty of information would be unjust, since the information should be regarded as the property of the subject who possesses it, and making him share that information would not be 'so different than forcing it to give away physical assets'.[40] This is in line with the general English reluctance to give recognition of any kind to general principles in contract law.[41]

Against this background, there is the acceptance across the EU of obligations to provide information. It is true that the imposition of a European general duty of information has been successful in the case of business-to-consumer relationships, whereas in the case of business-to-business relations, traditional national contract law approaches of member states have typically been maintained. This limits the impact of success of the development of a harmonised duty of information between common law and civil law jurisdictions. Nevertheless, the imposition of a universal duty of information in consumer contract law may have a spill-over effect on general contract law.[42]

Even in consumer contract law the remnants of the old traditions remain. For example, in certain member states, such as the UK, the new remedies for unfair

[38] PS Atiyah, *The Rise and Fall of freedom of contract* (Clarendon, 1985) 178.

[39] *Fox v Mackreth* (1788) 2 Cox Eq Cas 320, 320–21 (Lord Thurlow); *Arkwright v Newbold* (1881) 17 Ch D 301, 318, where it was held that 'No mere silence will ground the action of deceit'; *Smith v Hughes* (1867) LR 6 QB 597, 607 (Blackburn J): '[T]here is no legal obligation on the vendor to inform the purchaser that he is under a mistake, not induced by the act of the vendor'; *Turner v Green* [1895] 2 Ch 205; *Bradford Third Equitable Benefit Building Society v Borders* [1941] 2 All ER 205, 211: 'Mere silence, however morally wrong, will not support an action of deceit'.

[40] S Smith, *Atiyah's Introduction to the Law of Contract*, 6th edn (Oxford University Press, 2006) 245.

[41] S Whittaker, 'Theory and Practice of the "General Clause" in English Law: General Norms and the Structuring of Judicial Discretion' in S Grundmann and D Mazeaud (eds), *General Clauses and Standards in European Contract Law* (Kluwer Law International, 2006) 57–76.

[42] A Johnston, 'Spillovers from EU Law into National Law: (Un)intended Consequences for Private Law Relationship' in D Leczykiewicz and S Weatherill, *The Involvement of EU Law in Private Law Relationships* (Hart, 2013).

commercial practices exist only for misleading and aggressive practices, and not for misleading omissions.[43]

However, despite these limitations, it can be said that today the duty of information now exists for all types of consumer contracts, both those for sale as well as those concerning services.[44] Bearing in mind the fundamentally different initial approaches under common and under civil law, this represents an impressive success of EU consumer law. It is also an element of EU consumer law where the highest level of convergence among common law and civil law jurisdictions has been required.

B. Good Faith in Contract Law

EU consumer law has also contributed to the development of a common European good faith principle in consumer contract law. Good faith is an old concept of contract law, whose roots date back to ancient Roman law and to the famous concept of *bona fides*, which imposed certain general standards of behaviour on the parties while negotiating, concluding and executing contracts.[45] The fact that the majority of European contract laws are based on the foundations laid down by Roman law also resulted in the concept of good faith being widely accepted in the national legal systems of the majority of member states as one of their ruling.[46]

However, among the legal systems that have recognised a general principle of good faith in contract law, the formulation and wording of this principle differ, and it plays varying roles.[47] Moreover, national courts among the different member states also have an inconsistent jurisprudence when it comes to the interpretation of the meaning of good faith and its scope of application in practice.[48] Consequently, from the perspective of national contract laws, it is hardly possible to talk about a unified approach towards the principle of good faith and its substantial meaning and scope of application even in those countries that have adopted it as a general rule.

Contrary to the recognition of the duty of good faith as a general principle, some legal traditions have had a rather hostile attitude towards recognition of

[43] The Consumer Protection (Amendment) Regulations 2014.

[44] HW Micklitz, 'Unfair Commercial Practices and European Private law' in C Twigg-Flesner (ed), *The Cambridge Companion to European Union Private Law* (Cambridge University Press, 2010) 235.

[45] R Zimmermann, *The Law of Obligations: Roman Foundations of the Civil law traditions* (Clarendon, 1996).

[46] For a detailed analysis, see R Zimmermann and S Whittaker, *Good Faith in European Contract Law* (Cambridge University Press, 2000).

[47] cp eg Art 1337 of the Italian Civil Code, Art 1134 of the French Civil Code and Art 242 of the German Civil Code.

[48] H Beale, 'General Clauses and Specific Rules in the Principles of European Contract Law: The "Good Faith" Clause' in S Grundman and D Mazeaud (eds), *General Clauses and Standards in European Contract Law* (Kluwer Law International, 2006) 205–18.

good faith as a general principle and resisted its introduction into their national legal systems.[49] This is notably the case of English law, which has been, to start with, very sceptical, fearing the adoption of any kind of general clauses which would provide rather opaque and uncertain rules.[50] The presence of such a reluctance is particularly noticeable in the case of the general clause on good faith.[51] Teubner famously explained the view of English law on good faith as an infecting virus: 'British courts have energetically rejected this doctrine on several occasions, treating it like a contagious disease of alien origin'.[52]

The concept of good faith is closely connected to the core of national legal traditions and the related particularities which explain the hostile attitude of certain of member states towards the provision of a universally applicable principle of good faith.[53] Brownsword explains diverse approaches towards the general principle of good faith on the basis of diverse ruling values in societies from which a particular legal system has evolved. Accordingly, there are two possible ethics upon which the law of contract can be based: individualism and cooperativism.[54] The lack of a general principle of good faith is the consequence of prevailing individualist ethics.

In EU consumer law, the principle of good faith occurred for the first time in the text of the Directive 1993/13/EEC on Unfair Contract Terms as part of the general test aimed to be used for an assessment of fairness of a contract term in a contractual relationship between trader and consumer. Accordingly, '[a] contractual term which has not been individually negotiated shall be regarded as unfair if, contrary to the requirement of good faith, it causes a significant imbalance in the parties' rights and obligations arising under the contract, to the detriment of the consumer'.[55] Directive 1993/13/EEC on Unfair Contract Terms imposes only a minimum harmonisation principle, leaving it for the member states to further develop the rules on fairness of terms in consumer contracts.

It is noticeable that there are two principal parts of the general test: first, the stipulation of a contract term contrary to the requirements of good faith, and second, the causation of significant imbalance between the rights and obligation of the parties that is detrimental to the consumer.[56] Initially, it had been proposed

[49] D Ibbetson, *A Historical Introduction to the Law of Obligations* (Oxford University Press, 1999) 258.

[50] L Miller, 'After the unfair contract terms directive: Recent European Directives and English law' (2007) 3 *European Review of Contract Law* 88, 105.

[51] *Walford v Miles* [1992] AC 128 at 138.

[52] G Teubner, 'Legal Irritants: Good faith in British Law or How Unifying Law Ends up in new Divergences' (1998) 61 *MLR* 11.

[53] K Zweigert and H Kötz (n 10).

[54] R Brownsword, *Contract Law: Themes for the Twenty-First Century* (Butterworths, 2000) 30.

[55] Directive 93/13/EEC Art 3(1).

[56] Case C-237/02 *Freiburger Kommunalbauten GmbH Baugesellschaft & Co. KG v Ludger Hofstetter and Ulrike Hofstetter* [2004] ECR I-03403 para 19; Case C-243/08 *Pannon GSM Zrt. v Erzsébet Sustikné Győrfi* [2009] ECR I-04713 para 37; Case C-415/11 *Mohamed Aziz* (n 5) para 67.

that good faith would be used as a separate criterion for the assessment of fairness of contract terms, but in the end it was incorporated into the general criterion. This was the consequence of the opposition of some of the member states, such as the United Kingdom, which were not willing to accept good faith as a separate clause because they considered it an attempt to adopt good faith as a general European legal standard.[57]

Besides the Directive 93/13/EEC on Unfair Contract Terms, the concept of good faith is also mentioned in some subsequent European directives, though its practical role and importance is much less significant than in the case of unfair contract terms. The old Directive 97/7/EC on Distance Selling indicated good faith in the context of the required manner in which a trader is supposed to disclose necessary pieces of information to the consumer.[58] Interestingly, the CRD 2011/83/EU that fully repealed Directive 97/7/EC does not include a good faith clause. Directive 2002/65/EC on Distance Marketing of Financial Services uses the term 'good faith' in the context of a required manner of provision of pre-contractual information by a trader in the case of a distance contract.[59]

All of the old and currently pending projects on the unification of contract law in Europe also adopted good faith as one of the main principles of contract law. Accordingly, the principle of good faith and fair dealing was proposed as one of the pillars of the system of contracts proposed by the PECL.[60] Equally, the DCFR also emphasised the principle of good faith and fair dealing,[61] though with partially limited effects and applicability.[62] The same approach towards the role of good faith has been taken by the CESL according to which '[e]ach party has a duty to act in accordance with good faith and fair dealing'.[63]

Immediately after the adoption of Directive 93/13/EEC, it was commented by a common lawyer that the meaning of good faith as a European concept brought by this directive was 'mysterious'.[64] For instance, the Directive on Unfair Contract Terms has brought a general concept of good faith into Irish contract law, at least in relation to consumer contracts, but its meaning remained unclear to

[57] M Tenreiro, 'The Community Directive on Unfair Terms and National Legal Systems' (1995) 3 *European Review of Private Law* 273, 277.

[58] Directive 97/7/EC of the European Parliament and of the Council of 20 May 1997 on the protection of consumers in respect of distance contracts; Statement by the Council and the Parliament re Article 6(1); Statement by the Commission re Article 3(1), first indent [1997] OJ L144/19 Art 4(2).

[59] Directive 2002/65/EC of the European Parliament and of the Council of 23 September 2002 concerning the distance marketing of consumer financial services and amending Council Directive 90/619/EEC and Directives 97/7/EC and 98/27/EC [2002] OJ L271/16 Art 3(2).

[60] Art 1:201(1) of the PECL: 'Each party must act in accordance with good faith and fair dealing'.

[61] The most noticeable in Art I.-1:103 of the DCFR.

[62] M Mekki, 'Good faith and fair dealing in the DCFR' (2008) 4 *European Review of Contract Law* 338, 371.

[63] Art 2(1) of the proposed Optional Instrument.

[64] H Collins, 'Good faith in European Contract Law' (1994) 14 *Oxford Journal of Legal Studies* 229, 249.

the Irish courts.[65] Surprisingly, in spite of such a long presence of a good faith principle in EU consumer law and the necessity to interpret it, it has taken the CJEU a period of roughly two decades to explain the common European meaning of good faith. As a consequence of such lack of judicial activity of the CJEU, the meaning of good faith as provided by Directive 93/13/EEC on unfair contract terms remained unclear for years.[66]

The House of Lords had a chance twice (even arguably an obligation) to ask the CJEU for a preliminary reference on the meaning of good faith, but failed to do so.[67] However, even in a case where a preliminary reference was indeed made by the *Bundesgerichtshof*, the highest German civil court, on the fairness of a specific contract term under the provision of Directive 93/13/EEC on unfair contract terms, the CJEU, despite having the opportunity to address this question, declined to provide an answer as to whether that particular contract term was unfair. It realised it could not assess every complicated decision on unfairness and said it was the task of the national court. This remained in certain opacity surrounding the European meaning of good faith, though the CJEU has maintained its right to set down the general principles that need to guide national courts regarding the application of the rules.[68]

In accordance with its booming and fruitful jurisprudence in the area of unfair contract terms, the CJEU eventually provided clarification on what is to be understood under the notion of good faith. The Court's judgment in *Aziz* is of particular importance where it finally explained the meaning of good faith under Directive 93/13/EEC on unfair contract terms. In its judgment, the CJEU pointed out that while assessing fairness of a contract term, the national court shall understand 'contrary to the requirement of good faith', as a condition for a term to be declared unfair, as encompassing an assessment of 'whether the seller or supplier, dealing fairly and equitably with the consumer, could reasonably assume that the consumer would have agreed to such a term in individual contract negotiations'.[69] In other words, if the consumer would not have agreed, this would be proof that a particular term is contrary to the requirement of good faith and if the requirement of significant imbalance has been fulfilled, such a term shall be considered

[65] PA McDermott, 'The Europeanisation of Contract Law' in Mary Catherine Lucey and Cathrina Keville (eds), *Irish Perspectives on EC Law* (Round Hall, 2003) 177.

[66] C Twigg-Flesner, *The Europeanisation of Contract Law*, 2nd edn (Routledge, 2013) 93.

[67] Director-General of *Fair Trading v First National Bank* [2001] UKHL 52; *Office of Fair Trading v Abbey National plc and others* [2009] UKSC 6.

[68] Art 267 TFEU must be interpreted as meaning that the jurisdiction of the CJEU extends to the interpretation of the concept of 'unfair term' used in Art 3(1) of Council Directive 93/13/EEC of 5 April 1993 on unfair terms in consumer contracts and in the annex thereto, and to the criteria which the national court may or must apply when examining a contractual term in the light of the provisions of that Directive, bearing in mind that it is for that court to determine, in the light of those criteria, whether a particular contractual term is actually unfair in the circumstances of the case: Case C-137/08 *VB Penzugyi Lizing ZRT v Ferenc Schneider* [2010] ECR I-10847.

[69] Case C-415/11 *Mohamed Aziz* (n 5) para 69.

as unfair. It may be argued that this is in fact a test more pertinent to the question of significant imbalance. The consumer might not have agreed to such a term, but the seller could still be acting in good faith if they had justified reasons for using it.[70] But for present purposes, it is sufficient to note that the CJEU has set out criteria.

The same approach towards the meaning of the notion of good faith was confirmed in subsequent judgments of the CJEU in *Banco de Valencia*[71] and *Katalin,*[72] where the Court again pointed to the criterion of what the trader could have reasonably assumed from the consumer while negotiating and agreeing on a particular contract term as a criterion for assessment of fairness. Interestingly, the Court here idealises the image of consumers that the national courts shall take into consideration identifying that consumer as a person who knows what term is good for him and which is not good, and it is only the fact that such a term was not individually negotiated that caused a consumer to accept that term.

Besides explaining the meaning of good faith, the Court in *Aziz* also elaborated the ambiguous meaning of significant imbalance as the second essential component of general fairness test under the Directive 93/13/EEC on unfair contract terms, providing guidance in that aspect to the national courts. Accordingly, while assessing the existence of significant imbalance,

> it must in particular be considered what rules of national law would apply in the absence of an agreement by the parties in that regard. Such a comparative analysis will enable the national court to evaluate whether and, as the case may be, to what extent, the contract places the consumer in a legal situation less favourable than that provided for by the national law in force.[73]

Following the interpretation of the Court in *Aziz*, a contract term will be unfair if, first, in the event that it had not been stipulated, the consumer would have been in a more favourable situation and, second, if traders might have expected that consumers would not have agreed to the contract term if it had been negotiable. These two conditions must be fulfilled cumulatively.[74] This is how the European concept of good faith in consumer contract law is to be understood.

In summary, it can be concluded that the European concept of good faith has been developed through the provisions of Directive 93/13/EEC on Unfair Contract Terms and the interpretation of the CJEU. In such a manner, at least in the area of consumer contract law, the previously existing radically different approaches

[70] See G Howells, 'The European Union's Influence on English Consumer Contract Law' *George Washington University Law Review*, forthcoming.

[71] Joined Cases C-537/12 and C-116/13 *Banco Popular Español SA v Maria Teodolinda Rivas Quichimbo and Wilmar Edgar Cun Pérez (C-537/12) Banco de Valencia SA v Joaquín Valldeperas Tortosa and María Ángeles Miret Jaume* (*C-116/13*) [2013] ECR I-0000 para 66.

[72] Case C-342/13 *Katalin Sebestyén v Zsolt Csaba Kővári, OTP Bank, OTP Faktoring Követeléskezelő Zrt and Raiffeisen Bank Zrt* [2014] ECR I-0000 para 28.

[73] Case C-415/11 *Mohamed Aziz* (n 5) para 68.

[74] ibid para 67.

could be overcome. Even in the United Kingdom, though some judgments might be questionable on the facts,[75] the language used is that of the EU directive.[76]

C. The Average Consumer

The average consumer is the main benchmark in EU consumer law for assessing the behaviour of consumers. It unified previous different benchmarks among member states. The European notion of the average consumer was developed in freedom of movement case law and first defined in legislation by UCPD 2005/29/EC. Eventually, after the decision of the CJEU in *Kásler*, the standard of average consumer as a benchmark has also been spread to consumer contract law.[77]

The notion of the average consumer defines the substantive characteristics of a consumer as a legal standard establishing 'an idealised image of how a consumer behaves'.[78] In that aspect, the Directive defines average consumer as 'a consumer who is reasonably well-informed and reasonably observant and circumspect, taking into account social, cultural and linguistic factors, as interpreted by the European Court of Justice'.[79] This definition represents codification of the notion of an average consumer as already developed by the CJEU in a legislative text for reasons of coherency and legal certainty on the European level since it was identified that some member states were not applying such a test, but rather were still using their own national standards.[80]

The standard of average consumer is, as Weatherill describes it well, 'an attempt to navigate a course between the rich diversity of actual consumer behaviour and the need for an operational benchmark'.[81] The question is why the Commission opted for such a rather advanced standard of expected consumer behaviour when it had a chance to incorporate a more consumer friendly standard into the UCPD than the one developed by the CJEU.

The expected standard of behaviour developed through the CJEU case law is higher than the standard which had been previously adopted in some member states.[82] In other words, expectations related to the presumed consumer behaviour

[75] See bank charges case, *Office of Fair Trading v Abbey Nat'l* [2009] UKSC 6, [2010] 1 AC 696 (SC(E)).

[76] See especially *Dir Gen of Fair Trading v First Nat'l Bank* PLC [2001] UKHL 52, [2002] 1 AC 481; Howells (n 70).

[77] Case C-26/13, *Árpád Kásler and Hajnalka Káslerné Rábai v OTP Jelzálogbank Zrt* [2014] ECR I-0176 para 74.

[78] G Howells, 'The scope of European Consumer Law' (2005) 1 *European Review of Contract Law* 360, 366.

[79] Recital 18 of the UCPD.

[80] G Abbamonte, 'The UCPD and its general prohibition' in S Weatherill and U Bernitz (eds), *The Regulation of Unfair Commercial Practices under EC Directive 2005/29: New Rules and New Techniques* (Hart, 2007) 25.

[81] S Weatherill, 'Who is the "Average Consumer"' in Weatherill and Bernitz ibid 135.

[82] Case C-120/78 *Rewe Zentral v Bundesmonopolverwaltung für Branntwein (Cassis de Dijon)* [1979] ECR 00649; Case C-373/90 *Criminal proceedings against X (Nissan)* [1992] ECR I-00131; Case C-315/92

on the market were higher than those initially assumed by national consumer policies. This is not surprising, since the establishment of an average consumer as the unified European standard of expected consumer behaviour was not a product of European consumer policy, but rather a result of the tendency to abolish, as much as possible, all kinds of barriers for cross-border trades among member states.[83] However, what may be needed to remove national laws that protect anti-competitive practices, may not be same as the stand that one seeks to promote within the EU market.

The objective of consumer protection urges for the adoption of a more consumer-friendly standard, according to which an average consumer is seen as 'naïve and inexperienced', an argument put forth by Collins two decades ago.[84] On the contrary, the interests of internal markets advocate for the adoption of a standard that would establish as few regulatory obstacles as possible, to promote free movement of goods. Therefore, the acceptance of a higher standard of an average consumer could potentially hinder cross-border trade. This is why the average consumer, under such a meaning, was eventually approved as the general standard for assessment of fairness of commercial practice, taking into account the trade-offs between strengthening internal markets and achieving a high level of consumer protection.[85]

The standard of an average consumer in consumer contract law is to be used as a model of behaviour against which national courts have to verify whether a trader has duly fulfilled his obligations. In particular, the standard of a consumer is of utmost importance for two areas of consumer contract law: unfair contract terms and pre-contractual information requirements.

First, it is relevant for the assessment of fulfilment of the transparency requirements and fairness of contract terms, primarily in the context of Directive 93/13/EEC on unfair contract terms, and, whether a contract and its terms have been drafted in plain, intelligible language. This standard is used as a benchmark for the assessment of whether these criteria of contract terms have been fulfilled or not.[86] Second, for the verification of fulfilment of a trader's obligation to disclose all relevant information in plain, intelligible language imposed by all European directives in the area of consumer contract law, the standard is again used as a yardstick to verify whether these pre-contractual duties have been correctly fulfilled.[87]

Verband Sozialer Wettbewerb eV v Clinique Laboratoires SNC and Estée Lauder Cosmetics GmbH (1994) ECR I-00317; Case C-470/93 *Verein gegen Unwesen in Handel und Gewerbe Köln eV v Mars GmbH* [1995] ECR I-01923; Case C-210/96 *Gut Springenheide GmbH and Rudolf Tusky v Oberkreisdirektor des Kreises Steinfurt—Amt für Lebensmittelüberwachung* [1998] ECR I-04657.

[83] S Weatherill, *EU Consumer Law and Policy*, 2nd edn (Edward Elgar, 2013) 57.

[84] See H Collins, 'Good Faith in European Contract Law' (1994) 14 *Oxford Journal of Legal Studies* 229, 248.

[85] BB Duivenvoorde, *The Consumer Benchmarks in the Unfair Commercial Practices Directive* (Springer, 2016) 75.

[86] Directive 93/13/EEC Arts 4, 5.

[87] See eg CRD Arts 5, 6; Directive 2008/122/EC Arts 3, 4; Directive 2008/48 Arts 4–6.

The meaning of 'consumer', as a standard in consumer contract law, is relevant both for traders and for consumers. It provides traders with a guideline as to what manner they are obliged to behave in and how to fulfil the duties they are legally bound by, while consumers are made aware of the level of protection they are entitled to.[88] The necessity for having a unified meaning of the consumer in EU consumer contract law has become particularly important after the shift from minimum harmonisation to maximum harmonisation approach in consumer contract law. Reasons of legal certainty have still urged for adoption of a unified European standard.[89]

Besides sector-specific consumer contract directives which require the provision of information in a transparent manner, Directive 93/13/EEC imposes a high level of transparency requirement regarding contract terms. The transparency requirement goes together with the information requirements provided by other EU directives since their purpose is to ensure that consumers make well-informed decisions.[90]

Directive 93/13/EEC imposes strict requirements of full transparency of contract terms on traders. In all cases when the consumer is provided with the terms of the contract in writing, these terms have to be drafted in plain, intelligible language.[91] The assessment of fairness of the main subject matter of the contract and the stipulated price and remuneration are left out of the scope of the application of the directive, with the exception of the transparency obligation. Therefore, the so-called 'core terms' of a contract will be considered unfair if they are not provided in plain intelligible language.[92] Consequently, the transparency represents the minimum level of regulation that the European Union provides for core terms.[93] This is why in practice these rules play an important role.

The requirement of 'plain, intelligible language' is a standard that should be assessed on a case-by-case basis. Its purpose, as identified in *Commission v Spain* by Advocate General Geelhoed, is that the terms contained in general conditions have to be 'completely plain and intelligible to the consumer. Their meaning must not depend on which of a number of possible divergent interpretations is placed on them'.[94] Besides this form of protection, the directive adds another layer of

[88] V Mak, 'Policy choices in European consumer law' (2011) 7 *European Review of Contract Law* 257, 266.

[89] V Mak, 'Standards of Protection: In Search of the "Average Consumer" of EU Law in the Proposal of Consumer Rights Directive' (2011) 19 *European Review of Private Law* 25.

[90] See further on transparency and information requirements in EU consumer law in G Howells et al (eds), *Information Rights and Obligations: A Challenge for Party Autonomy and Transactional Fairness* (Ashgate, 2004).

[91] Directive 93/13/EEC Art 5.

[92] ibid Art 7(2).

[93] HW Micklitz, 'Reforming European Unfair Terms Legislation in Consumer Contracts' (2010) 6 *ERCL* 347, 366.

[94] Case C-70/03 *Commission v Spain* [2004] ECR I-07999 para 14.

protection stating that in case of any doubts about the meaning of a term, the one that is most favourable to the consumer will prevail.[95]

In its judgment in *Kásler*, the CJEU explicitly employed the standard of the average consumer who is reasonably well-informed, reasonably observant, and circumspect. The CJEU mandated national courts to adopt it as a benchmark for verifying whether a contract term has been drafted in a plain, intelligible manner.[96] The CJEU insisted the requirement of intelligibility should not be restricted to mere formal or grammatical intelligibility. Consumers needed to be able to discern what the terms really meant for them. This was the first instance in which the Court applied the benchmark of the average consumer, as defined by the UCPD 2005/29/EC, as a standard applicable to a case concerning unfair contract terms. Prior to the CJEU as the highest European judicial instance adopting this approach, a tendency to accept the average consumer as the applicable standard in consumer contract law could be observed in the case law of the national courts of some member states.[97] The approach of the Court in *Kásler* was confirmed in its subsequent decision in *CNP Assurances SA*, where the CJEU again identified the standard of the average consumer, as defined by the UCPD 2005/29/EC, as a benchmark to be used for the assessment of fairness of a contract term in consumer contracts.[98] However, as interpreted by the CJEU the standard seems rather protective as it is used to demand that contracts should be comprehended. It is unclear how this sits with the application of the criterion in its original context of unfair commercial practices.

The standard of the average consumer in consumer contract law seems implicitly recognised by the new CRD 2011/83/EU. This does not mention anywhere an average consumer or a generally applicable standard for the assessment of developed information duties under any other name. However, despite the fact that a generally applicable standard is not explicitly defined, this standard can be understood to underpin the CRD for it does provide a definition of a vulnerable consumer in the same manner as the UCPD. According to the directive, the standard of the 'vulnerable consumer' is to be applied in cases where consumers are particularly vulnerable due to 'their mental, physical or psychological infirmity, age or credulity in a way which the trader could reasonably be expected to foresee'.[99] Interestingly, such a provision did not exist in the CRD Proposal of 8 October 2008, and this was identified as a particularly weak point of the Proposal.[100]

[95] Directive 93/13/EEC Art 5.

[96] Case C-26/13 *Árpád Kásler and Hajnalka Káslerné Rábai v OTP Jelzálogbank Zrt* (n 77) para 74.

[97] BB Duivenvoorde, *The Consumer Benchmarks in the Unfair Commercial Practices Directive* (Springer, 2015) 224.

[98] Case C-94/14 *Jean-Claude Van Hove v CNP Assurances SA* [2015] ECR I-3892 para 47.

[99] CRD Recital 34.

[100] HW Micklitz and N Reich, 'Cronica de una muerte anunciada, the Commission Proposal for a Directive on Consumer Rights' (2009) 46 *Common Market Law Review* 471.

IV. Concluding Remarks

This chapter has shown how EU consumer law has managed to reconcile some of the fundamental differences between civil law and common law and develop some of the common European principles. In the case of consumer information this may be readily understood. Although the common and civil law adopted different general approaches to the duty to disclose pre-contractual information, once the policy of providing this to consumers was accepted, most member states were introducing new rules that did not conflict with existing legislation. The acceptance of good faith is more remarkable. There may exist differences in application, but most of these seem within the tolerable range which is implicit in the division of duties between the CJEU (as an interpreter of EU law) and national courts (as appliers of the law to the facts). The average consumer has now become the key standard for assessment of consumer behaviour when applying EU norms, though it seems to be applied with somewhat different consequences to unfair commercial practices than in the contract law sphere.

Overall, though the EU has achieved a remarkable degree of convergence in consumer contract law. This appears to continue in the field of digital goods.[101] The biggest challenge has of course been to bridge the gap between civil and common law traditions. The conference from which this chapter was derived took place as the Brexit result was announced. It will be interesting to follow the development of EU consumer law after Brexit, to determine its impact. Will Brexit make it easier to harmonise, with the major common law system removed? Will EU contract law be enhanced or diminished by any reduction in common law influence? What will be the impact on the European legacy of the English contract law, as well as the future development of English consumer contract law?

In the agenda that will follow the process of the United Kingdom exiting the European Union, no announced changes to consumer contract law have been mentioned.[102] Moreover, the United Kingdom introduced the new Consumer Rights Act 2015 dealing with the rights and remedies in relation to the supply of goods, digital content and services. This piece of legislation further aligns UK consumer law with the anticipation of potential development of EU consumer law. Before, the UK adopted the Consumer Contract Regulations 2013 which aligned UK Law with CRD 2011/83/EU. All this is expected to survive Brexit. UK consumer policy has been largely in line with EU consumer policy and has even gone beyond the level demanded at times. Moreover, one suspects industry will not want change merely for change sake. Besides, it is still not clear whether the

[101] DCD proposal.

[102] The White Paper, *The United Kingdom's exit from and new partnership with the European Union* (Cmnd 9417, 2017) hardly mentions EU consumer law, but where it does, seems to support what has been achieved: see para 8.36.

UK will continue to accept *acquis communautaire*. This might be a possibility as a number of non-EU member states follow European contract law.[103] Much is up for debate, but the EU imprint on the consumer contract law landscape is so deep that it is hard to imagine a wholesale reversal of policies that have achieved broad consensus support. It is a remarkable story of how the EU has managed to create an entire acquis that ensures that the whole of Europe speaks about consumer contract using the same terminology and policy framework.

[103] J Stuyck and M Durovic, 'External dimension of EU Consumer Law' in M Cremona and H Micklitz (eds), *External dimension of EU Private Law* (Oxford University Press, 2016).

10

Bridging the Gap: The CISG as a Successful Legal Hybrid between Common Law and Civil Law?

ANDRÉ JANSSEN AND NAVIN G AHUJA

I. Introduction

In the private law discourse, the differences between common law and civil law are often overemphasised.[1] Not infrequently is it said that the gap between these two legal worlds is irreconcilable, as they are just too different. However, the United Nations Convention on Contracts for the International Sale of Goods from 11 April 1980 (CISG) could prove that such an assumption is incorrect. Being an international legal hybrid combining common law elements and civil law ideas from different jurisdictions, the question is whether the Convention is just a 'toxic legal cocktail' or a successful synthesis that can help bridging the gap between the two leading legal systems. If the CISG is considered to be a successful international 'mixed legal system' which was drafted from scratch (as opposed to the *national* mixed legal systems, such as South Africa and Scotland) it then needs to be clarified whether it already plays or should play a significant role in the further development of private law on a European, national or international level.

This contribution will (1) shortly introduce the CISG as such, describing its history and development, aims, application and exclusion; (2) unfold the traits of the CISG and its origins by distinguishing civil law from common law elements and analysing how each of these systems influenced the Convention—the CISG as a legal hybrid; (3) analyse the standing of the CISG by explaining its application in legal practice and relevance as a legislative reference model; and (4) try to answer the question whether the success of the CISG is based on the assumption that it offers the best possible legal solution—the CISG as a *successful* legal hybrid? The final part concludes with the views of the authors.

[1] J Gordley, 'Common Law und Civil Law: eine überholte Unterscheidung' (1993) 1 *Zeitschrift für Europäisches Privatrecht* 498.

II. CISG Essentials

A. History and Development

After World War I, as the international trade community was redeveloping, it was observed by the famous German jurist Rabel that an international uniform sales law was needed. Whilst each state had its own national sales laws, in principle no other state was obliged to recognise or even apply them. Further, since international commercial transactions involved more than one jurisdiction, perhaps because the parties were from different states and also because the place of performance would likely be in a third state, determining the applicable substantial law was far from straight forward. Moreover, the parties' rights and obligations varied, depending on the law of the state applicable to the contract. However, the parties could avoid such uncertainty by including a choice-of-law clause in their contract, but that clause was again subject to private international law. Nevertheless, the fact was that at least one of the parties would be faced with the application of a foreign legal system of which it might have little or no knowledge.[2] In the words of Rabel:

> To avoid these complications and to substitute a reasonably concise body of clear and simple written rules could not be a loss, and still less would it be a loss to have to consult only one law commented on by the courts and scholars of the world instead of innumerable different foreign legislations.[3]

In 1926 the International Institute for the Unification of Private Law (UNIDROIT) agreed to Rabel's proposal for a uniform sales law, and subsequently in 1939 it accepted Rabel's so-called second draft. The project was then held back by World War II. However, by 1964 and after Rabel's death, with the involvement of a working group appointed by the Hague Conference, two conventions were finalised: the Uniform Law on the Formation of Contracts for the International Sale of Goods (ULF) and the Uniform Law on the International Sale of Goods (ULIS). However, only nine states,[4] the majority of which belonged to the European Economic Community, ratified the two conventions, and the practical relevance of these two conventions remained very limited. The United Nations Commission on International Trade Law (UNCITRAL) established in 1966, subsequently took over the project of an international sales law. UNCITRAL was comprised of representatives from 36 states,[5] most of whom specialised in international trade law.

[2] S Eiselen, 'Adoption of the Vienna Convention for the International Sale of Goods (the CISG) in South Africa' (1999) 116 *South African Law Journal, Part II* 327.

[3] E Rabel, 'Draft of an International Law of Sales' (1938) 5 *University of Chicago Law Review* 546.

[4] Belgium, Gambia, Israel, Italy, Luxemburg, the Netherlands, San Marino, Great Britain and Germany.

[5] From various regions such as Africa, Asia, Europe, North America and South America.

They analysed two main reasons for the two conventions lacking member states. First, it had been mostly European countries that participated in the drafting process. Secondly, the ULF and the ULIF appeared to be somewhat vague, complex and artificial to be considered and applicable worldwide, as they did not take other economic and legal factors into account (such as the concept of reasonable excuse that is available now in Article 44 CISG). Accordingly, UNCITRAL merged the two Conventions and tweaked the draft based on the feedback it received. In 1980, UNCITRAL presented the draft at the Vienna Conference. Forty-two out of 62 states accepted the text. By 1986, the minimum required number of states[6] had ratified the CISG. Consequently, in 1988 the CISG came into effect.

B. Aims

The main goal of the CISG is to provide harmony in the application of the law in the international sale of goods context and to prevent high costs arising from pre-contractual, performance and post-contractual stages of an international commercial transaction.[7] The Convention should minimise the uncertainty of legal rights and remedies and balance them regardless of the parties' bargaining power.[8] Whilst the CISG provides for basic default rules, it gives due importance to party autonomy, parties' intentions, conduct, and usages (see Articles 6, 8 and 9 CISG).[9] The objective of the CISG is to promote the development of international trade through the use of a uniform set of rules.[10] Although there remain some

[6] Art 99 of the CISG requires a minimum of 10 states to ratify, accept, approve or accede to the CISG in order for the CISG to enter into force.

[7] L Spagnolo, *CISG Exclusion and Legal Efficiency* (Kluwer Law International, 2014) 36–37.

[8] P Schlechtriem and P Butler, *UN Law on International Sale of Goods* (Springer-Verlag, 2009) 2.

[9] Art 6 of the CISG: 'The parties may exclude the application of this Convention or, subject to article 12, derogate from or vary the effect of any of its provisions'.

Art 8 of the CISG: '(1) For the purposes of this Convention statements made by and other conduct of a party are to be interpreted according to his intent where the other party knew or could not have been unaware what that intent was. (2) If the preceding paragraph is not applicable, statements made by and other conduct of a party are to be interpreted according to the understanding that a reasonable person of the same kind as the other party would have had in the same circumstances. (3) In determining the intent of a party or the understanding a reasonable person would have had, due consideration is to be given to all relevant circumstances of the case including the negotiations, any practices which the parties have established between themselves, usages and any subsequent conduct of the parties'.

Art 9 of the CISG: '(1) The parties are bound by any usage to which they have agreed and by any practices which they have established between themselves. (2) The parties are considered, unless otherwise agreed, to have impliedly made applicable to their contract or its formation a usage of which the parties knew or ought to have known and which in international trade is widely known to, and regularly observed by, parties to contracts of the type involved in the particular trade concerned'.

[10] Art 7(1) of the CISG: 'In the interpretation of this Convention, regard is to be had to its international character and to the need to promote uniformity in its application and the observance of good faith in international trade'.

important gaps in the Convention (see eg Articles 4 and 5 CISG)[11] and therefore it cannot be considered a self-sufficient system, the intention is to limit the applicability of other sets of rules alongside the CISG as far as possible. Its core aims can be found in the Preamble to the CISG,[12] which was agreed without much controversy at the 1980 Conference and led to 'broad acceptance of the principles underlying the Preamble'.[13]

C. Sphere of Application

According to Article 1(1) CISG,[14] and unless the parties opt-out of the CISG (Article 6 CISG), the Convention applies automatically to contracts concerning commercial sale of goods for money either where the parties whose places of business are in different contracting states and/or where the law of one of the contracting states is found to be applicable due to private international law rules. Contracts for goods to be manufactured or produced are also governed by the Convention (see Article 3 CISG).[15] However, there may be instances where the buyer supplies a substantial part of the materials necessary for the manufacturing,[16] or where the main obligation of the seller is to supply services rather than goods. In such cases the contract may be considered a contract for services (contract for

[11] Art 4 of the CISG: 'This Convention governs only the formation of the contract of sale and the rights and obligations of the seller and the buyer arising from such a contract. In particular, except as otherwise expressly provided in this Convention, it is not concerned with:

> (a) the validity of the contract or of any of its provisions or of any usage; (b) the effect which the contract may have on the property in the goods sold'.

Art 5 of the CISG: 'This Convention does not apply to the liability of the seller for death or personal injury caused by the goods to any person'.

[12] The preamble of the CISG reads: 'The States Parties to this convention, bearing in mind the broad objectives in the resolutions adopted by the sixth special session of the General Assembly of the United Nations on the establishment of a New International Economic Order, considering that the development of international trade on the basis of equality and mutual benefit is an important element in promoting friendly relations among States, being of the opinion that the adoption of uniform rules which govern contracts for the international sale of goods and take into account the different social, economic and legal systems would contribute to the removal of legal barriers in international trade and promote the development of international trade, have decreed as follows'.

[13] AH Kastely, 'Unification and Community: A Rhetorical Analysis of the United Nations Sales Convention' (1988) 8 *Northwestern Journal of International Law and Business* 586.

[14] Art 1(1) of the CISG: 'This Convention applies to contracts of sale of goods between parties whose places of business are in different States: (a) when the States are Contracting States; or (b) when the rules of private international law lead to the application of the law of a Contracting State'.

[15] Art 3 of the CISG: '(1) Contracts for the supply of goods to be manufactured or produced are to be considered sales unless the party who orders the goods undertakes to supply a substantial part of the materials necessary for such manufacture or production. (2) This Convention does not apply to contracts in which the preponderant part of the obligations of the party who furnishes the goods consists in the supply of labour or other services'.

[16] For example where the contract concerns the sale of handbags, the buyer supplies the calf leather, the lining, the zippers, the buckles, the thread, and the glue to the seller for the manufacture of the handbags.

work or labour) rather than a sales contract and thus would not be governed by the CISG.

The CISG governs according to Article 4 CISG the formation of the sales contract as well as the rights and obligations of the parties arising from such a contract.[17] Consequently, there are certain aspects of contract or sales law that are excluded from the Convention, which would ordinarily be available if domestic law was applicable. For example, any claim relating to the validity of the contract or any of the clauses within it is excluded for two possible reasons. First, the issue of validity in international sales was not common at the time of the drafting. Second, the drafters of the CISG 'viewed domestic laws on contract validity as the vehicle for a society's political, social, and economic philosophies'.[18] Another example concerns the passing of the property in the goods sold, as it seemed to be impossible to draft uniform rules on this aspect. The applicable law in this case might instead be the law that governs property.[19] Finally, under Article 5 CISG the liability of the seller for the death or personal injury caused by the goods is excluded, regardless of whether the injured person is the buyer or a third party.

III. Traits of the CISG and its Origins

A. The Concept of Civil Law and Common Law, and their Differences, in a Nutshell

The CISG finds its origins and influences in both the common law and civil law worlds, which have their own distinct features. During the drafting process of the Convention, considerable efforts went into bridging the gap between these two legal systems[20] and excluding any colloquial language or, according to some, 'domestic baggage',[21] such as 'consideration' or the 'Kaufmännisches Bestätigungsschreiben' (confirmation notice).[22] While drafting the CISG, instead of introducing a concept

[17] Art 4 of the CISG: 'This Convention governs only the formation of the contract of sale and the rights and obligations of the seller and the buyer arising from such a contract. In particular, except as otherwise expressly provided in this Convention, it is not concerned with: (a) the validity of the contract or of any of its provisions or of any usage …'.

[18] See 'Report of the Secretary-General: Formation and Validity of Contracts for the International Sale of Goods (A/CN.9/128, annex II)' (1977) VIII *Yearbook of the UN Commission on International Trade Law* 93.

[19] *Roder Zelt- und Hallenkonstruktionen GmbH v Rosedown Park Pty and Reginald Eustace* (1995) 57 FCR 216, 240 (FCA).

[20] J Basedow, 'Towards a Universal Doctrine of Breach of Contract: The Impact of the CISG' (2005) 25 *International Review of Law and Economics* 490.

[21] VM Rogers and AH Kritzer, 'A Uniform International Sales Law Terminology' in I Schwenzer and G Hager (eds), *Festschrift für Peter Schlechtriem zum 70. Geburtstag* (Mohr Siebeck, 2003) 223, 226.

[22] See more details under section III.D.iii.

from one legal system which representatives from the other legal system might find alien or curious, case scenarios were introduced. The representatives were then asked to vote on the desired outcome. The results enabled the representatives to take a stance, especially in 'difficult situations where starting with a legal draft would often produce alternative drafts, misunderstanding and impasse'.[23]

Most states today belong either to the common law system or to the civil law system. The common law legal system materialised in England during the Middle Ages, and was progressively implemented throughout the British colonies worldwide. The civil law legal system, on the other hand, from ancient Rome, was subsequently advanced in continental Europe and afterwards adopted by numerous countries outside the region such as Russia, Brazil and Japan. The common law legal system is based on the doctrine of judicial precedent (*stare decisis*). The opposing parties present their legal arguments, and the judge plays an active role by reaching a decision and providing its opinion and interpretation of limited statutes, which judgments subsequently become binding on lower courts. The civil law legal system in contrast is self-contained. It contains codes and statutes designed to cover all eventualities. Since the laws are comprehensive and explicit, the judge's role is customarily to determine the facts and accordingly apply the relevant code. His/her judgment does not give rise to any judicial precedent.

Of course this is a simplified 'black or white model', separating the world strictly into common and civil law. We are fully aware of the fact that the legal world of the twenty-first century is more diverse and complicated. There are national mixed jurisdictions, such as South Africa or Scotland; the English common law is different from eg the US system; civil law systems can be quite different from each other, and need further differentiations (eg Roman and German law tribe); and this simplified approach is disregarding the latest legal developments as for example the Europeanisation of national private law systems. Nonetheless, for this chapter we take the liberty to mainly use the presented simplified law model to keep this contribution somehow manageable.

Section III starts with a reflection of the common law influences on the Convention, followed by a similar reflection in respect of civil law influences. Section III goes on to deal with those cases in which the CISG actually rejected specific national legal ideas. It then discusses cases which shed light on those provisions of the CISG which do not originate in either common law or civil law systems, and instead demonstrate some unique new features previously unknown to both systems.

[23] JO Honnold, 'Uniform Laws for International Trade: Early "Care and Feeding" for Uniform Growth' (1995) 1 *International Trade and Business Law Journal* 5.

B. Common Law Influences

i. Some General Considerations

Rabel as the mastermind behind the idea to unify international sales law, started conducting a comparative analysis of various sales laws. His conclusion was that the common law legal system was 'most practicable and should be preferred'[24] in the context of a uniform international sales law. Hence, it is no wonder that the skeleton of the CISG, and especially the remedies part, reveal several common law ideas. At common law, where 'the debtor fails to do what he promised, he is liable in damages for "breach of contract" regardless of whether or not he himself or any of his assistants or subcontractors has been at fault'.[25] Further, it does not matter whether the debtor has wholly failed to perform as promised, has performed too late, or has performed unsatisfactorily, as failure to fulfil the promise will mean that the guarantee undertaken has not been observed and a 'breach of contract' has occurred.[26]

Moreover, the liability for non-performance is strict in nature. In other words, and unlike the original civil law tradition, damages can be sought without having to prove that the debtor was at fault.[27] Consequently, Rabel took the United Kingdom Sale of Goods Act 1893 as the foundation of his analysis.[28] In addition to the UK, the United States also had some influence, playing a (limited) role in the pre-development stage of the CISG until the early 1960s. Subsequently its representatives played a central role in the drafting and finalising of the text of the CISG.[29] The following examples illustrate some common law influences on the CISG.

ii. Common Law Roots Examples

a. Anticipatory Breach

Anticipatory breach of a contract is where it is apparent that one party will breach the contract prior to the date of performance. Regardless of whether or not the party is at fault, immediate remedies are available to the aggrieved party as a result of that transparency. Anticipatory breach originates in English

[24] U Magnus, 'The Vienna Sales Convention (CISG) between Civil and Common law—Best of all Worlds?' (2010) 3 *Journal of Civil Law Studies* 75.

[25] K Zweigert and H Kötz, *An Introduction to Comparative Law*, 3rd edn (Clarendon Press, 1998) 503.

[26] ibid.

[27] See eg for Germany § 280(1) of the German Civil Code: 'If the obligor breaches a duty arising from the obligation, the obligee may demand damages for the damage caused thereby. This does not apply if the obligor is not responsible for the breach of duty'.

[28] To date, the UK has not ratified the CISG.

[29] U Magnus, 'The Vienna Sales Convention (CISG) between Civil and Common law—Best of all Worlds?' (2010) 3 *Journal of Civil Law Studies* 79.

common law[30] while in civil law jurisdictions as the German one the concept was originally unknown (but see now § 323(4) of the German Civil Code after the so-called 'Schuldrechtsreform' of 2002).[31] The CISG deals with the anticipatory breach and provides for two different types of remedies. The first is where the aggrieved party is entitled to suspend the performance of its obligations under the contract (Article 71 CISG).[32] The other type is where the aggrieved party is entitled to declare the contract avoided (Article 72 CISG).[33] The former is similar to the American Uniform Commercial Code ('UCC', see §2-609(1) of the UCC),[34] while the latter is largely embedded in English common law.[35] Further, the former requires for it to be apparent that the party will not perform whereas the latter stresses that it must be clear that the party will commit a fundamental breach under Article 25 CISG.

b. Fundamental Breach Resulting in the Right to 'Avoid' the Contract

Article 81(1) CISG defines avoidance as releasing 'both parties from their obligations under it, subject to any damages which may be due'.[36] The question is whether any breach of contract automatically entitles the aggrieved party to terminate the contract. Under the CISG, a party may 'avoid' the contract and therefore discharge its further contractual obligations as a result of the other party having committed a fundamental breach (see Article 49(1)(a) CISG and Article 64 CISG).[37]

[30] See the leading English case *Hochster v De La Tour* [1853] EWHC QB J72.

[31] § 323(4) of the German Civil Code: 'The obligee may revoke the contract before performance is due if it is obvious that the requirements for revocation will be met.'

[32] Art 71(1) of the CISG: 'A party may suspend the performance of his obligations if, after the conclusion of the contract, it becomes apparent that the other party will not perform a substantial part of his obligations as a result of …'.

[33] Art 72(1) of the CISG: 'If prior to the date for performance of the contract it is clear that one of the parties will commit a fundamental breach of contract, the other party may declare the contract avoided'.

[34] §2-609(1) of the UCC: 'A contract for sale imposes an obligation on each party that the other's expectation of receiving due performance will not be impaired. When reasonable grounds for insecurity arise with respect to the performance of either party the other may in writing demand adequate assurance of due performance and until he receives such assurance may if commercially reasonable suspend any performance for which he has not already received the agreed return'.

[35] *Afovos Shipping Co SA v Romano Pagnan and Pietro Pagnan (The Afovos)* [1983] 1 WLR 195, Lord Diplock: 'it is to fundamental breaches alone that the doctrine of anticipatory breach is applicable'.

[36] Art 81 of the CISG: '(1) Avoidance of the contract releases both parties from their obligations under it, subject to any damages which may be due. Avoidance does not affect any provision of the contract for the settlement of disputes or any other provision of the contract governing the rights and obligations of the parties consequent upon the avoidance of the contract. (2) A party who has performed the contract either wholly or in part may claim restitution from the other party of whatever the first party has supplied or paid under the contract. If both parties are bound to make restitution, they must do so concurrently'.

[37] Art 49(1)(a) of the CISG: 'The buyer may declare the contract avoided if the failure by the seller to perform any of his obligations under the contract or this Convention amounts to a fundamental breach of contract'.

Art 64(1)(a) of the CISG: 'The seller may declare the contract avoided if the failure by the buyer to perform any of his obligations under the contract or this Convention amounts to a fundamental breach of contract'.

Whilst it can be viewed that the term 'fundamental breach' was derived from the English common law, it could only have been so in a literal sense.[38] The fundamental breach under English law was in fact developed 'to determine whether disclaimer clauses survived a particular breach of contract'.[39] It did not deal with the seriousness of a breach. English law only subsequently allowed for termination if the failure of performance 'goes to the root of the contract'.[40] The underlying reason for avoiding the contract only in the case of a fundamental breach under the CISG is to balance the parties' concerns. Furthermore, it reflects the old maxim '*favor contractus*'. A buyer needs certainty, whereas a seller requires 'protection against contracts cancelled on minor or capricious grounds, particularly where the goods have already been tendered to the buyer and there is no readily available alternative market or they could be disposed of at great cost to the seller'.[41] In many civil law systems, neither a fundamental breach nor a failure of performance which goes to the root of the contract is needed to terminate the contract. It is sufficient that the breach is not trivial (§ 323(5)2 of the German Civil Code),[42] or not of an insignificant nature (Art. 7:22(1)(a) of the Dutch Civil Code)[43] to justify avoidance of the contract.

c. Right of the Seller to Remedy

In case of non-conforming goods, the seller might want to remedy the defect by replacing or repairing the defective goods, while the buyer might have different intentions. Hence, the question arises as to whether the seller has the *right* to remedy. Under the CISG, he is entitled to remedy a defective delivery of goods. Such right is derived from §2-508 UCC (1977).[44] The English Sale of Goods Act,

[38] JO Honnold, *Uniform Law for International Sales*, 3rd edn (Kluwer and Taxation Publishers, 1999) 181.1.

[39] MR Will, 'Article 25' in CM Bianca and MJ Bonell, *Commentary on the International Sales Law* (Giuffrè, 1987) 209.

[40] AG Guest, *Benjamin's Sale of Goods*, 9th edn (Sweet & Maxwell, 2016) 12–018.

[41] JS Ziegel, 'The Remedial Provisions in the Vienna Sales Convention: Some Common Law Perspectives' in N Galston and H Smit (eds), *International Sales: The United Nations Convention on Contracts for the International Sale of Goods* (Bender, 1984) 9–12.

[42] § 323(5) of the German Civil Code: 'If the obligor has performed in part, the obligee may revoke the whole contract only if he has no interest in part performance. If the obligor has not performed in conformity with the contract, the obligee may not revoke the contract if the breach of duty is trivial'.

[43] Art 7:22(1)(a) of the Dutch Civil Code: 'If … the supplied object is not in conformity with that agreement, then the buyer has in addition the right to rescind the sale agreement, unless the lack of conformity, given its insignificant nature, does not justify such a rescission with its legal effects'.

[44] U Magnus, 'The Vienna Sales Convention (CISG) between Civil and Common law—Best of all Worlds?' (2010) 3 *Journal of Civil Law Studies* 80; §2-508 (1977) of the UCC: '(1) Where any tender or delivery by the seller is rejected because non-conforming and the time for performance has not yet expired, the seller may reasonably notify the buyer of his intention to cure and may then within the contract time make a conforming delivery. (2) Where the buyer rejects a non-conforming tender which the seller had reasonable grounds to believe would be acceptable with or without money allowance the seller may if he seasonably notifies the buyer have a further reasonable time to substitute a conforming tender'.

but also other civil law jurisdictions, originally did not explicitly provide such a right to the seller. The difference between the CISG and UCC in this context is that the latter entitles the buyer to reject the goods whereas the former allows the buyer to retain any right to claim damages. Further, the UCC entitles the seller to remedy the defect before the required delivery time, whereas the CISG has two separate sections. One allows an unrestricted right to remedy the defect until the date for delivery (Article 37 CISG),[45] while the other contains the right to remedy the defect after the required time for delivery (Article 48 CISG).[46] At the Vienna Conference, it was agreed by the majority that there was no right to remedy after the required time for delivery if the delay associated with the remedy constituted a fundamental breach of contract.[47]

C. Civil Law Influences

i. Some General Considerations

As seen, it is fair to say that the skeleton of the CISG derives from the (English) common law. Nonetheless, it has to be emphasised that the Convention has also several features which can be traced back (with some differences of course) to both common law and civil law. In such areas it was not really necessary 'to bridge a gap' but more to draft provisions which reflected the common ground of the two legal systems. Examples are the formation of contract part with its offer and acceptance mechanism (Articles 14 et seq CISG), the compensation principle including loss of profit and the rejection of punitive damages (Article 74 CISG),[48] and the obligation to mitigate losses (Article 77 CISG).[49] However, despite what just has

[45] Art 37 of the CISG: 'If the seller has delivered goods before the date for delivery, he may, up to that date, deliver any missing part or make up any deficiency in the quantity of the goods delivered, or deliver goods in replacement of any non-conforming goods delivered or remedy any lack of conformity in the goods delivered, provided that the exercise of this right does not cause the buyer unreasonable inconvenience or unreasonable expense. However, the buyer retains any right to claim damages as provided for in this Convention'.

[46] Art 48(1) of the CISG: 'Subject to article 49, the seller may, even after the date for delivery, remedy at his own expense any failure to perform his obligations, if he can do so without unreasonable delay and without causing the buyer unreasonable inconvenience or uncertainty of reimbursement by the seller of expenses advanced by the buyer. However, the buyer retains any right to claim damages as provided for in this Convention'.

[47] D Peacock, 'Avoidance and the Notion of Fundamental Breach Under the CISG' in GA Moens (ed), *International Trade and Business Law Review: Volume VIII* (Cavendish Publishing, 2003) 119.

[48] Art 74 of the CISG: 'Damages for breach of contract by one party consist of a sum equal to the loss, including loss of profit, suffered by the other party as a consequence of the breach. Such damages may not exceed the loss which the party in breach foresaw or ought to have foreseen at the time of the conclusion of the contract, in the light of the facts and matters of which he then knew or ought to have known, as a possible consequence of the breach of contract'.

[49] Art 77 of the CISG: 'A party who relies on a breach of contract must take such measures as are reasonable in the circumstances to mitigate the loss, including loss of profit, resulting from the breach. If he fails to take such measures, the party in breach may claim a reduction in the damages in the amount by which the loss should have been mitigated'.

been said the CISG also shows civil law elements which are not or hardly known in common law. Especially during the late drafting phase of the CISG, various traits of the civil law either were adopted or assisted in the development of some of the articles in the Convention. The following examples highlight some of the civil law influences on the CISG.

ii. Civil Law Roots Examples

a. Specific Performance

Where a contracting party is obliged to perform but chooses not to do so, specific performance compels that party to perform its obligations. The CISG foresees the right to require specific performance both for the buyer and the seller (see Article 46 CISG and Article 62 CISG).[50] Under civil law, in particular French and German law, the usual approach is that the aggrieved party's primary remedy would be for the contract to be performed. *Pacta sunt servanda*—promises need to be kept—is key in civil law: the debtor must do what he promised. The common law approach, on the other hand, is as already discussed to view damages as the primary remedy.[51] The financial value of the promise is the focal point here. Correspondingly, specific performance is considered an extraordinary equitable remedy under English law.[52] It only comes into play if damages are insufficient to satisfy the interests of the claimant (eg for the sale of land). The CISG leaned towards the civil law approach, adopting the remedy as an ordinary one. It combines the common law damages idea with the specific performance concept of the civil law.

Whilst specific performance under the Convention appears to be more readily available, the remedy is subject to the domestic law recognising such remedy (see Article 28 CISG).[53] Therefore, such remedy under the CISG could be considered a compromise between civil law countries, which ordinarily grant specific performance, and common law countries, which seldom allow for specific performance.[54] The reality, however, is that 'practical businessmen will not

[50] Art 46(1) of the CISG: 'The buyer may require performance by the seller of his obligations unless the buyer has resorted to a remedy which is inconsistent with this requirement'; Art 62 of the CISG: 'The seller may require the buyer to pay the price, take delivery or perform his other obligations, unless the seller has resorted to a remedy which is inconsistent with this requirement'.

[51] J Spanogle and P Winship, *International Sales Law* (Thomson Reuters, 2012) 333.

[52] S 52(1) of the English Sale of Goods Act 1979: 'In any action for breach of contract to deliver specific or ascertained goods the court may, if it thinks fit, on the plaintiff's application, by its judgment or decree direct that the contract shall be performed specifically, without giving the defendant the option of retaining the goods on payment of damages'.

[53] Art 28 of the CISG: 'If, in accordance with the provisions of this Convention, one party is entitled to require performance of any obligation by the other party, a court is not bound to enter a judgment for specific performance unless the court would do so under its own law in respect of similar contracts of sale not governed by this Convention'.

[54] A Janssen and M Spilker, 'CISG and International Arbitration' in LA DiMatteo (ed), *International Sales Law A Global Challenge* (Cambridge University Press, 2015) 152.

waste their time and money in expensive litigation to enforce international sales contracts.'[55] This might be the reason why Article 28 CISG plays almost no role whatsoever in legal practice.

b. Price Reduction

The CISG entitles the buyer to pay a reduced price if the goods delivered do not conform to the contract and the seller had not made any declaration of such non-conformity before delivering the goods (see Article 50 CISG).[56] The purpose was that 'it would be unjust for the seller to receive the full price for defective goods',[57] regardless of whether or not the seller is at fault. Further, such remedy is appropriate as it might be more difficult for the buyer to reject the goods. Accordingly, the buyer is required to merely make a declaration for the remedy to become applicable. The right to pay a reduced price is different from claiming damages. The buyer is entitled to seek both a price reduction and damages under the CISG. However, the damages sought would be reduced by the discounted amount by way of price reduction.[58] Such remedy was derived from Roman law '*actio quanti minoris*', which is echoed in civil law systems (see eg § 441 of the German Civil Code)[59] but is mainly unknown to the common law (eg the English Sale of Goods Act excluded the remedy of price reduction).[60]

c. *Nachfrist*-procedure

If a party to the contract has not performed its duty, ie if the seller does not deliver the goods or the buyer does not make the payment for the goods it received,

[55] JS Ziegel, 'The Remedial Provisions in the Vienna Sales Convention: Some Common Law Perspectives' in N Galston and H Smit (eds), *International Sales: The United Nations Convention on Contracts for the International Sale of Goods* (Bender, 1984) 9–11.

[56] Art 50 of the CISG: 'If the goods do not conform with the contract and whether or not the price has already been paid, the buyer may reduce the price in the same proportion as the value that the goods actually delivered had at the time of the delivery bears to the value that conforming goods would have had at that time. However, if the seller remedies any failure to perform his obligations in accordance with article 37 or article 48 or if the buyer refuses to accept performance by the seller in accordance with those articles, the buyer may not reduce the price'.

[57] A Kritzer, *Guide to Practical Applications of the United Nations Convention On Contracts for the International Sale of Goods* (Kluwer Law and Taxation Publishers, 1989) 375.

[58] Müller-Chen in I Schwenzer (ed), *Schlechtriem & Schwenzer Commentary on the UN Convention on the International Sale of Goods (CISG)*, 4th edn (Oxford University Press, 2016) 808.

[59] § 441 of the German Civil Code: '(1) Instead of revoking the agreement, the buyer may, by declaration to the seller, reduce the purchase price. The ground for exclusion under section 323(5) sentence 2 does not apply. (2) If more than one person comprises either the buyer or the seller, price reduction may be declared only by all or to all of them. (3) In the case of a price reduction, the purchase price is to be reduced in the proportion in which the value of the thing free of defects would, at the time when the contract was entered into, have had to the actual value. To the extent necessary, the price reduction is to be established by appraisal. (4) If the buyer has paid more than the reduced purchase price, the excess amount is to be reimbursed by the seller. Section 346(1) and section 347(1) apply with the necessary modifications'.

[60] Spanogle and Winship (n 51) 290.

the other party to the contract may fix an additional reasonable period of time for the defaulting party to fulfil its obligation (see Article 47(1) CISG and Article 63(1) CISG).[61] The fixing of the additional time is referred to as the *Nachfrist*, which found its origins in German law (see now § 281(1) of the German Civil Code and § 323(1) of the German Civil Code)[62] but which is unknown in the common law. The CISG contains a similar principle based on German law—albeit with some deviations, which cannot be discussed in detail here. The CISG requires a complete non-performance by the defaulting party. Part-performance will not invoke such right. Further, failure of the defaulting party to perform its obligations within the additional period entitles the aggrieved party to avoid the contract without proving that the breach is fundamental under Article 25 CISG (see Article 49(1)(b) CISG and Article 64(1)(b) CISG).[63] Where incomplete performance is concerned, it does not entitle the aggrieved party to avoid the contract unless the incomplete performance constitutes a fundamental breach. The right to fix an additional period is not mandatory under the Convention. Fixing an additional period of time is a right and not an obligation.[64] The contract can still be avoided if the delay in performance constitutes a fundamental breach.[65]

d. Examination and Notification

For those having a common law background one would expect that a buyer fulfils all his obligations upon making payment for the goods purchased and taking delivery. However, under the Convention, he has two additional obligations to fulfil if he does not want to lose his rights arising from the non-conformity

[61] Art 47(1) of the CISG: 'The buyer may fix an additional period of time of reasonable length for performance by the seller of his obligations'; Art 63(1) of the CISG: 'The seller may fix an additional period of time of reasonable length for performance by the buyer of his obligations'.

[62] § 281(1) of the German Civil Code: 'To the extent that the obligor does not render performance when it is due or does not render performance as owed, the obligee may, subject to the requirements of section 280 (1), demand damages in lieu of performance, if he has without result set a reasonable period for the obligor for performance or cure. If the obligor has performed only in part, the obligee may demand damages in lieu of complete performance only if he has no interest in the part performance. If the obligor has not rendered performance as owed, the obligee may not demand damages in lieu of performance if the breach of duty is immaterial'; § 323(1) of the German Civil Code: 'If, in the case of a reciprocal contract, the obligor does not render an act of performance which is due, or does not render it in conformity with the contract, then the obligee may revoke the contract, if he has specified, without result, an additional period for performance or cure'.

[63] Art 49(1)(b) of the CISG: 'The buyer may declare the contract avoided: in case of non-delivery, if the seller does not deliver the goods within the additional period of time fixed by the buyer in accordance with paragraph (1) of article 47 or declares that he will not deliver within the period so fixed'; Art 64(1)(b) of the CISG: 'The seller may declare the contract avoided: if the buyer does not, within the additional period of time fixed by the seller in accordance with paragraph (1) of article 63, perform his obligation to pay the price or take delivery of the goods, or if he declares that he will not do so within the period so fixed'.

[64] V Knapp in *Bianca-Bonell Commentary on the International Sales Law* (Giuffrè, 1987) 460.

[65] A Kritzer, *Guide to Practical Applications of the United Nations Convention On Contracts for the International Sale of Goods* (Kluwer Law and Taxation Publishers, 1989) 355, 425.

of the goods.[66] First, the buyer should examine the goods once handed over to him within a short period, regardless of whether or when he intends to utilise the goods (see Article 38(1) CISG).[67] Secondly, he should notify the seller of any non-conformity within a reasonable time, failing which the buyer loses in principle all his rights arising from the non-conformity (see Article 39(1) CISG).[68]

While traditional common law does not recognise any such obligations of the buyer (but see §2-607(3)(a) of the UCC),[69] and also some civil law jurisdictions do not foresee such an obligation to examine and to notify or only require the buyer to notify (eg Belgium, Italy or France), several civil law systems, as eg Austria, Germany (§377 of the German Commercial Code)[70] or the Netherlands (Article 7:13(1) of the Dutch Civil Code)[71] have identified this concept. German law in this regard heavily influenced the ULIS (which then was the starting point for drafting the CISG),[72] which required the buyer to examine the goods 'promptly within as short a period as possible'[73] (Article 38 ULIS) and to notify 'promptly after the buyer has discovered or ought to have discovered' the non-conformity

[66] See more detailed A Janssen, *Die Untersuchungs- und Rügepflicht im deutschen, niederländischen und internationalen Kaufrecht—Gemeinsamkeiten und Unterschiede* (Nomos-Verlag, 2001); A Janssen, 'Inspection and Notice of Non-Conformity' in LA DiMatteo et al (eds), *International Sales Law: Contract, Principles & Practice* (CH Beck, 2016) 443–82.

[67] Art 38(1) of the CISG: 'The buyer must examine the goods, or cause them to be examined, within as short a period as is practicable in the circumstances'.

[68] Art 39(1) of the CISG: 'The buyer loses the right to rely on a lack of conformity of the goods if he does not give notice to the seller specifying the nature of the lack of conformity within a reasonable time after he has discovered it or ought to have discovered it'. Only in cases of a reasonable excuse for the failure to give the required notice under Art 44 of the CISG the buyer can retain some rights.

[69] I Schwenzer and P Hachem, 'The CISG—Successes and Pitfalls' (2009) 57 *American Journal of Comparative Law* 469; §2-607(3)(a) of the UCC: 'the buyer must within a reasonable time after he discovers or should have discovered any breach notify the seller of breach or be barred from any remedy'.

[70] § 377 of the German Commercial Code: '(1) If a sale is a business transaction for both parties, then the buyer must promptly examine the goods after receipt from the seller, to the extent that this represents the ordinary business practice, and if a lack of conformity is discovered, promptly notify the seller thereof. (2) If the buyer omits to notify, the goods are deemed to be accepted unless a lack of conformity existed which was not recognizable by an examination. (3) If such a lack of conformity subsequently becomes apparent, then the notification must take place promptly after the discovery thereof; otherwise the goods will also be deemed accepted in respect of this lack of conformity. (4) For the assertion of rights by the buyer, the timely dispatch of the notification suffices. (5) If the seller fraudulently concealed the lack of conformity, it cannot rely on these provisions.'

[71] Art 7:23(1) of the Dutch Civil Code: 'The buyer can no longer claim that the supplied object is not in conformity with the sale agreement if he has not reported the lack of conformity to the seller with convenient speed after he has discovered or reasonably should have discovered it. However, if the object appears to be missing a quality that it should have according to the seller or if the lack of conformity concerns facts which the seller knew or ought to have known, but which he did not mention to the buyer, then the lack of conformity must be reported to the seller with convenient speed after it has been discovered. In the event of a consumer sale agreement, the lack of conformity must be reported by the buyer with convenient speed after it has been discovered, on the understanding that a report within a period of two months after that discovery is considered to be made in time'.

[72] I Schwenzer, 'The Noble Month (Articles 38, 39 CISG)—The Story Behind the Scenery' (2006) 7 *European Journal of Law Reform* 355.

[73] Art 38(1) ULIS: 'The buyer shall examine the goods or cause them to be examined promptly.'

(see Article 39 ULIS).[74] Under §377 of the German Commercial Code, both examination and notification have to be done without undue delay (‘*unverzüglich*’). However, since many domestic legal systems had no such requirement[75] and very few had any strict requirements at all,[76] it was essential for the CISG to require the buyer only to examine ‘within a short period as it is practicable in the circumstances’ (Article 38(1) of the CISG) and to notify ‘within a reasonable period after he has discovered it or ought to have discovered it’ (Article 39(1) of the CISG).

e. Good Faith

The proposition of good faith during the drafting of the CISG involved controversial discussions.[77] The debate was between representatives from common law and civil law states, between socialist and capitalist representatives, and between representatives from a similar socio-legal background.[78] One view was that the vague concept causes uncertainty, whereas the other was that it provides the necessary flexibility.[79] Numerous attempts were made in the wording of the principle, which finally resulted in the present form of Article 7(1) of the CISG. It says that in the interpretation of the CISG, ‘regard is to be had to its international character and to the need to promote uniformity in its application and the *observance of good faith in international trade.*’ The question is whether the purpose of this provision is only to provide uniformity in the *interpretation of the CISG provisions* itself or whether it goes beyond: is good faith also for a substantive principle to be applied to the form and performance of the contract? According to Schlechtriem (and others), the result is clear:

> … similar to the irresistible force of fundamental laws of nature such as the law of gravity, the principle that not only the interpretation of the Convention, but also the evaluation of the relations, rights and remedies of the parties, should be subject to the principle of good faith and fair dealing has found its way into the Convention, its understanding by the majority of legal writers and its application by the courts.[80]

Such application is similar with the observance of good faith or ‘*Treu und Glauben mit Rücksicht auf die Verkehrssitte*’, which was established in the German Civil Code law of 1900 (see §157 of the German Civil Code and §242 of the German

[74] Art 39(1) ULIS: ‘The buyer shall lose the right to rely on a lack of conformity of the goods if he has not given the seller notice thereof promptly after he has discovered the lack of conformity or ought to have discovered it’.

[75] For example under English law, s 35(1) of the Sale of Goods Act 1979 requires the buyer to notify the non-conformity to the seller if the buyer desires to avoid the contract.

[76] Schwenzer (n 72) 356.

[77] FG Mazzotta, ‘Good Faith Principle: Vaxata Quaestio’ in DiMatteo (n 54) 127.

[78] D Sim, ‘The Scope and Application of Good Faith in the Vienna Convention on Contracts for the International Sale of Goods’ in Pace International Law Review (ed), *Review of the Convention on Contracts for the International Sale of Goods (CISG) 2002–2003* (Kluwer Law International, 2004) 27.

[79] ibid 44.

[80] P Schlechtriem, ‘Good Faith in German Law and in International Uniform Laws’ (1997) 24 *Centro di studi e ricerche di diritto comparator e straniero, Saggi, Conferenze e Seminari* 3.

Civil Code).[81] For the English common law, it is well known that it does not (unlike the American UCC—see §1-304 of the UCC)[82] recognise any general principle of good faith.[83]

D. Rejection of Specific National Legal Ideas

So far, we have mainly discussed those features of the Convention where the drafters of the CISG have positively chosen either a common law or a civil law solution. Sometimes, however, it was in the first place not so much about choosing actively one solution but primarily an express and more often an implied *rejection of specific national legal ideas* which seem to be unfit for a working international and uniform sales law. We have chosen three examples to illustrate this category: consideration, the parol evidence rule, and finally the *Kaufmännisches Bestätigungsschreiben*.

i. Consideration

Offer and acceptance are fundamental elements that are required for creating a valid contract in most legal systems—regardless of whether they belong to common law or civil law.[84] The CISG accordingly contains the same requirements. On the other hand, under common law, consideration is required in addition to offer and acceptance to constitute a valid contract. Consideration is an 'act of forbearance or the promise thereof is the price for which the promise of the other is bought, and the promise thus given for it to be enforceable.'[85] Importantly, the doctrine of consideration was not incorporated into the CISG. The Secretariat Commentary specified that the text of Article 29(1)[86] of the CISG 'was intended to "eliminate" and "overrule" the Common Law requirement of consideration.'[87] Although the Convention does not expressly exclude the doctrine of consideration, it does not also state that the element of consideration is one of the requirements to enforce

[81] §157 of the German Civil Code: 'Contracts are to be interpreted as required by good faith, taking customary practice into consideration'.

§242 of the German Civil Code: 'An obligor has a duty to perform according to the requirements of good faith, taking customary practice into consideration'.

[82] §1-304 of the UCC: 'Every contract or duty within the Uniform Commercial Code imposes an obligation of good faith in its performance and enforcement'.

[83] Spagnolo (n 7) 174–75. However, due to the Europeanisation of the English law, good faith became more important also in England. Further developments after Brexit need to be seen.

[84] Morton Midtgaard Fogt, 'Contract Formation under the CISG: The Need for a Reform' in DiMatteo (n 54) 185.

[85] *Dunlop v Selfridge* [1915] AC 847.

[86] Art 29(1) of the CISG: 'A contract may be modified or terminated by the mere agreement of the parties'.

[87] P Butler, 'The Doctrines of Parol Evidence Rule and Consideration: A Deterrence to the Common Law Lawyer?' in SIAC, *Celebrating Success: 25 Years United Nations Convention on Contracts for the International Sale of Goods* (SIAC, 2006) 62.

the contract.[88] Regardless, as the title of the CISG denotes, there is almost always a transfer of goods in exchange for some payment, which thereby would constitute consideration anyway.

ii. Parol Evidence Rule

Regardless of how detailed a contract might appear to be, there is almost always some greater understanding between the parties that led them to conclude the contract, but that understanding might not be evident in the final written contract. Unlike most civil law countries, in the common law, courts apply the parol evidence rule. The parol evidence rule excludes evidence of such understandings, such as any prior oral or written agreement, negotiations, or previous practice or usage.[89] Such evidence is excluded from contradicting or varying any of the terms that the parties have intentionally agreed in the contract.[90] The purpose of the rule was to respect the importance the parties may have accorded to their writing.[91] However, it has been observed that 'the sacred cows of common law namely the inadmissibility of evidence of a pre-contractual nature and hence the subjective intent of parties are outdated and change is required.'[92] Although the CISG does not expressly refer to the parol evidence rule, it provides that contracts can be proved by any means (see Article 11 of the CISG).[93] Moreover, Article 8(3) of the CISG allows the courts to take into account 'all relevant circumstances of the case including negotiations, any practices which the parties have established between themselves, usages and any subsequent conduct of the parties' to determine the intent of another party.[94] The aim of the drafters of the CISG was for the intention of the parties to take priority over the contract itself.[95] Therefore, taking into account the negotiations and previous practices may assist in determining the parties' understanding of the contract.[96] Moreover, at the time of the drafting of the CISG, it was determined that the courts should not be restricted from reviewing all evidence.[97] Also, the parol evidence rule was already being constantly criticised

[88] JO Honnold, *Uniform Law for International Sales*, 3rd edn (Kluwer Law and Taxation Publishers, 1999) 204.4.

[89] Eg McKendrick in HG Beale (ed), *Chitty on Contracts*, 32nd edn, vol 1 (Sweet & Maxwell, 2015) 1071.

[90] Subject to some exceptions.

[91] Butler (n 87) 61.

[92] B Zeller, 'The Parol Evidence rule and the CISG—a comparative analysis' (2003) 36 *The Comparative and International Law Journal of Southern Africa* 308.

[93] Art 11 of the CISG: 'A contract of sale need not be concluded in or evidenced by writing and is not subject to any other requirements as to form. It may be proved by any means, including witnesses.'

[94] Art 8(3) of the CISG: 'In determining the intent of a party or the understanding a reasonable person would have had, due consideration is to be given to all relevant circumstances of the case including the negotiations, any practices which the parties have established between themselves, usages and any subsequent conduct of the parties.'

[95] Schmidt-Kessel and I Schwenzer in Schwenzer (n 58) 149.

[96] EA Farnsworth, 'Article 8' in Bianca and Bonell (n 39) 100.

[97] S Eiselen, 'The CISG as Bridge between Common and Civil Law' in DiMatteo (n 54) 625.

at that time.[98] Finally the CISG-AC, Opinion No 3: Parol Evidence Rule, Plain Meaning Rule, Contractual Merger Clause and the CISG supports this view, saying that 'The Parol Evidence Rule has not been incorporated into the CISG. The CISG governs the role and weight to be ascribed to contractual writing'.[99]

iii. Kaufmännisches Bestätigungsschreiben

Kaufmännisches Bestätigungsschreiben is a German principle of representing an agreement by confirmation notices.[100] It is mainly known in Germany, Austria and Switzerland. A typical scenario is where the parties (Y + Z) have an oral agreement and soon after, party Y sends to party Z a written confirmation of their agreement—however with a different content (eg about quantity or quality of the goods). If party Z does not agree with the written confirmation, then party Z is required to notify party Y, failing which, the written confirmation sent by party Y will be deemed the parties' agreement. Under the Convention, this specific feature of the Germanic law tribe is not applicable as such.[101] However, the *Kaufmännisches Bestätigungsschreiben* might be of relevance as usage or practice if the requirements of Article 9 of the CISG are met (eg Austrian seller and German buyer).[102]

E. No Clear Choice of the CISG and Previously Unknown New Features

Sometimes the CISG neither chose nor rejected a solution from common law or from civil law. Instead, the Convention gave room to the courts to decide the issue and which way to follow. This is for example the case for the battle of forms (conflicting standard contract terms) problem. While the English common law prefers the last-shot rule, the majority of the civil law courts seem to support the

[98] *Zell v American Seating Co* 138 F 2d 641, 644 (2d Cir 1943) (Frank J).

[99] CISG-AC Opinion no 3, Parol Evidence Rule, Plain Meaning Rule, Contractual Merger Clause and the CISG, 23 October 2004. Rapporteur: Professor Richard Hyland, Rutgers Law School, Camden, NJ, USA. Available at www.cisg.law.pace.edu/cisg/CISG-AC-op3.html.

[100] See S Kröll, 'Kaufmännisches Bestätigungsschreiben beim internationalen Warenkauf' (2003) 67 *RabelsZ* 448.

[101] Oberlandesgericht Köln CISG-Online no 127 (22.2.1994, 22 U 202/93); Oberlandesgericht Frankfurt/M. CISG-Online no 258 (5.7.1995, 9 U 81/94); Oberlandesgericht Dresden CISG-Online no 559 (9.7.1998, 7 U 720/98); M Esser, 'Commercial Letters of Confirmation in International Trade: Austrian, French, German and Swiss Law and Uniform Law under the 1980 Sales Convention' (1988) 18 *Georgia Journal of International and Comparative Law* 427.

[102] Art 9 of the CISG: '(1) The parties are bound by any usage to which they have agreed and by any practices which they have established between themselves. (2) The parties are considered, unless otherwise agreed, to have impliedly made applicable to their contract or its formation a usage of which the parties knew or ought to have known and which in international trade is widely known to, and regularly observed by, parties to contracts of the type involved in the particular trade concerned'.

knock-out rule.[103] Unlike Article 2.1.22 of the UNIDROIT Principles,[104] which chose the knock-out rule solution, the CISG did not explicitly settle this issue, even though it is a matter within the scope of the Convention. The disadvantage of this method can be seen from the battle of forms problem. Despite the rule of Article 7(1) of the CISG and the aim of a uniform interpretation of the convention, the issue is still far from being settled and numerous diverging court decisions and arbitral awards exist.[105]

The CISG also contains some new features which were previously unknown in common law and civil law. Here the drafters did not rely on a single legal system, but introduced a completely new idea. One example is the reasonable excuse under Article 44 of the CISG.[106] As already laid out before, according to Article 39(1) of the CISG the buyer normally loses all his rights arising from non-conformity if he fails to give the required notice. Article 44 of the CISG gives the buyer in this circumstance a loophole to escape the complete loss of all rights in case of a 'reasonable excuse for his failure to give the required notice'. If the buyer can prove the existence of such a reasonable excuse he retains the right to reduce the price and to claim damages (except for the loss of profits). This provision is a unique feature of the Convention and cannot be traced back to any other national law system, whether common law or civil law. The provision was introduced to make the strict rule of Article 39(1) CISG acceptable to those contracting countries in which the obligation to examine and to notify non-conformities is unknown or at least less strict.

F. Intermediate Result

The CISG is not dominated by one legal system. It contains both common law elements and civil law elements, so it is fair to say that the Convention is a legal hybrid or an international mixed legal system. Due to its history it is a quite unique

[103] See more detailed A Janssen, 'Kollidierende Allgemeine Geschäftsbedingungen im internationalen Kaufrecht (CISG)' (2002) 16 *Wirtschaftsrechtliche Blätter* 453–57.

[104] Art 2.1.22 of the UNIDROIT Principles: 'Where both parties use standard terms and reach agreement except on those terms, a contract is concluded on the basis of the agreed terms and of any standard terms which are common in substance unless one party clearly indicates in advance, or later and without undue delay informs the other party, that it does not intend to be bound by such a contract'.

[105] B Zeller, 'The CISG and the Battle of the Forms' in DiMatteo (n 54) 213–14; P Perales Viscasillas, 'The Role of the UNIDROIT Principles and the PECL in the Interpretation and Gap-filling of CISG' in A Janssen and O Meyer (eds), *CISG Methodology* (Sellier European Law Publishers, 2009) 295–96; K Wildner, 'Art. 19 CISG: The German Approach to the Battle of the Forms in International Contract Law: The Decision of the Federal Supreme Court of Germany of 9 January 2002' (2008) 20 *Pace International Law Review* 4.

[106] Art 44 of the CISG: 'Notwithstanding the provisions of paragraph (1) of article 39 and paragraph (1) of article 43, the buyer may reduce the price in accordance with article 50 or claim damages, except for loss of profit, if he has a reasonable excuse for his failure to give the required notice.'

private law legal laboratory. At some crucial legal crossroads the CISG provides a compromise between the two legal worlds—maybe the most obvious example is the combination of damages and specific performance both as 'main remedies'. To make the CISG solutions politically acceptable it was sometimes necessary for the drafters of the Convention to foresee some legal loopholes. The most obvious ones are arguably Article 28 of the CISG and Article 44 of the CISG. However, in practice the significance of the legal loopholes is very limited.

IV. Success of the CISG in Legal Practice and as a Legislative Reference Model

As of February 2018, 89 states worldwide from all five continents have adopted the CISG, and the number is growing continuously.[107] Moreover, nine of the 10 largest export and import nations are contracting states of the Convention (the UK being the exception).[108] Hence, it governs a large part of worldwide international trade. The CISG is available in six official languages,[109] all equally authoritative, and is also available in more than 30 unofficial translations.[110] It has correctly gained apparent international recognition as the 'first successful effort to harmonise international sales law on a world wide scale'[111] and Lookofsky says that the Convention is considered to be 'the most significant piece of substantive contract legislation in effect at the international level'.[112] But can we measure the success of the CISG? And if so, how? And what are the reasons that the Convention is considered to be a success? To find answers to these questions it is useful to distinguish between the standing of the CISG in legal practice and as a legislative reference model.

A. CISG in Legal Practice

i. CISG in Litigation

There is little doubt that the CISG has its position in international litigation and that it is not just a paper tiger. The Pace CISG Database reports over 2000

[107] See for a complete list of contracting states www.cisg.law.pace.edu/cisg/countries/cntries.html.

[108] P Butler, 'Choice of Law' in LA DiMatteo et al (eds), *International Sales Law: Contract, Principles & Practice* (CH Beck, 2016) 1027; India, another large trading nation, has also not adopted the CISG.

[109] Arabic, Chinese, English, French, Russian and Spanish.

[110] Texts of the CISG available at www.cisg.law.pace.edu/cisg/text/text.html.

[111] J Coetzee and M de Gama, 'Harmonisation of Sales Law: An International and Regional Perspective' (2006) 10 *Vindobona Journal of International Commercial Law & Arbitration* 17.

[112] J Lookofsky, 'The 1980 United Nations Convention on Contracts for the International Sale of Goods' in Herborts et al (eds), *International Encyclopedia of Laws—Contracts*, supp 29 (Kluwer Law International, 2000) 18.

published (and translated) court decisions.[113] According to a survey by Mistelis, 74 per cent of all reported CISG cases are decisions in litigation.[114] Awareness regarding the CISG as such seems to differ remarkably among legal practitioners worldwide. Meyer pointed out that while close to 80 per cent of all German, Austrian and Swiss lawyers surveyed suggested that they had experienced submission to CISG in litigation, Canadian, American and Australian lawyers were at the other extreme, ie most had had little, if any, exposure to it.[115]

Some general questions determining the actual relevance of the CISG in litigation remain unanswered. One problem is that we do not know the percentage of unreported cases. We can just assume that the actual number of CISG cases in litigation (and arbitration) is much higher than indicated at the Pace CISG Database. Another problem is that we do not know exactly how often the CISG is actually excluded under Article 6 CISG in legal practice.[116] According to Meyer's survey, 42 per cent of the legal practitioners in Germany are regularly excluding the CISG.[117] On the other hand, Spagnolo in 2014 indicated that litigation cases involving the CISG have been growing, and 'pro-CISG' jurisdictions such as China are increasing trade and have stronger bargaining power and thus, can require for the CISG to govern their contracts and not excluding its applicability.[118]

ii. CISG in Arbitration

Whether arbitral tribunals apply the Convention can only be ascertained through statistical investigations. The most detailed investigation of this kind was undertaken by Mistelis[119] on the basis of the Pace database.[120] He found that 26 per cent of all published cases were disputes in arbitration. However, considering the arbitral institutions' strict confidentiality policy, it is very likely that the real number of arbitration cases involving the CISG is marked higher. Mistelis estimates that significantly less than 5 per cent of the arbitration awards are published.[121] If he is correct, the figures relating to court decisions and arbitral awards on the CISG would change dramatically, with at least 70–80 per cent of CISG-related cases having been settled by arbitral tribunals.[122] Consequently, contrary to the published cases, almost four out of five CISG-related cases may be arbitration cases. In other

[113] See iicl.law.pace.edu/cisg/cisg.

[114] L Mistelis, 'CISG and Arbitration' in A Janssen and O Meyer (eds), *CISG Methodology* (Sellier European Law Publishers, 2009) 387–88.

[115] J Meyer, 'UN-Kaufrecht in der deutschen Anwaltspraxis' (2005) 69 *Rabels Zeitschrift für ausländisches und internationales Privatrecht* 485.

[116] See in general for this problem Spagnolo (n 7).

[117] Meyer (n 115) 470–71.

[118] Spagnolo (n 7) 212–21.

[119] Mistelis (n 114) 386. See also U Draetta, 'La Convenzione delle Nazioni Unite del 1980 sui contratti di vendita internazionale di beni mobili e l'arbitrato' (2011) 25 *Diritto del commercio internazionale* 633.

[120] See www.cisg.law.pace.edu/.

[121] Mistelis (n 114) 386–89.

[122] ibid.

words, even if there are no 'hard facts' for this assumption at the moment, one can conclude that there are hundreds of published and probably several thousands of non-published cases in international commercial arbitration which have applied the CISG.[123] Thus, from a purely statistical point of view, the Convention is often applied in arbitration.

B. CISG as a Legislative Reference Model

As seen, the CISG is fulfilling its primary aim: to give the parties quite a reliable law for the international sale of goods. However, over the years the Convention took on another, possibly even more important task (which the drafters arguably did not even foresee at that time): the CISG as a reference model for further legal development worldwide. We would like to give a short overview of where the CISG has been used as a legislative reference model at international law and soft law level, European Union level, and finally at national law level.

i. International Law and Soft Law Level

The CISG heavily influences private law development at an international law and soft law level. The two most famous soft law instruments for contract law, the PECL[124] and the UNIDROIT Principles of International Commercial Contracts (UNIDROIT Principles),[125] both contain numerous CISG ideas and brought them to general contract law level (as they are not intended to regulate sales law only). There is no doubt that the drafters of the PECL and UNIDROIT Principles used the CISG as a model of reference to develop their principles. And despite the fact that less than 20 per cent of African countries adopted the CISG, the General Commercial Law (UAGCL) under the Organization for the Harmonization of Business Law in Africa (OHADA) is largely based on the CISG.[126] The UAGCL superseded individual state laws all over Africa. The aim of OHADA was to promote a uniform commercial law while accommodating, inter alia, concepts of civil law, common law, Islamic law, and customary rules.[127]

[123] However, one has to take into account that national court decisions on the CISG are not always published either, and that this lack influences of course the statistics as well.

[124] JM Smits, 'Problems of Uniform Laws' in DiMatteo (n 54) 605; U Magnus, 'Tracing Methodology in the CISG: Dogmatic Foundations' in A Janssen and O Meyer (eds), *CISG Methodology* (Sellier European Law Publishers, 2009) 46.

[125] P Perales Viscasillas, 'UNIDROIT Principles of International Commercial Contracts: Sphere of Application and General Provisions' (1996) 13 *Arizona Journal of International and Comparative Law* 385; JM Smits, 'Problems of Uniform Laws' in DiMatteo (n 54) 605; T Neumann, *The Duty to Cooperate in International Sales: The Scope and Role of Article 80 CISG (Contributions on International Commercial Law—Beiträge zum Internationalen Wirtschaftsrecht)* (Sellier European Law Publishers, 2012) 20.

[126] S Kruisinga, *(Non-)conformity in the 1980 UN Convention on Contracts for the International Sale of Goods: a uniform concept?* (Intersentia, 2004) 23; Smits (n 124) 605; Magnus (n 124) 46.

[127] LG Castellani, 'Ensuring Harmonisation of Contract Law at Regional and Global Level: the United Nations Convention on Contracts for the International Sale of Goods and the Role of UNCITRAL' (2008) 13 *Uniform Law Review 1/2* 118–19.

ii. European Union Level

For the European Union the CISG has always been an important reference model for the further development of contract law in general and sales law in particular. The European Union not only considers the Convention as a model for general contract law (and not only sales law), but also extends the CISG ideas to situations outside the original B2B context (especially B2C). The most important example in this context is without any doubt the Consumer Sales Directive of 1999.[128] This directive was greatly influenced by the CISG, and it is openly admitted by the European Commission that the Convention was the main reference model for this Directive.[129] In particular, it adopted the rules concerning the non-conformity of the goods as well as the remedies under the CISG. This was implemented by every member state of the European Union. Additionally the (practically less influential) DCFR and the (since withdrawn) Draft for a Common European Sales Law (CESL) both had the CISG as their reference model. Last but not least the proposal for a Directive of the European Parliament and of the Council on certain aspects concerning contracts for the online and other distance sales of goods (OSD proposal) and the proposal for a Directive of the European Parliament and of the Council on certain aspects concerning contracts for the supply of digital content (DCD proposal) show clear CISG elements. Hence, the influence of the Convention on the further development of the European *acquis communautaire* will continue.

iii. National Law Level

Although the CISG is restricted to international sales in a B2B context, national states recognised it as a general contract law model law and a guide when restructuring their domestic private laws. Both the Dutch *Burgerlijk Wetboek* of 1992 and the CISG contain similar content as they were based on ULIS, which is one of the predecessors of the CISG.[130] The German Civil Code was amended by the *Gesetz zur Modernisierung des Schuldrechts* of 2002 (the biggest reform of German Civil Code ever since) to streamline its law of obligations with the CISG. Scandinavian countries[131] including Finland, Norway and Sweden revised their domestic Sale of Goods Acts upon ratification of the CISG in order to complement and mirror most of the contents of the CISG.[132] The People's Republic of China adopted the

[128] Directive 1999/44/EC of the European Parliament and of the Council of 25 May 1999 on certain aspects of the sale of consumer goods and associated guarantees OJ [1999] L171/12.

[129] MJ Bonell, 'The CISG, European Contract Law and the Development of a World Contract Law' (2008) 54 *American Journal of Comparative Law* 7.

[130] A Janssen, 'Application of the CISG in Dutch Courts' in F Ferrari (ed), *Quo Vadis CISG? Celebrating the 25th Anniversary of the United Nations Convention on Contracts for the International Sale of Goods* (Sellier, 2005) 130; SA Kruisinga, 'The Impact of Uniform Law on National Law: Limits and Possibilities—CISG and Its Incidence in Dutch Law' (2009) 13.2 *Electronic Journal of Comparative Law* 2, 20.

[131] Except Denmark.

[132] J Ramberg, 'The Vanishing Scandinavian Sales Law' (2009) 50 *Scandinavian Studies in Law* 258.

CISG in 1986. China's domestic contract law entered into effect in 1999.[133] During the drafting of the domestic Chinese contract law, the Convention was one of the main references to have been followed, often after examination of various foreign contract laws.[134]

V. Success of the CISG as the Best Possible Legal Solution?

The CISG is a success in legal practice and maybe even more as a legislative reference model. Is it therefore a 'perfect law'? Of course not. Nothing can be perfect. But is it at least the overall best solution? No, it is not. The CISG is a compromise between the different legal systems, countries and interests, and it goes without saying that a compromise is sometimes only the second-best solution. One example of the compromise character which results in a second-best solution is the question of the interest rate under Article 78 CISG. This provision states that 'if a party fails to pay the price or any other sum that is in arrears, the other party is entitled to interest on it'. It is easy to see that the CISG does not fix any kind of interest rate, a result which is of course unsatisfactory for both parties. The reason for this lacuna is that Article 78 CISG is a political compromise between western countries and Islamic countries where it is forbidden to claim interest.[135] The drafters were aware that this is not the overall best solution, but the best politically possible solution at that time. Hence, the CISG is neither a perfect law nor is it the best overall solution, and it is a matter of perspective whether the Convention is at least the best mixture of both legal worlds. The CISG might not be all that but it is for sure one thing: a functioning legal hybrid with comes regularly to widely accepted and acceptable solutions.

But is this functioning legal hybrid in danger as the Convention is aging? Did it or will it lose its functionality due to the process of aging? The CISG has not been amended since it came into effect in 1988, and the core of it is even older. Correspondingly it could be regarded as incapable of representing a comprehensive resolution of today's problems.[136] Further, UNCITRAL has not provided for any

[133] Contract Law of the People's Republic of China, adopted at the Second Session of the Ninth National People's Congress on 15 March 1999 and promulgated by Order No 15 of the President of the People's Republic of China on 15 March 1999.

[134] Ding Ding, 'China and CISG' in Michael R Will, *CISG and China: Theory and Practice* (Faculté de droit, Université de Geneve, 1999) 26.

[135] F Akaddaf, 'Application of the United Nations Convention on Contracts for the International Sale of Goods (CISG) to Arab Islamic Countries: Is the CISG Compatible with Islamic Law Principles?' (2001) 13 *Pace International Law Review* 46.

[136] A Rosett, 'Improving the Uniform Commercial Code' (1997) 24 *Centro di studi e ricerche di diritto comparator e straniero, Saggi, Conferenze e Seminari* 2.

process for amending the CISG. In order to amend any provision in a treaty or convention that affects all relevant states, it must be effected with the same formalities as required for the formation of the treaty or convention.[137] However, the CISG required 'more than two generations of international negotiation'[138] for its formation. It would be unthinkable to amend it with a similar process. Therefore, various articles in the Convention could end up becoming redundant or outdated. For example, the CISG provides that 'writing' includes telegram and telex, even though presently emails are widely used as a form of business communication.[139] However, it could be argued that as the social world evolves, the law is interpreted accordingly. For instance, the CISG Advisory-Council Opinion no 1 stated that the 'term "writing" in CISG now also includes any electronic communication retrievable in perceivable form.'[140] Thus, the CISG might be regarded as open-ended and flexible as opposed to being static. However, for some aspects it is harder to move the CISG to the twenty-first century especially when they deal with the sphere of applicability of the CISG. This is for example the case for the question whether an international download of digital content can be considered as a CISG contract as strictly speaking neither is digital content a 'good' nor is the contract a 'sales contract'.[141]

VI. Conclusion

The CISG is a unique legal hybrid or international mixed legal system, combining common law elements with civil law ideas. It is not dominated by one legal system and it has its very own 'legal character'. Even though the Convention is not perfect, and not even the best possible solution, or at least the best mix of common law and civil law, more than 3000 published cases have shown that it is in any event a functioning compromise which comes to widely accepted or acceptable solutions. The success of the CISG as a legislative reference model will continue on a worldwide scale. It is a 'legal lighthouse' in politically difficult times where words such as 'cooperation' or 'compromise' seem to have a negative connotation. The CISG shows that (legal) differences can be bridged and that a good compromise is a gain and not a loss for everybody. We assume Rabel would be very satisfied looking at

[137] Art 40 of the Vienna Convention of the Law of Treaties 1969.

[138] A Rosett, 'Critical Reflections on the United Nations Convention on Contracts for the International Sale of Goods' (1984) 45 *Ohio State Law Journal* 265.

[139] Art 13 of the CISG: 'For the purposes of this Convention "writing" includes telegram and telex'.

[140] CISG-AC Opinion no 1, Electronic Communications under CISG, 15 August 2003. Rapporteur: Professor Christina Ramberg, Gothenburg, Sweden, www.cisg.law.pace.edu/cisg/CISG-AC-op1.html#art13.

[141] J Mowbray, 'The Application of the United Nations Convention on Contracts for the International Sale of Goods to E-Commerce Transactions: The Implications for Asia' (2003) 7 *Vindobona Journal of International Commercial Law & Arbitration* 129.

his legal heritage. The CISG is applied on a daily basis, it brings jurists and especially scholars all over the world together, and every time a legal system takes the CISG as a legislative model the (legal) world comes a bit closer together. He would realise that the Convention is not only a bridge between common law and civil law, but it became a truly worldwide legal bridge. And that is probably the biggest achievement of the CISG.

11

The Sources and Effects of Contractual Terms: Towards an Approximation of Common Law and Civil Law

FRANCISCO DE ELIZALDE*

I. Introduction

It is self-evident that common law and civil law differ on key aspects of contract law. Nor need it be stated that the core objective of creating uniform laws at the European level is to eliminate those differences between the various national legislations that would represent a barrier to cross-border trade. This chapter attempts to demonstrate that, in one specific but decisive aspect of contract law, namely the content of the contract, a convergence between common law and civil law may be observed. It is meanwhile worth noting that this convergence occurs, on occasion, irrespective of the existence of uniform laws. Both circumstances have a bearing on an appropriate evaluation of the process of harmonisation.

It is widely accepted that the content of the contract constitutes a rule generating binding effects between the parties. Beyond this shared concept, though, common law and civil law have traditionally been considered as divergent legal families as regards the sources of the express and implied terms, and in connection with the effects that the terms generate—guarantees, duties and obligations derived from the contract. The hypothesis of this chapter is that convergence is occurring on both levels, in light of a functional perspective.

The chapter is structured in accordance with these two issues. The first section presents the traditional solutions of civil and common law, and their consequences

* I am very grateful to Gracia Pujadas for her invaluable help in the edition of this work. An extended version of this chapter, in Spanish, has been published under F de Elizalde, 'Una aproximación española y europea al contenido del contrato. Reflexiones a la luz de los Principios Latinoamericanos de Derecho de los Contratos' (2017) *Anuario de Derecho Civil*, 1139.

as regards the effects of terms. This presentation provides the suppositions behind the analysis of the current situation, which then follows. Lastly, the work explores the common evolution of the sources of contractual terms.

II. The Effects of Terms

A. Effects of Terms in Classic Civil Law

As Larenz explains, in continental law, the contract is 'primarily a standard of conduct, in accordance with which the obliged party must steer his actions'.[1] It is logical that, thus seen, the concept of contractual terms underlying traditional civil law would be that of 'a bond generating duties'.[2] The terms of the contract, according to this conceptual definition, are the source of obligations imposing on the debtor a legal duty of conduct, which must be performed, and comprises giving something or doing or refraining from doing something (Article 1088 Spanish Civil Code; Article 1101 French Civil Code),[3] along with duties accessory to that performance (§ 241.2 BGB). Meanwhile, although this is not here our concern, the unyielding link between terms and obligations entails that 'contractual liability would tend to be constructed with a certain degree of subjectivity, based on a breach of contractual duties … and in accordance with the requirement of fault'.[4] It is this aspect that the modernisation of the law of obligations and contracts aims to overcome, by means of the neutral notion of breach.[5]

The traditional attachment of continental law to legal duty as the effect of terms, places the parties in the position of creditor and debtor, in which the obligation and its circumstances take on the lead role. The contract would seem to be confined to the creation, modification, transfer or extinction of obligations, by means of a notion that is ratified, for example, in the reform of the French Civil Code of 2016 (Article 1101 Civil Code).

[1] K Larenz, *Derecho de Obligaciones*, vol I (Edersa, 1958) 85; K Larenz, *Lehrbuch des Shuldrechts*, vol I (CH Beck'sche Verlagsbuchhandlung, 1987) § 7, III p 91.

[2] AM Morales Moreno, 'Comentario al art. 35' in L Díez-Picazo (ed), *La Compraventa Internacional de Mercaderías. Comentario a la Convención de Viena* (Civitas, 1998) 290.

[3] In the original version of the French Civil Code. The reform of 2016 gives a new wording to the article in which, nevertheless, the reference to the obligation is still present.

[4] Morales Moreno (n 2) 290.

[5] AF Pantaleón Prieto, 'Las Nuevas Bases de la Responsabilidad Contractual' (1993) *Anuario de Derecho Civil 1720–1721*; AM Morales Moreno, *Incumplimiento del Contrato y Lucro Cesante: Discurso leído el día 8 de febrero de 2010 en su acto de recepción pública como Académico de Número* (Real Academia de Jurisprudencia y Legislación, 2010) 29–30; F Gómez Pomar, 'El Incumplimiento Contractual en Derecho Español' (2007) 3 *InDret* 7.

i. Initial Total and Absolute Impossibility of Performance

Following on from the above, one can understand how the possibility of performance has taken on such significance in continental law, and that committing to an obligation the performance of which is impossible has been seen as an obstacle that the terms can scarcely overcome. If the contract is a norm of conduct obliging the debtor to give, do or refrain from doing something, the logical consequence that would seem to follow on from this premise is that the debtor cannot oblige himself to an impossible performance, and as a result, initial impossibility would render the contract void, citing for this purpose the famed rule of Celsus: *impossibilium nulla obligatio est*.[6]

This solution would only cover initial total and absolute impossibility; in other words, if this arises when the contract is made (initial), affects the entire performance (total), and is impossible for any debtor (absolute, or objective). The rule is not, in general, invoked to cover circumstances where impossibility has subsequently arisen, is partial (unless this is equivalent to total impossibility because it affects the essence of the subject matter of the contract), nor what is known as subjective impossibility or inability, where performance is impossible for the debtor, but possible for others, except in the case of *intuitu personae*[7] performance. Lastly, as regards different modes, initial impossibility includes physical or material, and also legal impossibility.

The non-existence of a valid contract in cases of initial, total and absolute impossibility became widespread in the civil codes of the nineteenth and twentieth centuries. In Germany, the former §306 BGB established: 'A contract the performance of which is impossible, is null and void'.[8] This principle was supplemented by the likewise repealed §307 BGB, which incorporated into the German Civil Code Jhering's theory of *culpa in contrahendo*.[9] As a result, any person entering into a contract the performance of which would be impossible, and who was aware or should have been aware of that, was liable for the damages occasioned to the innocent party, subject to the limit of the negative interest.

In the Latin tradition, impossibility has been directly linked to the subject matter of the contract. In Spanish law, the Civil Code establishes that the subject matter (*objeto*) is an essential element of the contract (Article 1261 Civil Code), the absence of which dictates the nullity or, according to some authors, the non-existence, of the contract. In characterising the subject matter, Article 1271 of the Civil Code refers directly to legal impossibility when it is established that the things (subject matter of the contract) must not be *res extra commercium*, nor should the

[6] Cel D 50, 17, 185.

[7] V San Julián Puig, *El Objeto del Contrato* (Aranzadi, 1996) 270–72.

[8] Own translation.

[9] R Zimmermann, *The Law of Obligations. Roman Foundations of the Civilian Tradition* (Oxford University Press, 1996) 695.

services violate the law or good customs.[10] As regards material or physical impossibility, Article 1272 of the Civil Code provides that: 'Impossible things or services may not be the subject matter of a contract'. As a result, the initial impossibility of the thing or service, whether material or legal, results in the invalidity of the contract, as it would be bereft of subject matter.[11]

In France, the general regulation of the subject matter (*objet*) of the contract made reference, prior to the reform, only to the fact that the things must lie within the sphere of commerce, an expression intended to refer to legal possibility (former Article 1128 Civil Code). Unlike the Spanish Civil Code, the French *Code civil* did not, in characterising the subject matter of the contract, include any prohibition of material impossibility. This is confined, in the *Code civil*, to contracts of sale (Article 1601), establishing that if, when the sale is concluded, the subject matter has been totally lost or destroyed, then the contract will be null and void. Despite the above, French legal theory has interpreted Article 1601 of the *Code civil* in a broad sense, considering it to be applicable as well to contracts other than sales.[12] Following the reform of the Civil Code of 2016, the subject matter is no longer a requirement for a valid contract. However, Article 1163 of the Civil Code that deals with the content of the contract, demands that performance be possible, which leads on to similar results: a term requiring that something be given would be impossible to perform if the subject of the contract did not exist.

In Italy, the Civil Code (*Codice Civile*) acknowledges the subject matter (*oggetto*) as a requisite of the contract (Article 1325), which must be possible (Article 1346), without any distinction being made between material and legal possibility, otherwise the contract would be void (Article 1418). Article 1347 of the *Codice* establishes that a contract subject to a condition precedent or time period is valid if initially impossible performance becomes possible prior to fulfilment of the condition or the end of the time period.[13] However, if the initial impossibility endures, the contract would be invalid.

A detailed analysis of the issue reveals that initial impossibility covers various circumstances of differing practical value. At one extreme, which is essentially moot, we find the case of objects that are necessarily impossible: the classic example of the hippocentaurus.[14] There is ample consensus in comparative law that in this case the contract is void, either through application of the rules of subject matter, or otherwise because of the lack of seriousness in the agreement.

[10] A criticism to the things and services as the subject matter of contracts may be found in L Díez-Picazo, *Fundamentos del Derecho Civil Patrimonial*, vol I (Thomson Civitas, 2007) 97–200; San Julián Puig (n 7) 62–64.

[11] See STS (1ª) 4 November 1999 (RJ 1999, 8001).

[12] L Díez-Picazo, 'Sobre la Imposibilidad de la Prestación' in JM Abril Campoy and ME Amat Llari (eds), *Homenaje al Profesor Lluis Puig i Ferriol*, vol I (Tirant, 2006) 1089.

[13] The old § 308 BGB established a similar rule.

[14] Gai III, 97 a.

A different circumstance to the above, of greater practical relevance, is the case of an object that existed, but that disappears prior to the conclusion of the contract (*res extincta*), or even certain legal impossibilities. In such cases, the nullity of the contract is not a necessary consequence. As Zimmermann asserts, '*Impossibilium nulla obligatio est* neatly encapsulates the idea that nobody can be obliged to perform what he cannot perform. But this is not identical to the assertion that a contract aimed at an impossible performance is bound to be void'.[15] The validity of the contract could lie in the allocation, to the debtor, of the risk as to the existence of the object. On such a basis, the impossibility of specific performance need not necessarily deprive the creditor of the damages that would derive from a breach of contract.[16]

Ernst Rabel was one of the leading voices raised against the principle of the hitherto prevailing §306 BGB, focusing his criticism on an incorrect interpretation by the German codifier as regards the origin of the Roman *impossibilium nulla obligatio est* rule. According to Rabel, the emergence of the rule is to be found in the stipulations to give and, in particular, in ancient law governing contracts and bequests *per donationem*, the subjects of which were material property.[17] Betti adds that in an agricultural society such as that of Rome in the days of Classical law, the subject matter of contracts would be material things. As a result, it was logical that the aforementioned rule would lead to the invalidity of contracts that dealt with impossible objects.[18] For Zimmermann, *impossibilium nulla obligatio est* would only have applied strictly with regard to stipulations, and with numerous exceptions concerning contracts of sale.[19]

It is precisely in reference to sales that it becomes clear that Roman law had a different understanding of the rule to how it was later understood in the civil codes. In particular as regards legal impossibility, since physical impossibility would seem to have remained very much tied to the necessary material existence of the subject matter, even in the late periods of Roman law. I refer specifically to the passage of Licinius Rufinus containing the following assertion: '*Liberi hominis emptionem contrahi posse plerique existimaverunt, si modo inter ignorantes id fiat, quod idem placet etiam, si venditor sciat, emptor autem ignoret, quod si emptor sciens liberum esse emerit, nulla emptio contrahitur*'.[20] As a result, the purchase of a freeman would be valid, despite its legal impossibility, if the purchaser was unaware that the individual was not a slave. Hence the fact that an innocent purchaser (ignorant of the impossibility) was entitled to bring *actio empti*, to claim for damages.[21]

15 Zimmermann (n 9) 687.
16 Zimmermann (n 9) 696.
17 E Rabel, 'Origine de la Règle: *Impossibilium Nulla Obligatio*' in E Alglave et al (eds), *Mélanges Gérardin* (Sirey, 1907) 502.
18 E Betti, *Istituzioni de Diritto Romano*, vol II (CEDAM, 1962) 41.
19 Zimmermann (n 9) 689.
20 D 18, 1, 70.
21 Zimmermann (n 9) 242; Rabel (n 17) 511.

The generalisation of the *impossibilium nulla obligatio est* rule is attributed to the school of Rationalist Natural Law, and in German law, the Late Pandectists, on the basis of an understanding that the free will of the individual can only be applied to an action that said person is himself capable of performing. As a result, objective or even subjective impossibility, in other words the person's individual inability, would necessarily cause the contract to be invalid. The civil codes did not adopt this solution in the strictest sense, since while they incorporated initial objective impossibility as grounds for a contract to be void, they excluded cases of subjective impossibility from this stricture.[22]

The above confirms that for a practical jurist, as the Roman, initial impossibility did not constitute automatic grounds for a contract to be void, but rather, in certain cases *actio empti* was in fact permitted, an action that, in modern terminology, one could view as based on contractual liability. As a result, continuing with our contemporary concepts, contracts could on occasion be binding on an impossible performance. The explanation should be sought, perhaps (the sources are scant in this regard) in the enigmatic *praestare*, or guarantee as the content of the obligation, which would not be confined to dare or *facere*, unlike the solution offered by Rationalist Natural Law, followed by the authors of the civil codes.

The widespread imposition by the codification of civil law of invalidity derived from initial impossibility is rather the consequence of an incorrect linkage between freedom of will and the content of the contract, restricting terms to those which would be open to specific performance (obligations can only be established as regards that which can be given, done or refrained from). In reaching this conclusion, Rationalist Natural Law, or in German law the Late Pandectists,[23] would seem to have applied an excessively restrictive interpretation of moral philosophy and Canon law. These demand that the decision of a free man should be applied to a possible action, since an impossible action prevents will from achieving its purpose, and would therefore be a velleity. However,[24] if we hold that the bond regarding an impossible subject matter is not confined to its regulatory facet of duties (demanding performance in kind), but instead includes the guarantee of a factual situation, the non-existence of which confers entitlement to claim damages in certain cases, then there would seemingly be no difficulty in acknowledging that the contract would be valid. The possibility would lie, in this case, in the feasibility of fulfilling the compensation for damages resulting from the breach. I insist, however, that this was not the solution favoured by Codification.

[22] Zimmermann (n 9) 692–94. It appears that the rule was generalised in German law by Friedrich Mommsen, then received by Bernhard Windscheid and thereform, it was enshrined in the old §306 BGB. See, additionally, Rabel (n 17) 474; Díez-Picazo (n 12) 1091.

[23] Zimmermann (n 9) 692–94.

[24] St Thomas of Aquinas, *Summa Theologica*, I–II, q 13, Art 5. Available at: www.sacred-texts.com/chr/aquinas/summa/sum147.htm.

ii. Partial Impossibility Through Absence of Qualities

Similarly related to the problem of possible performance, we encounter the issue of initial but partial (not absolute) impossibility of performance. This covers two broad circumstances: the loss of a part of the subject matter (which does not concern us here), and more commonly, and of greater relevance, the initial lack in the subject matter of the qualities required by the contract.

a. The Absence of Presumed Qualities

The partial impossibility of performance, as a result of absent qualities, is liable to involve specific obligations, and occurs when the former are not present in the subject matter, when the contract is concluded. This obstacle does not, however, affect generic obligations, provided that the goods in question objectively exist (as we would otherwise be faced with a situation of absolute impossibility), and are not excessively delimited (which would make the subject matter a specific one due to individualisation).[25] In this type of obligation, the parties assume the imperishable qualities of the goods (*genus nunquam perit*) by agreement, or in the absence thereof, in accordance with the criteria of commerce.[26] The qualities do not constitute a problem of initial impossibility, because the subject matter (which is still ideal, and not specified) is always capable of possessing them.

The different solution of specific as opposed to generic obligations is justified by the possibility of performing *in natura*, in accordance with the definition of what is validly possible that underlies the Codification, inevitably tied to the concept of obligation and of subject matter, as accepted by the civil codes of the nineteenth century.

It should be recalled in this regard that, according to said legal texts, the contract is a standard of conduct that demands that the debtor performs by giving, doing or refraining from doing.[27] On the basis of this definition, it is understandable that one cannot demand that the debtor delivers an object with certain qualities that it does not possess. Under a specific obligation, the debtor can only hand over the thing as it exists in reality. If the contract requires specific qualities of the object that it lacks, the debtor will duly perform by delivering the thing (as it is). As regards the qualities, then a situation of initial partial impossibility of performance will arise, resulting in the absence of the debtor's bond with regard to said qualities. As Morales Moreno argues, 'the partial nature of the initial impossibility may explain that the duty of performance is confined to delivering the thing, while overlooking its qualities'.[28]

[25] JJ Vara Parra, 'La Imposibilidad Inicial' in S Sánchez Lorenzo (ed), *Derecho Contractual Comparado. Una Perspectiva Europea y Transnacional* (Thomson Reuters Civitas, 2013) 676.
[26] cp Art 327 Spanish Commercial Code.
[27] See above section II.A.
[28] AM Morales Moreno, 'Tres Modelos de Vinculación del Vendedor en las Cualidades de la Cosa' (2012) *Anuario de Derecho Civil* 9.

The need for performance to be initially possible, in specific obligations, is tied in with the consideration of the subject matter as an element that exists in real terms, a circumstance clearly highlighted in sales of specific objects. Here, the seller is obliged only to deliver the thing in the condition it has when the contract is concluded (Article 1468.I Spanish Civil Code, Article 1614 French Civil Code, and Article 1477 Italian Civil Code). In a generic sale, instead, an ideal concept of the subject matter is assumed: the seller is obliged to deliver the thing as it should be, according to the contract.[29]

As a result, in specific obligations, the subject matter of the contract is not what the parties determine, but the thing itself as it exists in reality. Continuing the example set out by Larenz (with regard to the regulations of the BGB in force up to the 2001 reform), if the parties to a contract for a specific purchase assume that the subject matter is a gold ring, the vendor discharges his duty of performance even if the ring does not possess this quality (in other words, if it is not gold). The reason lies in the fact that the seller does not undertake to deliver, in generic terms, a 'gold ring', but 'an individually determined ring', that the parties believed to be gold.[30] An obligation placed on the seller such that the contracted ring should possess a quality that it lacks would, under the traditional system of binding agreements, mean demanding performance that would *ab initio* be impossible.[31]

This line of argument is completed by means of a reference to the aedilitian remedies (or latent defects actions), a special regime of liability of the debtor, archetypal in onerous obligations to give (sales, leases, etc). According to this system, the debtor undertakes only to deliver the thing and to provide certain remedies in case of latent defects (Article 1461 Spanish Civil Code, Article 1603 French Civil Code and Article 1476 Italian Civil Code). The proof that the debtor under a specific obligation is not bound to deliver an object that would fulfil the presumed qualities of the thing, but rather the item that actually exists, is the result of the remedies available to the creditor. There are two such remedies (Articles 1486 Spanish Civil Code, Article 1644 French Civil Code):[32] *the actio redhibitoria*, which allows the contract to be rescinded, and the *actio quanti minoris*, which authorises a reduction in the price. Under the regime of such aedilitian remedies, the creditor cannot demand performance nor expectation damages, both of these being central remedies for breach. The cause of this limitation unquestionably lies in an absence of a binding obligation regarding the qualities of the object.

[29] AM Morales Moreno, 'Adaptación del Código Civil al Derecho Europeo: la Compraventa' in AM Morales Moreno, *La Modernización del Derecho de Obligaciones* (Thomson Civitas, 2006) 102.

[30] K Larenz, *Derecho de Obligaciones*, vol II (Edersa, 1959) 90.

[31] cp R Bercovitz Rodríguez-Cano, 'La Naturaleza de las Acciones Redhibitoria y Estimatoria en la Compraventa' (1969) *Anuario de Derecho Civil* 801, 833–34.

[32] The same is also true, to a certain extent, in Italy (Art 1492 CC). Notwithstanding, the general remedies for breach of contract are granted in the absence of qualities (Art 1497 CC), a case that is treated differently than that of defects.

The underlying reason is to be found in the aforementioned concept of the contract as a source of duties, in the necessary (initial and subsequent) possibility of performing them in kind, and in the impossibility that this could take place if the subject matter is specific and lacks the presumed qualities. The initial (partial) impossibility of performance, when the specific subject matter lacks qualities, justifies the absence of a binding obligation on the debtor regarding said qualities, according to the concept of the nineteenth-century civil codes. A consequence which, as explained above regarding absolute impossibility, could be reasonable with reference to specific performance, but on occasion would deprive the creditor of fair protection, by denying him the damages that would in fact be possible. Above all, if the contract implies that the debtor assumed, even implicitly, the risk of the absence of qualities in the subject matter.[33]

b. The Absence of Agreed Qualities

The scope of the conceptual assumption of Codification as regards the contract as a standard that results in duties and of the subject matter that actually exists, which lies at the foundation of the initial impossibility of performance, depends on the solution adopted as regards the qualities agreed by the parties.

One extreme view of such approaches would necessarily argue the partial invalidity of the contract, denying a bond as regards those qualities of the object that proved non-existent even if the obligation were to derive from an express agreement. If the debtor is bound only by what he can give, then it would be irrelevant whether the qualities were based on a contractual presumption, or instead an express agreement. At the most, the creditor would have access to the aedilitian remedies against latent defects, which are not based on a breach of contract.[34]

This is the solution derived from Article 1505 of the Peruvian Civil Code: 'There is liability for latent defects if the object lacks the qualities that were promised by the transferor and gave them value, or made them fit for the purpose of the purchase'. By virtue of this principle, the absence of promised or guaranteed qualities[35] would not give rise to a breach of contract, but would simply entitle the creditor to bring the resulting actions against latent defects (rescission and reduction of price). Article 2167 of the Argentinian Civil Code of Vélez Sársfield (repealed) ordered along the same lines:

> The contract may also make defects redhibitory which would otherwise not be, if the transferor guaranteed their absence, or guaranteed the quality of the thing supposed by the transferee. This guarantee arises even if it was not expressly stated, when the transferor positively asserted in the contract that the thing was free of defects, or possessed certain qualities, even if the transferee could easily become aware of the defect or lack of quality.

[33] cp in respect of absolute impossibility, J Ribot Igualada, 'La Imposibilidad Originaria del Objeto Contractual' (2015) 3 *Revista de Derecho Civil* 8.

[34] See above section II.A.ii.a.

[35] M de la Puente y Lavalle, *El contrato en General*, vol III (Palestra, 2001) 553.

Note that the expression 'guarantee' refers here to the aedilitian remedies, which is also known as 'guarantee or warranty against latent defects', a meaning that clearly differs from that of English law and, thus, should not be confused.

In general, setting aside for a moment the specific solutions of a particular legal system, the issue should be focused on the tension between initial partial impossibility and its consequences, on the one hand, and respect for freedom of contracts, on the other. If the theory of partial impossibility prevails, then the conventional guarantee or promise gives way, since it is deprived of the inherent efficacy of a term. An infringement of the guarantee would not constitute a breach of the contract, but at the most a defect that would be covered by a remedy against latent defects (aedilitian). On the contrary, the prevalence of freedom of contract regarding an accentuated vision of the initial impossibility constitutes recognition that the guarantee is incorporated within the contractual terms, with the consequent breach of contract in the event of defects in the subject of the contract.

As in the case of the *impossibilium nulla obligatio est* rule, the way the nineteenth-century civil codes understood the efficacy of a promise concerning the qualities of the item or subject matter of the contract, on occasion deprived of binding effects, is not consistent with its historical background.

If we analyse the contract of sale, we find that, in early Roman law, a stipulation as to the qualities of the object was valid, even if they were non-existent. The validity of a solemn promise granted the creditor, if the object lacked the promised qualities, entitlement to *actio empti*, corresponding to what in modern times is known as contractual liability.

With regard to the '*stipulatio*', Zimmermann and Morales Moreno, in separate studies,[36] analyse the validity in Roman law of those applying to states of facts (eg the promise that the slave was healthy), and the problem represented by potential initial impossibility of the obligation (eg if the slave was in fact sick).

Both authors pronounce themselves in favour of the validity of the stipulation, based on an understanding (according to Zimmermann) that the vendor was not guaranteeing the absence of the defect, nor the presence of a quality, but rather payment of damages if the reality did not correspond to his assertion;[37] or, for Morales Moreno, that 'the satisfaction of the creditor's interest … may be effected … by means of damages'.[38]

Both find their justification in a text by Ulpian, in which he upholds the validity of the stipulation in the following terms: 'I hold the following stipulation to be valid, namely: "That the slave is not a thief, is not a violator of graves, and is sound", for it contains the qualities that are in the interests of the purchaser of the slave. But if a guarantee is added to any of these statements, the stipulation will be all the more valid'.[39]

[36] Zimmermann (n 9) 310; Morales Moreno (n 29) 9–10.
[37] Zimmermann (n 9) 310.
[38] Morales Moreno (n 29) 10.
[39] Ulp D 21, 2, 31. Own translation.

The deduction drawn from the above is that Roman law accepted that one of the parties could be contractually bound by a state of facts (the qualities of the object), without this representing a problem of initial impossibility of the obligation.

The relationship between the promise (which must establish a binding obligation based on the qualities of the object) and the liability arising from latent defects (leading to a contrary result), along with the consequent confusion, may lie in the way in which Roman law itself evolved. At some point in the history of the Curule Aediles, apparently not at their founding,[40] the liability of the vendor (aedilitian) was extended to cover not only defects that he consciously or unconsciously failed to declare,[41] but also any assertions made or promises assumed (formally or informally) as regards the existence, in the item sold, of a quality, or the absence of a defect:[42] the '*dicta promissave*'.[43]

The Digest provides us with the distinction between a declaration or assertion *in contrahendo* ('*dictum*') of the vendor,[44] and a promise ('*promissum*'), the former being that which is 'spoken out loud' (unilaterally), while the latter 'may refer either to a simple promise, or to a public promise or a promise of stipulation'.[45] Both gave entitlement to aedilitian remedies.

Liability did not, however, attach to the vendor purely as a result of mere praise of the goods, the efficacy of which was distinguished from the '*dicta*' in which they were proffered 'boastfully'.[46] The delimitation between the two would have been done by reference to *Ius civile*.[47]

A purchaser suffering harm through the '*dicta*' and promises of the vendor could opt either for aedilitian protection and the remedies this granted, which could be exercised before curule jurisdiction in the cases lying within the scope of application of the edict, as regards the object, or otherwise civil law actions before the corresponding jurisdiction.[48]

In post-Classical law, the jurisdiction of the Curule Aediles no longer existed, and the propensity of the Byzantine jurists to generalise rules[49] led to the extension

[40] R Monier, *La Garantie Contre les Vices Cachés dans la Vente Romaine* (Sirey, 1930) 51.

[41] M Kaser, *Derecho Romano Privado* (Reus, 1968) 195.

[42] Zimmermann (n 9) 315.

[43] Ulp D 21, 1, 1, 1; Gai D 21, 1, 18, pr; Ulp D 21, 1, 38, 10.

[44] cp Monier (n 40) 55.

[45] Ulp D 21, 1, 19, 2. As regards *dicta*, the cited Ulp 21, 1, 19, 2 adds after 'spoken out loud', the expression 'and terminated by the words themselves', but the latter would be interpolated; cp Monier (n 40) 55.

[46] Ulp D 21, 1, 19, 3.

[47] It is argued whether the phrase '*quod eius praestari oportere dicetur*', of Ulp D 21, 1, 1, 1, points to the *Ius civile*, in the sense that liability for '*dicta*' was established by *Ius civile*, or if, on the contrary, the *Ius honorarium* had its own criteria. See B Nicholas, 'Dicta Promissave' in D Daube (ed), *Studies in the Roman Law of Sale. Dedicated to the Memory of Francis de Zulueta* (Clarendon Press, 1959) 95–101.

[48] cp AM Morales Moreno, 'El Alcance Protector de las Acciones Edilicias' (1980) *Anuario de Derecho Civil* 597.

[49] P Stein, 'Medieval Discussions of the Buyer's Actions for Physical Defects' in D Daube (ed), *Studies in the Roman Law of Sale. Dedicated to the Memory of Francis de Zulueta* (Clarendon Press, 1959) 103.

of the scope of application of aedilitian remedies to any type of object sold (not only slaves and livestock, as had originally been the case).[50]

There was, furthermore, some confusion between aedilitian remedies and *actio empti*, which meant that recourse could be made to either in actions for rescission and reduction of price, even against a vendor acting in good faith,[51] with the distinction being retained as regards damages concerning bad faith sellers, who would be subject to *actio empti*.[52]

All the above may justify the reference to promises to be found in certain civil codes in relation to the actions against latent defects (aedilitian remedies). In the case of Spain, the somehow more recent precedent of García Goyena (who drafted the Civil Code proposal of 1851) may have been influential as he argued that aedilitian remedies covered promises.[53] At present, however, the Supreme Court constantly upholds the validity and binding force of an express agreement (based on Article 1255 Civil Code), a violation of which constitutes a breach of contract.[54] It should nonetheless be pointed out that the survival of the regime against latent defects has on occasion prompted the Spanish courts to exercise a lax interpretation of certain contractual promises, which did not give rise to a clear and express regime of conventional guarantee.[55]

In German law, although the *impossibilium nulla obligatio est* rule held sway there, the prevalence of the agreement was traditionally accepted, while confining the consequences of a breach to damages. In practice, the former §459.2 BGB (in force until 31 December 2001), in connection with §463 of the same legal text, allowed the purchaser to demand compensation for damages if the vendor had given assurances of a particular quality, which was absent when the risk associated with the thing was transferred. The expression 'assurance' (*Zusicherung*) by the vendor 'demands rather more than a mere assertion or asseveration. It requires the recognisable intention of the vendor to enter into an obligation, in other words, to accept liability for defects in the quality of the thing',[56] making this assurance

[50] F Schulz, *Classical Roman Law* (Clarendon Press, 1954) 538, who believes that Ulp D 21, 1, 1 is interpolated and was falsely attributed to Labeo. Monier (n 40) 161–62, is of the same opinion.

[51] Ulp D 19, 1, 13. The text would have been interpolated to make the vendor of good faith liable under the *actio empti*, as suggested by Monier (n 40) 147–54. It is argued whether the liability of the seller acting in good faith preceded Justinian, as Zimmermann (n 9) 321–22 claims, against the competing argument of A D'Ors, *Derecho Privado Romano* (Eunsa, 1997) para 49, p 558. AM Honoré, 'The History of the Aedilitian Actions from Roman to Roman-Dutch Law', in *Studies in the Roman Law of Sale. Dedicated to the Memory of Francis de Zulueta* (Clarendon Press, 1959) 139, acknowledges that it is a debated matter.

[52] Ulp D 19, 1, 13, pr; cp Morales Moreno (n 48) 598.

[53] F García Goyena, *Concordancias, Motivos y Comentarios del Código Civil Español*, vol III (Sociedad Tipográfica-Editorial, 1852) 397.

[54] In this vein, SSTS (1ª) 12 March 1999 (RJ 1999, 2144), 18 March 1999 (RJ 1999, 8979), 11 July 2000 (RJ 2000, 6683), 16 November 2001 (RJ 2001, 9458), 3 December 2003 (RJ 2003, 8520), 19 July 2004 (RJ 2004, 4387), 1 September 2006 (RJ 2006, 6065), 11 June 2008 (RJ 2008, 3561), 10 June 2010 (RJ 2010, 2675) and 8 September 2015 (RJ 2015, 4753).

[55] See STS (1ª) 20 November 2008 (RJ 2009, 283) or STS (1ª) 30 March 2011 (RJ 2011, 3133).

[56] Larenz (n 30) 65.

similar to a promise. The reform of the BGB, as will be shown below, eliminated the consequences of initial impossibility as regards the validity of the contract, along with the aedilitian remedies (against latent defects), and its response to the binding efficacy of the agreement as to qualities is therefore even more robust today, with the spectrum of remedies having been extended.

Italian law reaches a particular conclusion, in a context marked by the distinction between latent defects and the absence of qualities, considering that these are different cases of the unfitness of the subject matter of the contract. Article 1497 of the *Codice* establishes that a lack of promised qualities results in a breach of contract, an assertion that must be nuanced by certain features common to the aedilitian remedies applicable to latent defects (limitation, for example), an unsatisfactory solution that has prompted the creation and expansion of the case law emanated doctrine of *aliud pro alio*.

B. Contractual Terms in English Law: Guarantees

The starting point in English law as regards contractual terms differs from the assumption made by traditional continental law. In common law, the debtor is under no principal obligation to comply with duties of conduct—although he may be. Instead, he guarantees a result. Atiyah asserts that a term of the contract: 'may be either (i) a statement about a state of facts, or (ii) a promise that something (not necessarily in the control of the promisor) will or will not happen in the future, or (iii) a conditional clause. Clauses of the first two kinds are often called promises'.[57] Atiyah holds the view that the word 'undertaking' better conveys the concept than 'promise',[58] to which Zweigert and Kötz seem to agree, as, according to them, in common law every contract is treated as containing a guarantee.[59]

As a result, the guarantee is present in all of the facets of the promise. If it comprises commitment to acting or refraining from doing (obligation, in continental terminology), the debtor guarantees satisfaction of the interest of the creditor in all cases, without the option of claiming an impossibility of performance. This satisfaction generally takes place, if performance itself is not possible, by payment of damages. In English law, specific performance is a rather exceptional remedy, the result of the moderation of equity. As a consequence, damages resulting from the guarantee take the form of the natural satisfaction of the contractually binding expectations.

As regards the second class of promise, a contractual undertaking as to a factual circumstance, Atiyah emphasises that lawyers, unlike philosophers, have never had any difficulty in 'holding that a person can promise (or undertake) a state of

[57] PS Atiyah, *An Introduction to the Law of Contract*, 6th edn (Oxford University Press, 1995) 169.
[58] ibid.
[59] K Zweigert and H Kötz, *An Introduction to Comparative Law* (Clarendon Press, 1998) 503.

facts, as distinguished from promising to do something in the future'[60] (an obligation in the continental sense). The indisputable function of the contract in common law as an instrument for the allocation of risks between the parties[61] allows a term as to a factual situation to be valid, with one of the parties guaranteeing its correctness.[62]

What the above reveals is that, in English law, initial impossibility would be worthy only of (lesser) consideration as a 'mistake', a vice in consent, the consequence of which, in that legal system, is that the contract would be void.[63] Whether the performance guaranteed is possible, or the promised factual situation corresponds to the reality are, per se, irrelevant as to the validity of the contract. This is, however, affected if the agreement is undermined by a mistake.[64] I reiterate, though, that outside this rather exceptional circumstance, a guarantee of impossible conduct or as regards a non-existent factual state is valid. To the extent that, in order to avoid the severe consequences of mistake, the courts grant significant pre-eminence to the contract and, by means of interpretation, they recurrently allocate the risks of mistake to one of the parties, thereby favouring the validity of the agreement.[65]

What is of interest for the evolution of the civil law is that in English law, not only can the parties agree a guarantee as to a performance that is *ab initio* impossible, or regarding a factual situation that may or may not exist, but on occasion this guarantee is the result of default rules and even mandatory law. This is the case of certain implicit legal guarantees known as 'implied terms in law'. The quintessential example of the latter, regarding the qualities of things, is the Sale of Goods Act 1979 (SGA 1979), which to a great extent covers rules included in the previous Sale of Goods Act 1893.

Section 14(2) SGA 1979[66] incorporates within the content of the contract, as an implied term, the guarantee that the goods sold would be of satisfactory quality, in the case of a professional seller, it being irrelevant whether the object transferred

[60] Atiyah (n 57) 169–70.

[61] J Beatson, *Anson's Law of Contract* (Oxford University Press, 1998) 3.

[62] This outcome, that now appears natural, has not always been contractual. D Ibbetson, *A Historical Introduction to the Law of Obligations* (Oxford University Press, 2006) 223, relates that until the mid-eighteenth century, the breach of a warranty led to an action in tort.

[63] The conditions that an action for mistake should meet in English law are considerably stricter than its continental counterparts. However, various groups of cases that would entail an error in the civil law (based on statements, not a lack of disclosure) could be treated under misrepresentation in English law. See GH Treitel and E Peel, *The Law of Contract*, 13th edn (Sweet & Maxwell, 2011) paras 8-001–8-020, paras 8-042–8-043.

[64] ibid, para 8-002; *Couturier v Hastie* (1856) 5 HLC 673. This is also how s 6 Sale of Goods Act 1979 (SGA 1979) is to be interpreted, according to Treitel and Peel (n 63) para 8-009.

[65] See the decision of the High Court of Australia in *McRae v Commonwealth Disposals Commission* (1951) 84 CLR 377, and the qualifications in the English case *Great Peace Shipping Ltd v Tsavliris Salvage (International) Ltd (The Great Peace)* [2002] EWCA Civ 1407.

[66] The fitness for purpose of the subject matter of the contract is one of the most relevant issues for the buyer. According to PS Atiyah et al, *The Sale of Goods* (Longman, 2001) 156, s 14(2) SGA 1979 is the 'very heart of the law of sale'.

does or does not correspond to the branch of commerce in which the vendor typically engages.[67] The undertaking on the seller arises in the more severe form of a 'condition' (as per section 14(6) SGA 1979), which allows the buyer not only to claim for damages in the event of a breach resulting from the unfitness of the object, but also grants termination of the contract.

The quality of the goods includes, through the requirements of this implied condition, and in the case in question: fitness for all the purposes for which goods of the kind in question are commonly supplied; appearance and finish; freedom from minor defects; safety; and the durability of the goods (section 14(2B) SGA 1979). For its part, section 14(3) SGA 1979 imposes an implied term that a professional seller guarantees the fitness of the goods for a particular purpose (other than that for which they are commonly supplied), whether expressly or implicitly indicated by the buyer. This thus covers the guarantee of objective and subjective fitness of the goods acquired. The subject matter of the contract is defined in accordance with its ideal existence, it being irrelevant for the validity of the contract whether the thing possesses the promised qualities *ab initio*. The contract is valid, and the vendor is bound by it, even if the real object lacks said qualities.

The guarantee included in section 14 SGA is a default rule, with the peculiarity that the parties may disregard this only if the term restricting or eliminating its effects is reasonable, as per section 6(3) Unfair Contract Terms Act 1977 (UCTA 1977). However, if the contract is concluded between a professional and a consumer, the implied term is mandatory. This was established in section 6(2) UCTA 1977, in connection with section 14 SGA 1979 and now results from section 31 Consumer Rights Act 2015 (CRA 2015), as regards section 9 of the same Act.

It should be clarified that implied guarantees are not confined to the circumstances mentioned in the SGA 1979 or the CRA 2015. The Supply of Goods and Services Act 1982 (section 4) and the Supply of Goods (Implied Terms) Act 1973 (section 10) demand that the goods be fit for purpose, including a qualitative standard similar to that of the SGA 1979, in any contract transferring or agreeing on the transfer of property of goods or hire-purchase agreements. Similarly, case law has imposed the aforementioned 'implied terms in law' in different contracts, such as certain property leases.[68]

From the above, one first deduces the natural and solid nature of guarantees in English law. Secondly, and more significantly, it is clear that not only are the parties

[67] Under the Sale of Goods Act 1893 it was argued whether the implied term bounded non-professional sellers. Lord Wilberforce in *Ashington Piggeries Ltd v Christopher Hill Ltd* [1972] AC 441, clarified that it did not. The Supply of Goods (Implied Terms) Act 1973 reformed the old law in the sense of the current s 14(2) SGA. See M Bridge, *The Sale of Goods* (Oxford University Press, 2009) para 7.34 pp 418–19. In respect of habitual dealing in the type of goods sold, in *Stevenson & another v Rogers* [1999] 1 All ER 613 it was held not to be necessary for a sale to be considered undertaken in the course of business. See Atiyah et al (n 66) 160.

[68] *Liverpool City Council v Irwin* [1977] AC 239.

entitled to agree on a guarantee that would assign to one of them the risks derived from the non-existence of the goods or of certain qualities in them, but that the legal system itself allocates this risk, in certain circumstances.

III. The Guarantee as the Backdrop for the Modernisation of the Civil Law

A. Regarding the Acceptance of Guarantees in Civil Law

The so-called process of 'modernisation' of the law of contracts, or of obligations and contracts, seeking to adapt nineteenth-century rules and principles to the current era, is having a particularly noticeable effect on the countries of continental Europe. It is not meant by this that English law remains unchanged, quite the contrary, but rather that because of its particular system of sources, the evolution of the legal system occurs more gradually than in civil law countries. In the latter, the rigidity of the civil codes has prompted a reflection as to their reform, with the aim of imbuing with legal certainty modern contractual reality, which on many occasions is not properly catered for by the existing framework of these codes. As is known, this reform has already taken place in Germany, the Netherlands, and recently in France.[69] Reform proposals have been drawn up in other Western European countries, but for the moment they lack binding effect.[70] The failure to update the civil codes has, in many contexts, been redressed through case law, a task that is not always a simple one in legal systems in which judges do not develop regulatory policy.

Modernisation impacts on various aspects of the legal framework governing contracts, of which for the purposes of this study we are concerned solely with the contractual terms. In this regard, the law has evolved considerably, and this has had significant consequences,[71] since the terms determine the rules binding the parties to a contract. However, this aspect has received considerably less attention from scholars than other aspects of the general theory of contract law, such as breach.

[69] In Germany, the modernisation process resulted in the reform of the BGB, which was ordered by the *Gesetz zur Modernisierung des Schuldrechts*, 26 November 2001, Bundesgesetzblatt [2001] I, 3138. In the Netherlands, a new Civil Code was enacted in 1992. In France, as in Germany, modernisation was conducted through a reform of the Civil Code, established by the Ordonnance nº 2016-131 du 10 février 2016 portant réforme du droit des contrats, du régime général et de la preuve des obligations, JORF nº 35 du 11 février 2016. Countries in Eastern Europe have enacted new Codes as a result of the fall of communism, such as Estonia (1992), Latvia (1997), Lithuania (2000), Slovenia (2001), Croatia (2005 and 2008), Romania (2011), Czech Republic (2014) and Hungary (2014).

[70] In Spain, the most recent initiative is the 'Propuesta de Anteproyecto de ley de Modernización del Derecho de obligaciones y contratos', *Boletín del Ministerio de Justicia*, año XLIII, enero 2009.

[71] See F de Elizalde, *El contenido del contrato* (Thomson Reuters Aranzadi, 2015).

This results, perhaps, from the fact that modernisation of terms has occurred in specific contracts, or when the evolution has been driven by case law, without a clear identification with the terms of a contract, as a more general concept.

The modernisation of contract law, as regards terms, is dictated largely by two far-reaching changes concerning the *status quo ante*: (i) the enhancement of non-voluntary sources of contractual terms, above all good faith (in civil law), the standards derived from case law (in common law), and in both legal traditions, mandatory and non-mandatory legislation; and (ii) a recognition of the guarantee as binding content, which means moving beyond the concept of the contract as a source only of duties of performance. The first of these changes (the renewal of non-voluntary sources) affects both English law and the civil law. The second (guarantee), meanwhile, is inherent to the latter, since as already indicated, it has been present in common law since ancient times.

Before setting out the main rules derived from the aforementioned transformations, it is important to emphasise the novelty that the recognition of the guarantee as a term constitutes for civil law. Its significance is such that, as we will see, the enhancement of non-voluntary sources of terms (the other fundamental change) results in recognition of the binding force of the guarantee. This is justified by the needs of modern contracts, within the context of which the legitimate expectations of the parties become increasingly binding. Commerce is more and more reluctant to accept contracts that do not cover such expectations, as may occur in a regime tied to the contract as a source of performance duties (give, do, refrain from doing). Among other (numerous and diverse) reasons, the nineteenth-century definition of the contract explains the abundant usage, in the legal practice of continental law, of Anglo-Saxon contractual models that serve to alleviate this specific lack (through the typical representations and warranties clauses),[72] but which ultimately give rise to other problems by incorporating what are in truth 'alien' contracts, in the expression of De Nova,[73] in continental legal systems.

[72] In common law, contractual warranties are designed to alter the 'caveat emptor' rule that applies in the absence of a legal guarantee (eg the implied terms in law enshrined in the SGA 1979). The representations allow for pre-contractual remedies and its inclusion in contracts responds to historical reasons. Before the Misrepresentation Act 1967, the law did not allow the claimant to choose between an action for rescission based on a misrepresentation and an action for breach of contract if the representation had been included in the contract as a term. This rule was circumvented by agreement. The law changed with the mentioned Misrepresentation Act 1967 s 1.

[73] G De Nova, *Il contratto alieno* (Giappichelli, 2010) 47 ff. 'Alien' contracts are not innominate ones but rather typical contracts (eg sales) with a foreign structure and regulation. As regards sales, it is further reasoned by G De Nova, *Il Sale Purchase Agreement: Un Contratto Commentato* (Giappichelli, 2016) 11, that 'l'interprete di uno SPA debe) decodificare il testo del contratto secondo le categorie giuridiche e linguistiche del diritto angloamericano, e riqualificare le sue norme secondo le categorie giuridiche del … diritto italiano'. The reception of foreign contractual models does not only affect the civil law. Those models, mainly of American and English origin, have also impacted on the practice of other common law systems, where they are also considered to be legal transplants. See A Afsharipour, 'Legal Transplants in the Law of the Deal: M&A Agreements in India' (2015) 469 *Legal Studies Research Paper Series, University of California, Davis, School of Law* 19, 26, ssrn.com/abstract=2686718.

There can be no denying the influence that common law has exerted on civil law countries in the acceptance of the guarantee as a term, and most particularly as regards its recognition as a default rule or, to a lesser extent, mandatory law. As it has been highlighted, it is an inherent feature of common law to accept contractual guarantees, with even those that apply to non-existent factual circumstances (such as qualities that the thing does not possess) being deemed valid. The acceptance of this rule in continental systems would seem to lie at the basis of modernisation.

While it is always difficult to calibrate the influence of the different factors in generating an outcome, it is commonly held that the United Nations Convention on Contracts for the International Sale of Goods (CISG) represents a solid cornerstone for the convergence of legal systems that, through the influence of common law, ultimately incorporate the guarantee (in this case, the conformity of the goods with the contract) in those countries of the civil law that have adopted the Convention. Within the European context, the Principles of European Contract Law (PECL), with their rejection of the initial impossibility of performance as grounds for invalidity (Article 4:102) and Directive 99/44/EC,[74] which incorporated the guarantee of conformity in consumer sales, consolidated this course.

It should come as no surprise, given the above, that the reform of Germany's BGB should have incorporated not only the principle of conformity (in sales and work contracts, as per §433 and following and §633 BGB) but should also have reformed §276 BGB, located in the general part governing the law of obligations, in order expressly to include liability derived from a guarantee.[75] The French reform (2016) is less clear. The new Article 1166 Civil Code takes into account the legitimate expectations of the parties in determining the qualities that may be demanded in performance, which could be interpreted as a guarantee. However, it also leaves unaltered the traditional aedilitian remedies (the peculiar system against latent defects), that on the contrary does not guarantee said qualities, even if case law has progressively eroded this through exceptions. In countries such as Spain and Italy, where parliament has not taken the initiative to reform, case law has likewise driven recognition of the guarantee, in addition to the aforementioned international and European legislation.

B. In Particular, as Regards the Guarantee of Conformity

The problem of partial (not absolute) initial impossibility of performance arises in traditional civil codes, as explained above,[76] when a contract obliges the giving

[74] Directive 1999/44/EC of the European Parliament and of the Council of 25 May 1999 on certain aspects of the sale of consumer goods and associated guarantees [1999] OJ L171/12.

[75] See R Zimmermann, *The New German Law of Obligations* (Oxford University Press, 2006) 50–51.

[76] See above section II.A.ii.

of a specific thing, the archetype being sales. Here, the seller is obliged to deliver the thing as it exists in reality, without being bound by the fitness of the object (comprising its qualities). Any latent defects that the thing might reveal provide entitlement only to the special aedilitian regime, which grants two remedies: rescission of the contract or reduction of price.

The evolution of continental law in this regard has been seen in the recognition of a guarantee by means of which the vendor is bound to deliver a thing with the fitness that the purchaser may reasonably expect. As a result, modern sales no longer consider the object as it exists in reality, but in accordance with its design by the contract, supplemented by legal criteria. This thus overcomes the problems of initial impossibility of performance and the lack of qualities in the thing entails, in general, a breach of contract.

The transformation of the legal systems has occurred, at the European and international level, by means of the so-called principle or guarantee of conformity. Furthermore, case law of various European countries has admitted the guarantee of fitness of the object through the doctrine of *aliud pro alio* (Spain, Italy), or others of similar effect, such as in France the *défaut de délivrance conforme*.[77]

The 'principle of conformity'[78] refers to a legal requirement that obliges the seller of an object to ensure that it conforms to the contract. By application of this principle, the delivery of an object which differs from that agreed upon by the parties,[79] or is unfit for purpose as defined by legal criteria (implied terms), represents a breach of said contract.[80] This concept is embodied in the CISG, which, with regard to the binding qualities or characteristics of goods,[81] seeks to bridge the differences between the civil and common law traditions.[82]

The demand for conformity extends, in the European Union, to internal sales, but only of consumer goods, by means of Directive 1999/44/EC.[83] In

[77] See F de Elizalde, 'Should the implied term concerning quality be generalized? Present and future of the principle of conformity in Europe' (2017) 25 *European Review of Private Law* 71, 90–93. For further information see: in France, G Venandet et al, 'Art 1604' in G Venandet et al (eds), *Code Civil* (Dalloz, 2016) 2180–86; in Spain, Elizalde (n 71) ch 2; and in Italy, G Perlingieri, 'Art 1490' in G Perlingieri (ed), *Codice civile annotato con la dottrina e la giurisprudenza*, vol IV-1 (Edizioni Scientifiche Italiane, 2010) 1271–81.

[78] As called by Recitals (7) and (8) of Dir 1999/44/EC.

[79] San Julián Puig (n 7) 89.

[80] N Fenoy Picón, *El Sistema de Protección del Comprador* (Colegio de Registradores de la Propiedad y Mercantiles de España, 2006) 23: 'the seller breaches the contract if the item he delivers (the real object) does not conform with the subject matter designed by the contract (the ideal object). This breach is called lack of conformity or non-conformity of the delivered item'. Own translation.

[81] To this respect, CISG Art 35.1 establishes that: 'The seller must deliver goods which are of the quantity, quality and description required by the contract and which are contained or packaged in the manner required by the contract'.

[82] cp I Schwenzer and P Hachem, 'The CISG—Successes and Pitfalls' (2009) 57 *American Journal of Comparative Law* 457, 462. Nevertheless, to this respect, the solution is closer to the common law. See, for example, SGA 1979 s 14. See M Bridge, 'The UK Sale of Goods Act, the CISG and the UNIDROIT Principles' in P Šarčević and P Volken (eds), *The International Sale of Goods Revisited* (Kluwer, 2001) 147–49, who draws a comparison between CISG Art 35 and SGA 1979 s 14.

[83] Directive 1999/44/EC Art 2.1.

some jurisdictions, such as in Italy and Portugal, the guarantee of conformity applies to consumer leases,[84] and German law governs not only sales (whether consumer goods or not, and whether movable or immovable), but also work (construction, etc) contracts.[85] The principle of conformity has been enshrined in the DCFR,[86] recognised in the CESL Regulation Proposal and also in the Proposal for a Directive on certain aspects for the online and other distance sales of goods (OSD proposal).

The principle of conformity entails a different manner (in comparison with the traditions of civil law) of relating the qualities of the object to the terms, with the former acquiring binding force and being guaranteed. This is, then, a different regime from that which results from the aedilitian remedies, which assumes a lack of any binding obligation on the debtor as regards the qualities of the object. The principle of conformity and aedilitian remedies therefore reflect incompatible regulatory solutions.[87]

The extent of the qualities that may be demanded in the object (conformity) is firstly dictated by agreement, and in default thereof, by legal criteria which supplement the terms, establishing that the object must be fit for normal use or for a particular purpose known by the seller. The fitness for purpose of the subject matter of the contract becomes a term, reflecting a notable evolution as regards traditional civil law.

IV. The Sources of Terms; The Binding Effects of Pre-contractual Information

There is also a second, significant cause behind the evolution of terms: the binding nature of pre-contractual information (*rectius: in contrahendo*), in other words, what the parties convey or fail to disclose (regarding the latter, if they were obliged to do so) before the contract is concluded. If certain requirements to be mentioned *ut infra* are fulfilled, this information is guaranteed in the contract, becoming a term thereof, a novel aspect that affects both English law and the countries of the civil law tradition.

The engine of change is information itself. It is a commonplace that we live in a so-called 'Information Society', in which the relevance of information is increasingly crucial to contracts. This is because of the complexity of products and services, as well as being due to the information asymmetries that arise from this.

[84] In Italy, see Art 128.1 of the Consumer Code 2005 and in Portugal, see Art 1º-A.2. Decree-Law 67/2003 (as revised by Decree-Law 84/2008).

[85] BGB paras 434, 633.

[86] Arts IV.A.- 2:301 ff (sales); IV.B.- 3:102 ff (lease of goods); IV.C.- 3:104 ff (construction); IV.C.- 5:106 (storage) and IV.C.- 6:104 (design).

[87] Fenoy Picón (n 80) 41–42; Morales Moreno (n 2) 294.

The debate, in European contract law, seems to have been focused on whether the parties (or rather, one of them) should disclose information, a duty that is increasingly demanded by European consumer legislation[88] and also, beyond B2C relations, such as the MiFID Directives.[89] Mandated disclosure has been subject to serious criticism as regards its efficacy in solving the asymmetries generated by information.[90] Among other arguments, critics question the use of pre-contractual duties of information as the recipients seem not to read it. Additionally, from an English law perspective, the lack of a general principle of good faith poses a real problem as to the generalisation of duties to disclose information beyond contracts *uberrima fidei*, and thus constitutes an obstacle to a European common core.

However, the assessment of information could differ if we analyse it from another perspective. This involves moving away from the most extensive treatment of pre-contractual information, which considers it to be related to intention. In effect, the underlying grounds of pre-contractual duties of information, and also the criticism thereof, lies in the idea that they are designed to improve the quality of agreement.

This is the same position that traditional contract law assumed in respect of the other kind of information: not that which should be disclosed, but the information that is effectively disclosed by the parties. I refer here to statements, that may either be public (such as advertising) or private, including in the latter case statements made when negotiating a contract such as, for example, those representing the qualities of an object or the financial situation of a company the shares of which are being bought.

In the nineteenth-century concept of the contract (and we include here both the common law and the civil law traditions), fundamentally based on the principle of free will, agreement is the prevalent source of terms. Default rules do exist, to an extent, but their function is confined to supplementing possible gaps in the contract.[91]

Within this conceptual framework, it may be understood that the only binding undertaking that the parties may assume would be the result of their agreement.

[88] Among many others, UCPD 2005/29/EC.

[89] Directive 2004/39/EC of the European Parliament and of the Council of 21 April 2004 on markets in financial instruments amending Council Directives 85/611/EEC and 93/6/EEC and Directive 2000/12/EC of the European Parliament and of the Council and repealing Council Directive 93/22/EEC (MiFID I) [2004] OJ L145/1; Directive 2014/65/EU of the European Parliament and of the Council of 15 May 2014 on markets in financial instruments and amending Directive 2002/92/EC and Directive 2011/61/EU (MiFID II) [2014] OJ L173/349.

[90] See O Ben-Shahar and C Schneider, *The Failure of Mandated Disclosure* (2010) Olin Working Papers, University of Chicago Law & Economics: papers.ssrn.com/sol3/papers.cfm?abstract_id=1567284; O Ben-Shahar and C Schneider, *More Than You Wanted to Know. The Failure of Mandated Disclosure* (Princeton University Press, 2016).

[91] F de Castro y Bravo, 'Notas Sobre las Limitaciones Intrínsecas de la Autonomía de la Voluntad' (1982) *Anuario de Derecho Civil* 1060.

As a consequence, information not included within the contract as an express term would not be binding. This applies whether agreement is determined in accordance with subjective or objective criteria.[92] Information that is incorrect or is omitted may give rise to a vice of consent resulting in rescission of the contract, but not a binding term as regards the factual situation on which the aggrieved party relied.

The move beyond this approach centred on agreement is dictated by the re-emergence of the non-voluntary sources of the contract, including not only default rules *in se*, but also conduct *in contrahendo* by the parties in relationship with the former (in consumer contracts, the relationship arises with mandatory law). The growing protection of the legitimate expectations of the parties has extended the contractual guarantee to include pre-contractual information that generates reliance.[93]

The major proposals for a European contract law, namely, the PECL and the DCFR, clearly move away from the aforementioned standpoint (intention) when it comes to pre-contractual information, by proposing that that information may be binding when the protection of reliance so requires. In this respect, Article 6:101(1) PECL (Statements giving rise to contractual obligations) establishes:

> A statement made by one party before or when the contract is concluded is to be treated as giving rise to a contractual obligation if that is how the other party reasonably understood it in the circumstances, taking into account:
>
> (a) the apparent importance of the statement to the other party;
> (b) whether the party was making the statement in the course of business; and
> (c) the relative expertise of the parties.

Article II 9:102(1) DCFR uses an almost verbatim wording. Directive 99/44/EC enshrines a similar rule, although limited to public statements and drafted in a different way that makes statements binding, as a rule, unless there is a lack of actual and reasonable reliance (Article 2.4). This rule was incorporated and generalised to all sales in German law (§ 434.1 BGB). In other legal systems, such as in Spain, a similar outcome (beyond consumer law) has been brought about by the courts, which attribute binding effects to statements, based on good faith.[94] In France, cases with coinciding factual backgrounds have been resolved on the basis of '*non-conformité*', that assumes a breach of term.[95]

[92] AM Morales Moreno, 'Información Publicitaria y Protección del Consumidor (Reflexiones Sobre el Art 8º de la LGCU)' in AM Morales Moreno, *La Modernización del Derecho de Obligaciones* (Thomson Civitas, 2006) 233.

[93] For a development of this, see Elizalde (n 77) chs 6–9.

[94] See among others, SSTS (1ª) 21 July 1993 (RJ 1993, 6176); 15 June 2000 (RJ 2000, 4418); 23 May 2003 (RJ 2003, 5215); 29 September 2004 (RJ 2004, 5688).

[95] See Venandet et al (n 77) 2180–86.

In the aforementioned cases, it is quite clear that the pre-contractual information becomes binding by force of law, and not because of agreement. In the case of Directive 99/44/EC and German or Spanish law, this is plain. And it is also noticeable that reliance has a say, as not all pre-contractual information is binding.[96]

In the case of the proposals, references to: (i) the importance of the information given to the other party, (ii) the issue of whether the party was making the statement in the course of business, or (iii) the relative expertise of the parties, provide the clue as to a non-voluntary source of terms, especially, in connection with the subjective test of interpretation adopted by the proposals as a primary criterion (Article 5:101(1) PECL and Article II. 8:101(1) DCFR). The law does not consider the latter when binding the party as regards a statement.

In English law, however (notwithstanding the changes brought about by European legislation), the binding effects of pre-contractual information has grown through the interpretation of the contract, formally based on the agreement of the parties. Nonetheless, in various works Professor Atiyah raises his voice against the literal meaning of the words employed by the English courts (which base the incorporation of pre-contractual information to the contract on agreement), holding that the expression 'intention of the parties' does not, in this context, mean what it says.[97]

Atiyah argues that judges rarely examine the intention of the parties in order to rule on the cases of this type that are brought before them. What is found in case law is constant recourse to objective elements (eg the fact that the party making the declaration was a professional seller of goods, or as the owner of the land had a greater opportunity to discover the accuracy of the information conveyed), in order to establish, on the basis thereof, whether one of the parties should be bound by his statements.[98] This is consistent with the objective criterion of contractual interpretation that presides in English law. The interpretation of the contract, taking into consideration not just its literal meaning, but also the criterion of a reasonable person, allows for the protection of reliance placed on pre-contractual statements, by making them binding.

[96] However, the Package Travel Directive finds a term from pre-contractual information more readily. See Art 3, Council Directive (EC) 90/314 of 13 June 1990 on package travel, package holidays and package tours [1990] OJ 158/59. The norm that will replace it contains a similar rule. See Art 6, Directive (EU) 2015/2302 of the European Parliament and Council of 25 November 2015 on package travel and linked travel arrangements, amending Regulation (EC) No 2006/2004 and Directive 2011/83/EU of the European Parliament and of the Council and repealing Council Directive 90/314/EEC, [2015] OJ L326/1.

[97] I am referring to the following works: Atiyah (n 57) 180–81; PS Atiyah, 'Misrepresentation, Warranty and Estoppel' in PS Atiyah (ed), *Essays on Contract* (Clarendon Paperbacks, 1996) 277–88, 300–02; PS Atiyah, 'The Binding Nature of Contractual Obligations. The Move From Agreement to Reliance in English Law and the Exclusion of Liability Relating to Defective Goods', in D Harris and D Tallon (eds), *Contract Law Today. Anglo-French Comparisons* (Clarendon Press, 1989) 30–33; PS Atiyah, *The Rise and Fall of the Freedom of Contract* (Clarendon Press, 1979) 772.

[98] Atiyah (n 57) 180–81.

English legal theory accepts such objective criteria, although they are typically presented as parameters to determine agreement, summarised by means of two elements: (i) the importance of the declaration for the recipient, and (ii) the position of the parties as regards the information, concerning the ease with which they can ascertain its accuracy.[99] These criteria are present, as said, in the aforementioned Articles 6:101 (1) PECL and II 9:102(1) DCFR.

If we bring in the proviso raised by Professor Atiyah and put it in relation with the objective criterion employed by English law in interpreting agreement (the standard of a reasonable person),[100] the deduction is that the binding effect of statements (when this occurs) is, in truth, established on the basis of objective parameters that are not connected with common intention, in the subjective sense.

Agreement would seem to be a convenient label employed in accordance with the case to attach liability to the issuer of the declaration or otherwise, which in reality depends on a legal allocation of risk (derived from the courts which, in common law, are involved in regulatory policy or, as applicable, legislation).[101] And this legal rule, which justifies the binding nature of pre-contractual information, would serve to guarantee the protection of the reasonable reliance of the recipient of the information,[102] an aspect mentioned by Lord Nourse in *Harlingdon and Leinster v Christopher Hull.*[103]

The binding nature of pre-contractual information, through the objective interpretation of the contract, is a formula to which other countries of the civil law tradition have had recourse, as in the case of Germany. German law adopts a two-fold approach. The more recent, as already mentioned, serving directly to regulate the incorporation of information within the terms, as occurs with regard to public statements in a contract of sale (§434.1 BGB). In parallel, and with a longer tradition, case law acknowledges that information *in contrahendo* may be contractually binding, if this would be the result of an objective or good faith interpretation of the contract, as a consequence of §157 BGB.

As a result, German courts have reached similar conclusions to those of English law in comparable cases, placing value on the importance of information and the

[99] See Treitel and Peel (n 63) para 9-046; J Cartwright, *Misrepresentation, Mistake and Non-Disclosure* (Sweet & Maxwell, 2007) paras 8.08–8.11; DK Allen, *Misrepresentation* (Sweet & Maxwell, 1988) 100–05.

[100] Especially as from the case *Investors Compensation Scheme v West Bromwich Builiding Society* [1997] UKHL 28.

[101] Atiyah (n 97) 'Misrepresentation' 276. A historical approach to this technique may be found in Ibbetson (n 62) 224. In respect of the use of interpretation as an instrument for policy change, see C Mitchell, 'Interpreting Commercial Contracts: The Policing Role of Context in English Law' in L DiMatteo and M Hogg (eds), *Comparative Contract Law. British and American Perspectives* (Oxford University Press, 2016) 157–69.

[102] Atiyah (n 97) *The Rise and Fall* 771–78; Atiyah (n 97) 'Misrepresentation' 279, 287.

[103] *Harlingdon and Leinster Enterprises Ltd v Christopher Hull Fine Art Ltd* [1989] EWCA Civ 4. 'The description must have a sufficient influence in the sale to become an essential term of the contract and the correlative of influence is reliance … I would say that there cannot be a contract for the sale of goods by description where it is not within the *reasonable* contemplation of the parties that the buyer is relying on the description'.

position of the parties regarding the information, in making pre-contractual statements binding if, according to these parameters, the reliance of the recipient is deemed worthy of protection.[104] And, in Germany, more strikingly than in English law, the source of the undertaking is good faith (a legal standard), rather than the common intention of the parties, the determination of which is governed by another specific legal rule (§133 BGB).

Overall, it would seem that, in respect of sources of terms, the existing soft and hard European contract law rules serve to clarify the real grounds for the binding effects of information. These grounds show the augmentation of reliance-based liabilities, beyond the scope of intention.

Whether one considers that the source is directly the law itself, or instead an objective interpretation of the contract, a common pattern may be perceived across Europe: that pre-contractual information may become a term of the contract when the recipient of the information has placed an actual and reasonable reliance on it. In the words of the proposals and those of English law, this is expressed as taking into account: (i) the importance of the information and (ii) the position of the parties in respect of it.

However, not all information that creates a reasonable reliance will become binding. In fact, many pre-contractual statements that induce a party to enter into a contract are not. An additional requirement is needed, such as every time that a risk is allocated under a contract. A recognised source of terms—either voluntary or non-voluntary—should order that allocation. I refer, in this case, to either legislation (such as Directive 99/44/EC, the BGB, section 13 SGA, etc), good faith in civil law as a source of norms, or, in common law, case law, as judges have a say in the creation of legal rules. Without these, an allocation of risk derived from a pre-contractual information may not be established.

V. Conclusions

The process of harmonisation of European contract law should not be assessed exclusively on the basis of hard law. This perspective neglects the significant effects of soft law in the transformation of national legal systems, which has frequently occurred by both the adoption of a new set of rules modelled on the European proposals, and by the influence of the latter in the reasoning of judicial decisions. In the same vein, the aforementioned proposals have helped to express, in clear rules, the modern boundaries of contractual terms. In certain instances, they have proved to be particularly useful for stakeholders in understanding national case law, to the benefit of legal certainty.

[104] See H Unberath, 'Contents and Effects' in S Leible and M Lehmann (eds), *European Contract Law and German Law* (Wolters Kluwer, 2014) 302.

However, an accurate assessment of harmonisation needs to be three-fold, including not only European hard and soft law, but also the analysis of the different national legal solutions that result from common factual problems. From this functional standpoint, it is also noticeable that civil law and the common law have significantly bridged the gap, at least in respect of the subject matter of this work: contractual terms.

Both legal traditions seem to be moving rapidly (within the always slow pace of law) towards a different underlying notion of contractual justice. Recalling a graphic expression from Hamilton, mutatis mutandis, the nineteenth-century absolute monarchy of intention is giving place to a parliamentary structure in which the legitimate expectations of the parties are increasingly being guaranteed.[105] Modern rules on contract terms reflect this notion, and the whole process of harmonisation should be credited for its attachment to reality.

105 WH Hamilton, 'The Ancient Maxim Caveat Emptor' (1931) 40 *Yale Law Journal* 1133, 1187.

Part IV

Uniform Rules as a Model for Non-EU Countries

12

European Contract Law and Asian Contract Law

MATEJA DUROVIC

I. Introduction

European contract law certainly represents the most advanced model of regional harmonisation of contract law.[1] As such, it has had a significant impact on the development of contract laws in a number of countries outside the European Union.[2] This is particularly true in the area of consumer contract law, as these rules make up a major part of the body of European contract law.[3] Besides the influence on the content of the national contract laws of countries throughout the world, the development of European contract law has been widely used as an inspiration and a model for the regional harmonisation of contract laws. This has also been the case with Asian contract law. The harmonisation of European contract law has been a project characterised by great successes, but also by a number of failures. For that reason, the examination of the experience gained in the case of European contract law may be of great benefit for any other regional initiative for the harmonisation of contract law. Accordingly, this chapter focuses on the examination of what the Asian example of the harmonisation of contract law may learn from the European model.

This chapter does not cover all of the countries and territories of the Asian continent, but only the 16 contract law jurisdictions of Eastern and South-Eastern Asia. Ten countries form the Association of the Southeast Asian Nations (ASEAN): Vietnam, Cambodia, Thailand, Brunei, Malaysia, Indonesia, Singapore, Laos, Myanmar and the Philippines; while China, Taiwan, Macau SAR, Hong Kong SAR, South Korea and Japan constitute the six contract law regimes of Eastern Asia.

[1] L Miller, *The Emergence of EU Contract Law: Exploring Europeanization* (Oxford University Press, 2011).

[2] M Heidemann, *Methodology of Uniform Contract Law* (Springer, 2010) 36–37.

[3] J Stuyck and M Durovic, 'External dimension of EU Consumer Law' in M Cremona and H Micklitz (eds), *External dimension of EU Private Law* (Oxford University Press, 2015) 247.

These 16 jurisdictions have been chosen as among them there currently exists an initiative to harmonise contract laws. This initiative has also been inspired by European contract law. As this is still only an initiative at an early stage of development, this chapter will use the process of the harmonisation of European contract law in order to demonstrate what Asian contract law can learn from the European model. The European case clearly demonstrates that harmonisation is not an easy task, but rather a difficult exercise, with diverse challenges and obstacles to be addressed and resolved. For that reason, it may be beneficial for Asian contract law to learn from the positive and negative experiences gained through the establishment of European contract law.

II. The Asian Contract Law Initiative

Eastern and South-Eastern Asia is a part of the world with an increasing number of commercial and consumer transactions among different jurisdictions.[4] The development of cross-border commercial activities has also been followed by a closer cooperation of contract law scholars interested in providing a regulatory response to the development of cross-border trade. One of the products of such cooperation between legal scholars has been the launch of an initiative for the harmonisation of contract law in the region. Thus far, this initiative has been a purely academic project without the organised political support of the jurisdictions involved. Some interstate support for the establishment of a common supranational contract law exists only in the case of the 10 countries of the ASEAN, but does not involve the remaining six jurisdictions of Eastern Asia.

The main purpose of the initiatives among the Asian contract law scholars has been to develop the Principles of Asian Contract Law (PACL). As may be observed at the outset from their name, the development of the PACL has been inspired by the Principles of European Contract Law (PECL). The PACL are the private, academic initiative of a number of contract law scholars coming from South-Eastern and Eastern Asian jurisdictions. It has been envisaged as providing a set of supranational rules which are designed in such a manner as to secure a convenient and functional application by the Asian parties and courts.[5] The development of the PACL project commenced in 2009.[6] As a first result, in 2010, the Draft Articles of the PACL dealing with the non-performance of a contract have been published.[7]

[4] B Zeller, 'Facilitating Regional Economic Integration: ASEAN, ATIGA and the CISG' in I Schwenzer and L Spagnolo (eds), *Towards Uniformity: the 2nd annual MAA Schlechtriem CISG conference* (Eleven International Publishing, 2011) 255–67.

[5] YJ Lee et al, *A Study on Draft Articles Principles of Asian Contract Law Performance and Non-Performance, Research Institute for Asia Private Law* (Research Institute for Asia Private Law, 2016) 3.

[6] S Han, 'Principles of Asian Contract Law: An Endeavour or Regional Harmonisation of Contract Law in East Asia' (2013) 58 *Villanova Law Review* 4, 589, 590.

[7] Lee et al (n 5).

The PACL is intended to reflect the particularities of national Asian contract laws, but in such a manner as to represent a legal response to globalisation through the establishment of rules which would fit into global laws and transactional practices. In that sense, the PACL drafters have identified four principal goals of the PACL. The first is to serve as a model law for the reform of the national contract laws of Eastern and South-Eastern Asian jurisdictions. The second aim is to provide help to the national courts and arbitrations in cases where they need to make a decision regarding the applicable law to cross border commercial transactions. The third purpose is to be a 'soft law' and as such to be used as the applicable law to the contractual transactions by the parties themselves. The fourth goal of the PACL is to be a widely developed academic project which would touch upon and compare similarities and differences which exist among contract laws of the jurisdictions of Eastern and South-Eastern Asia.[8]

Besides the PACL, there are also other initiatives in the region related to the harmonisation of contract law. These primarily include diverse forums for the exchange of contract law experiences and examination of the existing similarities and differences. It was for exactly that purpose that in 2006 the Asian Law Institute (ASLI) was established in Singapore. The principal purpose of the ASLI is to foster Asian legal scholarship and to facilitate greater interaction amongst legal scholars in Asia and those working on Asian law-related issues. In the same year (2006), another important institution, the Research Institute for Asian Private Law, was established. The Research Institute has focused its research on Asian private law and the common values among different jurisdictions of the Asian countries.

The latest among the academic projects is the 'Studies in the contract laws of Asia'. This project has gathered leading contract law scholars from the jurisdictions of Eastern and South-Eastern Asia. This initiative is less ambitious. It is hoped to contribute to a better understanding of the contract law in the region through the provision of a complete study of contract law in the region. The results of the study are to be presented in six volumes, eventually identifying similarities and differences among the national contract laws. It is the first study ever of that kind in the English language, and is to be published by Oxford University Press, underlining its significance. The comparison is performed primarily through the application of a functional method and comparing diverse national contract law notions of the same or similar purpose.[9]

Each of the six volumes deals with one of the six specific contract law topics: remedies, formation of contract, contract contents, invalidity of contracts, contract ending, and public policy and illegality. The first, on remedies, was published in early 2016; the second is currently being prepared for publication, and the others are intended to be issued in the future.[10] Two major purposes of

[8] ibid 1–2.

[9] K Zweigert and H Kötz, *An Introduction to Comparative Law*, T Weir tr, 3rd edn (Oxford University Press, 1998) 33–34.

[10] M Chen-Wishart, A Loke and B Ong (eds), *Studies in the Contract Laws of Asia, Remedies for Breach of Contract* (Oxford University Press, 2016).

this important project have clearly been identified. The first is to contribute to the dialogue among the contract laws of different jurisdictions in Asia; the second purpose is to enable the interaction with the contract laws of the Western hemisphere.[11] The results of this study will represent compelling material for any future discussion on the harmonisation of contract law in Eastern and South-Eastern Asia.

III. The Challenges of the Harmonisation Process

Ideas about the establishment of supranational contract laws are primarily the legacy of the twentieth century. The initiatives for the harmonisation of contract laws among diverse jurisdictions followed the development and explosion of global production and trade, as well as the increase of cross-border commercial and consumer transactions. In that setting, the presence of different contract law regimes among diverse jurisdictions has also been seen as an obstacle to the development of cross-border trade and the fostering of economic activities. The regulatory answer to this obstacle was to diminish these differences, through the harmonisation of national contract laws.[12] This view has been used as the most important argument in promoting the harmonisation of contract laws.

Namely, what businesses and consumers look for while performing cross-border commercial transactions is legal certainty, to know which rules will apply, and the content of these rules. The harmonisation of contract law contributes to legal certainty, as relevant market players are more familiar with the applicable laws and rules they need to follow, so they more readily perform cross-border transactions, as has been claimed, which increases mutual trust among market participants.[13] The harmonisation also leads to the reduction of transaction costs in cross-border trade as the same contract rules may apply to a number of contracting parties from different jurisdictions, which addresses the problem of compliance. The harmonised contract law instrument always needs to respond adequately to the development of technology, society and any other kinds of changes and all of the contemporary challenges.

Besides addressing the needs of cross-border commerce, the drafting and development of supranational contract law have also been seen as an inspiring and challenging academic activity for legal scholars throughout the world.[14]

[11] M Chen-Wishart, A Loke and B Ong, 'Introduction' in (n 10) 1.

[12] R Goode, 'Contract and Commercial Law: The Logic and Limits of Harmonisation' (2010) 7 *Electronic Journal of Comparative Law* 4.

[13] H Collins, 'Transaction costs and Subsidiarity in European Contract Law' in S Grundmann and J Stuyck (eds) *An Academic Green Paper on European Contract Law* (Kluwer Law International, 2002) 270.

[14] Draft Common Frame of Reference (DCFR).

Accordingly, a number of different initiatives on the harmonisation of contract law have occurred as a result of the activity of legal scholars.

The harmonisation of contract law may also represent a political project, supported by particular governments, for different reasons. For instance, in the European Union, the European Civil Code was advocated with the explanation that it would represent proof of a higher level of unity among the European nations. Similar ideas have been presented in the case of the 10 South-Eastern Asian countries, where the establishment of the ASEAN contract law was discussed as part of the harmonisation of trade laws.[15] The harmonisation of the contract laws of the 16 jurisdictions has also been identified as an instrument for the facilitation of cross-border trade.[16] The harmonisation of contract law as a result of the trade needs and as a consequence of the academic activity and political initiative are not separated from each other, but are typically closely connected.[17] However, as it now stands, the initiative for the harmonisation of contract law in Eastern and South-Eastern Asia still seems, prevailingly, to be an idea driven by academics, rather than being either the idea of market players or a political project.

The Asian academics, as the initiators of the contract law harmonisation, have emphasised the necessity of the establishment of Asian contract law principles.[18] If in the case of Asia, the goal of harmonisation is to make Asian contract laws closer to each other, the question which arises is what its authors aim to achieve in practice.[19] Viewed from the perspective of the Eastern and South-Eastern Asian jurisdictions, the differences among contract law regimes may be seen as obstacles to the further growth of cross-border trade among diverse jurisdictions. The new contract law instruments may shape the legal, economic and social development of the region. Essentially, it is important to note that any harmonised contract law instrument would need to address the particularities of the Asian culture and its different legal traditions.[20]

A high level of caution however is always required. The requirements of legal certainty dictate that the harmonisation of contract law should be performed in such a manner that it clarifies legal complexity, not that it increases it further.[21] This is why a particularly important question that needs to be examined in

[15] Joint Communique of the 6th ASEAN Law Ministers Meeting (ALAWMM), 19–20 September 2005.

[16] R Amoussou-Guenou, 'Perspective of ASEAN (Asian) Principles of Contract Law' (2004) Conference Drafting of International Commercial Contracts, Hanoi, December 2004, p 14.

[17] (n 14).

[18] YJ Lee, 'Basic Guideline for the Principles of Asian Contract Law' (2009) 3 *Asia Private Law Review* 325–41.

[19] S Koo Myong, 'Scope of Damages' (2010) 4 *Asia Private Law* 396.

[20] GF Bell, 'New challenges for the uniformisation of laws: how the CISG is challenged by "Asian values" and Islamic law' in I Schwenzer and L Spagnolo (eds), *Towards Uniformity: the 2nd annual MAA Schlechtriem CISG conference* (Eleven International Publishing, 2015).

[21] Qi Zhou, 'Harmonisation of European Contract Law: Default and Mandatory Rules' in LA DiMatteo et al, *Commercial Contract Law Transatlantic Perspective* (Cambridge University Press, 2013) 526.

detail concerns the potential value added by the Asian harmonised contract law instrument.

A recent study of the Singapore Academy of Law, carried out on the basis of data collected from approximately 500 lawyers involved in diverse forms of cross-border transactions, showed that in 48 per cent of cross-border transactions, English law was stipulated as the applicable law. This was followed by Singapore law, at 25 per cent, New York law in 7 per cent of cases, and Hong Kong law in 3 per cent of the transactions.[22] It is possible to observe that English law regulates almost half of the transactions. These observations suggest that promoters of a harmonised contract law instrument in Asia should first check with the relevant stakeholders whether there is a need for the creation of a harmonised commercial contract law instrument, and solicit recommendations regarding the features of this new set of rules. In particular, the question would be whether a business would use it in practice, of course under the condition that the contract law instrument is drafted in such a manner as to suit businesses. Businesses would need to have some incentive to use the new set of rules; otherwise it will simply remain a black letter law. In that sense, the experience with the three versions of the UNIDROIT Principles of International Contracts (1994, 2004 and 2010 versions) should always be remembered, as this contract law instrument is hardly ever used in practice as the applicable law.

In the area of consumer contract law, the situation seems to be a bit different than in the case of commercial contract law. The harmonisation of consumer contract law also needs to be concerned with the fact that the contractual relationship between a trader and a consumer is one in which inequality of bargaining power exists between the parties. This is something that a harmonised contract law instrument should certainly adequately address and for this reason consumer contract law has much more regulatory character than the commercial contract law.[23] Freedom of contract is herein more restricted. Consumers have much less choice when it comes to choosing the applicable law, in cross-border transactions. This is something that is traditionally decided by businesses through their standard terms and conditions. As a result of the fact that they are not sure which contract law will regulate their transaction and what the content of that law is, consumers are less willing to perform cross-border consumer transactions.

The example of European contract law has demonstrated that the harmonisation of consumer contract law among the member states has led to an increase in cross-border trade among the member states, as consumers gain confidence to perform cross-border transactions.[24] European contract law is constantly evolving in an attempt to provide an adequate regulatory response to the development

[22] Singapore Academy of Law, 'Study on governing law and jurisdictional choices in cross-border transactions' (2016) available at www.sal.org.sg/Documents/SAL_Singapore_Law_Survey.pdf.

[23] HW Micklitz, 'The Regulatory Character of EU Consumer and Contract Law' in C Twigg Flesner, *Research Handbook on EU Consumer and Contract Law* (Edward Elgar, 2016).

[24] HW Micklitz et al, *European Consumer Law*, 2nd edn (Intersentia, 2014).

of the society and changes in the techniques of the market, eg the digital age.[25] The development of European contract law has also increased the general level of consumer protection in the European Union. In the case of Asia, the 16 contract law jurisdictions of Eastern and South-Eastern Asia have, as a general observation, very scant rules on consumer contract law. Some of the Asian jurisdictions have started developing consumer contract laws, already being inspired by European contract law.

The Chinese Consumer Contracts Act 2000 and the Malaysian Consumer Protection Act 1999, which was amended in 2010 to add the provisions on unfair contract terms, are both heavily inspired by the EU Directive 1993/13/EEC on Unfair Contract Terms. The new 2011 Vietnamese consumer law was also heavily influenced by European contract law and its rules on consumer contracts. In addition to this, some of the jurisdictions have developed their consumer law rules purely to encourage commercial transactions by consumers from the other jurisdictions. An example is Hong Kong SAR, which developed certain consumer contract law rules in order to protect consumers from mainland China wishing to shop in Hong Kong SAR.[26]

However, the adoption of a harmonised contract law instrument is just the first step towards the substantial harmonisation of contract law. For that purpose, the second step is of essential importance, as it requires preserving the uniformity in the application of the supranational contract law in practice.[27] This is because proper harmonisation cannot be achieved without the existence of a common judicial body responsible for interpreting the harmonised legal instrument.[28] The court and its judges need to be independent of the influence of national legal traditions and contract law concepts which are embedded in the contract law traditions from which the judges come.

In that sense European contract law may represent a useful example, as the ECJ has, in the last three decades, provided a number of important decisions in which it provided unified, autonomous explanations of a number of contract law notions under European contract law. For instance, such was the case with respect to the notions of the invitation to purchase or the average consumer as the principal standard used in European contract law.

All in all, it may be concluded that the need for and legal design of a harmonised commercial contract legal instrument needs to be carefully considered. In particular, this needs to be checked with businesses, as they are the intended users of this legal instrument. On the other hand, as consumer contract law is an area of law which is still developing in Asia, it may be argued that there is more of a need for the development of a harmonised consumer contract law instrument, than a commercial contract law instrument. This instrument would not only facilitate

[25] A de Franceschi, *European Contract Law and Digital Service Market* (Intersentia, 2016).
[26] Trade Descriptions (Unfair Trade Practices) (Amendment) Ordinance 2012.
[27] I Schwenzer (ed), *Commentary on the CISG* (Oxford University Press, 2016) 6–7.
[28] Heidemann (n 2) 54.

the performance of cross-border consumer transactions, but also improve the overall wellbeing of consumers in Asia. In that sense, European contract law might be a useful model, as it represents the most advanced example of harmonised consumer contract law, aimed at securing a high level of consumer protection.[29] Likewise, it seems that the harmonisation of consumer contract law is an easier task in cases where the national rules are still, to a large extent, missing. This is well demonstrated by the example of European contract law in which one observes that it is an easier task to harmonise consumer contract law than commercial contract law, especially in cases when the rules are still not fully developed.

IV. Convergence of Legal Systems

The presence of differences among the contract law traditions which constitute the obstacles to further development of cross-border trade has been used as a major argument advocating harmonisation. However, the related question is regarding the effects of the existence of these differences on the process of harmonisation, and whether convergence is possible at all. As an initial observation, the example of European contract law shows well that dealing with the diversity of contract laws is a possibility, but also that this is a very difficult and time-consuming task. Also, particular care needs to be taken about a number of factors throughout the process, especially ensuring that the project pursued and the goal are not overambitious, as this could be a direct cause of the failure of the entire project.

In the area of contract law, a general distinction is made among three legal traditions: civil law, common law and mixed law. All three legal traditions are present in the 16 jurisdictions of Eastern and South-Eastern Asia. A majority of the contract laws belong to the civil law legal tradition (Japan, South Korea, PR China, Indonesia, Macau SAR, Taiwan, Laos, Cambodia, Vietnam), with particularly strong influence from German contract law. Common law has also had an important role in the development of contract law in Asia (Hong Kong SAR, Singapore, Malaysia, Brunei). In certain jurisdictions, both the civil law and the common law traditions have played an important role in the development of the national contract laws (Philippines, Thailand).

In addition to this, some of the national contract laws have been influenced by other important factors, as is the case of socialism as a ruling ideology in PR China, or prevailing religious beliefs (in Malaysia and Indonesia). Also, these jurisdictions exhibit huge differences when it comes to the language in which these contract law instruments are written, each being written in the official languages of the jurisdiction.

[29] J Stuyck, *1993—Twenty Years Later. The Evolution of Consumer Law in the European Union* (Intersentia, 2013).

It is possible to observe that the contract laws of the jurisdictions of Eastern and South-Eastern Asia have been materially influenced and shaped by different foreign laws. The reasons for that influence are different. One reason is the colonial past, which is the case for Hong Kong SAR, Taiwan and Indonesia. The second reason is that some of the contract laws were used as a best model for the development of the national contract law traditions, as was the example with Thailand or Japan. However, the transplantation of the foreign laws has traditionally been done taking into consideration the particularities of the national history, society, religion and other values.[30] Consequently, a trend recently observed has been the influence on contract laws in Asia of European contract law as a result of the tendency to strengthen trade relations with the European Union and its member states, as is the case with Vietnam, where European contract law was rather imposed as a condition for the development of mutual trade.[31]

Interestingly, among the 16 Asian contract law jurisdictions examined, there are also some examples of double-transplants of contract law. That is the case, for instance, in South Korea and Taiwan, whose contract laws were materially influenced by Japanese contract law during those countries' periods of Japanese occupation. For that reason, contract laws in these two jurisdictions also resemble the German contract law. Another example is Malaysia, which has developed its contract law taking Indian contract law, and thus English contract law, as a model.

For the harmonisation of contract law, the presence of material differences among national contract laws, particularly if they belong to different legal families (eg civil law vs common law), represents a major challenge. For that reason, it has even been argued that harmonisation among contract laws belonging to diverse legal families is actually not possible at all. The European Union was singled out as a concrete example of such impossibility with the explanation that the basics of contract laws are so different that no convergence is possible.[32]

However, the development of European contract law in the last three decades and its acceptance and incorporation into national contract laws by such a large number of countries has shown that this argument can hardly be accepted as valid and that convergence is, in reality, possible. Of course, convergence is not an easy task. In the case of European contract law the process of drafting and the evolution of contract law were faced with challenges brought about by the existence of differences among the national contract law regimes belonging to civil law, common law and mixed legal systems. Some other factors, such as religion or political ideology, also played an important role.

[30] M Chen-Wishart, 'Comparative Asian Contract Law on the Remedies for Breach of Contract: Transplant, Convergence, and Divergence' (n 10) 426.

[31] Stuyck and Durovic (n 3) 247.

[32] P Legrand, 'European Legal Systems are not converging' (1996) 45 *International and Comparative Law Quarterly* 52.

However, the experiences gained from European contract law show that only a partial convergence seems possible. European contract law is still not complete a legal instrument, but needs to be supplemented by the provisions of the national contract laws as in certain areas, where differences are so radical, compromises could not be reached. Some of the aspects of different approaches towards contract law turned out to be irreconcilable and thus, a compromise among all relevant stakeholders could not be reached.

This is the case with, for instance, the rules on pre-contractual liability, good faith or consent defects. These are the areas where the civil and common law approaches are radically different.[33] In that sense, European contract law had more success, as in some but not all areas, the irreconcilability was successfully overcome. This is the case, for instance, with the imposition of a general pre-contractual duty of information which is a completely new approach for English contract law. However, this does not apply to all contracts, only to consumer contracts. Again, convergence is easier in areas which are innovative, as is the case with consumer contract law.

The harmonised contract law instrument should also use innovative legal terminology in order to avoid confusion with the existing national contract law concepts. This is well demonstrated in the case of European contract law, where a completely new legal terminology has been developed in order to make a clear separation between European contract law and the national contract law concepts of the EU member states.[34]

The legal language is also important for another reason: namely, the existence of language diversity presents an additional challenge for the harmonisation of contract law. In that context, what must be borne in mind is the number of official languages in the 16 jurisdictions of Eastern and South-Eastern Asia. In this context, the question of the languages in which the official version of a potential common contract law instrument for the 16 jurisdictions should be issued is most important. Different language versions of the same document may be understood in a different manner, and produce diverse results in practice. Incidental to this is the question of which official version shall prevail in case of conflict between two official language versions.

All in all, the example of European contract law demonstrates that the convergence of different legal traditions is possible. However, the attainment of full convergence seems an overambitious and impossible task due to radically different approaches in certain areas of contract law. For this reason, European contract law is not a complete legal instrument, but is supplemented with the provisions of the national contract laws. This is something that needs to be taken into

[33] J Cartwright and MW Hesselink, *Precontractual liability in European Private Law* (Cambridge University Press, 2011); R Zimmermann and S Whittaker, *Good Faith in European Contract Law* (Cambridge University Press, 2000); R Sefton-Green, *Mistake, Fraud and Duties to Inform* (Cambridge University Press, 2005).

[34] M Durovic, *European Law on Unfair Commercial Practices and Contract Law* (Hart Publishing, 2016) 197.

consideration in case of Asian contract law. Also, the question of official language versions of the harmonised legal instrument is an important one that needs to be carefully thought out.

V. Legal Nature of Asian Contract Law

The development of supranational contract law also requires a policy decision regarding the legal nature of the contract law instrument. When developing a supranational contract law instrument, there is always a policy dilemma regarding whether to opt for binding legislation or to rather go for a soft law instrument.[35] Both options have their advantages and disadvantages. The choice is closely linked with the question of competence and possibility. In other words, the promoters of harmonisation always need to check what in reality can be passed.

The main advantage of opting for a soft law instrument is that it is an easier option, as it does not preclude any of the existing contract law rules, but establishes a parallel one. As it interferes significantly less with the national legal order, it is much easier to reach the necessary consensus, and to pass it. For the same reason, soft law instrument will be more complete as it is easier to include provisions where there are different approaches of the national contract laws.

However, the major problem with a soft law instrument is how to secure its usage application in practice. The promotion of a contract law instrument is a very difficult task, especially in the commercial relations where the parties have at their disposal contract laws that they are used to and familiar with, as is the case with the Vienna Convention on Contracts for the International Sale of Goods (CISG) or English contract law, both of which are extensively used in Asia as the applicable law. For this reason, for the success of the harmonisation process, it is certainly much more desirable to opt for a binding legal instrument. The success herein is not to be only understood as the achievement of high level of harmonisation, but should also refer to the application of the harmonised rules in practice as the set of rules which regulate a contractual relationship.

The body of European contract law consists of a number of binding pieces of legislation, adopted through a complex system in which a number of the European institutions and the member states take part. The complex process for the adoption of pieces of legislation also means that it is not easy to secure political support and reach a compromise. The binding pieces of legislation are, typically, the directives that regulate contract law in a fragmented manner.[36] The directives deal with specific types of consumer contracts (package travel, timeshare, consumer credit), consumer contracts which are concluded in a particular manner

[35] F Ferrari, 'International Uniform Law Conventions, Lex Mercatoria and Unidroit Principles' (2000) 5 *Uniform Law Review* 3.

[36] J Smits, 'Coherence and Fragmentation in the Law of Contract' in P Letto-Vanamo, *Coherence and Fragmentation in European Private Law* (Sellier, 2012) 18 ff.

(distance contracts, doorstep selling contracts) or specific elements of consumer contracts (fairness of contract terms). All of these European directives represent hard law, ie the EU member states have to implement their provisions into their national legal systems properly and in a timely manner and to apply them in practice. Otherwise, in case of failure to do so, the European Commission is entitled to take action against that EU member state before the CJEU.[37] In the area of contract law, a number of such cases have already been recorded.[38]

The European example also demonstrates well how the question of the legal nature is tightly linked with the questions of competence and which legal nature may be adopted at all. In the case of the European Union, the constitutional basis and competence for the development of European contract law is disputable.[39] The CJEU, as the highest judicial instance in the EU, has also emphasised that the EU competence for adoption of the common legislation is not absolute, but limited.[40] The lack of clear competence and the political support from the relevant stakeholders were the main reasons why different drafts and legislative proposals and academic projects in the area of contract law projects on the European level have failed.[41] These include the idea of the European Civil Code and some other massive projects such as the PECL, the DCFR or the CESL.

However, despite their failure to become binding law, these projects in practice have had an impact on the Europeanisation of contract law.[42] In reality, they have become soft law. Accordingly, the provisions of the DCFR have been applied in the case law of the CJEU, however, not so much in the judgments, but primarily in the opinions of the Advocate Generals.[43] The national courts of some EU member states, in particular the supreme courts, have also referred to the DCFR in their decisions, as was the case with the courts in Spain, Estonia and Sweden.[44] Also, the DCFR and the CESL have been widely used as a model law for redevelopment of the national contract laws of the EU member states.[45]

[37] Art 258 of the Treaty of the Functioning of the European Union.

[38] Case C-144/99 *Commission v Netherlands* [2001] ECR I-3541 para 17; Case C-478/99 *Commission v Sweden* [2002] ECR I-4147; Case C-70/03 *Commission v Spain* [2004] ECR I-07999.

[39] S Vogenauer and S Weatherill, 'The European Community's Competence to Pursue the Harmonisation of Contract Law—an Empirical Contribution to the Debate' in S Vogenauer and S Weatherill (eds), *The Harmonisation of Europan Contract Law—Implications for European Private Laws, Business and Legal Practice* (Hart Publishing, 2006) 125–26.

[40] Case C-376/98 *Federal Republic of Germany v European Parliament and Council of the European Union (Tobacco Advertising I)* [2000] ECR I-08419.

[41] MW Hesselink, 'The Politics of European Civil Code' (2004) 10 *European Law Journal* 675.

[42] cp S Vogenauer, 'The DCFR and the CESL as Models for Law Reform' in G Dannemann and S Vogenauer (eds), *The Common European Sales Law in Context* (Oxford University Press, 2013) 732.

[43] Opinion of Advocate General in Case C-180/06 *Renate Ilsinger v Martin Dreschers* [2009] ECR I-03961; Opinion of Advocate General in Case C-540/08 *Mediaprint Zeitungs- und Zeitschriftenverlag v Österreich-Zeitungsverlag GmbH* [2010] ECR I-10909.

[44] G Kalouta, 'The DCFR in the Courts' in M Andenas and D Fairgrieve, *Courts and Comparative Law* (Oxford University Press, 2015) 717.

[45] S Vogenauer, 'The DCFR and the CESL as models for Law Reform' in Dannemann and Vogenauer (n 42).

In addition to this, they have had an impact outside the borders of the European Union. This is the case with the reform of the Chinese contract law in 1999, which was affected by European contract law—primarily the provisions of the PECL. One concrete example of this impact is Article 2:301 PECL on negotiations contrary to good faith, which was transplanted into Chinese law. The Korean Civil Code was reformed with strong influence from the PECL.[46] Likewise, the PECL was used as inspiration for the adoption of the ASEAN contract law in the 10 countries of South-Eastern Asia.[47] It is true that these documents were successful as model laws, due to their high quality and the authority of their drafters, but their effects would certainly be much greater if they had been adopted as binding laws.

The proposers of the PACL have imagined it to be a soft law instrument, primarily to be used as a model law. Soft law, being a less ambitious project which interferes less with the existing national contract laws, is certainly an easier and faster option. However, in the case of soft law, parties need to be strongly motivated to opt for it, given the competition among all possible applicable contract laws. If there is not a particularly strong reason to choose the PACL, they will never opt for it. Education and information about particular contract law regimes in that sense is a necessary prerequisite. Contractual parties need to have an incentive to use a particular model. However, a good quality of the harmonised contract law instrument is also necessary in the case of opting for hard law as being in line with the principle of party autonomy, parties may always exclude its application and opt for some other contract law regime.

The dilemma between opting for soft law or hard law is not an easy one to resolve. What first needs to be verified is which options are possible at all. Soft law is certainly an easier and less ambitious alternative which is always possible, even when political support from the governments is missing. However, irrespective of the choice made, a particular harmonised contract law instrument still needs to be promoted among market players in order to be used in practice.

VI. Conclusions

This chapter has examined the initiative for the development of an Asian contract law in light of the experience that may be gained from the European contract law. Similarly to the example of the European jurisdictions, the national contract laws of the 16 jurisdictions of Eastern and South-Eastern Asia belong to different legal traditions and show a high level of difference as a result of a number of different

[46] YJ Lee, 'A Study on Draft Articles Principles of Asian Contract Law Performance and Non-Performance' (2016) *Research Institute for Asia Private Law* 8.

[47] See thac.or.th/en/wp-content/uploads/ASEAN-Principles-of-Contract-Law.pdf.

factors. The European example shows that the reconciliation of the differences among the 16 contract laws is feasible and that convergence is, to some extent, possible. However, only a partial convergence is to be attempted. This is because certain areas of contract laws, where radically different approaches are deeply embedded in the national legal traditions, can hardly be converged.

Accordingly, the initiative for an Asian contract law needs to take care not to be over-ambitious. Otherwise, the success of the project is in danger. The European example may also show that harmonisation may be easier in the more innovative areas of law such as in the area of consumer contract law or digital contracts. It is much more difficult to touch upon traditional contract law concepts which are deeply embedded in the core of national legal traditions.

The question of convergence is less relevant if the promoters of an Asian contract law, when it comes to the legal nature of the harmonised contract law instrument, opt for soft law rather than for a binding convention, which seems to be their target. Binding law instruments, as is the case with European directives, secure a higher level of harmonisation of contract law. However, it is much more difficult to reach consensus regarding the adoption of binding legislation. For this reason, a model law appears to be an easier policy alternative. This is because a model law is not seen as a danger to the national contract law orders. Still, the main challenge is how to secure the usage of the model law in practice. Otherwise, the question is what their purpose is at all. The European model shows that one of the principal factors is the level of excellence of the model law, but still the model law needs to be promoted. However, due to the sensitivity of consumer contract law, business-to-consumer relations should ideally be regulated by a supranational binding instrument.

The European example also shows that for the preservation of uniformity, particular attention should be paid to the interpretation of the supranational contract law instrument that needs to secure the uniformity. The terms of the Asian contract law must never be interpreted in the context they have in the contract law of a particular jurisdiction, but must have a supranational meaning. For that purpose, the existence of a supranational court in charge of the interpretation of the supranational contract law instrument is highly recommended, as is well demonstrated by the active role that the CJEU plays in cases of European contract law. The question of the interpretation is also tightly connected with the language issue, as particular care needs to be taken also of the language of the harmonised contract law instrument, as significant language diversity is also present in Asia.

13

The Two Spirits of the PLACL

IÑIGO DE LA MAZA GAZMURI

I. Introduction

The aim of this work is rather modest. First, I am interested in gathering some background on the Latin American Principles of the Contract (PLACL). In doing so, I will narrate—albeit very briefly—the origin of this project and the way in which it has been developed. At the same time, without lingering too much on their obvious differences, I will presently advance an assessment of the obvious differences between the ways in which this project and another with similar objectives—the Principles of European Contract Law (PECL)—have been developed.

Secondly, I will try to show that the PLACL, so to speak, are motivated by two different purposes. The first one consists of systematising certain coincidences that may possibly be detected among the contract laws of the region. The second can be explained as an attempt to promote a shift from one understanding of the contract—with inevitable, and at times relevant nuances from country to country,[1] characteristic of the codification process of the eighteenth and nineteenth centuries—to another whose origins can be traced more conspicuously to the Vienna Convention on the International Sale of Goods (CISG). I will try to show how these two purposes were captured in the current PLACL text.

Thirdly, I will try to show some of the results that the coexistence of these two purposes in the PLACL text brought about.

[1] The codes of the region developed at different times, between the middle of the nineteenth century and the beginning of the twenty-first century. Surprisingly, however, in contract law it is possible to note a cluster of relevant similarities between them. On this, see C Pizarro (ed), *El derecho de los contratos en Latinoamérica* (Foundation pour le Droit Continental, 2012). Paying enough attention to this cluster, what is apparent is that the contract law of the region, despite the differences between the various countries, remains in some way anchored to the contract paradigm of the codification of the eighteenth and nineteenth centuries. On this paradigm, see AM Morales Moreno, *Claves de la Modernización del derecho contractual* (Ibañez, Centro de Estudios de Derecho Comparado, 2016).

II. Some Background

According to Pizarro, the history of the PLACL begins in 2009 in Rennes, France, during the International Congress on the Transformations of Contract Law.[2] A group of Latin American professors in attendance thought of suggesting to Professor Michel Grimaldi the elaboration of a set of Latin American Principles of Contract Law.

The request they made to Professor Grimaldi, and through him to the *Fondation pour le Droit Continental*, must be contextualised in a certain uneasiness among select French scholars brought about by the reports of the World Bank about the laws of contract proper to the continental tradition.[3]

Pizarro points out that when the idea was suggested, they received immediate support from Professor Grimaldi, and it was agreed to work out a detailed work project. Working on this detailed project, the Latin American professors in Rennes considered that there were two fundamental aspects that had to form the basis of the project. The first was the need to identify a 'regional legal identity' that would prevent the PLACL from being a mere copy of other existing principles. The second mandate that should be executed through the preparation of the PLACL was to improve what had already been achieved through other soft law instruments of contract law.[4]

In order to enquire into the regional legal identity, a questionnaire of 40 questions was elaborated to cover the main legal issues that arise during the contractual process.[5] The function of the questionnaire was to gather information about how the various countries of the region faced contract law. This questionnaire was answered through reports by delegations from Argentina, Brazil, Colombia, Chile, Paraguay, Uruguay and Venezuela.[6]

The first meeting, held in Bogotá in October 2010, aimed specifically at discussing the results of the various reports.

From then on, the work meetings began to happen, annually or bi-annually. The working method consisted of asking the different professors in the group to prepare proposals for the articles referring to the different topics. These were then discussed during the meetings until a certain consensus was reached or, in the end, in the absence of such consensus, the different options were put to the vote.

During 2013 a first draft of the PLACL was produced. This first draft was divided into seven parts. The first, called 'Preliminary', was concerned with the

[2] Pizarro (n 1) 15.

[3] ibid.

[4] ibid 16.

[5] For example, it was inquired about the general principles of contract law, the training rules, the contracts for adhesion, hypotheses of pre-contractual liability, the validity and form of contracts, the effects of the contract, the notion of non-compliance and remedies against breach of contract.

[6] Regarding the participants, see Pizarro (n 1) 11–16.

application of these principles and some general principles. The second, under the heading 'Contract Formation', formalised the procedure for meeting the offer and acceptance—'the vitiation of the contract and the regime of contractual inefficiency'. The next part, 'Contract interpretation', grouped seven rules on the subject. The fifth part, 'On the Simulation of Contracts', regulated this phenomenon. The sixth part, referring to the effects of the contract, formalised the unilateral termination of the contract in favour of third parties and the theory of the risks. The last two parts concerned compliance with the contract and the remedies.

Substantially, this scheme has been maintained, until the last version available as of December 2017. However, there have been some significant changes. The first of these is that, concerning the conditions for validity, the cause and the subject matter were incorporated as essential elements of the contract. The second is that rules on agency and on the alteration of circumstances were incorporated. In this way, the current version of the PLACL is composed of a preliminary chapter, which deals with the scope and general principles. A second chapter on contract formation includes the vices of the contract and the rules on the subject matter, cause and solemnities of the contract. The third chapter is dedicated to the nullity of the contract, and the fourth to simulation. The fifth chapter, 'Effects of the contract against third parties', formalises agency and stipulation in favour of another. Chapters six and seven deal with the interpretation and fulfilment of contractual obligations respectively. The eighth chapter discusses non-compliance with contractual obligations and, in relation to this, regulates both non-performance and remedies, which in the PLACL are called *medios de tutela del acreedor*. This incredibly wide range of topics has been condensed into 120 articles.

Finally, despite the fact that the PLACL are still in a draft form, with the texts currently in force in the respective periods, they have been discussed in the Law Faculty at Diego Portales University during 2013 and 2015, the Law Faculty at Oxford University during 2014, and the Law Faculty at Universidad Autónoma de Madrid during 2016. Likewise, they have attracted the attention of scholars. In this way, works on these principles have been published—one during 2013,[7] two in 2014[8] and three in 2016.[9]

[7] JM Eyzaguirre and J Rodríguez, 'Expansión y límites de la buena fe objetiva—a propósito del «Proyecto de Principios Latinoamericanos de derecho de los contratos»' (2013) *Revista Chilena de Derecho Privado* 21.

[8] A Ferrante, '¿Es correcta la elección del método de cálculo de la reducción del precio en los Principios latinoamericanos de Contratos?' (2014) *Revista Chilena de Derecho Privado* 22; A Morales, 'Los principios latinoamericanos de derecho de los contratos. Un debate abierto sobre las grandes cuestiones jurídicas de la contratación' (2014) LXVII *Anuario de Derecho Civil* I 227.

[9] A Vidal, 'La pretensión de cumplimiento específico de las obligaciones no dinerarias y los costes excesivos para el deudor como límite a su ejercicio' in *Estudios de Derecho Civil X* (Thomson Reuters-La Ley, 2015) 555–67; A Vidal, 'Incumplimiento contractual y pretensión de cumplimiento específico en

III. The Two Spirits of PLACL

Beyond the obvious soft law character that the PLACL are assigned in the preliminary chapter and their claim to be used as a kind of *lex mercatoria*, there is an interesting question regarding other objectives of the PLACL that are not explicit.

The issue can be formulated in the following way: do the PLACL intend to present the existing contract law in the region systematically at the level of principles or, instead, to promote a shift towards some more or less recent developments in contract law at the European level? Of course, another option is to deal with both at the same time, although as I will examine in section IV of this chapter, this last option entails significant risks at the level of internal coherence.

A first possibility is that this is a kind of restatement of the contract law at the Latin American level. In other words, it would be a question of detecting the coincidences that exist in the diverse civil codes and of presenting them, with the generality that is a characteristic of some principles, in a systematised way.

A second possibility consists of something different and more ambitious. Without losing sight of the contract legislation available in Latin America, it is about trying to bring it closer to the understanding of the contractual phenomenon that permeates the CISG, the Dutch Civil Code, Directive 1999/44/EC,[10] the amendment of the German law of obligations of 2002, and to a certain extent the recent amendment of the French Civil Code. This understanding also permeates, in an extremely conspicuous manner, the main soft law instruments at the level of uniform law and at the level of comparative law.[11] Following a relatively widely shared terminology in Latin America, I will call this new paradigm, 'modern law of obligations'.[12]

The truth is that everything indicates that, somehow, the idea is to do both at the same time.

On the one hand, the reference to the search for a 'Latin American legal identity' seems to indicate an intense commitment to the civil codes of the region. This explains formally at least that in the PLACL the cause, subject matter and the way in which each of them is conceived are still considered essential elements of the contract.

los principios latinoamericanos de derecho de contratos (PLDC)' in A Vaquer, E Bosch and MP Sánchez (eds), *El derecho común europeo de la compraventa y la modernización del derecho de contratos* (Atelier, 2015) 745–67; I de la Maza Gazmuri, 'El error en los Principios Latinoamericanos de Derecho de los Contratos' in Vaquer, Bosch and Sánchez (ibid) 789–800.

[10] Directive 1999/44/EC of the European Parliament and of the Council of May 25 1999 on certain aspects of the sale and guarantees of consumer goods [1999] OJ L171/12.

[11] At the level of soft law the following can be considered: the PECL, the UNIDROIT Principles, the DCFR and the CESL proposal.

[12] See AM Morales Moreno, *La modernización del derecho de obligaciones* (Thomson Reuters, 2006).

Thus, Article 9 of the PLACL provides that: 'consent, subject-matter, and cause are the essential elements required to form a contract'.

Article 38 of the PLACL provides the following:

(1) The subject-matter of a contract must be ascertained or ascertainable, possible, and lawful.

(2) It is unlawful when it is prohibited by law or when it is contrary to good morals or to public policy.

Finally, under Article 39:

(1) All obligations require a cause. A cause is presumed to exist as long as it is not proven otherwise, even if it is not expressed.

(2) The cause of the contract must be lawful.

Something similar happens with the distinction between absolute and relative nullity in Article 40.

The same reason is probably useful in explaining the fact that in the PLACL, unlike the UNIDROIT Principles or PECL, anticipatory breach is not considered. Likewise, it seems to be this kind of 'Latin American legal identity' which explains that Article 93 of the PLACL refers to the 'exception of contract not fulfilled' when considering suspension.

On the other hand, however, it would require a significant degree of blindness not to notice the enormous influence that the CISG, the UNIDROIT Principles and PECL have on the design of the PLACL text.

Thus, for example, in structural terms the performance of obligations is not disciplined with regard to ways of extinguishing obligations as is the case, for example, in the Chilean and Colombian civil codes.

In addition, always within the structural area, the means of relief for the creditor are singly identified in Article 93, as follows:

(1) In the event of non-performance, the obligee may, at its discretion and as appropriate, exercise one of the following means of relief for the non-performance:

(a) Specific performance;
(b) Price reduction;
(c) Termination of the contract;
(d) Defence of the unperformed contract; and
(e) Damages.

(2) Damages may be claimed separately or in conjunction with the remaining means of relief.

As can be seen, there are at least three relevant differences in the design that, in general, the codes of the region present. First, the remedies are not determined by the type of obligation in question (giving, doing and not doing).

Second, the special regimes of protection of the creditor (eg *vices caches*, eviction, and measure) are eliminated, and, finally, suspension is explicitly established as a means of relief and the price reduction is generalised.

In terms of content now, it is difficult to exaggerate the influence of this modern law of obligations in the PLACL. For example, with regard to freedom of contract, Article 5 of the PLACL provides: 'The parties are free to enter into contracts and to determine their content, so long as this does not violate the law or public policy'.

In turn, Article 1.1 of the UNIDROIT Principles provides: 'The parties are free to enter into a contract and to determine its content'.

In terms of formation of consent, there is a close resemblance to the CISG. Thus, for example, in abandoning the 'mirror-image rule',[13] the resemblance is quite evident, considering Articles 19 of the CISG and 25 of the PLACL. The first two subparagraphs of Article 19 provide as follows:

(1) A reply to an offer which purports to be an acceptance but contains additions, limitations or other modifications is a rejection of the offer and constitutes a counter-offer.

(2) However, a reply to an offer which purports to be an acceptance but contains additional or different terms which do not materially alter the terms of the offer constitutes an acceptance, unless the offeror, without undue delay, objects orally to the discrepancy or dispatches a notice to that effect. If he does not so object, the terms of the contract are the terms of the offer with the modifications contained in the acceptance.

Meanwhile, Article 25 of the PLACL provides:

(1) A reply to an offer that contains additions, limitations, or modifications constitutes a counter-offer.

(2) However, if the terms of the offer are not materially altered, the reply constitutes an acceptance, and the contract will be concluded with such additions, limitations or modifications.

(3) Even when the limitations or modifications do not materially alter the terms of the offer, the reply will be understood as a rejection in the following cases:

(a) When the offer expressly demands full or partial acceptance of the proposed terms.
(b) When the offeror without delay informs the offeree of its objection to the changes.

[13] S Durany, 'Sobre la necesidad de que la adaptación coincida en todo con la oferta: el espejo roto' (1990) XLIII-4 *Anuario de Derecho Civil* 1011.

As regards vices of consent, the similarities between Article 29 of the PLACL, Article 3.2.2 of the UNIDROIT Principles and Article 4:103 of the PECL are sufficiently obvious. Article 29 of the PLACL provides:

(1) Mistake vitiates a contract when:

(a) It is caused by information supplied by the other party.
(b) The other party knew or should have known of the mistake and did not disclose it against good faith.
(c) Both parties made the same mistake.

(2) In these cases, the contract is null if the mistake can be excused or the risk of its existence was not or ought not to have been assumed by the person who made it.

Meanwhile, the literal wording of Article 3.2.2 of the UNIDROIT Principles provides as follows:

(1) A party may only avoid the contract for mistake if, when the contract was concluded, the mistake was of such importance that a reasonable person in the same situation as the party in error would only have concluded the contract on materially different terms or would not have concluded it at all if the true state of affairs had been known, and

(a) the other party made the same mistake, or caused the mistake, or knew or ought to have known of the mistake and it was contrary to reasonable commercial standards of fair dealing to leave the mistaken party in error; or
(b) the other party had not at the time of avoidance reasonably acted in reliance on the contract.

(2) However, a party may not avoid the contract if

(a) it was grossly negligent in committing the mistake; or
(b) the mistake relates to a matter in regard to which the risk of mistake was assumed or, having regard to the circumstances, should be borne by the mistaken party

Finally, Article 4:103 of the PECL reads:

(1) A party may avoid a contract for mistake of fact or law existing when the contract was concluded if:

(a)(i) the mistake was caused by information given by the other party; or
(ii) the other party knew or ought to have known of the mistake and it was contrary to good faith and fair dealing to leave the mistaken party in error; or
(iii) the other party made the same mistake, and

(b) the other party knew or ought to have known that the mistaken party, had it known the truth, would not have entered the contract or would have done so only on fundamentally different terms.

(2) However a party may not avoid the contract if:

(a) in the circumstances its mistake was inexcusable, or
(b) the risk of the mistake was assumed, or in the circumstances should be borne, by it.

Something similar occurs when the notion of non-performance contained in Article 85 of the PLACL[14] is compared to the definition of non-performance, Article 7.1.1 of the UNIDROIT Principles,[15] and its essential nature, regulated in Article 86 of the PLACL and Article 7.3.1 of the UNIDROIT Principles.[16]

These examples should suffice. The PLACL involve, on the one hand, an attempt to systematise some of the convergences that can be detected in contract law in Latin America. This is not all, however. It is also a question of promoting a movement from the law of contracts, whose inspiration (more or less direct) was the process of codification of the late eighteenth and nineteenth centuries,[17] towards a different understanding of the contractual phenomenon—that of the modern law of obligations.[18]

[14] See definition below, section IV.A.

[15] 'Non-performance is failure by a party to perform any of its obligations under the contract, including defective performance or late performance'.

[16] '(1) A party may terminate the contract where the failure of the other party to perform an obligation under the contract amounts to a fundamental non-performance.

(2) In determining whether a failure to perform an obligation amounts to a fundamental non-performance regard shall be had, in particular, to whether

(a) the non-performance substantially deprives the aggrieved party of what it was entitled to expect under the contract unless the other party did not foresee and could not reasonably have foreseen such result;
(b) strict compliance with the obligation which has not been performed is of essence under the contract;
(c) the non-performance is intentional or reckless;
(d) the non-performance gives the aggrieved party reason to believe that it cannot rely on the other party's future performance;
(e) the non-performing party will suffer disproportionate loss as a result of the preparation or performance if the contract is terminated.

(3) In the case of delay the aggrieved party may also terminate the contract if the other party fails to perform before the time allowed it under Article 7.1.5 has expired'.

[17] Of course there exists a generalisation that applied specifically to each civil code of the region, which can be very inaccurate because, as the Chilean Civil Code is dated 1857, the current Argentinian Civil and Commercial Code is dated 2016. Nevertheless, as far as contract law is concerned, even the Argentinian model is more attached to the codified paradigm than to the CISG.

[18] The differences between the two models of regulation of the contractual phenomenon have been detailed in Morales Moreno (n 1).

The results that can be generated by the simultaneous presence of these two purposes—to systematise, where possible, contract law in the region and to seek a shift to a diverse contractual paradigm—are manifold. I am not interested in considering them all. For the scope of this assessment I will consider no more than three in the next section.

IV. Systematising and Shifting: Some Results

As I have pointed out, I am not interested in presenting and comprehensively examining all possible outcomes that the presence of the two spirits of the PLACL can bring about. What I intend to do in this section is to show three possible results and illustrate them with examples from the PLACL.

A. Collaboration

I will call the first result 'collaboration'. The distinguishing characteristic of this result is that the shift towards the contractual model of the modern law of obligations contributes to improve some aspects that, as a rule, are considered defective in the codified contract law. However, this contribution does not alter—at least not significantly—the understanding of that contract law.

In the PLACL this collaboration, it seems to me, can take two forms. I will call the first one 'development' and the second one 'ordination'.

By development, I will signify here something like completing the plan of the legislator. That is to say, it is to add certain aspects that the codifier omitted but that plausibly could have been added and that, in this way, legal operators consider in general.

I think that good examples of development are found first in Articles 5 to 7 of the PLACL under the heading 'General principles'. No one seems to doubt that the same principles underlie the rules that shape contract law. Likewise, there seems to be no doubt that these principles cover at least freedom of contract, binding force of contract and good faith. However, the civil codes in the region are often not particularly explicit in their regulation of principles of law. Thus, for example, as regards good faith, the only ones that seem to formulate it in a really explicit way are the old Argentinian Civil Code[19] and the current Brazilian code. The first of these, in Article 1198, provided the following: 'Los contratos deben

[19] In the case of the PLACL, in general, the old Argentinian Civil Code was used, so the articles cited in this work correspond to it.

celebrarse, interpretarse y ejecutarse de buena fe y de acuerdo con lo que ver o símilmente las partes entendieron o pudieron entender, obrando con cuidado y previsión'.

In the case of the PLACL, in general, the old Argentinian Civil Code was used, so the articles cited in this work correspond to it.

Meanwhile, the Brazilian Civil Code, in Article 422, provides that: 'Os contratantes são obrigados a guardar, assimna conclusão do contrato, comoemsua execução, os princípios de probidade e boa fé'.

However, in other civil codes, such as those of Chile and Colombia, the provision is limited to noting that contracts must be carried out in good faith.[20] Additionally, there is no general rule of contract law in the Paraguayan, Uruguayan or Venezuelan civil codes.

As regards autonomy of will and binding force of contracts, the situation is also dissimilar. However, in general, with the exception of Article 944 of the Argentinian Civil Code and, to a certain extent, Article 11 of the Paraguayan Civil Code, they do not explicitly appear in the codes. Thus, for example, in the Chilean and Colombian civil codes, both principles are generally recognised in relation to the rule of mandatory force of the contract.[21]

Section 2 of the preliminary chapter of PLACL collaborates with the civil codes in terms of developing them, explicitly expressing the principles of contract law on which there is agreement in the region.[22]

A second example of collaboration through development can be found in section 2 of chapter 2 of the PLACL, under the title 'Of the negotiation of the contract', in which certain behaviours that are demandable of the parties during the negotiation of the contract are particularised, regulating the withdrawal of negotiations and the duty of confidentiality. In the civil codes of the region it is possible to find some that do not refer to the pre-contractual liability, as is the case of the Chilean, Colombian, Uruguayan and Venezuelan codes and others that refer to the requirements of good faith during the pre-contractual period, but that do not attempt to particularise them. This is the case of the Argentinian,[23] Brazilian[24] and Paraguayan civil codes.[25]

Once again, the collaboration of the PLACL here consists of developing standards through the particularisation of certain behaviours demanded during the negotiation of the contract.[26]

[20] See Arts 1546 Chilean CC and 1603 Colombian CC.

[21] See eg Arts 1159 Venezuelan CC, 154 Chilean CC, 1602 Colombian CC. More explicit, however, is Art 11 of the Uruguayan CC.

[22] On the agreement Pizarro (n 1) 19–23, 117–24, 207–14, 297–99, 379–88, 485–91 and 561–65.

[23] See Art 1109.

[24] See Arts 186–87.

[25] See Art 689.

[26] In the design of these rules, the influence of the UNIDROIT Principles and PECL is evident.

A third example of collaboration through development is found in Article 85 of the PLACL, which defines non-performance as follows:

(1) Non-performance is a failure to perform in the agreed manner.
(2) Defective performance includes all forms of non-conformity between which was agreed and that was performed by the obligor.
(3) Non-performance by the obligor includes the persons it employs to perform the obligation.
(4) There shall be no grounds for damages if non-performance is not attributable to the obligor.

The collaboration here is particularly evident with respect to civil codes such as the Argentinian, Brazilian, Paraguayan, Venezuelan, Chilean or Colombian codes, which do not define non-performance,[27] but the closest they reach—in the case of the last two—is a taxonomy of non-performance as regards the remedy of damages, in the following terms: 'La indemnización de perjuicios comprende el daño emergente y el lucro cesante, ya provengan de no haberse cumplido la obligación, o de haberse cumplido imperfectamente, o de haberse retardado el cumplimiento'.[28]

The fourth example of this type of collaboration is found in Article 86 of the PLACL; its tenor is as follows:

Non-performance shall be understood as fundamental when:

(a) The parties have agreed that it is with respect to specific obligations or specific events of non-performance.
(b) The non-performance is intentional.
(c) The conduct of the non-performing party gives the obligee reason to believe that it cannot rely on the other party's future performance.
(d) It substantially deprives the obligee of what it was entitled to expect according to that which was foreseeable for the parties at the time the contract was concluded.

Development in this case consists of explaining something about what is agreed upon in the region—namely, that no particular contractual breach allows termination—but which civil codes do not usually explicitly state or develop. In fact, from the codes to which the questionnaire refers, only the Paraguayan code in Article 724 states that the non-performance must be relevant to the termination of the contract; none of the others contains a similar statement.[29]

[27] The Paraguayan CC, in contrast, defines it in its Art 1342, as 'failure to fulfil the obligation or delay in the execution'.
[28] Arts 1556 Chilean CC and 1613 Colombian CC.
[29] See eg Art 1489 Chilean CC.

Finally, a fifth assumption of this kind of collaboration is found in Article 102, regarding the mitigation of losses. Its tenor is as follows:

(1) Compensation is subject to reduction when the obligee has failed to take reasonable steps to mitigate loss in good faith. Reduction shall correspond to the amount by which the loss could have been mitigated.
(2) In any event, the aggrieved party shall be entitled to compensation for what has been allocated towards mitigating the loss.

It is a development because even though it is considered that there is a close relationship between the demands of the general principle of good faith to the parties, the fact is that with the exception of Peru and Bolivia, that followed the lead of the Italian Civil Code, there are other codes in the region that explicitly and generally reflect mitigation of damage by the creditor.[30]

The second method of collaboration is ordination, which may be understood as occurring when something that already existed in the codes of the region, and is presented in a more systematic way, lacks an appropriate order. I believe that the most obvious manifestation of this second method of collaboration is found in Article 93 of the PLACL, which has already been transcribed above. The function of this precept is to present, in a single article, the remedies against breach of contract. This arrangement renders usefulness because, in general, the codes of the region apply them in a dispersed way, omitting the treatment of some and reserving others to certain types of contract (conspicuously, sale).

Thus, for example, the Chilean Civil Code distinguishes between non-performance with obligations to do or not to do, and does not contain an explicit rule regarding obligations to give.[31] Secondly, termination is considered in relation to the conditional obligations.[32] Thirdly, reduction of the price is treated with regard to the discipline of partial impossibility,[33] measure (*cabida*),[34] eviction[35] and latent defects[36] in the contract of sale and purchase. Fourthly, the Chilean Civil Code does not deal with suspension, but this has been derived from a rule of damages, the *exceptio non adimpleti contractus*.[37]

B. Modification

The second result that can be produced by the relationship between the two purposes that motivate the PLACL is, as it were, less innocent than collaboration.

30 L San Martín, 'La carga del perjudicado de evitar o mitigar el daño' (2012) *Universidad Externado de Colombia* 29.
31 See Arts 1553 and 1555.
32 See Art 1489.
33 See Art 1814.
34 See Art 1832.
35 See Art 1852.
36 See Art 1860.
37 See Art 1552.

It is the modification of plots of contract law in terms that cannot be said to develop the plan of the legislator, but rather to alter it in a relatively incompatible way with the contractual paradigm prevailing at the time those codes came into effect.

The examples of this result are, in my view at least, more limited than when it deals with the collaborative relationship.

This happens, at least partially, because looking at things dispassionately, it is possible to consider that there is a contractual paradigm in the region. The existence of the 'mirror-image rule', the essential elements of the contract, or the relationship between non-performance and original impossibility might be examples of such a paradigm. The same cannot however be said with respect to other areas, such as the excessive disproportion referred to in Article 37 of the PLACL.[38]

In some cases, such as the Colombian and the Chilean examples, it may be considered that Article 37 modifies the understanding of the commutative requirement in force in both codes, which limits the protection provided by *laesio enormis* to certain *numerus clausus* cases established by the legislation.[39] However this does not happen, for example, in the case of the Argentinian,[40] Brazilian[41] and Paraguayan[42] civil codes.

In what cases can it be affirmed, then, that there has been a change that alters, in general, the contractual paradigm in the region?

In my opinion, some of the most obvious candidates would have been the modification of the mirror-image rule in the formation of consent, the suppression of the cause and the subject matter as essential elements of the contract, the establishment of a nullity without the need for a judicial declaration, the establishment of a notion of breach that absorbed all possible deviations in the performance of the contract, and the possibility of an anticipated termination of the contract.

Of all these possible candidates, the only one that clearly appears is the modification of the mirror-image rule. This is Article 25 of the PLACL, which has

[38] (1) A party may seek the adaptation of a contract or any of its clauses, or to annul the contract, if it or they give the other party an excessive advantage in contravention of the requirements of good faith.

(2) All circumstances must be taken into account when considering the existence of gross disparity, in particular the dependence of the aggrieved party and its extraordinary economic distress, urgent needs, ignorance or lack of experience.

Moreover, the relationship of trust existing between the parties as well as the nature and purpose of the contract must be taken into consideration.

(3) Upon request of the aggrieved party, the judge may adapt the contract in order to make it consistent with the agreement that would have been reached by the parties in accordance with good faith.

(4) The party against which an action of nullity is brought may also request adaptation in accordance with the previous paragraph, provided it promptly informs the other party of this decision.

[39] Thus, eg sale of real estate, interests, penalty clauses, partitions.

[40] See Art 954.

[41] See Art 157.

[42] See Art 671.

already been transcribed above and allows the contract to be formed even with discrepancies between the parties.

On the other hand, while nullity still requires judicial declaration,[43] the cause and the subject matter, as will be seen, continue to enjoy good health. As far as the notion of breach is concerned, although apparently broad, the fact is that it is by no means obvious that it covers all possible deviations. There is a problem of ambiguity here, which will be reviewed immediately.

Perhaps, with regard to remedies, the fact that they may be described as modalities of specific performance, the repair and replacement (Article 87) may be considered as a modification generalising the reduction of the price as a general remedy (Article 88) and that termination may operate by communication (Article 90).

C. Ambiguity

I will name as ambiguity the third result of the relationship between the two purposes of the PLACL.

I believe that there is ambiguity when, in the solution of a given problem, rules may be applied, some of which correspond to the contractual paradigm of the codes of the region and others instead to the CISG paradigm, and when trying to apply them together they are incompatible and, as a result, there is a certain indeterminacy as to which solution is to be applied.

It seems to me that the question is perfectly illustrated if we consider a case that, in the abstract, is capable of being classified as an original impossibility of contract and of error. The case can be one in which a thing that does not exist (nor is expected to exist) is sold. The question, then, under the PLACL, is how—if indeed there is a way—would the position of the buyer be protected?

It is convenient to start with the contractual paradigm in force in the region in this regard. Everything indicates that this would be a case of original impossibility due to lack of subject matter. Thus, for example, it happens in Article 953 of the Argentinian Civil Code or in Article 166 of the Brazilian Civil Code. On the other hand, with regard to the contract of sale, the first paragraph of Article 1814 of the Chilean Civil Code provides as follows: 'La venta de una cosa que al tiempo de perfeccionarse el contrato se supone existente y no existe, no produce efecto alguno'. The same provision is found in the first paragraph of Article 1870 of the Colombian Civil Code.

Instead, in what I have called the CISG paradigm, the subject matter conceived in this way has lost all relevance. To understand this, we can start with Articles 2:101 PECL and 3.1.2 of the UNIDROIT Principles.

[43] Art 42: 'Nullity may be invoked through an action or a defence'.

The first of these provides the following:

(1) A contract is concluded if:
  (a) the parties intend to be legally bound, and
  (b) they reach a sufficient agreement without any further requirement.
(2) A contract need not be concluded or evidenced in writing nor is it subject to any other requirement as to form. The contract may be proved by any means, including witnesses.

Similarly, Article 3.1.2 of the UNIDROIT Principles states: 'A contract is concluded, modified or terminated by the mere agreement of the parties, without any further requirement'.

Commenting on this precept, Huber indicates that it is clear that it aims to exclude cause and consideration as requirements of the contract.[44]

On the other hand, the commentary on Article 4:103 PECL points out:

> In some legal systems a contract which, unknown to the parties, is impossible to perform, for example, because of the absence of an *object* or because the seller has no right to dispose of the goods it is purporting to sell, may be ineffective. Under the Principles this approach is not taken. Very often such cases will be ones of fundamental mistake under which either party affected may avoid the contract, but there may be cases when a party should be treated as taking the risk of impossibility and therefore should not be entitled to avoid the contract.[45]

In this way, we can assume that in the CISG paradigm, the initial impossibility is resolved either as a case of error or as one of non-performance. On the other hand, as already seen, in the civil codes of the region, it is resolved as a case of absolute nullity due to lack of subject matter.

With this data, the question is this: how do the PLACL solve the problem? The answer, in my opinion, is ambiguous.

As we have seen, in the PLACL, the subject matter is an essential element of the contract. If it fails—a typical case of initial impossibility—everything indicates that we would face a case of absolute nullity. This, of course, does not happen in the PECL or in the UNIDROIT Principles. For the former, the case of lack of subject matter can be solved under the rules of error or non-performance.[46] The UNIDROIT Principles, on the other hand, would have to resort to the rules of non-performance.[47]

The point is that in the PLACL, both the notions of error and non-performance closely follow the PECL and the UNIDROIT Principles. It is worth remembering the notion of error of the PLACL: 'Ignorance or an

[44] M Huber, 'Commentary Article 3.1.2' in S Vogenauer (ed), *Commentary on the UNIDROIT Principles of International Commercial Contracts (PICC)*, 2nd edn (Oxford University Press, 2015) 467.
[45] PECL Pts I and II p 228. Italics in the original.
[46] See Art 4:119 PECL.
[47] See Art 3.2.4 UNIDROIT Principles.

erroneous assumption relating to facts or to law when of such importance that a reasonable person in the same situation would not have concluded the contract or would have done so on materially different terms'.

Everything indicates that if a person would have known that the thing he is acquiring does not exist, he would not have contracted. Therefore, the definition of error covers the case of lack of subject matter.

If one now remembers the notion of non-performance with Article 85 of the PLACL: '[N]on-performance is a failure to perform in the agreed manner', it seems evident that if the thing that is owed does not exist, the debtor will not comply with his obligation, therefore the hypothesis of lack of subject matter is also covered by the rules of non-performance.

Thus, it is not clear what space is left for the subject matter as an essential element of the contract.

Another illustration of the ambiguity that produces the coexistence of the two purposes in the PLACL appears in relation to the cause.

With regard to the cause, it has been pointed out that one of its functions has been to contribute to solving the problems caused by the alteration of circumstances (hardship). The point, however, is that this is explained by the absence of a rule that, in the respective civil code, may solve the problem in a more technically precise way. Well, the point is that in the current version of the PLACL there are rules in section 2 of chapter 8 on hardship that seek to resolve the issue more precisely.[48] In this way, there are two figures designed to solve the same question. It is, however, a much less controversial case than that of the subject matter since everything seems to indicate that, in the face of a case of altered circumstances, the rules that must prevail are those of Article 90 which turn the cause, at least in this respect, into something superfluous.

V. Conclusion

There are two driving forces within PLACL: one which aspires to systematise contract law in Latin America, and the other which seeks a certain modification

[48] 'Artículo 90. Concepto de imprevisión.

Si la ejecución del contrato se torna excesivamente onerosa, a causa de un cambio de circunstancias posterior a su perfección, cuyo acaecimiento no fue previsto o no era razonable preverlo, la parte afectada tiene derecho a requerir la renegociación del contrato.

Artículo 91. Efectos de la imprevisión.

Transcurrido un plazo razonable, si las partes no alcanzan un acuerdo, cualquiera podrá demandar la adaptación del contrato a las circunstancias sobrevinientes o la resolución.

Artículo 92. De la frustración del fin del contrato.

La frustración definitiva de la causa por un cambio de circunstancias existentes a la época de la perfección, imprevisto para las partes y que supera el riesgo asumido por aquella afectada, la autoriza a resolverlo.'

that will align the PLACL with certain relatively recent developments that have taken place in Europe.

The coexistence of these two aims has produced certain results in the text of the PLACL. Probably the most challenging is a certain ambiguity with respect to certain issues whose resolution will determine which way the balance tips—toward harmonisation, or toward the modernisation of contract law.

Resolving these ambiguities is still a pending issue. Likewise, the fate of the PLACL remains to be seen. Perhaps a more modest and realistic claim is that they constitute a foundation upon which an academic discussion could begin, in relation to the desired end for contract law in the region.

14

The Effects of European Harmonisation on Turkish Contract Law

IŞIK ÖNAY

I. Introduction

Having adapted the Swiss Civil Code and Code of Obligations into its own legal system, Turkish law has always been open to influences from Europe in the area of private law. In the last two decades, there have been important changes of legislation concerning Turkish contract law.

This chapter aims to (i) provide a brief overview of the development of Turkish contract law to give the reader a context; (ii) analyse and contrast selected novelties under the new Turkish Code of Obligations and other legislation to determine the extent to which these were influenced by the trends in European harmonisation of contract law.

II. A Brief Overview of the Development of Turkish Contract Law

The European influence on Turkish law dates back to the second half of the nineteenth century. Within the framework of the so-called *Tanzimat* reforms, the Ottoman Empire enacted legal reforms, among others. The rise of trade and capitalism necessitated the introduction of a modern legal system, since the Sharia-based legal system then in place was unable to address the problems caused by these new developments.[1] Inspired by the French revolution,[2] the Ottoman

[1] B Tanör, *Osmanlı-Türk Anayasal Gelişmeleri*, 26th edn (Yapı Kredi Yayınları, 2016) 98.

[2] AC Yıldırım, 'Ottoman Mecelle as a Secular Uniform Law Instrument' (2015) 10 *International Journal of Turcologia* 27, 33.

Empire joined the codification movement which started in Europe. The first step was the adaptation of the first three books of the French Commercial Code of 1807, which resulted in the enactment of the Ottoman Code of Commerce (*Kanunname-i Ticaret*) in 1850 and the Ottoman Code of Maritime Law (*Ticaret-i Bahriye Kanunnamesi*), which was also based on primarily French, but also Dutch, Prussian and Sardinian laws.[3]

The next step was to draft a civil code. Three alternatives were considered to that end, the first of which was to adopt the French *Code civil*. It was the Grand Vizier Ali Paşa who suggested such an approach to Sultan Abdülaziz in 1869.[4] A second suggestion, put by Hasan Fehmi Efendi, was to draft a purely Islamic code, bereft of any secular influence.[5] Eventually Sultan Abdülaziz decided to adopt a third alternative suggested by Ahmet Cevdet Paşa, which is considered a compromise between the aforementioned two suggestions.[6] *Mecelle-i Ahkâm-ı Adliyye (Mecelle)*, a code which was influenced by both the Hanafi school of Sunni Islam reasoning[7] and the French *Code civil*,[8] was drafted between 1869 and 1876. It consisted of 16 books and 1851 articles and regulated law of obligations, law of property and law of civil procedure. Each book was presented to Sultan Abdülaziz once drafted and entered in force only after his approval.[9]

The *Mecelle* remained in force until it was abolished upon the reception of the Swiss Civil Code and the Swiss Code of Obligations in 1926. There were several attempts to amend the *Mecelle*, and in 1923 a commission was tasked to draft a new civil code. However, these attempts failed and in 1925 Mahmut Esat Bozkurt, who acted as Minister of Justice from 1924 to 1930, dissolved the commission and announced the government's intention to adopt a western code.[10] Eventually Turkey decided to adopt the Swiss Civil Code and Code of Obligations, and the

[3] İ Ortaylı, *Batılılaşma Yolunda*, 7th edn (Merkez Kitaplar, 2007) 141; Yıldırım (n 2) 31; H Veldet, 'Kanunlaştırma Hareketleri ve Tanzimat' in *Tanzimat* (MEB Yayınları, 1999) 196–99; YM Atamer, 'Rezeption und Weiterentwicklung des schweizerischen Zivilgesetzbuches in der Türkei' (2008) 72 *Rabels Zeitschrift für ausländisches und internationales Privatrecht* 723; SS Onar, 'Osmanlı Hukukunda İslâm Hukukunun Bir Kısmının Codification'u Mecelle' (1954) XX *İstanbul Üniversitesi Hukuk Fakültesi Mecmuası* 57, 60.

[4] Veldet (n 3) 199–202.

[5] Yıldırım (n 2) 36.

[6] ibid 36; For more on the discussion in the nineteenth-century debate over whether to adopt the French *Code civil* or to draft the *Mecelle*, see S Örsten Esirgen, 'Osmanlı Devleti'nde medeni kanun tartışmaları: Mecelle mi, Fransız Medeni Kanunu mu?' (2011) 29 *Osmanlı Tarihi Araştırma ve Uygulama Merkezi Dergisi* 31.

[7] Atamer (n 3) 725; Onar (n 3) 84; Veldet (n 3) 192; C Osmanağaoğlu Karahasanoğlu, 'Mecelle-i Ahkam-ı Adliyye'nin Yürürlüğe Girişi ve Türk Hukuk Tarihi Bakımından Önemi' (2011) 29 *Ankara Üniversitesi Osmanlı Tarihi Araştırma ve Uygulama Merkezi Dergisi* 93, 102.

[8] For more on the French influence on the *Mecelle* see Veldet (n 3) 195; Yıldırım (n 2) 33–36. Despite this influence, it is important to note that the *Mecelle* does not recognise party autonomy in contract law (Onar (n 3) 71).

[9] For more on the general principles and individual books of the *Mecelle* and their entries into force see C Osmanağaoğlu Karahasanoğlu (n 7) 97–102; Onar (n 3) 65–71.

[10] Atamer (n 3) 729; Onar (n 3) 85.

Turkish Civil Code[11] and Code of Obligations[12] entered into force as of 4 October 1926. This choice was based on various reasons. Firstly and most importantly, many Turkish lawyers including the Minister of Justice himself were educated in French-speaking cantons of Switzerland and therefore were well acquainted with Swiss law.[13] Secondly, the Swiss codes were the most recent ones, and were much simpler in terms of language and were more compatible with a secular system when compared to their contemporary counterparts in Europe.[14]

There were several attempts to draft a new civil code, starting from the 1950s.[15] However, these attempts did not lead to a new legislation, but only to some changes of the then-current legislation, until the new Turkish Civil Code[16] (TCC) was adopted by the parliament on 22 November 2001 and entered into force as of 1 January 2002. The introduction of a new code of obligations took a further decade. The new Turkish Code of Obligations[17] (TCO) entered into force as of 1 July 2012 together with the new Turkish Commercial Code (TComC). Another important development concerning contract law was the introduction of the Law on Consumer Protection[18] in 1995, which was later replaced by a new Law on Consumer Protection[19] (LoCP) entering into force on 28 May 2014. Lastly it should be noted that Turkey is a contracting state to the United Nations Convention on International Sale of Goods (CISG), and CISG has been a part of Turkish law since 1 August 2011.[20]

III. Effects of European Harmonisation on Turkish Contract Law

As explained above, this chapter aims to explore whether the development of Turkish contract law is in any way affected by European harmonisation of contract law. To this end, a selection of recent changes in contract law will be analysed with regard to their similarities and differences to the legal instruments created during European harmonisation of contract law.

[11] Law no 743 (OG, 4.4.1926, no 339).

[12] Law no 818 (OG, 8.5.1926, no 366).

[13] Atamer (n 3) 731; K Oğuzman and N Barlas, *Medenî Hukuk*, 21st edn (Vedat Kitapçılık, 2015) N 97; R Serozan, *Medeni Hukuk*, 6th edn (Vedat Kitapçılık, 2016) 65.

[14] Oğuzman and Barlas (n 13) N 98; Atamer (n 3) 731–33; Serozan (n 13) 64.

[15] Oğuzman and Barlas (n 13) N 102 ff.

[16] Law no 4721 (OG, 8.12.2001, no 24607).

[17] Law no 6098 (OG, 4.2.2011, no 27836).

[18] Law no 4077 (OG, 8.3.1995, no 22221).

[19] Law no 6502 (OG, 28.11.2013, no 28835).

[20] See Law no 5870 (OG 14.4.2009, no 27200) and the Council of Ministers Decision no 2010/247 (OG, 7.4.2010, 27545). Instruments of ratification, acceptance, approval and accession were deposited with the Secretary-General of the United Nations in accordance with CISG Art 91(4) on 7 July 2010 and therefore CISG came into force on 1.8.2011 (see CISG Art 99(2)).

IV. Selected Novelties in the Turkish Code of Obligations

A good starting point before addressing selected novelties in the TCO is its general preamble, which explicitly mentions the international and regional harmonisation efforts in the area of law of obligations. UNIDROIT (International Institute for the Unification of Private Law) and UNCITRAL (United Nations Commission on International Trade Law) are mentioned as institutions contributing to the studies on harmonisation. The general preamble also refers to the European Commission's 'Action Plan on a More Coherent European Contract Law'[21] and its Communication 'European Contract Law and the revision of the Acquis: The Way Forward'.[22] Furthermore the preamble lists the following as the most important products of these harmonisation efforts: Principles of International Commercial Contracts (UNIDROIT Principles); United Nations Convention on Contracts for the International Sale of Goods (CISG); Principles of European Contract Law (PECL) and Principles of European Tort Law (PETL). The preamble goes on to say that although the new code is not entirely based on these instruments, they were taken into account in the drafting of the new code. The following analysis aims to assess the accuracy of this statement in the preamble by taking selected novelties concerning contract law and comparing those with the aforementioned instruments.

V. Unsolicited Goods (TCO Article 7)

The article in the TCO concerning the sending of unsolicited goods can be translated as follows: 'The delivery of unsolicited goods does not constitute an offer. The recipient is not obliged to return or to preserve the goods'.

No such rule was found in the old Code of Obligations, and therefore it is a novelty. The aim of introducing such a rule was to punish and discourage sellers who turn to aggressive marketing techniques to pressure consumers into buying goods hence raising their profits.[23]

[21] Communication from the Commission to the European Parliament and the Council of 12 February 2003 'A more coherent European contract law—An action plan' COM(2003) 68 final.

[22] Communication from the Commission to the European Parliament and the Council of 11 October 2004 'European Contract Law and the Revision of the Acquis: The Way Forward' COM(2004) 651 final.

[23] MM İnceoğlu and B Başoğlu, 'Sipariş Edilmemiş Malların Gönderilmesi' in Bİ Engin, B Baysal and T Aydın Ünver (eds), *Prof Dr Rona Serozan'a Armağan* (Oniki Levha Yayıncılık, 2010) 982; MK Oğuzman and MT Öz, *Borçlar Hukuku Genel Hükümler*, vol 1, 13th edn (Vedat Kitapçılık, 2015), N 187.

Similar rules were introduced in legislations of EU member states[24] due to Article 9 of the Distance Contracts Directive,[25] which required member states (i) to prohibit the supply of goods or services to a consumer without their being ordered by the consumer beforehand, where such supply involves a demand for payment and (ii) to exempt the consumer from the provision of any consideration in cases of unsolicited supply, the absence of a response not constituting consent. The article was later amended by Article 15 of the Unfair Commercial Practices Directive[26] and finally the Distance Contracts Directive was replaced by the Directive on Consumer Rights,[27] Article 27 of which states the following:

> The consumer shall be exempted from the obligation to provide any consideration in cases of unsolicited supply of goods, water, gas, electricity, district heating or digital content or unsolicited provision of services, prohibited by Article 5(5) and point 29 of Annex I to Directive 2005/29/EC. In such cases, the absence of a response from the consumer following such an unsolicited supply or provision shall not constitute consent.

A rule on unsolicited goods is also present in the Draft Common Frame of Reference (DCFR) II-3:401:

(1) If a business delivers unsolicited goods to, or performs unsolicited services for, a consumer:

(a) no contract arises from the consumer's failure to respond or from any other action or inaction by the consumer in relation to the goods and services; and
(b) no non-contractual obligation arises from the consumer's acquisition, retention, rejection or use of the goods or receipt of benefit from the services.

(2) Sub-paragraph (b) of the preceding paragraph does not apply if the goods or services were supplied:

(a) by way of benevolent intervention in another's affairs; or
(b) in error or in such other circumstances that there is a right to reversal of an unjustified enrichment.

(3) This Article is subject to the rules on delivery of excess quantity under a contract for the sale of goods.

(4) For the purposes of paragraph (1) delivery occurs when the consumer obtains physical control over the goods.

[24] For examples from Germany and Austria respectively see §241a BGB and §864(2) ABGB.
[25] Directive 97/7/EC of the European Parliament and of the Council of 20 May 1997 on the protection of consumers in respect of distance contracts [1997] OJ L144/19.
[26] UCPD 2005/29/EC.
[27] CRD 2011/83/EU.

Based on the aforementioned, the introduction of an article regulating unsolicited goods into TCO seems to be in line with the trend in European harmonisation efforts. It must however be noted that the drafting of TCO Article 7 was not a product of a thorough analysis of trends in European private law, but a mere translation of Article 6a of the Swiss Code of Obligations (SCO), which has been in force since 1 July 1991. This is also acknowledged by the legislator itself in the explanatory notes on TCO Article 7.

There are a few problematic issues with TCO Article 7, worth mentioning in comparison with its counterparts in European private law. Firstly, Article 7 does not contain any exception to the rule, whereas DCFR II-3:401, SCO 6a, § 241a (2) BGB, 864 (2) ABGB all state that that the recipient of unsolicited goods may indeed face non-contractual claims, if it is clear to the recipient that the goods were sent mistakenly. The initial draft of the TCO Article 7 contained a similar second paragraph, however this was removed in parliamentary debate. The rationale behind this was to encourage diligent behaviour on part of senders of such goods.[28] Despite the absence of an express rule, the same conclusion may still be reached under Turkish law by imposing on the recipient a duty to inform the sender, where it is obvious that the goods were sent mistakenly. Such duty may be based on the good faith and fair dealing principle regulated under TCC Article 2.[29]

A second derogation from the trends of European private law concerns the scope of the article regarding the persons involved. DCFR II-3:401 and §241a(2) BGB require the recipient to be a consumer, whereas this is not the case for either Turkish or Swiss law. It is however rightly argued that the scope of the article shall be limited to consumers, by way of teleological interpretation.[30] This problem is further complicated with the new LoCP, which entered into force two years later than the TCO. LoCP Article 7 contains a similar article for unsolicited goods and services, which is parallel to the Consumers Rights Directive.[31] In order to reach the desirable outcome that the rule only applies to consumers, one could easily argue that the legislator limited the application of the rule to consumers, by introducing a rule that is more recent and specific when compared to the rule in TCO (*lex posterior specialis derogat legi priori generali*).[32]

The scope of Article 7 with regard to the subject matter of the contract seems to be limited to goods.[33] This however is not the case in DCFR, Directive on

[28] İnceoğlu and Başoğlu (n 23) 996–97.

[29] ibid 1020; HN Nomer, *Borçlar Hukuku Genel Hükümler*, 14th edn (Beta, 2015) N 22; M Şeker, '6098 sayılı Türk Borçlar Kanununa Göre Ismarlanmamış Şeyin Gönderilmesi (BK.7)' 2013/2 *İstanbul Ticaret Üniversitesi Sosyal Bilimler Dergisi* 81, 92.

[30] İnceoğlu and Başoğlu (n 23) 997–99; Nomer (n 29) N 22; N Yavuz, *Türk Borçlar Kanunu'nun Getirdiği Yenilikler ve Değişiklikler*, 2nd edn (Adalet Yayınevi, 2012) 34.

[31] 'In cases when unsolicited goods or services are sent or provided, the consumer shall not be subject to any claim. In these cases, the consumer remaining silent, using the good or the service does not amount to an acceptance to form a contract. The consumer is under no obligation to return or preserve the good.'

[32] Nomer (n 29) N 22.

[33] İnceoğlu and Başoğlu (n 23) 1000–02.

Consumer Rights or BGB, which also include services within the scope. Although the exclusion of services from TCO Article 7 is difficult to justify, this problem seems to have been solved by the LoCP, which expressly includes unsolicited services within its scope.

Another critique of Article 7 concerns its wording. The article states that the delivery of unsolicited goods is not an offer. This formulation may however, in certain cases, work against the recipient, whom the article aims to protect. Assuming that the recipient is happy with the product and the price, the statement by the recipient that he/she wishes to buy the product will constitute the offer and the sender will be able to reject the offer and ask for a higher price.[34] This is not the case in the DCFR and Consumer Rights Directive, where it is merely stated that the failure to respond is not acceptance. This problem could be overcome by the argument that such rejection would constitute an act in contradiction to its previous conduct on sender's part (*venire contra factum proprium*). Nonetheless, again, this problem seems to be solved by LoCP Article 7, which merely states that silence or use on part of the consumer, who has been provided with unsolicited good or services, does not amount to an acceptance to form a contract.

As explained above, the inclusion of an article regulating unsolicited goods into TCO seems to be in line with the European harmonisation efforts. However it seems very unlikely that the legislator took the developments in European private law into account in the drafting of the article, which seems to be a replica of the SCO Article 6a and is prone to problems, which might have been avoided by a thorough analysis of European legislation. In my opinion the introduction of LoCP Article 7 is a welcome change, rendering TCO Article 7 inapplicable to consumer transactions. Since the application of TCO Article 7 shall already be limited to consumer transactions by teleological interpretation, the introduction of LoCP Article 7 is to be considered an implicit revocation of TCO Article 7.

VI. Standard Terms (TCO Articles 20–25)

Articles 20–25 of TCO regulate standard terms and were not to be found in the former code. Prior to the TCO's entry into force, the regulation of standard terms was limited to consumer transactions. Provisions on standard terms were present in the former Law on Consumer Protection, and this is also the case in the LoCP (Article 5), which is currently in force. The provisions in the legislation on consumer protection are regulated under the heading 'unfair terms' and are heavily influenced by the EC Directive[35] on unfair terms in consumer contracts.

[34] Oğuzman and Öz (n 23) N 187.

[35] Council Directive 93/13/EEC of 5 April 1993 on unfair terms in consumer contracts [1993] OJ L95/29.

Another provision on standard terms is to be found under TComC Article 55 in the context of unfair competition. The provisions in LoCP and TComC are considered as *lex specialis* vis-à-vis the provisions in TCO and are applicable to respectively consumer or commercial transactions.[36] It should however be noted that the existence of TComC Article 55 does not preclude the application of TCO Articles 20–25 to commercial transactions.[37]

The introduction of a regulation on standard terms into TCO, widening the scope of the control on standard terms to non-consumers is a welcome change and seems to be in line with the trends in European countries (eg §§305–10 BGB; §§879(3) and 864a ABGB).[38] The instruments drafted with the aim of harmonising European contract law also contain provisions on standard terms (DCFR II-1:109, 9:103(1), 9:408, 9:403; PECL 2:209(3); UNIDROIT Principles Articles 2.1.19(2), 2.1.20, 4.6).

TCO Article 20 defines the concept of standard terms as terms presented to one of the parties that were formulated by the other party alone, in advance, with the intention to be used in multiple similar contracts. This definition is very much in line with the definitions provided under DCFR II-1:109,[39] PECL 2:209(3)[40] and UNIDROIT Principles Article 2.1.19.[41] The definition of an unfair term per LoCP Article 5 however seems to be wider in scope, considering that it does not include the requirements of having been drafted in advance and the intention of use for multiple contracts. A similar definition is also provided under Article 3 of the EC Directive on Unfair Terms in Consumer Contracts.[42]

TCO Article 21(1) states that standard terms, which are to the detriment of the recipient of those, only become part of the contract if the supplying party expressly informs the other party about the existence of these terms and makes it

[36] Oğuzman and Öz (n 23) N 501–502.

[37] YM Atamer, 'Genel İşlem Koşulu mu Bireysel Pazarlıkla Kurulan Sözleşme mi? Tüketici ve Tacir İşlemleri Açısından Karşılaştırmalı Olarak Başvurulabilecek Değerlendirme Kriterleri' in Ç Kırca (ed), *Yeni Türk Borçlar Kanunu ve Yeni Türk Ticaret Kanunu Sempozyumu—Makaleler Tebliğler* (Vedat Kitapçılık, 2013) 103, fn 2; E Büyüksagis, 'Turkish Contract Law Reform: Standard Terms, Unforeseen Circumstances, and Judicial Intervention' 17 *European Busineness Organisation Law Review* 423, 439; Oğuzman and Öz (n 23) N 502; cp G Antalya, *Borçlar Hukuku Genel Hükümler*, vol 1 (Legal Yayınevi, 2012) 296: The author argues that TCO Art(s) 20–25 are not applicable to commercial transactions.

[38] YM Atamer, 'Yeni Türk Borçlar Kanunu Hükümleri Uyarınca Genel İşlem Koşullarının Denetlenmesi- TKHK M.6 ve TTK M. 55, F. 1, (f) ile Karşılaştırmalı Olarak' in B Şit (ed), *Türk Hukukunda Genel İşlem Şartları Sempozyumu* (Banka ve Ticaret Hukuku Araştırma Enstitüsü, 2011) 10; Büyüksagis (n 37) 432 ff.

[39] 'A "standard term" is a term which has been formulated in advance for several transactions involving different parties and which has not been individually negotiated by the parties'.

[40] 'General conditions of contract are terms which have been formulated in advance for an indefinite number of contracts of a certain nature, and which have not been individually negotiated between the parties.'

[41] 'Standard terms are provisions which are prepared in advance for general and repeated use by one party and which are actually used without negotiation with the other party'.

[42] Atamer (n 38) 20.

possible for the other party to examine these. The DCFR contains a similar rule under DCFR II-9:103(1).[43] TCO Article 21(1) is rightly criticised for requiring the standard terms to be to the detriment of the recipient, although this stage of the control on standard terms (incorporation test) shall merely pertain to whether the standard terms are included within the contract or not.[44] The control over the content of standard terms is regulated under TCO Article 25 and shall only be relevant if standard terms overcome the incorporation test per TCO Article 21 and become part of the contract.

According to TCO Article 21(2), surprising clauses in standard terms do not become part of the contract even if the formulating party expressly informed the other party about the existence of standard terms and took necessary steps to provide access to those. Such clauses can only be considered part of the contract provided that these were expressly explained to and agreed by the other party.[45] A similar rule is also found under UNIDROIT Principles Article 2.1.20(1).[46]

TCO Article 22 states that in cases where standard terms are not considered part of the contract, the rest of the contract shall not be affected by the invalidity of standard terms. DCFR contains a similar rule under II-9:408(2).[47] TCO Article 23 concerns interpretation of standard terms and adopts the *contra proferentem* rule. Accordingly, standard terms shall in doubt be interpreted to the disadvantage of the party who has formulated those. The same rule is also present under PICC 4.6[48] and DCFR II-8:103[49] as general principles of contract interpretation. TCO Article 25 forbids the inclusion of clauses in the standard terms that are to the detriment of the other party in a way that contradicts good faith and fair dealing.

The new articles of TCO on standard terms seem at first glance to be influenced by European harmonisation. The explanatory notes on TCO Articles 20–25 do indeed refer to EU legislation and the German Civil Code (BGB). However, a closer look reveals that the articles in TCO are not as detailed as the ones in BGB (§§305–10). A good example is TCO Article 25 on the reasonableness test for

43 'Terms supplied by one party and not individually negotiated may be invoked against the other party only if the other party was aware of them, or if the party supplying the terms took reasonable steps to draw the other party's attention to them, before or when the contract was concluded'.

44 Atamer (n 38) 27–28.

45 ibid 29–30; Oğuzman and Öz (n 23) N 513; Büyüksagis (n 37) 433.

46 'No term contained in standard terms which is of such a character that the other party could not reasonably have expected it, is effective unless it has been expressly accepted by that party'.

47 'If the contract can reasonably be maintained without the unfair term, the other terms remain binding on the parties'.

48 'If contract terms supplied by one party are unclear, an interpretation against that party is preferred'.

49 '(1) Where there is doubt about the meaning of a term not individually negotiated, an interpretation of the term against the party who supplied it is to be preferred. (2) Where there is doubt about the meaning of any other term, and that term has been established under the dominant influence of one party, an interpretation of the term against that party is to be preferred'.

contents of standard terms, which is drafted in a very vague manner, leading to a lack of legal certainty.[50] This is neither the case in BGB (§§307–09) nor in DCFR (II-9:403–08).

One shortcoming of the rules on standard terms is the fact that the rules do not make a distinction based on the type of contract. DCFR contains different provisions for contracts between businesses (DCFR II-9:405), non-business parties (DCFR II-9:404) and businesses and consumers (DCFR II-9:403). BGB also distinguishes between types of contracts in determining the scope of application for the rules on standard terms (BGB §310). Such a distinction does make sense, because the degree of ideal protection differs depending on the type of contract.[51] For example the incorporation test is usually deemed unnecessary for business-to-business contracts, as businesses cannot be expected to warn the other party about standard terms and take necessary steps to provide access in the urgency of daily business life.[52]

Another criticism directed at the TCO regarding its provisions on standard terms concerns the dichotomy created by two different sets of rules. The TCO's provisions have been criticised as the already existing rules under the legislation on consumer protection were not properly observed during the drafting of the new rules.[53]

A prima facie look leaves the impression that by introducing rules on standard terms into the TCO, the legislator was influenced by European harmonisation. Nonetheless a closer look again reveals that the legislator failed to make proper use of the experience accumulated during the studies for harmonisation.

VII. Unfair Exploitation/Gross Disparity (TCO Article 28)

Another novelty in the new code concerns unfair exploitation. Article 28 of TCO provides that if there is gross disparity between the obligations of the parties, which is deliberately caused by one of the parties taking advantage of the other party's distress, urgent needs, inexperience or ignorance, the disadvantaged party may either avoid or adapt the contract, to correct the disparity.

The old TCO already had a provision (Article 21) on unfair exploitation, and entitled the exploited party to avoid the contract. The novelty in the new code is

[50] Atamer (n 38) 41–42; Büyüksagis (n 37) 440.

[51] E Kuntalp, 'Bankalar ve Genel İşlem Koşulları' (Türk Hukukunda Genel İşlem Şartları Sempozyumu, 08.04.2011) 93. On the different criteria to be applied to business-to-business contracts and business-to-consumer contracts, see Atamer (n 37) 26 ff.

[52] Atamer (n 38) 35.

[53] ibid 10, 71.

an additional right granted to the exploited party. It is difficult to determine the source of inspiration for this change, as the explanatory notes on the article are silent on that matter. However, it must be noted that the prevailing opinion in both the Turkish[54] and the Swiss[55] doctrines and before the Swiss Federal Court[56] allowed for such an adaptation, despite the lack of an express regulation. Therefore, it is very likely that the change is a reaction of the legislator to views expressed in legal literature. Nonetheless the right to adapt in cases of unfair exploitation/gross disparity is also granted under UNIDROIT Principles (3.2.7), PECL (4:109) and DCFR (II-7:207), and the change is in line with trends embraced during European harmonisation of contract law.

VIII. Hardship (TCO Article 138)

TCO Article 138 states that if the performance becomes extremely onerous due to an unexpected change of circumstances after the formation of contract, and if such change is not attributable to the debtor, the debtor may ask the court to adapt the contract to the changed circumstances, or may terminate the contract if such adaptation is not viable.

Although the former TCO did not contain such a regulation in the general part on contracts,[57] the same principle was embraced both by the scholars[58] and courts[59] relying on the good faith and fair dealing principle under TCC Article 2 II. Therefore the regulation is considered to be a mere inclusion of a principle adopted by legal scholars and case law into the new code.[60]

Although the explanatory notes on the article only refer to the German theory of *Wegfall der Geschäftsgrundlage*, similar provisions on hardship are also available under DCFR III-1:110, PECL 6:111, UNIDROIT Principles Articles 6.2.2–6.2.3 and CESL Article 89. In contrast to those articles, TCO Article 138 does not expressly require parties to negotiate before the contract may be subject to adaptation or termination.[61]

[54] N Kocayusufpaşaoğlu, *Borçlar Hukukuna Giriş—Hukuki İşlem, Sözleşme*, 5th edn (Filiz Kitabevi, 2010) § 39 N 28.

[55] P Gauch et al, *Schweizerisches Obligationenrecht Allgemeiner Teil*, vol 1, 9th edn (Schultess, 2008) N 754.

[56] BGE 123 III 292.

[57] A similar provision regulating hardship was provided for contracts for work under Art 365(2) of the former TCO. A counterpart of this article is still in force under TCO Art 480(2).

[58] Büyüksagis (n 37) 442.

[59] Yarg 13 HD, 12.2.1981, 147/932; Yarg HGK, 18.11.1998, 13-815/835.

[60] Oğuzman and Öz (n 23) N 1836.

[61] Büyüksagis (n 37) 443–44; cp R Serozan, *Borçlar Hukuku Genel Bölüm—İfa, İfa Engelleri, Haksız Zenginleşme* (6th edn, Filiz Kitabevi 2014) §20 N 9.

IX. Passing of Risk in Sales Contracts (TCO Article 208)

One of the most fundamental changes that the TCO introduced regards passing of risk in sales contracts. The previous code (Article 183) adopted the Roman principle *periculum est emptoris*, and therefore the buyer bore the risk once the contract was concluded. Although this rule is still maintained by Swiss law (Article 185 OR),[62] the Turkish legislator decided to take the transfer of possession as the event that as a rule transfers the risk and benefits of the good to the buyer.[63] TCO Article 208(1) provides that unless stated otherwise by law or in the contract, the risk is deemed to pass when the buyer acquires possession of the personal property.

The deciding moment for the transfer of the risk in the sale of real (immovable) property on the other hand is set as the moment of registration into the land registry. However according to TCO Article 245(1), if the parties have agreed to carry out the delivery at a time after the registration, risks and benefits of the real property are deemed to pass at the time of delivery. TCO Article 245(2) requires such agreement to be in writing.

TCO Article 208(2) provides an exception to the rule, whereby the risk is deemed to pass to the buyer if the buyer defaults in accepting delivery of the goods. TCO Article 208(3) provides another exception to the rule. Accordingly, if the seller sends the goods to another place than the place of performance at the buyer's request, risks and benefits pass with the delivery of the goods to the carrier. If fungible goods are sold, the goods need to be identified in these exceptional cases for the risk to pass (also see CISG Article 67(2); DCFR IV-A 5:102(2)). This requirement seems to be omitted by the legislator, but shall nevertheless be observed in the application of the article.[64]

The explanatory notes on TCO Article 208 refer to CISG and BGB. The notes justify the change of rule by pointing to criticisms directed at the old rule (*periculum est emptoris*) in legal literature and the fact that transfer possession is the deciding moment regarding the passing of risk for personal property in rules regulating international trade.

[62] See H Honsell, *Schweizerisches Obligationenrecht—Besonderer Teil* (Stämpfli Verlag, 2010) 52 ff.

[63] T Ansay and I Önay, 'Sales of Personal Property' in T Ansay and EC Schneider (eds), *Introduction to Turkish Business Law*, 2nd edn (Kluwer International, 2014) 25–26.

[64] YM Atamer, 'Taşınır Satımı Sözleşmesi' in MM İnceoğlu (ed), *Türk Borçlar Kanunu Sempozyumu—Makaleler—Tebliğler* (Oniki Levha Yayıncılık, 2012) 193–94: The author suggests the application of CISG Art 67(2) to domestic sales by analogy. HN Nomer and Bİ Engin, *Türk Borçlar Kanunu Şerhi—Özel Borç İlişkileri—Cilt 1: Satış Sözleşmesi—1. Fasikül*, 3rd edn (Seçkin Yayıncılık, 2016) Art 208 N 40 and 43.

The change in the rule governing passing of risk in sales contracts is a welcome one as it has corrected a rule which has been criticised for being unjust.[65] The change also seems to be in line with European and international trends regarding the issue (see DCFR IV-A 5:102(1);[66] CISG Article 67(1);[67] CESL 142–43).

X. Law on Consumer Protection

Consumer protection is the area of contract law where Turkish law is most extensively influenced by European harmonisation. Article 172 of the Turkish Constitution of 1982 states that the state shall take measures to protect and inform consumers and shall encourage their initiatives to protect themselves. However, Turkey's first legislation on consumer protection[68] was introduced as late as 1995, when Turkey and the EU established a Customs Union, obliging Turkey to align its legislation with EU in terms of consumer protection.

As EU's relationship with Turkey progressed, Turkey kept aligning its legislation with EU law. To this end, a major revision[69] was undertaken in 2003.[70] Although there were several revision attempts after 2003,[71] it was only in 2013 that a new Law on Consumer Protection (LoCP)[72] was introduced. The general preamble of LoCP, which entered into force on 28 May 2014, states that the new law aims to implement the following directives into Turkish law:

— Council Directive 87/357/EEC of 25 June 1987 on the approximation of the laws of the Member States concerning products which, appearing to be other than they are, endanger the health or safety of consumers [1987] OJ L192/49;

— Council Directive 90/314/EEC of 13 June 1990 on package travel, package holidays and package tours [1990] OJ L158/59;

[65] Atamer (n 64) 188–190; Nomer and Engin (n 64) Art 208 N 5.

[66] 'The risk passes when the buyer takes over the goods or the documents representing them'.

[67] 'If the contract of sale involves carriage of the goods and the seller is not bound to hand them over at a particular place, the risk passes to the buyer when the goods are handed over to the first carrier for transmission to the buyer in accordance with the contract of sale. If the seller is bound to hand the goods over to a carrier at a particular place, the risk does not pass to the buyer until the goods are handed over to the carrier at that place. The fact that the seller is authorised to retain documents controlling the disposition of the goods does not affect the passage of the risk'.

[68] Law no 4077 (OG, 8.3.1995, no 22221).

[69] Law no 4822 amending the Law on Consumer Protection (OG, 14.3.2003, 25048).

[70] For a thorough analysis of Law no 4077 in comparison with EU directives see YM Atamer and HW Micklitz, 'The Implementation of the EU Consumer Protection Directives' 27 *Penn State International Law Review* 551.

[71] ibid 606–07.

[72] Law no 6502 (OG, 28.11.2013, no 28835).

- Council Directive 93/13/EEC of 5 April 1993 on unfair terms in consumer contracts [1993] OJ L95/29;
- Directive 98/6/EC of the European Parliament and of the Council of 16 February 1998 on consumer protection in the indication of the prices of products offered to consumers [1998] OJ L80/27;
- Directive 1999/44/EC of the European Parliament and of the Council of 25 May 1999 on certain aspects of the sale of consumer goods and associated guarantees [1999] OJ L171/12;
- Directive 2002/65/EC of the European Parliament and of the Council of 23 September 2002 concerning the distance marketing of consumer financial services and amending Council Directive 90/619/EEC and Directives 97/7/EC and 98/27/EC [2002] OJ L 271/16;
- Directive 2005/29/EC of the European Parliament and of the Council of 11 May 2005 concerning unfair business-to-consumer commercial practices in the internal market and amending Council Directive 84/450/EEC, Directives 97/7/EC, 98/27/EC and 2002/65/EC of the European Parliament and of the Council and Regulation (EC) No 2006/2004 of the European Parliament and of the Council [2002] OJ L149/22;
- Directive 2006/114/EC of the European Parliament and of the Council of 12 December 2006 concerning misleading and comparative advertising [2006] OJ L 376/21;
- Directive 2008/48/EC of the European Parliament and of the Council of 23 April 2008 on credit agreements for consumers and repealing Council Directive 87/102/EEC [2008] OJ L133/66;
- Directive 2008/122/EC of the European Parliament and of the Council of 14 January 2009 on the protection of consumers in respect of certain aspects of timeshare, long-term holiday product, resale and exchange contracts, [2008] OJ L33/10;
- Directive 2009/22/EC of the European Parliament and of the Council of 23 April 2009 on injunctions for the protection of consumers' interests [2009] OJ L110/269;
- Directive 2011/83/EU of the European Parliament and of the Council of 25 October 2011 on consumer rights, amending Council Directive 93/13/EEC and Directive 1999/44/EC of the European Parliament and of the Council and repealing Council Directive 85/577/EEC and Directive 97/7/EC of the European Parliament and of the Council [2011] OJ L304/64;
- Commission Recommendation 98/257/EC of 30 March 1998 on the principles applicable to the bodies responsible for out-of-court settlement of consumer disputes [1998] OJ L115/31;
- Commission Recommendation 2001/310/EC of 4 April 2001 on the principles for out-of-court bodies involved in the consensual resolution of consumer disputes [2001] OJ L109/56.

XI. Late Payment in the Provision of Goods and Services (TComC Article 1530)

TComC Article 1530 is inspired by the Directive on Combating Late Payment in Commercial Transactions (2011/7/EU).[73] The aim of this article is to discourage late payments in commercial transactions among businesses. The need for such a regulation became apparent as certain big enterprises started to use late payments as a method of financing. This habit particularly harmed micro-SMEs, eg those providing goods for supermarkets, and led to an increase in the number of bankruptcies. To prevent this trend of late payment and to establish a new trend of prompt payment, Article 1530 regulates payment periods, conditions for default, interest rates in a way to discourage late payments.[74]

Since TComC Article 1530 is very much in line with Directive 2011/7/EU, I will not elaborate on details of it. However, some derogations from the directive and inconsistencies with Turkish contract law are worthy of note.

Firstly, the scope of the article seems to differ from the directive in two aspects. The scope of the article is limited to transactions made for supply of goods and services between commercial enterprises (TComC Article 1530(2)).[75] Since the definition of commercial enterprise per TComC Article 11(1) excludes small business owners (tradesmen) and liberal professions, the scope of TComC Article 1530 seems to be narrower than the scope of Directive 2011/7/EU, which is applicable to commercial transactions between undertakings.[76] Article 2(3) of the directive defines undertaking as 'any organisation, other than a public authority, acting in the course of its independent economic or professional activity, even where that activity is carried out by a single person'.

A second derogation from the directive regarding the article's scope pertains to public authorities. In contrast to the directive (Article 4), transactions between public authorities and undertakings are not explicitly covered by the article.[77]

[73] Directive 2011/7/EU of the European Parliament and of the Council of 16 February 2011 on combating late payment in commercial transactions [2011] OJ L48/1.

[74] YM Atamer and G Okutan Nilsson, 'Para Alacaklısının Geç Ödemelere Karşı Korunmasına İlişkin Yeni TK M. 1530 Düzenlemesi ve Uygulama Alanı' XXIX *Banka ve Ticaret Hukuku Dergisi* 31, 33–35; H Ülgen et al, *Ticari İşletme Hukuku* (On İki Levha Yayıncılık, 2015) N 615; S Ayan, '6102 Sayılı Türk Ticaret Kanunu'nun 1530. Maddesi Gereğince Borçlunun Temerrüdü' 12 *Dokuz Eylül Üniversitesi Hukuk Fakültesi Dergisi* 717, 720–25; AH Dural, 'Ticari İşletmeler Arasındaki Mal ve Hizmet Tedariki Sözleşmelerine İlişkin Yeni Ticaret Kanunu'nun 1530. Maddesi' (Yeni Türk Ticaret Kanunu'nun Ticari İşletme Hukuku Alanında Getirdiği Yenilikler Sempozyumu—25–26.11.2011) 119–20.

[75] Ülgen and others (n 74) N 615.

[76] Atamer and Okutan Nilsson (n 74) 64–66: the authors argue that Art 1530 shall be interpreted in line with the directive to include small business-owners (tradesmen); however they admit that liberal professions fall outside the scope of the article, but point to a need for a change of legislation to cover those as well. For an interpretation of the article including liberal professions within the scope see Dural (n 74) 122.

[77] Dural (n 74) 122.

Nevertheless activities undertaken by public authorities shall fall under the scope of the article as long as these are of a private law nature. Activities of a public law nature would however not be covered by the article.[78]

It must also be noted that TCO Article 1530(2) contains a statement, which is difficult to reconcile with general principles of Turkish contract law. Although fault is not a requirement for default under the TCO, and interest for default in monetary obligations can be claimed in the absence of fault on the debtor's part, TComC 1530(2) seems to require fault for default. This inconsistency is caused by the direct translation of Article 3(1)(b) of the Directive.[79] Some scholars argue that despite its wording, the article shall be read in accordance with the general principles of Turkish contract law,[80] whereas others argue that fault is only required to trigger the consequences of default under TComC Article 1530, in particular the increased default interest rate. According to the latter view, in the absence of fault on the debtor's part the creditor would be able to resort to the general provisions regulating default but not to those regulated under TComC Article 1530.[81]

Another problem caused by the (this time inaccurate) translation concerns the calculation of interest rates. Article 2(6) of the directive defines 'statutory interest rate' as simple interest for late payment at a rate which is equal to the sum of the reference rate and at least eight percentage points. TComC Article 1530(7) on the other hand states that the statutory interest rate for late payment within the context of TComC Article 1530 is to be determined by the Central Bank of the Republic of Turkey on January each year and requires this rate to be at least 8 per cent more than the default interest rate applicable to commercial transactions. Although some scholars argued for a teleological interpretation in line with the Directive, which would serve the purpose of discouraging late payment,[82] the Central Bank adopted a literal interpretation.[83] As of 1 January 2017, the Central Bank of the Republic of Turkey set the interest rate as 10.75 per cent.

XII. Conclusion

The analysis of selected novelties in Turkish contract law above reveals that the changes are mostly in the same direction as the products of European harmonisation.

[78] Atamer and Okutan Nilsson (n 74); P Çağlayan, 'Avrupa Birliği Yönergeleri ve Alman Hukukundaki Deneyimler Işığında Mal ve Hizmet Tedarikinde Geç Ödemenin Sonuçları (TK 1530)' XXVII *Banka ve Ticaret Hukuku Dergisi* 173, 218.

[79] '[T]he creditor is entitled to interest for late payment without the necessity of a reminder, where the following conditions are satisfied: … (b) the creditor has not received the amount due on time, *unless the debtor is not responsible for the delay*' (emphasis added).

[80] Ayan (n 74) 769 ff; Atamer and Okutan Nilsson (n 74) 59–60.

[81] Çağlayan (n 78) 230 ff.

[82] Atamer and Okutan Nilsson (n 74) 56–57; A Kendigelen, *Yeni Türk Ticaret Kanunu—Değişiklikler, Yenilikler ve İlk Tespitler*, 3 edn (On İki Levha Yayıncılık, 2016) 604 fn 39.

[83] Ülgen and others (n 74) N 631.

It would however be an overstatement to conclude that the instruments aiming to harmonise European contract law have been thoroughly analysed and the trends in European contract law have been taken into account in the drafting of the TCO. Some of the novelties in the TCO seem to be indirectly influenced by European harmonisation (eg TCO Article 7, which is taken from Article 6a of the Swiss Code of Obligations, and TCO Articles 20–25, which are taken partly from the BGB) and prone to problems, which may have been avoided, had the revision been based on a thorough analysis of European trends. Others seem to be the inclusion of principles already offered and applied by courts and scholars under the old Code of Obligations into the new one (eg rules on unfair exploitation and hardship). Direct influences on the other hand come from EU law and are mostly found in the area of consumer protection law where the legislator has consistently been updating the legislation to align Turkish law with the acquis. TComC Article 1530 is another example of the influence of EU law on Turkish contract law.

In introducing a new code, the legislator had the opportunity to observe the trends in European contract law and to 'Europeanise' Turkish contract law in the modern sense. Nevertheless, the legislator refrained from introducing fundamental changes to the system of contract law and was particularly criticised for not reviewing the consequences of non-performance, as was done with the *Schuldrechtsmodernisierungsgesetz* in Germany.[84] On a brighter note, legal scholars in Turkey are inclined to follow the developments in European private law, and these trends may be taken into account in the interpretation and application of the rules in force.

[84] R Serozan, *Borçlar Hukuku Genel Bölüm—İfa, İfa Engelleri, Haksız Zenginleşme*, 6th edn (Filiz Kitabevi, 2014) § 11 N 14 ff; Serozan (fn 13)*k* § 3 N 33a.

15

An American Perspective on the European Harmonisation of Contract Law

LARRY A DIMATTEO

I. Introduction

This chapter will frame the evolution of European contract law, namely, the drafting of the Principles of European Contract Law (PECL) and the Draft Common Frame of Reference (DCFR), in the context of the evolution of the American Uniform Commercial Code (UCC). In addition, I will look to the promise of the future with the creation of the European Law Institute (ELI) and the likely revisiting of the proposed Common European Sales Law (CESL). My hope for the ELI is from the vantage point of the American Law Institute's (ALI) influence on American law-making and harmonisation of law.

This chapter is founded on two imperfect analogies. The first analogy is accepting the United States and the European Union (EU) as federations of states. Of course, the level of sovereignty of the countries of the EU is of a much higher order than the federalism espoused in the US Constitution, in which residual power rests with the states and not the Federal government. From the perspective of contract law harmonisation, the analogy serves a purpose in that each American state and territory possesses its own common law of contracts, buttressed by self-contained and independent state court systems.

The second pseudo-analogy is the movement to enact a common European contract law and the movement in the United States to enact a uniform commercial law. The difference being that the harmonisation effort in the EU has been at the federal level, and the harmonisation of commercial law in the United States was undertaken at the state level. The analogy works, in that private law supported by independent court systems reside at the state level in both legal systems. The first question worth asking is why need the harmonisation of contract law be viewed as an EU endeavour? Just as the United States rejected the idea of a Federal commercial law or a Federal common law (*Erie* Doctrine), why can't harmonisation occur at the state level in Europe? The reasons seem apparent. The American states are bound by a common legal tradition, while Europe has numerous legal traditions at work. However, when looking closer, we find that the common law tradition of the United States has an outlier in the civil law tradition of Louisiana, and the EU is dominated by the civil law tradition, with outliers being the common law traditions of the United Kingdom (pending its exit from the EU) and Ireland. But, in the end, there is much more diversity in the EU with the differences exhibited between the Franco-Roman and Germanic law families, as well as differences between countries within the same civil law family, and finally, the uniqueness of the Nordic legal systems.

Another difference is that the United States put in place at the end of the nineteenth century an institutional framework for the development of harmonised law at the state level. This now century-old infrastructure is represented by the National Conference of Commissioners on Uniform State Laws (NCCUSL) and the American Law Institute (ALI). These sponsoring organisations, one private and the other quasi-governmental, continue to draft model laws, one of which, the Uniform Commercial Code (UCC), is accepted as the most successful harmonisation of law projects in US history. This is a process of law-making, with the creation of the European Law Institute that should be more fully investigated. To mimic the US model, the ELI would work for harmonisation through national legislative bodies, and not at the EU level. But, for such an effort to work, the ELI would need to be coupled with an NCCUSL-like institution with ties to national legislative bodies.

II. Paying Homage

In a book of this type, it is important to pay homage to those that have devoted a good part of their careers to the harmonisation of private law, especially in the harmonisation of contract law. There are too many to mention here, and without any disrespect intended to some great scholars that I may miss, I will discuss just a few.

All modern efforts to unify private law, especially as regards the sale of goods, are greatly indebted to Ernst Rabel. Rabel completed his habilitation in 1902, with his work 'The seller's liability for failure to deliver conforming goods' (*Die Haftung des Verkäufers wegen Mangels im Rechte*). He was the first director of the Kaiser Wilhelm Institute for Foreign and International Private Law in Berlin, beginning in 1926. In the postwar period it became the Max Planck Institute for Comparative and International Private Law, and was relocated to Hamburg in 1956. He also served as a member of the Institute for the Unification of Private Law in Rome beginning in 1927.[1] Rabel had a decisive influence on the development

[1] Global Sales Law, 'Curriculum Vitae Prof Dr Ernst Rabel', globalsaleslaw.org/index.cfm?pageID=649.

of a modern, systematic comparative law methodology. He was influential in the development of the 'functional' or 'contextual' methodology that became standard in Europe, the United States, and elsewhere. His method was based upon a distrust of the ability to formally compare language and concepts from different legal systems. David Gerber states that Rabel's methodology was based on his belief that 'meaningful comparisons could be achieved only by reference to the underlying social problems to which the language was related.'[2] His distrust of the coherency of language followed the logic of the philosopher Ludwig Wittgenstein ('the world is the totality of facts, not of things'),[3] and presaged the rise of contextualism in contract interpretation, at least in the common law.

Rabel, though a lifelong Catholic, was eventually forced to resign his professorship in Berlin because of his Jewish heritage and migrated to the United States in 1939. He continued his work and supported himself through research grants that he received from the American Law Institute (ALI), the University of Michigan, and Harvard Law School.[4] In 1942 Rabel and fellow German Karl Loewenstein were among those invited by the ALI to join an international experts' committee charged with preparing a global restatement of 'essential human rights'. The document that the ALI committee formulated later was an important point of reference in the drafting of the United Nations' Universal Declaration of Human Rights. He eventually became a US citizen, and while in the United States he completed his seminal four-volume work, *The Conflict of Laws: A Comparative Study*.[5]

I would next like to pay homage to two Rudolfs—one from the common law and the other from the civil law. I am referring to the efforts of Rudolf Schlesinger at Cornell, and Rodolfo Sacco at Torino, and their work on the common core comparative law methodology.[6] And I would be remiss not to acknowledge Ole Lando's monumental efforts in drafting the Principles of European Contract Law (PECL).

Other more contemporary efforts should also be noted here, including in no particular order, the work of Michael Joachim Bonell in the drafting of the UNIDROIT Principles; Christian von Bar and his Study Group on a European Civil Code; the work of the Acquis Group; and the work of Reinhard Zimmermann.

[2] D Gerber, 'Sculpting the Agenda of Comparative Law: Ernst Rabel and the Façade of Language' in A Riles (ed), *Rethinking the Masters of Comparative Law* (Hart Publishing, 2001) 190.

[3] L Wittgenstein, *Philosophical Investigations*, GE Anscombe tr (Basil Blackwell, 1953).

[4] M Rheinstein, 'In Memory of Ernst Rabel' (1956) 5 *The American Journal of Comparative Law* 185.

[5] E Rabel, *The Conflict of Laws: A Comparative Study*, vols 1–4 (University of Michigan Press, 1958); D Clark, 'The Influence of Ernst Rabel on American Law' in M Lutter, E Stiefel and M Hoeflich (eds), *Der Einfluss deutscher Emigranten auf die Rechtsentwicklung in den USA und in Deutschland* (Mohr, 1993) 107.

[6] Rudolf Schlesinger (ed), *Formation of Contracts: A Study on the Common Core of Legal Systems* (Oceana Publications Inc and Stevens & Sons, 1968); The common core approach has been used as a standard methodology in comparative law studies: M Bussani and U Mattei, 'The Common Core Approach to European Private Law' (1997) 3 *Colum J Eur L* 339; R Sacco, 'Legal Formants: A Dynamic Approach to Comparative Law' (1991) 39 *Am J Comp L* 21; K Zweigert and H Kötz, *Introduction to Comparative Law*, T Weir (tr), 2nd edn (Clarendon Press, 1987) 28, 33.

Beginning in the 1980s, with the continued integration of European countries, all of these scholars and groups had the vision of developing a trans-European contract law, as well as broader private law and civil code projects. Building on the comparative law work of those mentioned earlier, the Principles of European Contract Law took a comparative law approach without prioritising any individual legal system. The Principles were drawn up by a private group of European academics led by Ole Lando, including Ulrich Drobnig, Reinhard Zimmermann and Hugh Beale, among others. The main focus of the PECL is to find a common core of contract law rules that could be used by all European States. In structure the PECL are similar to the Restatements of US law.

Lando noted that the EU Parliament has called for preparatory work on a European Civil Code[7] and has 'stressed how important it is to standardise the law of obligations', beginning with the law of contracts.[8] 1994, the year the EU Parliament was calling for such preparatory work, also marked the Governing Council of the International Institute for the Unification of Private Law (UNIDROIT) giving its approval to publication of the Principles of International Commercial Contracts (UNIDROIT Principles), and the Commission on European Contract Law concluded its work on the first part of the Principles of European Contract Law.[9] It should be noted that the UNIDROIT Principles Steering Committee was established in 1971, meaning that it took 23 years to complete and publish the document, while the work of the CECL began in 1982, with publication of Part I in 1995, Part II in 1999 and Part III in 2002—a total of 20 years of work.

The reasons in favour of the harmonisation of contract law are summarised as: the riskiness of entering foreign markets, especially by small and medium-sized enterprises (SMEs); differences in national contract laws are obstacles to the free movement of goods, persons and services, and are thereby antithetical to a fully functional common market; and the partial harmonisation through directives, although beneficial, adds more complexity and acts as a further obstacle due to its piecemeal approach.[10] Lando refers to other 'federalised' or multiple jurisdiction entities such as the United States, United Kingdom, and Canada. He rebuts the argument that such legal systems support the argument against the need for a harmonised law of contracts, by noting the harmonisation of contract law within those systems. In the case of the United States, the contract laws between the states have been harmonised through the passage of a litany of model laws including the UCC.[11] I would further argue that the UCC has not only harmonised

[7] Resolution A2-157/89 on action to bring into line the private law of the Member States [1989] OJ C158/400; Resolution A3-0329/94 on the harmonisation of certain sectors of the private law of the Member States [1994] OJ C205/518.

[8] O Lando, 'The Rules of European Contract Law', www.cisg.law.pace.edu/cisg/biblio/lando2.html#1.

[9] MJ Bonell, 'The UNIDROIT Principles of International Commercial Contracts and the principles of European Contract Law: Similar Rules for the same Purposes?' (1996) 26 *Uniform Law Review* 229.

[10] Lando (n 8) 127–28.

[11] ibid.

commercial law, but also that of the common law among the states, as principles found in the Code, such as the principles of good faith, fair dealing, unconscionability, impracticability, and contextual interpretation have been adopted by analogy into the common law.[12]

Given that a majority of members of the Commission on European Contract Law (CECL) were practising lawyers, it is not surprising that a functional approach should be used in drafting the PECL.[13] Ole Lando notes that although the functional approach was utilised, it was only the beginning point in the drafting process. As an example of the functional approach, he notes that: 'functional more than conceptual considerations determine whether *culpa in contrahendo* sounds in contract or tort.'[14] However, the CECL 'not only consider[ed] the results of the cases, but it also pays attention to the concepts and methods used to reach the results.'[15] The combination of outcome and method analyses were needed to achieve its 'main task, which is to propose rules, not to state existing laws'.[16]

As noted above, Lando has acknowledged that the model of the American Restatement projects was used in the drafting of PECL.[17] He noted that due to the diversity in the common law in the United States and even greater diversity among European national laws, the power of PECL, as well as the American Restatements, is related to their degree of persuasiveness in selecting or creating and advancing the best options among a choice of rules.

The Acquis Group is made up of more than 40 legal scholars; to mention a few, including some personal friends, they include Gianmaria Ajani and Barbara Pasa from the University of Turin, Hans Schulte-Nölke from the University of Osnabruck, Reiner Schulze from the University of Muenster, Matthias Storme from the KU Leuven, Christian Twigg-Flesner from the University of Hull, and Fryderyk Zoll from Cracow.[18]

The Study Group on a European Civil Code, led by Christian von Bar, is a network of academics, from across the EU, conducting comparative law research in private law in the various legal jurisdictions of the member states. Its aim is stated as producing a codified set of Principles of European Law for the law of obligations and core aspects of the law of property.[19]

Most of these groups and a multitude of conferences were inspired by the work of the Lando Commission. In 2005, these groups were brought together by the

[12] Q Zhou and L DiMatteo, 'Three Sales Laws and the Common Law of Contracts' in L DiMatteo and M Hogg (eds), *Comparative Contract Law: British and American Perspectives* (Oxford University Press, 2016).

[13] O Lando, 'The Common Core of European Private Law and the Principles of European Contract Law' (1998) 21 *Hastings International and Comparative Law Review* 809.

[14] ibid 813.

[15] ibid.

[16] ibid 822.

[17] Lando (n 8) 131.

[18] Acquis Research Group, 'Existing European Private Law' www.acquis-group.jura.uni-snabrueck.de/ag/dms/ag/dms.php.

[19] Study group on a European Civil Code, www.sgecc.net.

European Commission as a Joint Network on European Private Law and charged with drawing up a Common Frame of Reference. The Study Group on a European Civil Code and the Acquis Group took leading roles.

A further step towards a European private law was the foundation of the European Law Institute (ELI) in Paris in May 2011. The ELI was set up primarily by legal academics, but addresses all areas of the law and branches of the profession. The chairs of the ELI Founding Committee were Irmgard Griss, President of the Austrian Supreme Court and President of the Association of Supreme Court Presidents in the European Union and Reinhard Zimmermann.[20]

At the EU level, the work of Dirk Staudenmayer and the European Commission for Contract and Consumer Law should be noted, including their efforts relating to insurance contracts, digital contract rules, and cloud computing contracts. The conclusion of the Commission was that uniform private law rules remain a worthwhile goal on behalf of merchants and consumers. It states that:

> All economic transactions are based on contracts. This is why the differences in the contracts rules on how a contract is concluded or terminated, or on how the delivery of a faulty product has to be remedied, are felt in the daily life of both traders and consumers. For traders, these differences generate additional complexity and costs, notably when they want to export their products and services to several EU Member States. For consumers, these differences make it more difficult to shop in countries other than their own, in particular when shopping online.[21]

The work on the sale and supply of goods, including rules on digital content, embodied in the CESL, remains a timely avenue for harmonisation. Such efforts, whether or not initially successful, establish the bedrock for more successful ventures in the future. A historical example is the myriad of revisions needed before the American UCC was adopted.

It is important, given the worthiness and importance of uniform rules, that a long-term view be taken—from both backward-looking and future-looking perspectives. The core question is 'whether the whole process of drafting uniform rules is still worthy to pursue?' At a purely conceptual level, the answer is simply that if we believe that uniform contract rules are important in the European context, then they are worth pursuing. At the present moment, with some calling the EU project into question (such as the Brexit vote to leave the EU), it is important to look at other reference points. One reference point is found in the negotiation and enactment of the American UCC. The next section briefly explains the story behind the drafting and enactment of the UCC.

[20] Max Planck Institute for Comparative and International Private Law, www.mpipriv.de/en/pub/research/european_private_law_and_priva/maxeup.cfm#i48904.

[21] European Commission for Contract and Consumer Law, ec.europa.eu/justice/contract/index_en.htm.

III. Story of the American Commercial Code

The American UCC can be seen as representative of the market economy's need for specialised rules. But, in the end, it served to generalise, modernise, and harmonise a chaotic system of specialised rules adopted in part by the different American states. The UCC replaced an ad hoc series of model laws, not universally adopted by the different states, that included: the Uniform Sales Act, Negotiable Instruments Law, Uniform Warehouse Receipts Act, Uniform Bills of Lading Act, Uniform Stock Transfer Act, the Uniform Trust Receipts Act, and numerous other statutes.[22] The National Conference of Commissioners on Uniform State Laws (NCCUSL) promulgated the first of these uniform acts with the Negotiable Instruments Law of 1896 and the Uniform Sales Act of 1906. By analogy, a European contract law could organise and replace the numerous existing private law directives.

In 1940, NCCUSL decided to begin work on a new uniform sales law, which the American Law Institute joined in 1942. The impetus for the project was the threat of the US government enacting a Federal sales law.[23] Soon thereafter, the sales law project was expanded to a commercial code project, with Karl Llewellyn as Chief Reporter. The American Bar Association also reviewed and commented on drafts of the UCC, with the finished document published in 1952. The UCC was discussed in a number of state legislatures but ultimately rejected, which began a project of revision. A few courts recognised the UCC as equivalent to a Restatement as a 'stamp of approval of a large body of American scholarship'.[24] Pennsylvania was the first state to enact the UCC, on 1 April 1953, but no other state followed suit, leading to a further revision effort. Progress in enacting the UCC came to a standstill, with all eyes looking to New York, where the state-sponsored Law Commission undertook a three-year study of the Code, eventually concluding in 1956 that:

> (1) The 'preponderance' of the arguments for or against codification 'is in favor of careful and foresighted codification of all or major parts of commercial law.' (2) Such a commercial code 'would be of greater value to the public and the legal profession than the enactment, even with revisions, of separate uniform laws.' (3) Such a code 'is attainable with a reasonable amount of effort and within a reasonable amount of time.' (4) The Uniform Commercial Code 'is not satisfactory in its present form.' (5) The Uniform Commercial Code 'cannot be made satisfactory without comprehensive re-examination and revision in the light of all critical comment obtainable.'[25]

[22] R Braucher, 'The Legislative History of the Uniform Commercial Code' (1958) 58 *Columbia Law Review* 798.

[23] Proposed Federal Sales Act HR No 8176, 76th Cong, 3d Sess (1940), reprinted in 'Symposium: The Proposed Federal Sales Act' (1940) 26 *Va L Rev* 537.

[24] Braucher (n 22) 801 (citing *Fairbanks, Morse & Co v Consolidated Fisheries Co*, 190 F.2d 817, 822 n 9 (3d Cir 1951)).

[25] Braucher (n 22) 803–04 (citing 1956 NY Report 65(A) 57–58).

The Editorial Board of the UCC began a new revision of the Code, ending with the publication of a revised version with updated 'official comments' in 1958. The use of Official Comments was part of the drafting process from the very beginning. The sponsors of the UCC believed it imperative that Official Comments were needed to 'make clear what changes were made in the law and why, and that the Code should expressly refer to those Comments as a guide in its construction and application.'[26] A provision was provided that established that any conflict between the text and the Comments should be resolved in favour of the text. New York rejected the idea that the Comments were a part of the legislative instrument. Nonetheless, courts have often referred to the Comments when applying the Code's formal provisions.

It was not until New York's enactment, as the premier commercial law state, of the Code in 1964 that the dam burst, leading to its enactment by all 50 states, as well as the District of Columbia, US Virgin Islands, and Puerto Rico, with the lone exception of Louisiana's opting out of Article 2 (Law of Sales). The major thematic change resulting from the many debates and revisions of the UCC related to the mandatory nature of its rules. The UCC as initially drafted made all its rules mandatory except for ones that expressly stated: 'unless otherwise agreed' by the contracting parties. This was reversed with the insertion in section 1-102(3), which recognised freedom of contract as the dominant principle making almost all of the rules non-mandatory in nature. The major exceptions to the non-mandatory nature of UCC rules were the general principles of good faith, fair dealing, commercial reasonableness, and the doctrine of unconscionability, as well as formal requirements, namely the statute of frauds.

There are lessons to be learned in analysing the drafting, enactment and the evolution of the UCC for the process of enacting a European contract law. First, was the perseverance needed in campaigning for its enactment, which included the willingness to listen and make revisions and to actively lobby for its adoption. Second, is that most such laws quickly become obsolete, as the business world continually produces novel ways of contracting. This was apparent in the drafting of the UCC, when it was determined that the Official Comments to the 1952 Draft had become somewhat obsolete by the time of the 1958 Draft. Structures were put in place to combat the problem of obsolescence. The sponsors of the UCC provided mechanisms for the Code to be self-amending and open to a process of formal revisions. The latter dealt with future avoidance of political issues by the foundation laid down in the long-term negotiation of the UCC provisions that allowed for legislative acceptance of its later revisions. All nine of the UCC articles have been revised, except for Article 2 (sale of goods), and additional 'sub-articles' have been added unanimously in response to changes in technology and the market place, including the adoption of Article 2A on the lease of goods and Article 4A

[26] Braucher (n 22) 809.

on wire transfers. The two major failures have been the rejection by the states of the 2003 Revision of Article 2 and the failure to come to agreement on an addition relating to the licensing of goods (Article 2B).

Article 2 is still working after six decades of its drafting because of its self-amending qualities. This is no real surprise, since Karl Llewellyn, a purveyor of the German Civil Code (BGB), wrote Article 2 as well as Article 1 (General Provisions). It is in Article 2 that we see the UCC's most innovative qualities, including the duty of good faith, doctrines of unconscionability (unfairness) and impracticability (hardship), as well as the contextual interpretation of contracts, and to a lesser extent, the acceptance of the firm offer and written confirmation rules. But, its resilience and ability to refresh itself comes from the core belief that the law is found in commercial practice. The triad of the ubiquitous use of the reasonableness standard in Article 2's gap-filling provisions, the embrace of contextual evidence, and the malleability of the good faith principle, allow Article 2 to keep working and working. The importance of standards and principles, alongside the inevitable fixed rules relating to formation and breach, are essential to a well-functioning and evolving general contract law.

The final lesson to be learned from the history of the UCC is found in its preamble that recognises an ambitious set of goals. Unlike the UK Sale of Goods Act 1979, whose purpose was expressly stated as the clarification of existing law, the UCC states that its purposes include simplification of the law governing commercial transactions; continued expansion of commercial practices through custom, usage, and agreement of the parties; and uniformity among the various jurisdictions. In addition, the Code mandates that it 'shall be liberally construed and applied to promote its underlying purposes and policies'.[27] This makes up the essence of a forward-looking body of commercial law.

The goals of past efforts, such as the PECL project, have included the facilitation of cross-border trade, establishing an infrastructure for EU rules governing contracts, providing guidelines for national courts and legislatures, and bridging the civil–common law divide, and should be used as benchmarks in assessing the worthiness of future projects and in judging the outcomes of such projects. Some of the chapters of this book provide examples of this type of goal-setting and benchmarking.

There are four final points I would like to discuss. The first point is how do general and specialised rules relate to the harmonisation of contract law; the second point relates to the relationship between harmonisation and diversity, as discussed by Hugh Beale in Chapter 2; the third point is the role of European legal education as it relates to harmonisation; and the final point is the preference for mandatory, universal European contract law versus an optional instrument.

[27] Uniform Commercial Code §1-102.

IV. General and Specialised Contract Rules

How does one define contract law and its many species? When are specialised rules needed, or when is something best left to general contract law? When does a set of fixed rules need to be carved out of the general principles of contract law? For the purposes of enacting a European contract law, why does this matter? The evolution of United States contract law provides an example. But first the story must go back to the origins of American law in English common law. The old English writ system provided specialised causes of action. It was not until much later that a general law of contracts was recognised and built up by the common law. With the Industrial Revolution and the specialisation of goods and financial instruments, the need for specialised rules became clear. Thus, history shows that a contractual legal system can exist as bodies of specialised rules or as a system of general contract law. The key marker is the stage of economic development that a contract law system operates within. The writ system was quite sophisticated in an agrarian, barter economy. In the modern era, a fully integrated, advanced market economy needs both a general contract law and specialised bodies of rules. Such areas as secured transactions and negotiable instruments, and the economic needs they serve, could not function without sets of highly formalised and coherent rules.

Beginning in the later part of the nineteenth century, the United States witnessed a disaggregation of the common law of contracts, but it also retained general contract law as a set of default rules for both non-specialised areas of contract law and as a backdrop of general default rules for the specialised areas of contract law. In contrast, the European Union has enacted numerous bodies of specialised private law rules with no common general contract law to support the specialised rules.

The old dilemma of what came first—the egg (specialised rules) or the chicken (general contract law)—can be answered simply by saying they both came first, given the cyclical nature of legal evolution. Nathan Isaacs in the early twentieth century advanced the argument that Maine's progression thesis[28] was, in fact, cyclical in nature. In a 1917 article in the University of Pennsylvania Law Review ('The Law and the Law of Change'),[29] Isaacs sketched out a cycle theory of legal development and argued that it possessed the descriptive power to be applicable to civil, common, and Talmudic law. The ideas of stages, described differently by

[28] H Sumner Maine, *Ancient Law* (C Scribner, 1864).

[29] Isaacs' cycle theory of legal evolution is explored in his two-part article: N Isaacs, '"The Law" and the Law of Change: A Tentative Study of Comparative Jurisprudence' (1917) 65 *University of Pennsylvania Law Review* 665, 748; LA DiMatteo and S Flaks, 'Beyond Rules' (2010) 47 *Houston Law Review* 305.

different theorists, is found in Maine's work; its cyclical nature is Isaacs' refinement of an idea that legal development progresses through a never-ending series of cycles involving codification, legislation through the courts, equity and fictions, and then back to codification. Within these cycles are pendulums that swing back and forth between formalism and contextualism, facilitation (freedom of contract) and regulation (fairness), and shifts between the efficacy of rules and the flexibility of standards-principles. All of these dichotomies are false, in the sense that in any era of legal development there are degrees of each end of the dichotomies. Put simply, the dichotomies are in reality places along a continuum.

For our purposes, Isaacs' insights provide a scenario. First, it does not matter whether private law begins with a general contract law followed by bodies of specialised rules for different transaction types,[30] or whether it begins with bodies of specialised rules followed by the development of general contract law principles. Because of political concerns in the European context, it may be best to begin with a contract law, which focuses on its facilitative nature rather than its regulatory nature. This may mean a body of mostly fixed rules, assisted with some general principles. In the area of formalism versus contextualism, modern laws of contracts have become more contextualised, but at the same time some areas of contract law continue to require highly formalised rule structures. Finally, no matter where one begins on these various continuums, courts will invariably swing between strict rule application and the development of general principles or standards in the search for the proper balance between freedom and justice.

As fixed rules are applied to new developments in business and technology, eventually exceptions to the rules are needed to prevent injustice in similarly situated cases. Eventually, the litany of rules, exceptions to the rules, and exceptions to the exceptions, leads to hopeless confusion and uncertainty. The conceptual structure of law is held together by legal fictions and equitable adjustments. In the end, general standards and principles and new codifications need to be reasserted to clarify and simplify the law. It then begins anew; as standards and principles are applied, injustice will appear in sets of similarly situated cases, resulting in the creation of more specialised rules.

Isaacs' cycles can be used to place the development and enactment of European contract law in a longer-term context. Isaacs' cycles looked at legal development through a prism that sees the law's evolution through centuries and millennia of time. I believe that in any system of federated states, and as long as the European Union remains in existence, the historical cycles outlined above will take their course. Political reasons may make this an inopportune time for the enactment

[30] The concept of transaction types is a core concept in Llewellynian legal thought. See LA DiMatteo, 'Reason and Context: A Dual Track Theory of Interpretation' (2004) 109 *Penn State Law Review* 397.

of a general European contract law, but the work on such projects must continue. European contract law may need to advance slowly and more quietly, through small victories, such as a digital content law, followed by a sales law, a general contract law, and in the not so near future, a general civil code.

V. Commercial and Consumer Contract Law

The areas of consumer contract law versus general contract law adds an additional layer of complexity between national and EU law, but also presents an opportunity for uniform rules in order to reset the balance in the common market between these two related legal regimes. It should always be borne in mind that the difference between consumer and commercial contract law is a matter of degree and not of kind. The integrity of both is based upon the balancing of efficiency (benefit-cost) and effectiveness (solving problems) in the development of consumer and commercial contract rules. Both areas suffer, from time to time, from market failures. The proof is the fact that the regulation of contracts and the regulatory function of contract law are ever evolving and never fixed. The only question is how best to attack such failures and abuses—by the current marketplace of regulation; through new regulations addressing the perceived dangers presented by the Internet, electronic platforms, and the misuse of information; or a decrease or restructuring of regulation due to the accessibility of information and self-corrective measures facilitated by non-governmental watchdog groups. This is the tension that needs to be studied and reconsidered over time. Is more regulation of certain types of contracts needed, or is less needed? Should regulations be delayed, given the speed of technological change, to weigh their benefits to an innovation-driven economy; the costs to that economy by new regulations not fully thought-out and vetted before enactment; and the costs to consumers of abuse of these new ways of doing business? And, is the abuse likely to be short-term, but self-correcting in the long-term?

VI. Harmonisation and Diversity

In the end, uniform rules of private law allow for the working out of national legal inefficiencies through Pan-European rules—bridging the gap between common and civil law systems (and between civil law systems) by emphasising 'core' values, distinguishing true divergences from mere misunderstanding; distinguishing divergence in the letter of the law from convergence in practice and legal outcomes; and the problem of speaking of different legal languages, but achieving similar outcomes. The final question that needs to be addressed is how much harmonisation is needed (descriptive element) and how much divergence should be allowed (normative element)? As Hugh Beale has asserted, there needs to be a balancing between uniformity and diversity. If the French require the right of taste in a documentary sale of wine or cheese, so be it!

VII. Relationship of Legal Education and Harmonisation of Law

The harmonisation of legal education and of business law, centring on contract law, is needed to create 'European' lawyers able to assist their clients wherever their clients do business in Europe. The EU has never been better positioned to build a European contract law, due to the Europeanisation of many of its law schools. One sees in law school curricula many courses on European law and comparative law, as well as the proliferation of specialised degrees, especially at the Masters of Law level relating to international trade, European law, and so forth. The Europeanisation of legal education makes today's European law graduates and future lawyers and judges better equipped to understand, interpret, and apply a European contract law. Thus, the intellectual infrastructure will be in place when a European contract law becomes a reality.

VIII. Opting-in and Opting-out of a European Contract Law

Behavioural decision theory (behavioural law and economics) has shown that framing how an instrument applies profoundly influences whether it will be widely or lightly used. If the use of a common European contract law is a preferred outcome, than it should be adopted as a mandatory instrument, and not as an optional one. It seems that the CESL's framing as an optional instrument was more of a political decision than an optimal decision to advance the goal of the harmonisation of contract law. Maybe, the advancement of an optional instrument is the best strategy at this time to continue the progress towards private law harmonisation. But, from a purely academic or intellectual view, to have the desired impact it would be best if not in the near future, then as an ultimate goal to seek a mandatory or opt-out instrument. Again, if it is wished to 'encourage' the use of a harmonising instrument, the decision-maker should be required to opt-out of the application of that instrument. An optional instrument frames the status quo as the use of national law, while an opt-out instrument sets the status quo as the use of trans-European contract law. This was the case with the CISG; if the CISG was an opt-in instrument, it is implausible that it would have had much of a real world impact, and there would be far fewer CISG case decisions.

It should be stressed that contract law is itself an optional legal regime, in that the parties retain the power of creating their own contract law through the negotiation of express terms at odds with contract law's default rules. In the European context, it would be best to draft a contract law with a minimal amount of mandatory rules, so that private parties may freely negotiate out of the law. At the same time, the instrument should require the parties to expressly opt-out in order to increase the impact and use of the common rules.

IX. Conclusion

The progression from the PECL, DCFR, and proposed, but ultimately rejected CESL, has advanced the idea of a trans-European contract law. However, their use in the enactment of a European contract law seems remote at the present time. The question posed is whether the goals set forth in PECL—that harmonisation of contract law will facilitate cross-border trade and bridge the gap between the civil law and common law, as well as across the different civil law systems—still hold true? The answer is strongly in the affirmative.

My conclusion is that unlike other areas of law, the harmonisation of contract law is a worthy and a feasible effort, given the universal nature of transactions and transactional law. It is an important project in the European sense; the legal continuity of private law within the common market meets the threshold of any utilitarian analysis where the benefits of homogeneity outweigh the costs to national sovereignty. In the free trade era, the functionality of the EU as a single market provides Europe with a competitive advantage externally by its lowering of transaction costs internally. At the current moment, the harmonisation effort has encountered some strong headwinds, such as the political uncertainty of the EU itself. Nonetheless, the increased functionality of the common market should not be swept aside in the current tide of nationalism, since all parties benefit economically from such harmonisation efforts, whether in the development of uniform rules or through a better understanding of each other's laws.

Efforts need to continue both on the 'political' and academic fronts. The strongest argument for further harmonisation efforts is a stage one adoption of the CESL in the area of licensing and digital content. The role of academic research in support of such efforts, in developing alternatives, and in expanding the framework of uniform law has never been more important. 'All hands should be on deck' in this academic undertaking, including law and economics, behavioural law and economics, empirical legal research (an underutilised tool in private law research), and feminist jurisprudence. So now is not the time to be discouraged; now is the time to double down on the noble vision of a trans-European contract law regime.

INDEX

www.ingramcontent.com/pod-product-compliance
Ingram Content Group UK Ltd.
Pitfield, Milton Keynes, MK11 3LW, UK
UKHW022222151225
9585UKWH00003B/110

9 781509 916283